Associated Press

Stylebook
and Briefing on Media Law

with Internet Guide and Glossary

Editor
Norm Goldstein
apstylebook@ap.org

Published by
THE ASSOCIATED PRESS
50 Rockefeller Plaza
New York, NY 10020

Library of Congress Catalog Card Number: **91-070484**
ISBN: **0-917360-20-6**

Typesetting and design by 18:29, LLC
Printed in the United States of America
Printed by Banta Book Group

First Edition, August 1977

36th Edition, 2001

CONTENTS

PHOTO CAPTIONS

FILING THE WIRE

FILING PRACTICES

PROOFREADERS' MARKS

ABOUT THE AP

AP PUBLICATIONS

**In Memory
of
CHRISTOPHER W. FRENCH
1940-1989**

FOREWORD

Work on this Stylebook began in mid-1975. The orders were: Make clear and simple rules, permit few exceptions to the rules, and rely heavily on the chosen dictionary as the arbiter of conflicts.

As work progressed, we became convinced that while style would remain the chief purpose, there were many factual references we should include to make things a bit easier for busy editors.

So we have a Stylebook, but also a reference work.

As for the "style" itself, we thought at the outset that it wouldn't be possible to please everyone. Of course, we were right.

Journalists approach these style questions with varying degrees of passion.

Some don't think it is really important. Some agree that basically there should be uniformity for reading ease if nothing else. Still others are prepared to duel over a wayward lowercase.

We encountered all three of these types and, in their special ways, all were helpful.

It is customary at this place to thank those whose aid and counsel produced the volume that follows.

That list is long. It ranges from the staff of The Associated Press to editors and writers on member newspapers, to other individuals and groups with special interests in some subjects. In particular we sought and received many member views on a variety of difficult questions so that this book could reflect what members wanted.

We are particularly grateful to those newspaper editors who agreed to review the final draft and give us their comments as well as those of their staffs.

The completed book incorporates many of their suggestions.

We have tried to make the Stylebook current and trust it will be a lasting work. But language changes, and we will review entries annually, making necessary changes by wire notes during the review period.

Each new printing of the Stylebook will incorporate the changes that have been announced on the wires.

LOUIS D. BOCCARDI
President and
Chief Executive Officer

STYLEBOOK

STYLEBOOK KEY

This updated and revised version of The Associated Press Stylebook has been organized like a dictionary. Need the acronym for a government agency? Look under the agency's name. Should you capitalize a word? Check the word itself or the **capitalization** entry. What's the format for baseball boxes? See **baseball**.

Following is a key to the entries:

airport Capitalize as part of a proper name: *La Guardia Airport, Newark International Airport.*

The first name of an individual and the word *international* may be deleted from a formal airport name while the remainder is capitalized: *John F. Kennedy International Airport, Kennedy International Airport,* or *Kennedy Airport.* Use whichever is appropriate in the context.

Do not make up names, however. There is no *Boston Airport,* for example. The *Boston airport* (lowercase *airport*) would be acceptable if for some reason the proper name, *Logan International Airport,* were not used.

airtight

air traffic controller (no hyphen.)

airways The system of routes that the federal government has established for airplane traffic.

See the **airline, airlines** entry for its use in carriers' names.

Alabama Abbrev.: *Ala.* See **state names**.

Entry words, in alphabetical order, are in **boldface**. They represent the accepted word forms unless otherwise indicated.

Text explains usage.

Examples of correct and incorrect usage are in italics.

Many entries simply give the correct spelling, hyphenation and/or capitalization.

Abbrev. indicates the correct abbreviation of a word.

Related topics are in **boldface**.

Other abbreviations used in the Stylebook:

n.: noun form	**adj.:** adjectives
v.: verb form	**adv.:** adverbs

AAA Formerly the American Automobile Association. On second reference, *the automobile association* or *the association* is acceptable.

Headquarters is in Heathrow, Fla.

a, an Use the article *a* before consonant sounds: *a historic event*, *a one-year term* (sounds as if it begins with a *w*), *a united stand* (sounds like *you*).

Use the article *an* before vowel sounds: *an energy crisis*, *an honorable man* (the *h* is silent), *an NBA record* (sounds like it begins with the letter *e*), *an 1890s celebration.*

a- The rules of **prefixes** apply, but in general no hyphen. Some examples:

achromatic   atonal

A&P Acceptable in all references for *Great Atlantic & Pacific Tea Co. Inc.* Headquarters is in Montvale, N.J.

AARP Use only the initials; it's the official name of the American Association of Retired Persons.

abbreviations and acronyms The notation *abbrev.* is used in this book to identify the abbreviated form that may be used for a word in some contexts.

A few universally recognized abbreviations are required in some circumstances. Some others are acceptable depending on the context. But in general, avoid alphabet soup. Do not use abbreviations or acronyms which the reader would not quickly recognize.

Guidance on how to use a particular abbreviation or acronym is provided in entries alphabetized according to the sequence of letters in the word or phrase.

Some general principles:

BEFORE A NAME: Abbreviate the following titles when used before a full name outside direct quotations: *Dr., Gov., Lt. Gov., Mr., Mrs., Rep., the Rev., Sen.* and certain military designations listed in the **military titles** entry. Spell out all except *Dr., Mr., Mrs.* and *Ms.* when they are used before a name in direct quotations.

For guidelines on how to use titles, see **courtesy titles; legislative titles; military titles; religious titles;** and the entries for the most commonly used titles.

AFTER A NAME: Abbreviate *junior* or *senior* after an individual's name. Abbreviate *company, corporation, incorporated* and *limited* when used after the name of a corporate entity. See entries under these words and **company names.**

In some cases, an academic degree may be abbreviated after an individual's name. See **academic degrees**.

WITH DATES OR NUMERALS: Use the abbreviations *A.D., B.C., a.m., p.m., No.*, and abbreviate certain months when used with the day of the month.
Right: *In 450 B.C.; at 9:30 a.m.; in room No. 6; on Sept. 16.*
Wrong: *Early this a.m. he asked for the No. of your room.* The abbreviations are correct only with figures.
Right: *Early this morning he asked for the number of your room.*
See **months** and individual entries for these other terms.

IN NUMBERED ADDRESSES: Abbreviate *avenue, boulevard* and *street* in numbered addresses: *He lives on Pennsylvania Avenue. He lives at 1600 Pennsylvania Ave.*
See **addresses**.

STATES: The names of certain states and the *United States* are abbreviated with periods in some circumstances.
See **state names; datelines;** and individual entries.

ACCEPTABLE BUT NOT RE-QUIRED: Some organizations and government agencies are widely recognized by their initials: *CIA, FBI, GOP.*
If the entry for such an organization notes that an abbreviation is acceptable in all references or on second reference, that does not mean that its use should be automatic. Let the context determine, for example, whether to use *Federal Bureau of Investigation* or *FBI.*
See **second reference**.

AVOID AWKWARD CON-STRUCTIONS: Do not follow an organization's full name with an abbreviation or acronym in parentheses or set off by dashes. If an abbreviation or acronym would not be clear on second reference without this arrangement, do not use it.
Names not commonly before the public should not be reduced to acronyms solely to save a few words.

SPECIAL CASES: Many abbreviations are desirable in tabulations and certain types of technical writing. See individual entries.

CAPS, PERIODS: Use capital letters and periods according to the listings in this book. For words not in this book, use the first-listed abbreviation in Webster's New World Dictionary. If an abbreviation not listed in this book or in the dictionary achieves widespread acceptance, use capital letters. Omit periods unless the result would spell an unrelated word.

ABC Acceptable in all references for *American Broadcasting Cos.* (the plural is part of the corporate name).
Divisions are *ABC News, ABC Radio* and *ABC-TV.*

ABCs

able-bodied

ABM, ABMs Acceptable in all references for *anti-ballistic missile(s)*, but the term should be defined in the story.
Avoid the redundant phrase *ABM missiles.*

A-bomb Use *atomic bomb* unless a direct quotation is involved.

See **Hiroshima**.

Aborigine Capitalize when referring to Australian indigenous people.

abortion Use *anti-abortion* instead of *pro-life* and *abortion rights* instead of *pro-abortion* or *pro-choice*. Avoid *abortionist*, which connotes a person who performs clandestine abortions; use a term such as *abortion doctor* or *abortion practitioner*.

aboveboard

absent-minded

absent without leave *AWOL* is acceptable on second reference.

academic degrees If mention of degrees is necessary to establish someone's credentials, the preferred form is to avoid an abbreviation and use instead a phrase such as: *John Jones, who has a doctorate in psychology.*

Use an apostrophe in *bachelor's degree, a master's*, etc., but there is no possessive in *Bachelor of Arts* or *Master of Science*.

Use such abbreviations as *B.A., M.A., LL.D.* and *Ph.D.* only when the need to identify many individuals by degree on first reference would make the preferred form cumbersome. Use these abbreviations only after a full name — never after just a last name.

When used after a name, an academic abbreviation is set off by commas: *Daniel Moynihan, Ph.D., spoke.*

Do not precede a name with a courtesy title for an academic degree and follow it with the abbreviation for the degree in the same reference:

Wrong: *Dr. Pam Jones, Ph.D.*
Right: *Dr. Pam Jones, a chemist.*

See **doctor**.

academic departments Use lowercase except for words that are proper nouns or adjectives: *the department of history, the history department, the department of English, the English department*, or when *department* is part of the official and formal name: *University of Connecticut Department of Medicine*.

academic titles Capitalize and spell out formal titles such as *chancellor, chairman*, etc., when they precede a name. Lowercase elsewhere.

Lowercase modifiers such as *department* in *department Chairman Jerome Wiesner.*

See **doctor** and **titles**.

academy See **military academies**.

Academy Awards Presented annually by the Academy of Motion Picture Arts and Sciences. Also known as the *Oscars*.

Lowercase *the academy* and *the awards* whenever they stand alone.

accept, except *Accept* means to receive.

Except means to exclude.

accommodate

accused A person is *accused of*, not *with*, a crime.

To avoid any suggestion that an individual is being judged before a trial, do not use a phrase such as *accused slayer John Jones*, use *John Jones, accused of the slaying*.

For guidelines on related words, see **allege**; **arrest**; and **indict**.

Ace A trademark for a brand of elastic bandage.

acknowledgment

acre Equal to 43,560 square feet or 4,840 square yards. The metric equivalent is .4 (two-fifths) of a hectare or 4,047 square meters.

One square mile is 640 acres.

To convert to hectares, multiply by .4 (5 acres x .4 equals 2 hectares).

See **hectare**.

acronyms See the **abbreviations and acronyms** entry.

act Capitalize when part of the name for pending or implemented legislation: *the Taft-Hartley Act*.

acting Always lowercase, but capitalize any formal title that may follow before a name: *acting Mayor Peter Barry*.

See **titles**.

act numbers Use Arabic figures and capitalize *act*: *Act 1*; *Act 2, Scene 2*. But: *the first act, the second act*.

actor (man) **actress** (woman)

Actors' Equity Association

Headquarters is in New York.

A.D. Acceptable in all references for *anno Domini*: in the year of the Lord.

Because the full phrase would read *in the year of the Lord 96*, the abbreviation *A.D.* goes before the figure for the year: *A.D. 96*.

Do not write: *The fourth century A.D. The fourth century* is sufficient. If *A.D.* is not specified with a year, the year is presumed to be A.D.

See **B.C.**

-added Follow this form in sports stories: *The $50,000-added sweepstakes*.

addresses Use the abbreviations *Ave.*, *Blvd.* and *St.* only with a numbered address: *1600 Pennsylvania Ave.* Spell them out and capitalize when part of a formal street name without a number: *Pennsylvania Avenue*. Lowercase and spell out when used alone or with more than one street name: *Massachusetts and Pennsylvania avenues*.

All similar words (*alley, drive, road, terrace,* etc.) always are spelled out. Capitalize them when part of a formal name without a number; lowercase when used alone or with two or more names.

Always use figures for an address number: *9 Morningside Circle*.

Spell out and capitalize *First* through *Ninth* when used as street names; use figures with two letters for *10th* and above: *7 Fifth Ave., 100 21st St.*

Abbreviate compass points used to indicate directional ends of a street or quadrants of a city in a numbered address: *222 E. 42nd St., 562 W. 43rd St., 600 K St. N.W.* Do not abbreviate if the number is omitted: *East 42nd Street, West 43rd Street, K Street Northwest*.

See **highway designations**.

adjectives The abbreviation *adj.* is used in this book to identify the spelling of the adjectival forms of words that frequently are misspelled.

The **comma** entry provides guidance on punctuating a series of adjectives.

The **hyphen** entry provides guidance on handling compound modifiers used before a noun.

ad-lib (n., v., adj.)

administration Lowercase: *the administration, the president's administration, the governor's administration, the Reagan administration.*

See the **government, junta, regime** entry for distinctions that apply in using these terms and *administration.*

administrative law judge This is the federal title for the position formerly known as *hearing examiner.* Capitalize it when used as a formal title before a name.

To avoid the long title, seek a construction that sets the title off by commas: *The administrative law judge, John Williams, disagreed.*

administrator Never abbreviate. Capitalize when used as a formal title before a name.
See **titles**.

admiral See **military titles**.

admissible

admit, admitted These words may in some contexts give the erroneous connotation of wrongdoing.

A person who announces that he is a homosexual, for example, may be acknowledging it to the world, not admitting it. *Said* is usually sufficient.

ad nauseam

adopt, approve, enact, pass Amendments, ordinances, resolutions and rules are adopted or approved.
Bills are *passed.*
Laws are *enacted.*

Adrenalin A trademark for the synthetic or chemically extracted forms of epinephrine, a substance produced by the adrenal glands.

The nonproprietary terms are *epinephrine hydrochloride* or *adrenaline.*

Adventist See **Seventh-day Adventist Church**.

adverbs The abbreviation *adv.* is used in this book to identify the spelling of adverbial forms of words frequently misspelled.

See the **hyphen** entry in the **Punctuation** chapter for guidelines on when an adverb should be followed by a hyphen in constructing a compound modifier.

adverse, averse *Adverse* means unfavorable: *He predicted adverse weather.*

Averse means reluctant, opposed: *She is averse to change.*

adviser Not *advisor.*

advisory

Aer Lingus The headquarters of this airline is in Dublin, Ireland.

Aeroflot The headquarters of this airline is in Moscow.

Aeromexico This airline formerly was known as Aeronaves de Mexico.

Headquarters is in Mexico City.

aesthetic

affect, effect *Affect*, as a verb, means to influence: *The game will affect the standings.*

Affect, as a noun, is best avoided. It occasionally is used in psychology to describe an emotion, but there is no need for it in everyday language.

Effect, as a verb, means to cause: *He will effect many changes in the company.*

Effect, as a noun, means result: *The effect was overwhelming. He miscalculated the effect of his actions. It was a law of little effect.*

Afghan (adj.) *Afghani* is the *Afghan* unit of currency.

AFL-CIO Acceptable in all references for the *American Federation of Labor and Congress of Industrial Organizations.*

A-frame

African Of or pertaining to Africa, or any of its peoples or languages. Do not use the word as a synonym for *black* or *Negro.*

In some countries of Africa, *colored* is used to describe those of mixed white and black ancestry. In other societies *colored* is considered a derogatory word.

Because of the ambiguity, avoid the term in favor of a phrase such as *mixed racial ancestry.* If the word cannot be avoided, place it in quotation marks and provide its meaning.
See **colored**.

African-American The preferred term is *black*. Use *African-American* only in quotations or the names of organizations or if individuals describe themselves so.
See **black**.

after- No hyphen after this prefix when it is used to form a noun:
aftereffect   afterthought
Follow *after* with a hyphen when it is used to form compound modifiers:
after-dinner drink   after-theater snack

afterward Not *afterwards.*

Agency for International Development *AID* is acceptable on second reference.

agenda A list. It takes singular verbs and pronouns: *The agenda has run its course.*
The plural is *agendas.*

agent Lowercase unless it is a formal title used before a name.

In the FBI, the formal title is *special agent.* Use *Special Agent William Smith* if appropriate in a special context. Otherwise, make it *agent William Smith* or *FBI agent William Smith.*
See **titles.**

ages Always use figures. When the context does not require *years* or *years old*, the figure is presumed to be *years.*

Ages expressed as adjectives before a noun or as substitutes for a noun use hyphens.

Examples: *A 5-year-old boy,* but *the boy is 5 years old. The boy, 7, has a sister, 10. The woman, 26, has a daughter 2 months old. The law is 8 years old. The race is for 3-year-olds.*

The woman is in her 30s (no apostrophe).

See also **boy**; **girl**; **infant**; and **youth**.

See **comma** in **punctuation guidelines**.

ages of history See the **historical periods and events** entry.

agnostic, atheist An *agnostic* is a person who believes it is impossible to know whether there is a God.

An *atheist* is a person who believes there is no God.

aid, aide *Aid* is assistance.

An *aide* is a person who serves as an assistant.

aide-de-camp, aides-de-camp A military officer who serves as assistant and confidential secretary to a superior.

AIDS Acceptable in all references for *acquired immune deficiency syndrome*, sometimes written as *acquired immunodeficiency syndrome*.

AIDS is an affliction in which a virus has weakened the body's immune system and cancer or serious infections have occurred. *AIDS* is spread most often through sexual contact; contaminated needles or syringes shared by drug abusers; infected blood or blood products; and from pregnant women to their offspring.

The scientific name for the virus is human immunodeficiency virus, or HIV. The most common type of the virus is often designated HIV-1 to distinguish it from another type called HIV-2.

National *AIDS* statistics, which are updated monthly, are available from the federal government's Centers for Disease Control and Prevention in Atlanta.

A note about *AIDS* tests: Routine *AIDS* tests look for the presence of antibodies the body has made to defend against the *AIDS* virus. A positive antibody test is evidence of an infection with the *AIDS* virus. People who test positive are often described as being *HIV-positive*. (Hyphenate *HIV-positive* only when used as a compound adjective. *HIV virus* is redundant.)

A positive result does not mean the person tested has *AIDS*. People infected with the virus do not have *AIDS* until they develop serious symptoms. Many remain infected but apparently healthy for years.

AIDS antibody tests should be distinguished from tests for the *AIDS* virus itself. The presence of the *AIDS* virus can be confirmed by laboratory cultures or by the much more sensitive polymerase chain reaction, or PCR, test.

ain't A dialectical or substandard contraction. Use it only in quoted matter or special contexts.

air base Two words. Follow the practice of the U.S. Air Force, which uses *air force base* as part of the proper name for its bases in the United States and *air base* for its installations abroad.

On second reference: *the Air Force base*, *the air base*, or *the base*.

Do not abbreviate, even in datelines:

LACKLAND AIR FORCE BASE, Texas (AP) —

Air Canada Headquarters is in Montreal.

air-condition, air-conditioned (v. and adj.) The nouns are: *air conditioner, air conditioning*.

aircraft names Use a hyphen when changing from letters to figures; no hyphen when adding a letter after figures.

Some examples for aircraft often in the news: *B-1, BAC-111, C-5A, DC-10, FH-227, F-15 Eagle, F-16 Falcon, L-1011, MiG-21, Tu-144, 727-100C, 747, 747B, VC-10. Airbus A300* or *A300* (no hyphen) is an exception.

This hyphenation principle is the one used most frequently by manufacturers and users. Apply it in all cases for consistency. For other elements of a name, use the form adopted by the manufacturer or user. If in doubt, consult Jane's All the World's Aircraft.

NO QUOTES: Do not use quotation marks for aircraft with names: *Air Force One, the Spirit of St. Louis, Concorde.*

PLURALS: *DC-10s, 747s.* But: *747B's.* (As noted in **plurals**, the apostrophe is used in forming the plural of a single letter.)

SEQUENCE: Use Arabic figures to establish the sequence of aircraft, spacecraft and missiles: *Apollo 10.* Do not use hyphens.

aircraft terms Use *engine*, not *motor*, for the units that propel aircraft: a *twin-engine* plane (not *twin engined*).

Use *jet plane* or *jetliner* to describe only those aircraft driven solely by jet engines. Use *turboprop* to describe an aircraft on which the jet engine is geared to a propeller. Turboprops sometimes are called *propjets.*

Jet planes in commercial use include the *BAC-111; Boeing 707, 727, 737, 747; the Convair 880; the DC-8, DC-9,* and *DC-10; the L-1011;* and *the VC-10.*

See the **engine, motor** entry.

air force Capitalize when referring to U.S. forces: *the U.S. Air Force, the Air Force, Air Force regulations.* Do not use the abbreviation *USAF.*

Congress established the Army Air Forces (note the *s*) in 1941. Prior to that, the air arm was known as the U.S. Army Air Corps. The U.S. Air Force (no *s*) was created as a separate service in 1947.

Use lowercase for the forces of other nations: *the Israeli air force.*

This approach has been adopted for consistency, because many foreign nations do not use *air force* as the proper name.

See the **military academies** and **military titles** entries.

air force base See **air base**.

Air Force One The Air Force applies this name to any of its aircraft the president of the United States may be using.

In ordinary usage, however, *Air Force One* is the name of the Air Force plane normally reserved for the president's use.

Air France Headquarters is in Paris.

Air-India The hyphen is part of the formal name.

Headquarters is in Bombay, India.

Air Jamaica Headquarters is in Kingston, Jamaica.

airline, airlines Capitalize *airlines*, *air lines* and *airways* when used as part of a proper airline name.

Major airlines are listed in this book separately by name.

Companies that use *airlines* include Alitalia, American, Continental, Hawaiian, Japan, Northwest, Trans World, United and Western.

Delta uses *air lines*.

Companies that use *airways* include British and Qantas.

Companies that use none of these include Aer Lingus, Aeromexico, Air Canada, Air France, Air-India, Air Jamaica, Hughes Airwest, Iberia, KLM and Western Alaska.

On second reference, use just the proper name (*Delta*), an abbreviation if applicable (*TWA*), or *the airline*. Use *airlines* when referring to more than one line.

Do not use *air line*, *air lines* or *airways* in generic references to an airline.

airmail

airman See **military titles**.

Air National Guard

airport Capitalize as part of a proper name: *La Guardia Airport*, *Newark International Airport*.

The first name of an individual and the word *international* may be deleted from a formal airport name while the remainder is capitalized: *John F. Kennedy International Airport*, *Kennedy International Airport*, or *Kennedy Airport*. Use whichever is appropriate in the context.

Do not make up names, however. There is no *Boston Airport*, for example. The *Boston airport* (lowercase *airport*) would be acceptable if for some reason the proper name, *Logan International Airport*, were not used.

airtight

air traffic controller (no hyphen)

airways The system of routes that the federal government has established for airplane traffic.

See the **airline, airlines** entry for its use in carriers' names.

aka (no spacing is an exception to Webster's)

Alabama Abbrev.: *Ala.* See **state names**.

a la carte

a la king, a la mode

Alaska Do not abbreviate. Largest land area of the 50 states. See **state names**.

Alaska Standard Time The time zone used in all of Alaska, except the western Aleutian Islands and St. Lawrence Island, which are on *Hawaii-Aleutian Standard Time*.

There is also an *Alaska Daylight Time*.

See **time zones**.

Alberta A province of western Canada. Do not abbreviate. See **datelines**.

albino, albinos

Alcoa Inc. *Alcoa* is acceptable in all references to the formerly named Aluminum Company of America.

Alcoa also is a city in Tennessee.

alcoholic Use *recovering*, not *reformed*, in referring to those afflicted with the disease of alcoholism.

alderman Do not abbreviate. See **legislative titles**.

alert See **weather terms**.

Al Fatah A Palestinian guerrilla organization. Drop the article *Al* if preceded by an English article: *the Fatah statement, a Fatah leader*.

align

Alitalia Airlines Headquarters is in Rome.

all- Use a hyphen:
all-around (not all-round) all-out
all-clear   all-star
See **all right** and the **all time, all-time** entries.

Allahu akbar The Arabic phrase for "God is great."

allege The word must be used with great care.
Some guidelines:
—Avoid any suggestion that the writer is making an allegation.
—Specify the source of an allegation. In a criminal case, it should be an arrest record, an indictment or the statement of a public official connected with the case.
—Use *alleged bribe* or similar phrase when necessary to make it clear that an unproved action is not being treated as fact. Be sure that the source of the charge is specified elsewhere in the story.
—Avoid redundant uses of *alleged*. It is proper to say: *The district attorney alleged that she took*

a bribe. Or: *The district attorney accused her of taking a bribe.* But not: *The district attorney accused her of allegedly taking a bribe.*
—Do not use *alleged* to describe an event that is known to have occurred, when the dispute is over who participated in it. Do not say: *He attended the alleged meeting* when what you mean is: *He allegedly attended the meeting.*
—Do not use *alleged* as a routine qualifier. Instead, use a word such as *apparent, ostensible* or *reputed.*
For guidelines on related words, see **accused; arrest;** and **indict**.

Allegheny Mountains Or simply: *the Alleghenies.*

alley Do not abbreviate. See **addresses**.

allies, allied Capitalize *allies* or *allied* only when referring to the combination of the United States and its Allies during World War I or World War II: *The Allies defeated Germany. He was in the Allied invasion of France.*

allot, allotted, allotting

all right (adv.) Never *alright*. Hyphenate only if used colloquially as a compound modifier: *He is an all-right guy.*

all time, all-time An *all-time high,* but *the greatest runner of all time.*
Avoid the redundant phrase *all-time record.*

allude, refer To *allude* to something is to speak of it without specifically mentioning it.

To *refer* is to mention it directly.

allusion, illusion *Allusion* means an indirect reference: *The allusion was to his opponent's war record.*

Illusion means an unreal or false impression: *The scenic director created the illusion of choppy seas.*

alma mater

almost never Do not use the phrase. Instead use *seldom* or *hardly ever.*

also-ran (n.)

altar, alter An *altar* is a tablelike platform used in a religious service.

To alter is to change.

Aluminum Company of America Now Alcoa Inc. See **Alcoa**.

alumnus, alumni, alumna, alumnae Use *alumnus* (*alumni* in the plural) when referring to a man who has attended a school.

Use *alumna* (*alumnae* in the plural) for similar references to a woman.

Use *alumni* when referring to a group of men and women.

Alzheimer's disease This is a progressive, irreversible neurological disorder. Most victims are older than 65, but Alzheimer's can strike in the 40s or 50s.

Symptoms include gradual memory loss, impairment of judgment, disorientation, personality change, difficulty in learning and loss of language skills.

No cure is known.

AM Acceptable in all references to the *amplitude modulation* system of radio transmission.

a.m., p.m. Lowercase, with periods. Avoid the redundant *10 a.m. this morning.*

Amalgamated Transit Union Use this full name on first reference.

Headquarters is in Washington.

ambassador Use for both men and women. Capitalize as a formal title before a name. See **titles**.

amendments to the Constitution Use *First Amendment*, *10th Amendment*, etc.

Colloquial references to the Fifth Amendment's protection against self-incrimination are best avoided, but where appropriate: *He took the Fifth seven times.*

America West Headquarters is in Tempe, Ariz.

American An acceptable description for a resident of the United States. It also may be applied to any resident or citizen of nations in North or South America.

American Airlines Headquarters is in Fort Worth, Texas.

American Baptist Association See **Baptist churches**.

American Baptist Churches in the U.S.A. See **Baptist churches**.

American Bar Association *ABA* is acceptable on second reference. Also: *the bar association, the association.*

Headquarters is in Chicago.

American Broadcasting Cos. See ABC.

American Civil Liberties Union
ACLU is acceptable on second reference.

Headquarters is in New York.

American Federation of Government Employees
Use this full name on first reference to prevent confusion with other unions that represent government workers.

Headquarters is in Washington.

American Federation of Labor and Congress of Industrial Organizations
AFL-CIO is acceptable in all references.

Headquarters is in Washington.

American Federation of Musicians
Use this full name on first reference.

The shortened form *Musicians' union* is acceptable on second reference.

Headquarters is in New York.

American Federation of State, County and Municipal Employees
Use this full name on first reference to prevent confusion with other unions that represent government workers.

Headquarters is in Washington.

American Federation of Teachers
Use this full name on first reference to prevent confusion with other unions that represent teachers.

Headquarters is in Washington.

American Federation of Television and Radio Artists
AFTRA is acceptable on second reference.

Headquarters is in New York.

American Hospital Association
AHA is acceptable on second reference. Also: *the hospital association, the association.*

Headquarters is in Chicago.

Americanisms
Words and phrases that have become part of the English language as spoken in the United States are listed with a star in Webster's New World Dictionary.

Most Americanisms are acceptable in news stories, but let the context be the guide.

See **word selection**.

American Legion
Capitalize also *the Legion* in second reference. Members are *Legionnaires*, just as members of the Lions Club are *Lions*.

Legion and *Legionnaires* are capitalized because they are not being used in their common noun sense. A *legion* (lowercase) is a large group of soldiers or, by derivation, a large number of items: *His friends are legion.* A *legionnaire* (lowercase) is a member of such a legion.

See the **fraternal organizations and service clubs** entry.

American Medical Association
AMA is acceptable on second reference. Also: *the medical association, the association.*

Headquarters is in Chicago.

American Newspaper Publishers Association
See **Newspaper Association of America**.

American Petroleum Institute *API* is acceptable on second reference.

Headquarters is in Washington.

American Postal Workers Union This union represents clerks and similar employees who work inside post offices.

Use the full name on first reference to prevent confusion with the National Association of Letter Carriers. The shortened form *Postal Workers union* is acceptable on second reference.

Headquarters is in Washington.

American Press Institute *API* is acceptable on second reference.

Headquarters is in Reston, Va.

American Society for the Prevention of Cruelty to Animals This organization is limited to the five boroughs of New York City and neighboring Suffolk County in providing animal adoption services, although it has offices elsewhere that offer legal advice and other services to other animal welfare organizations. *ASPCA* is acceptable on second reference.

See **Society for the Prevention of Cruelty to Animals.**

American Society of Composers, Authors and Publishers *ASCAP* is acceptable on second reference.

Headquarters is in New York.

American Stock Exchange In second reference: *the American Exchange, the Amex,* or *the exchange.*

American Telephone & Telegraph Co. See **AT&T Corp.**

American Veterans of World War II, Korea and Vietnam *AMVETS* is acceptable in all references.

Headquarters is in Washington.

Amex See **American Stock Exchange.**

amid Not *amidst.*

amidships

ammunition See **weapons.**

amnesty See the entry that reads **pardon, parole, probation.**

amok Not *amuck.*

among, between The maxim that *between* introduces two items and *among* introduces more than two covers most questions about how to use these words: *The funds were divided among Ford, Carter and McCarthy.*

However, *between* is the correct word when expressing the relationships of three or more items considered one pair at a time: *Negotiations on a debate format are under way between the network and the Ford, Carter and McCarthy committees.*

As with all prepositions, any pronouns that follow these words must be in the objective case: *among us, between him and her, between you and me.*

ampersand (&) See entry in **Punctuation** section.

amplitude modulation *AM* is acceptable in all references.

Amtrak This acronym, drawn from the words *American travel by track*, may be used in all references to the *National Railroad Passenger Corp.* Do not use *AMTRAK*.

The corporation was established by Congress in 1970 to take over intercity passenger operations from railroads that wanted to drop passenger service. Amtrak contracts with railroads for the use of their tracks and of certain other operating equipment and crews.

Amtrak is subsidized in part by federal funds appropriated yearly by Congress and administered through the Department of Transportation.

Amtrak should not be confused with *Conrail* (see separate entry). However, the legislation that established Conrail provided for Amtrak to gradually take over ownership of certain trackage in the Boston-Washington corridor and from Philadelphia to Harrisburg.

Amtrak headquarters is in Washington.

AMVETS Acceptable in all references for *American Veterans of World War II, Korea and Vietnam.*

anchorman, anchorwoman (not anchor or co-anchor)

anemia, anemic

Anglican Communion This is the name for the worldwide association of the 22 separate national Anglican churches.

Each national church is independent. A special position of honor is accorded to the archbishop of Canterbury, as the preeminent officer in the original Anglican body, the Church of England.

The test of membership in the Anglican Communion traditionally has been whether a church has been in communion with the See of Canterbury. No legislative or juridical ties exist, however.

BELIEFS: Anglicans believe in the Trinity, the humanity and divinity of Christ, the virginity of Mary, salvation through Christ, and everlasting heaven and hell.

A principal difference between Roman Catholics and Anglicans is still the dispute that led to the formation of the Church of England — refusal to acknowledge that the pope, as bishop of Rome, has ruling authority over other bishops. See **catholic, catholicism**.

ANGLICAN CHURCHES: Members of the Anglican Communion, in addition to the Church of England, include the Scottish Episcopal Church, the Anglican Church of Canada, and, in the United States, the Protestant Episcopal Church.

See **Episcopal Church**.

Anglo- Always capitalized. No hyphen when the word that follows is in lowercase:

Anglomania   Anglophobe
Anglophile

Use a hyphen when the word that follows is capitalized:

Anglo-American   Anglo-Indian
Anglo-Catholic   Anglo-Saxon

angry *At* someone or *with* someone.

animals Do not apply a personal pronoun to an animal unless its sex has been established or the animal has a name: *The dog was scared; it barked. Rover* *was scared; he barked. The cat, which was scared, ran to its basket. Susie the cat, who was scared, ran to her basket. The bull tosses his horns.*

Capitalize the name of a specific animal, and use Roman numerals to show sequence: *Bowser, Whirlaway II.*

For breed names, follow the spelling and capitalization in Webster's New World Dictionary. For breeds not listed in the dictionary, capitalize words derived from proper nouns; use lowercase elsewhere: *basset hound, Boston terrier.*

anno Domini See **A.D.**

annual An event cannot be described as *annual* until it has been held in at least two successive years.

Do not use the term *first annual.* Instead, note that sponsors plan to hold an event annually.

annual meeting Lowercase in all uses.

anoint

another *Another* is not a synonym for *additional*; it refers to an element that somehow duplicates a previously stated quantity.

Right: *Ten people took the test; another 10 refused.*

Wrong: *Ten people took the test; another 20 refused.*

Right: *Ten people took the test; 20 others refused.*

Antarctic, Antarctica, Antarctic Ocean

ante- The rules in prefixes apply, but in general, no hyphen. Some examples:

antebellum   antedate

anthems See **composition titles**. Lowercase the term *national anthem.*

anti- Hyphenate all except the following words, which have specific meanings of their own:

antibiotic	antipasto
antibody	antiperspirant
anticlimax	antiphon
antidote	antiphony
antifreeze	antiseptic
antigen	antiserum
antihistamine	antithesis
antiknock	antitoxin
antimatter	antitrust
antimony	antitussive
antiparticle*	

*And similar terms in physics such as *antiproton.*

This approach has been adopted in the interests of readability and easily remembered consistency.

Hyphenated words, many of them exceptions to Webster's New World, include:

anti-aircraft	anti-labor
anti-bias	anti-Semitic
anti-inflation	anti-social
anti-intellectual	anti-war

See **Antichrist, anti-Christ**.

Antichrist, anti-Christ *Antichrist* is the proper name for the individual the Bible says will challenge Christ.

The adjective *anti-Christ* would be applied to someone or something opposed to Christ.

anticipate, expect *Anticipate* means to expect and prepare for something; *expect* does not include the notion of preparation:

They expect a record crowd. They have anticipated it by adding more seats to the auditorium.

Antiochian Orthodox Christian Archdiocese of North America Formed in

1975 by the merger of the Antiochian Orthodox Christian Archdiocese of New York and All North America and the Archdiocese of Toledo, Ohio, and Dependencies in North America. It is under the jurisdiction of the patriarch of Antioch.

See **Eastern Orthodox churches**.

anybody, any body, anyone, any one One word for an indefinite reference: *Anyone can do that.*

Two words when the emphasis is on singling out one element of a group: *Any one of them may speak up.*

AOL Time Warner Inc. A merger of America Online and Time Warner Inc., approved in January 2000.

Time Warner holdings included CNN, Time magazine, TBS, TNT, Cartoon Network, HBO, Warner Music Group, Fortune, Sports Illustrated, Entertainment Weekly and Looney Tunes. The online company AOL owned Netscape Communications, MovieFone, CompuServe and a stake in Hughes Electronics, a maker of electronic equipment.

AP Use in logotypes. Acceptable on second reference for *The Associated Press.*

Do not capitalize *the* when it precedes *AP*.

See **Associated Press**.

apostolic delegate, papal nuncio An *apostolic delegate* is a Roman Catholic diplomat chosen by the pope to be his envoy to the church in a nation that does not have formal diplomatic relations with the Vatican.

A *papal nuncio* is the pope's envoy to a nation with which the Vatican has diplomatic relations.

apostrophe (') See entry in **Punctuation** section.

Appalachia In the broadest sense, the word applies to the entire region along the Appalachian Mountains, which extend from Maine into northern Alabama.

In a sense that often suggests economic depression and poverty, the reference is to sections of eastern Tennessee, eastern Kentucky, southeastern Ohio and the western portion of West Virginia.

The Appalachian Regional Commission, established by federal law in 1965, has a mandate to foster development in 397 counties in 13 states — all of West Virginia and parts of Alabama, Georgia, Kentucky, Maryland, Mississippi, New York, North Carolina, Ohio, Pennsylvania, South Carolina, Tennessee and Virginia.

When the word *Appalachia* is used, specify the extent of the area in question.

Appalachian Mountains Or simply: *the Appalachians.*

appeals court See **U.S. Court of Appeals**.

apposition A decision on whether to put commas around a word, phrase or clause used in apposition depends on whether it is essential to the meaning of the sentence (no commas) or not essential (use commas).

See the **essential phrases, nonessential phrases** entry for examples.

approve See the entry that reads **adopt, approve, enact, pass**.

April See **months**.

April Fools' Day

Aqua-Lung A trademark for an underwater breathing apparatus.

See **scuba**.

Arabic names In general, use an English spelling that approximates the way a name sounds in Arabic.

If an individual has a preferred spelling in English, use that. If usage has established a particular spelling, use that.

Problems in transliteration of Arabic names often are traceable to pronunciations that vary from region to region. The *g*, for example, is pronounced like the *g* of *go* in North Africa, but like the *j* of *joy* in the Arab Peninsula. Thus it is *Gamal* in Egypt and *Jamal* in nations on the peninsula. Follow local practice in deciding which letter to use.

Arabs commonly are known by two names (*Fuad Butros*), or by three (*Ahmed Zaki Yamani*). Follow the individual's preference on first reference. On second reference, use only the final name in the sequence.

The articles *al-* or *el-* may be used or dropped depending on the person's preference or established usage. *Osama el-Baz, el-Baz* or *Moammar Gadhafi, Gadhafi*.

The Arabic word for son (ibn or bin depending on personal preference and the nation) is sometimes part of a name (*Rashid bin Humaid*). On second reference, use only the final word in the name: Humaid.

The word *abu*, meaning *father of*, occasionally is used as a last name (*Abdul Mohsen Abu Maizer*). Capitalize and repeat it on second reference: *Abu Maizer*.

The titles *king, emir, sheik* and *imam* are used, but *prince* usually replaces *emir*. Some Arabs are known only by the title and a given name on first reference (*King Hussein*). Others are known by a complete name (*Sheik Sabah Salem Sabah*). Follow the common usage on first reference. On second reference, drop the title, using only the given name if it stood alone (*Hussein*) or the final name in the sequence if more than one was used on first reference (*Sabah*). Make an exception to this procedure for second reference if an individual commonly is known by some other one of the names used on first reference.

The *al*, when found in front of many newspaper names, means *the*. It should be capitalized, as in *The New York Times, El Pais, Die Welt*.

Arabic numerals The numerical figures *1, 2, 3, 4, 5, 6, 7, 8, 9, 10*.

In general, use Arabic forms unless denoting the sequence of wars or establishing a personal sequence for people or animals. See **Roman numerals**.

Separate entries list more details and examples. For a full list, see the **numerals** entry.

arbitrate, mediate Both terms are used in reports about labor negotiations, but they should not be interchanged.

One who *arbitrates* hears evidence from all people concerned, then hands down a decision.

One who *mediates* listens to arguments of both parties and tries by the exercise of reason or persuasion to bring them to an agreement.

arch- No hyphen after this prefix unless it precedes a capitalized word:

archbishop   arch-Republican
archenemy   archrival

archaeology

archbishop See **Episcopal Church; Roman Catholic Church;** and **religious titles**.

archbishop of Canterbury In general, lowercase *archbishop* unless it is used before the name of the individual who holds the office.

Capitalize *Archbishop of Canterbury* standing alone only when it is used in a story that also refers to members of Britain's nobility. See the **nobility** entry for the relevant guidelines.

archdiocese Capitalize as part of a proper name: *the Archdiocese of Chicago, the Chicago Archdiocese*. Lowercase when it stands alone.

See the entry for the particular denomination in question.

arctic (lowercase for adjective meaning frigid; capitalize for region around the North Pole), **Arctic Circle, arctic fox, Arctic Ocean**

are A unit of surface measure in the metric system, equal to 100 square meters.

An *are* is equal to approximately 1,076.4 square feet or 119.6 square yards.

See **hectare** and **metric system**.

area codes See **telephone numbers**.

Arizona Abbrev.: *Ariz.* See **state names**.

Arkansas Abbrev.: *Ark.* See **state names**.

Armenian Church of America The term encompasses two independent dioceses that cooperate in some activities: the Eastern Diocese of the Armenian Church of America, for areas outside California, and the Western Diocese of the Armenian Church of America, which serves California.

See **Eastern Orthodox Churches**.

Armistice Day It is now *Veterans Day*.

army Capitalize when referring to U.S. forces: *the U.S. Army, the Army, Army regulations*. Do not use the abbreviation *USA*.

Use lowercase for the forces of other nations: *the French army*.

This approach has been adopted for consistency, because many foreign nations do not use *army* as the proper name.

See **military academies** and **military titles**.

arrest To avoid any suggestion that someone is being judged before a trial, do not use a phrase such as *arrested for killing*. Instead, use *arrested on a charge of killing*.

For guidelines on related words, see **accuse; allege;** and **indict**.

arrive It requires the preposition *at*. Do not omit, as airline dispatchers often do in: *He will arrive La Guardia.*

artifact

artificial intelligence Ideally, computers that think like humans. Currently, computers cannot apply experience, logic, and prediction to problem-solving. They act only on instructions, either from the program or from the user.

artillery See **weapons**.

artworks See **composition titles**.

as See **like, as**.

ashcan, ashtray

Ash Wednesday The first day of Lent, 46 days before Easter.

See **Easter** and **Lent**.

Asian, Asiatic Use *Asian* or *Asians* when referring to people.

Some Asians regard *Asiatic* as offensive when applied to people.

Asian flu

Asian subcontinent In popular usage the term applies to Bangladesh, Bhutan, India, Nepal, Pakistan, Sikkim and the island nation of Sri Lanka (formerly Ceylon) at the southeastern tip of India.

For definitions of the terms that apply to other parts of Asia, see **Far East; Middle East**; and **Southeast Asia**.

as if The preferred form, but *as though* is acceptable.

assassin, killer, murderer

An *assassin* is a politically motivated killer.

A *killer* is anyone who kills with a motive of any kind.

A *murderer* is one who is convicted of murder in a court of law.

See **execute** and the **homicide, murder, manslaughter** entry.

assassination, date of A prominent person is shot one day and dies the next. Which day was he assassinated? The day he was attacked.

assault, battery Popularly, *assault* almost always implies physical contact and sudden, intense violence.

Legally, however, *assault* means simply to threaten violence, as in pointing a pistol at an individual without firing it. *Assault and battery* is the legal term when the victim was touched by the assaulter or something the assaulter put in motion.

assembly Capitalize when part of the proper name for the lower house of a legislature: *the California Assembly*. Retain capitalization if the state name is dropped but the reference is specific:

SACRAMENTO, Calif. (AP) — The state Assembly ...

If a legislature is known as a general assembly: *the Missouri General Assembly, the General Assembly, the assembly. Legislature* also may be used as the proper name, however. See **legislature**.

Lowercase all plural uses: *the California and New York assemblies.*

assemblyman, assembly-woman Do not abbreviate. See legislative titles.

assistant Do not abbreviate. Capitalize only when part of a formal title before a name: *Assistant Secretary of State George Ball.* Whenever practical, however, an appositional construction should be used: *George Ball, assistant secretary of state.*
See **titles**.

associate Never abbreviate. Apply the same capitalization norms listed under **assistant**.

Associated Press, The The newsgathering cooperative dating from 1848.
Use *The Associated Press* on first reference (the capitalized article is part of the formal name).
On second reference, *AP* or *the AP* (no capital on *the*) may be used.
The address is 50 Rockefeller Plaza, New York, NY 10020. The telephone number is (212) 621-1500.
The World Wide Web address is www.ap.org.
The following are service names used most frequently by the AP.

DataFeature
DataSpeed
DataStream
DataStream 500 Stocks
DigitalStocks
GraphicsNet
Newsfeatures
NewsPhoto
NewsPower
Network News
PhotoColor
PhotoExpress
PhotoStream
SelectStocks

SportsStats
See the **AP** entry.

Association Do not abbreviate. Capitalize as part of a proper name: *American Medical Association.*

astronaut It is not a formal title. Do not capitalize when used before a name: *astronaut John Glenn.*

AT&T Corp. The full name of the business formerly known as American Telephone & Telegraph Co.
Headquarters is in New York.

Atchison, Topeka & Santa Fe Railway A subsidiary of Burlington Northern Santa Fe Corp.
Headquarters is in Fort Worth, Texas.

atheist See the **agnostic, atheist** entry.

athlete's foot, athlete's heart

Atlanta The city in Georgia stands alone in datelines.

Atlantic Ocean

Atlantic Richfield Co. *Arco* is acceptable on second reference.
Headquarters is in Los Angeles.

Atlantic Standard Time, Atlantic Daylight Time Used in the Maritime Provinces of Canada and in Puerto Rico.
See **time zones**.

at large Usually two words for an individual representing more than a single district: *con-*

gressman at large, councilman at large.

But it is *ambassador-at-large* for an ambassador assigned to no particular country.

Atomic Age It began Dec. 2, 1942, at the University of Chicago with the creation of the first self-sustaining nuclear chain reaction.

Atomic Energy Commission It no longer exists. See **Nuclear Regulatory Commission**.

attache It is not a formal title. Always lowercase.

attorney, lawyer In common usage the words are interchangeable.

Technically, however, an *attorney* is someone (usually, but not necessarily, a lawyer) empowered to act for another. Such an individual occasionally is called an *attorney in fact.*

A *lawyer* is a person admitted to practice in a court system. Such an individual occasionally is called an *attorney at law.*

Do not abbreviate. Do not capitalize unless it is an officeholder's title: *defense attorney Perry Mason, attorney Perry Mason, District Attorney Hamilton Burger.*

See **lawyer**.

attorney general, attorneys general Never abbreviate. Capitalize only when used as a title before a name: *Attorney General Griffin B. Bell.*

See **titles**.

augur A transitive verb. Do not follow it with the preposition for: *The tea leaves augur a time of success.*

August See **months**.

author A noun used for both men and women. Do not use it as a verb.

automaker, automakers

automatic See **pistol** and **weapons** entries.

automobiles Capitalize brand names: *Buick, Ford, Mustang, Accord, Toyota, Taurus, Saturn.* Lowercase generic terms: *Sunfire convertible, Windstar minivan.*

Auto-Train Corp. A private company that hauls passengers and their cars, leasing rails and equipment owned by other companies.

Headquarters is in Washington.

autoworker, autoworkers One word when used generically.

But *Auto Worker* when referring specifically to the membership and the activities of the United Automobile, Aerospace and Agricultural Implement Workers of America.

autumn See **seasons**.

avenue Abbreviate only with a numbered address. See **addresses**.

average, mean, median, norm *Average* refers to the result obtained by dividing a sum by the number of quantities added together: *The average of 7, 9, 17 is 33 divided by 3, or 11.*

Mean commonly designates a figure intermediate between two extremes, determined by adding the series of numbers and dividing the sum by the number of cases: *The mean temperature of five days with temperatures of 67, 62, 68, 69, 64 is 66.*

Median is the middle number of points in a series arranged in order of size: *The median grade in the group of 50, 55, 85, 88, 92 is 85. The average is 74.*

Norm implies a standard of average performance for a given group: *The child was below the norm for his age in reading comprehension.*

average of The phrase takes a plural verb in a construction such as: *An average of 100 new jobs are created daily.*

averse See **adverse, averse**.

Avianca The headquarters of this airline is in Bogota, Colombia.

aviator Use for both men and women.

awards and decorations Capitalize them: *Bronze Star, Medal of Honor*, etc.

See **Nobel Prize** and **Pulitzer Prize**.

awe-struck

awhile, a while *He plans to stay awhile.*

He plans to stay for a while.

AWOL Acceptable on second reference for *absent without leave.*

ax Not *axe.*

The verb forms: *ax, axed, axing.*

Axis The alliance of Germany, Italy and Japan during World War II.

B

Baby Bells A collective description of the regional telephone companies formed out of the breakup of the Bell System of AT&T. Avoid except in quotes.

baby boomer Lowercase, no hyphen.

baby-sit, baby-sitting, baby-sat, baby sitter

baccalaureate

bachelor of arts, bachelor of science A *bachelor's degree* or *bachelor's* is acceptable in any reference.

See **academic degrees** for guidelines on when the abbreviations *B.A.* or *B.S.* are acceptable.

back up (v.) **backup** (n. and adj.)

backward Not backwards.

back yard (n.) **backyard** (adj.)

bad, badly *Bad* should not be used as an adverb. It does not lose its status as an adjective, however, in a sentence such as *I feel bad.* Such a statement is the idiomatic equivalent of *I am in bad health.* An alternative, *I feel badly*, could be interpreted as

meaning that your sense of touch was bad.

See the **good, well** entry.

Bahamas In datelines, give the name of the city or town followed by *Bahamas:*
NASSAU, Bahamas (AP) —
In stories, use *Bahamas, the Bahamas or the Bahama Islands* as the construction of a sentence dictates.

Identify a specific island in the text if relevant.

bail *Bail* is money or property that will be forfeited to the court if an accused individual fails to appear for trial. It may be posted as follows:

—The accused may deposit with the court the full amount or its equivalent in collateral such as a deed to property.

—A friend or relative may make such a deposit with the court.

—The accused may pay a professional bail bondsman a percentage of the total figure. The bondsman, in turn, guarantees the court that it will receive from him the full amount in the event the individual fails to appear for trial.

It is correct in all cases to say that an accused *posted bail* or *posted a bail bond* (the money held by the court is a form of bond). When a distinction is desired, say that the individual *posted his own bail*, that *bail was posted by a friend or relative*, or that *bail was obtained through a bondsman.*

Bakelite A trademark for a type of plastic resin.

baker's dozen It means 13.

Bakery, Confectionery, Tobacco Workers and Grain Millers International Union The shortened form *Bakery Workers union* is acceptable in all references.

Headquarters is in Washington.

balance of payments, balance of trade The *balance of payments* is the difference between the amount of money that leaves a nation and the amount that enters it during a period of time.

The *balance of payments* is determined by computing the amount of money a nation and its citizens send abroad for all purposes — including goods and services purchased, travel, loans, foreign aid, etc. — and subtracting from it the amount that foreign nations send into the nation for similar purposes.

The *balance of trade* is the difference between the monetary value of the goods a nation imports and the goods it exports.

An example illustrating the difference between the two:

The United States and its citizens might send $10 billion abroad — $5 billion for goods, $3 billion for loans and foreign aid, $1 billion for services and $1 billion for tourism and other purposes.

Other nations might send $9 billion into the United States — $6 billion for U.S. goods, $2 billion for services and $1 billion for tourism and other purposes.

The United States would have a *balance-of-payments* deficit of $1 billion but a *balance-of-trade* surplus of $1 billion.

ball carrier

ballclub, ballpark, ballplayer, ballroom

ball point pen

baloney Foolish or exaggerated talk.

The sausage or luncheon meat is *bologna.*

Baltimore The city in Maryland stands alone in datelines.

Band-Aid A trademark for a type of adhesive bandage.

BankAmerica Corp. A merger of BankAmerica and NationsBank.

Headquarters is in Charlotte, N.C.

bankruptcy See entry in **Business Guidelines**.

baptism See **sacraments**.

baptist, Baptist A person who baptizes is a *baptist* (lowercase).

A *Baptist* (uppercase) is a person who is a member of the Protestant denomination described in the next entry.

Baptist churches It is incorrect to apply the term *church* to any Baptist unit except the local church.

The largest of the more than 20 Baptist bodies in the United States is the Southern Baptist Convention. It has more than 12 million members, most of them in the South, although it has churches in 50 states.

The largest Northern body is American Baptist Churches in the U.S.A., with about 1.5 million members.

Blacks predominate in three other large Baptist bodies, the National Baptist Convention of America, the National Baptist Convention U.S.A. Inc., and the Progressive National Baptist Convention Inc.

The roster of Baptist bodies in the United States also includes the Baptist General Conference, the Conservative Baptist Association of America, the General Association of Regular Baptist Churches, the General Association of General Baptists, and the North American Baptist General Conference.

The Baptist World Alliance, a voluntary association of Baptist bodies throughout the world, organizes the Baptist World Congress meetings generally held every five years. Headquarters is in Washington.

CLERGY: All members of the Baptist clergy may be referred to as *ministers*. *Pastor* applies if a minister leads a congregation.

On first reference, use *the Rev.* before the name of a man or woman. On second reference, use only the last name.

See **religious titles**.

See **religious movements** for definitions of some descriptive terms that often apply to Baptists but are not limited to them.

barbecue Not *barbeque* or *Bar-B-Q*.

barbiturate

barmaid

bar mitzvah The Jewish religious ritual and family celebration that marks a boy's 13th birthday. Judaism regards the age of 13 as the benchmark of religious maturity. *Bar mitzvah* translates as "one who is responsible for the Commandments."

Some congregations have instituted the *bas mitzvah* or *bat mitzvah*, a similar ceremony for girls.

baron, baroness See **nobility**.

barrel A standard barrel in U.S. measure contains 31.5 gallons.

A standard barrel in British and Canadian measure contains 36 imperial gallons.

In international dealings with crude oil, a standard barrel contains 42 U.S. gallons or 35 imperial gallons.

See the **oil** entry for guidelines on computing the volume and weight of petroleum products.

barrel, barreled, barreling

barrel-chested, barrelhouse Also: *double-barreled shotgun*.

barrister See **lawyer**.

barroom

BASIC A computer programming language. Acronym for *Beginners' All-Purpose Symbolic In-*

struction Code. Use of acronym on first reference is acceptable if it is identified as a programming language.

battalion Capitalize when used with a figure to form a name: *the 3rd Battalion, the 10th Battalion.*

battlefield Also: *battlefront, battleground, battleship.* But *battle station.*

Bavarian cream

bay Capitalize as an integral part of a proper name: *Hudson Bay, San Francisco Bay.*

Capitalize also *San Francisco Bay area* or *the Bay area* as the popular name for the nine-county region that has San Francisco as its focal point.

bazaar A fair. *Bizarre* means unusual.

B.C. Acceptable in all references to a calendar year in the period *before Christ.*

Because the full phrase would be *in the year 43 before Christ,* the abbreviation *B.C.* is placed after the figure for the year: *43 B.C.*

See **A.D.**

because, since Use *because* to denote a specific cause-effect relationship: *He went because he was told.*

Since is acceptable in a causal sense when the first event in a sequence led logically to the second but was not its direct cause: *They went to the game, since they had been given the tickets.*

before Christ See **B.C.**

Beijing The city in China (formerly Peking) stands alone in datelines.

Belize The former British Honduras.

bellwether

benefit, benefited, benefiting

Benelux Belgium, the Netherlands and Luxembourg.

If *Benelux* is used, explain that it is an inclusive word for these three nations.

Ben-Gurion International Airport
Located at Lod, Israel, about 10 miles south of Tel Aviv. See **airport.**

Benzedrine A trademark for a type of pep pill or stimulant.

Berlin Stands alone in datelines.

Berlin Wall On second reference, *the wall.*

Bermuda collar, Bermuda grass, Bermuda shorts

beside, besides *Beside* means at the side of.
Besides means in addition to.

besiege

best seller (n.)

betting odds Use figures and a hyphen: *The odds were 5-4, he won despite 3-2 odds against him.*

The word *to* seldom is necessary, but when it appears it should be hyphenated in all constructions: *3-to-2 odds, odds of 3-to-2, the odds were 3-to-2.*

bettor A person who bets.

between See the **among, between** entry.

bi- The rules in **prefixes** apply, but in general, no hyphen. Some examples:

bifocal	bimonthly
bilateral	bipartisan
bilingual	

biannual, biennial *Biannual* means twice a year and is a synonym for the word semiannual.

Biennial means every two years.

Bible Capitalize, without quotation marks, when referring to the Scriptures in the Old Testament or the New Testament. Capitalize also related terms such as the *Gospels, Gospel of St. Mark, the Scriptures, the Holy Scriptures.*

Lowercase *biblical* in all uses.

Lowercase *bible* as a nonreligious term: *My dictionary is my bible.*

Do not abbreviate individual books of the Bible.

Old Testament is a Christian designation; Hebrew Bible or Jewish Bible is the appropriate term for stories dealing with Judaism alone.

The standard names and order of Old Testament books as they appear in Protestant Bibles are: Genesis, Exodus, Leviticus, Numbers, Deuteronomy, Joshua, Judges, Ruth, 1 Samuel, 2 Samuel, 1 Kings, 2 Kings, 1 Chronicles, 2 Chronicles, Ezra, Nehemiah, Esther, Job, Psalms, Proverbs, Ecclesiastes, Song of Solomon, Isaiah, Jeremiah, Lamentations, Ezekiel, Daniel, Hosea, Joel, Amos, Obadiah, Jonah, Micah, Nahum, Habakkuk, Zephaniah, Haggai, Zechariah, Malachi.

Jewish Bibles contain the same 39 books, in different order. Roman Catholic Bibles follow a different order, usually use some different names, and include the seven Deuterocanonical books (called the Apocrypha by Protestants): Tobit, Judith, 1 Maccabees, 2 Maccabees, Wisdom, Sirach, Baruch.

The books of the New Testament, in order: Matthew, Mark, Luke, John, Acts, Romans, 1 Corinthians, 2 Corinthians, Galatians, Ephesians, Philippians, Colossians, 1 Thessalonians, 2 Thessalonians, 1 Timothy, 2 Timothy, Titus, Philemon, Hebrews, James, 1 Peter, 2 Peter, 1 John, 2 John, 3 John, Jude, Revelation.

Citation listing the number of chapter and verse(s) use this form: *Matthew 3:16, Luke 21:1-13, 1 Peter 2:1.*

Bible Belt Those sections of the United States, especially in the South and Middle West, where fundamentalist religious beliefs prevail. Use with care, because in certain contexts it can give offense.

See **religious movements**.

bicycle

big-bang theory The theory that the universe began with the explosion of a superdense primeval atom and has been expanding ever since.

The **oscillating theory**, another hypothesis, maintains that expansion eventually will stop, followed by contraction to a superdense atom, followed by another big bang.

The **steady-state theory**, an alternative hypothesis, maintains that the universe always has existed and that matter constantly is being created to replace matter that is constantly being destroyed.

Big Board Acceptable on second reference for *the New York Stock Exchange*.

big brother One's older brother is a *big brother*. *Big Brother* (capitalized) means under the watchful eye of big government, from George Orwell's "1984."

Capitalize also in reference to members of Big Brothers-Big Sisters of America Inc. The organization has headquarters in Philadelphia.

Big Three automakers A phrase generally referring to General Motors, Ford and Chrysler (a unit of DaimlerChrysler).

bigwig

billion A thousand million.

For forms, see the **millions, billions** entry.

Bill of Rights The first 10 amendments to the Constitution.

bimonthly Means every other month. *Semimonthly* means twice a month.

birthday Capitalize as part of the name for a holiday: *Washington's Birthday*. Lowercase in other uses.

bishop See **religious titles** and the entry for the denomination in question.

biweekly Means every other week. *Semiweekly* means twice a week.

bizarre Unusual. A fair is a *bazaar*.

black Preferred usage for those of the Negro race. (Use *Negro* only in names of organizations or in quotations.) Do not use *colored* as a synonym. See the **colored** entry.

Black Muslims See **Muslim(s)**.

blackout, brownout A *blackout* is a total power failure over a large area or the concealing of lights that might be visible to enemy raiders.

The term *rotating blackout* is used by electric companies to describe a situation in which electric power to some sections temporarily is cut off on a rotating basis to assure that voltage will meet minimum standards in other sections.

A *brownout* is a small, temporary voltage reduction, usually from 2 percent to 8 percent, implemented to conserve electric power.

blast off (v.) **blastoff** (n. and adj.)

Blessed Sacrament, Blessed Virgin

blind See **disabled, handicapped, impaired**.

blizzard See **weather terms**.

bloc, block A *bloc* is a coalition of people, groups or nations with the same purpose or goal.

Block has more than a dozen definitions, but a political alliance is not one of them.

blond, blonde Use *blond* as a noun for males and as an adjective for all applications: She has *blond* hair.

Use *blonde* as a noun for females.

bloodhound

Bloody Mary A drink made of vodka and tomato juice. The name is derived from the nickname for Mary I of England.

blue blood (n.) **blue-blooded** (adj.)

blue chip stock Stock in a company known for its long-established record of making money and paying dividends.

B'nai B'rith See the **fraternal organizations and service clubs** entry.

board Capitalize only when an integral part of a proper name. See **capitalization**.

board of aldermen See **city council**.

board of directors, board of trustees Always lowercase. See the **organizations and institutions** entry.

board of supervisors See **city council**.

boats, ships A *boat* is a watercraft of any size but generally is used to indicate a small craft. A *ship* is a large, seagoing vessel.

The word *boat* is used, however, in some words that apply to large craft: *ferryboat, PT boat, gunboat*.

Use Arabic or Roman numerals in the names of boats and ships: *the Queen Elizabeth 2* or *QE2; Titan I, Titan II*.

The reference for military ships is Jane's Fighting Ships; for nonmilitary ships, Lloyd's Register of Shipping.

Boeing Co. Formerly Boeing Aircraft Co.

Headquarters is in Chicago.

boldface Use boldface type for the slug lines, bylines and underlines for bylines atop a story, and for separate subhead lines if needed within a story.

Do not use boldface for individual words within a paragraph.

bologna The sausage. *Baloney* is foolish or exaggerated talk.

bona fide

bonbon

bonds See **loan terminology** in Business guidelines and style section.

boo-boo

book titles See **composition titles**.

Books on Tape A trademark for a brand of audiotapes. Use a generic term such as audiotape or audiocassette.

borscht

Bosporus, the Not the Bosporus Strait.

Boston The city in Massachusetts stands alone in datelines.

Boston brown bread, Boston cream pie, Boston terrier

boulevard Abbreviated only with a numbered address. See **addresses**.

boundary

bowlegged

box office (n.) **box-office** (adj.)

boy Applicable until 18th birthday is reached. Use *man* or *young man* afterward.

boycott, embargo A *boycott* is an organized refusal to buy a particular product or service, or to deal with a particular merchant or group of merchants.

An *embargo* is a legal restriction against trade. It usually prohibits goods from entering or leaving a country.

boyfriend, girlfriend

Boy Scouts The full name of the national organization is *Boy Scouts of America*. Headquarters is in Irving, Texas.

Cub Scouting is for boys 8 through 10. Members are *Cub Scouts* or *Cubs*.

Boy Scouting is for boys 11 through 17. Members are *Boy Scouts* or *Scouts*.

Exploring is a separate program open to boys and girls from high school age through 20. Members are *Explorers*, not *Explorer Scouts*. Members of units that stress nautical programs are *Sea Explorers*.

See **Girl Scouts**.

BP Amoco PLC Formerly British Petroleum. *BP* is acceptable on second reference.

Headquarters is in London.

bra Acceptable in all references for *brassiere*.

brackets See entry in **Punctuation** chapter.

Brahman, Brahmin *Brahman* applies to the priestly Hindu caste and a breed of cattle.

Brahmin applies to aristocracy in general: *Boston Brahmin*.

brand names When they are used, capitalize them.

Brand names normally should be used only if they are essential to a story.

Sometimes, however, the use of a brand name may not be essential but is acceptable because it lends an air of reality to a story: *He fished a Camel from his shirt pocket* may be preferable to the less specific cigarette.

When a company sponsors an event such as a tennis tournament, use the company's name for the event in first reference and the generic term in subsequent references: *The Buick Women's Open; the $200,000 women's tennis tournament, the tournament*.

Also use a separate paragraph to provide the name of a sponsor when the brand name is not part of the formal title.

Brand name is a nonlegal term for *service mark* or *trademark*. See entries under those words.

brand-new (adj.)

break in (v.) **break-in** (n. and adj.)

break up (v.) **breakup** (n. and adj.)

Bricklayers, Masons and Plasterers' International Union of America The shortened form *Bricklayers union* is acceptable in all references.

Headquarters is in Washington.

bride, bridegroom, bridesmaid *Bride* is appropriate in wedding stories, but use *wife* or *spouse* in other circumstances.

brigadier See **military titles**.

Bright's disease After Dr. Richard Bright, the London physician who first diagnosed this form of kidney disease.

Brill's disease After Nathan E. Brill, a U.S. physician. A form of epidemic typhus fever in which the disease recurs years after the original infection.

Britain Acceptable in all references for *Great Britain*, which consists of England, Scotland and Wales.

See **United Kingdom**.

British, Briton(s) The people of Great Britain: the English, the Scottish, the Welsh.

British Airways The successor to British European Airways and British Overseas Airways Corp.

Headquarters is in Hounslow, England.

British Broadcasting Corp. *BBC* is acceptable in all references within contexts such as a television column. Otherwise, do not use *BBC* until second reference.

British Columbia The Canadian province bounded on the west by the Pacific Ocean. Do not abbreviate.

See **datelines**.

British Commonwealth See **Commonwealth, the**.

British Petroleum See **BP Amoco PLC**.

British thermal unit The amount of heat required to increase the temperature of a pound of water 1 degree Fahrenheit. *Btu* (the same for singular and plural) is acceptable on second reference.

British ton See **ton**.

British Virgin Islands Use with a community name in datelines on stories from these islands. Do not abbreviate.

Specify an individual island in the text if relevant.

See **datelines**.

broadcast The past tense also is *broadcast*, not *broadcasted*.

Broadway, off-Broadway, off-off-Broadway When applied to stage productions, these terms refer to distinctions made by union contracts, not to location of a theater.

Actors' Equity Association and unions representing craft workers have one set of pay scales for *Broadway* productions (generally those in New York City theaters of 300 or more seats) and a lower scale for smaller theaters, classified as *off-Broadway* houses.

The term *off-off-Broadway* refers to workshop productions that may use Equity members for a limited time at substandard pay. Other unions maintain a hands-off policy, agreeing with the Equity attitude that actors should have an opportunity to whet their talents in offbeat roles without losing their Equity memberships.

broccoli

Bromo Seltzer A trademark for a brand of bicarbonate of soda.

Bronze Age The age characterized by the development of bronze tools and weapons, from 3500 to 1000 B.C. Regarded as coming between the Stone Age and the Iron Age.

brother See **Roman Catholic Church**.

Brotherhood of Locomotive Engineers *BLE* is acceptable on second reference.

Headquarters is in Cleveland.

brothers Abbreviate as *Bros.* in formal company names: *Warner Bros.*

For possessives: *Warner Bros.' profits.*

brownout See the **blackout, brownout** entry.

brunet, brunette Use *brunet* as a noun for males, and as the adjective for both sexes.

Use *brunette* as a noun for females.

brussels sprouts

Btu The same in singular and plural. See **British thermal unit**.

Budapest The capital of Hungary. In datelines, follow it with *Hungary.*

Buddha, Buddhism A major religion founded in India about 500 B.C. by Buddha. Buddha, which means enlightened one, was the name given to Gautama Siddhartha by his followers.

Buddhism has about 325 million followers, mostly in India, Tibet, China, Japan, Korea and Southeast Asia. About 2 million practice Buddhism in North America.

Buddhists believe that correct thinking and self-denial will enable the soul to reach nirvana, a state of release into ultimate enlightenment and peace. Until nirvana is reached, believers cannot be freed from the cycle of death and rebirth.

There are four major groups within Buddhism.

—Hinayana or Theravada: Followers stress monastic discipline and attainment of nirvana by the individual through meditation. It is dominant among Buddhists in Burma, Cambodia, Laos, Thailand and Sri Lanka.

—Mahayana: Followers lay stress on idealism. The ideal life is that of virtue and wisdom. The sect is found mostly in Japan, Korea and eastern China.

—Mantrayana: Major centers for this group are in the Himalayas, Mongolia and Japan. It is similar to Mahayana but also has a structure of spiritual leaders and disciples, believes in various evil spirits and deities, uses magic, and has secret rituals.

—Zen: Followers seek enlightenment through introspection and intuition. The doctrines are again similar to Mahayana and like Mantrayana there is a loose structure of leaders and disciples. This group is found mostly in Japan.

Bufferin A trademark for buffered aspirin.

bug, tap A concealed listening device designed to pick up sounds in a room, an automobile, or such is a *bug*.

A *tap* is a device attached to a telephone circuit to pick up conversations on the line.

building Never abbreviate. Capitalize the proper names of buildings, including the word *building* if it is an integral part of the proper name: *the Empire State Building*.

build up (v.) **buildup** (n. and adj.)

bullet See **weapons**.

bullfight, bullfighter, bullfighting

bullpen One word, for the place where baseball pitchers warm up, and for a pen that holds cattle.

bull's-eye

bureau Capitalize when part of the formal name for an organization or agency: *the Bureau of Labor Statistics, the Newspaper Advertising Bureau.*

Lowercase when used alone or to designate a corporate subdivision: *the Washington bureau of The Associated Press.*

burglary, larceny, robbery, theft Legal definitions of *burglary* vary, but in general a *burglary* involves entering a building (not necessarily by breaking in) and remaining unlawfully with the intention of committing a crime.

Larceny is the legal term for the wrongful taking of property. Its nonlegal equivalents are *stealing* or *theft*.

Robbery in the legal sense involves the use of violence or threat in committing larceny. In a wider sense it means to plunder or rifle, and may thus be used even if a person was not present: *His house was robbed while he was away.*

Theft describes a larceny that did not involve threat, violence or plundering.

USAGE NOTE: You *rob* a person, bank, house, etc., but you *steal* the money or the jewels.

bus, buses Transportation vehicles. The verb forms: *bus, bused, busing.*

See **buss, busses**.

bushel A unit of dry measure equal to 4 pecks or 32 dry quarts. The metric equivalent is approximately 35.2 liters.

To convert to liters, multiply by 35.2 (5 bushels x 35.2 equals 176 liters).

See **liter**.

business editor Capitalize when used as a formal title before a name. See **titles**.

business names See **company names**.

buss, busses Kisses. The verb forms: *buss, bussed, bussing.*

See **bus, buses**.

by- The rules in prefixes apply, but in general, no hyphen. Some examples:

byline	byproduct
bypass	bystreet

By-election is an exception. See the next entry.

by-election A special election held between regularly scheduled elections. The term most often is associated with special elections to the British House of Commons.

bylaw

bylines Use only if the reporter was in the datelined community to gather the information reported.

Nicknames should not be used unless they specifically are requested by the writer.

C

cabinet Capitalize references to a specific body of advisers heading executive departments for a president, king, governor, etc.: *The president-elect said he has not made his Cabinet selections.*

The capital letter distinguishes the word from the common noun meaning cupboard, which is lowercase.

See **department** for a listing of all the U.S. Cabinet departments.

Cabinet titles Capitalize the full title when used before a name; lowercase in other uses: *Secretary of State Cyrus R. Vance,* but *Juanita M. Kreps, secretary of commerce.*

See **titles**.

cactus, cactuses

cadet See **military academies**.

Caesarean section

caliber The form: *.38-caliber pistol.*

See **weapons**.

California Abbrev.: *Calif.* See **state names**.

call letters Use all caps. Use hyphens to separate the type of station from the basic call letters: *WBZ-AM, WBZ-FM, WBZ-TV.*

Until the summer of 1976, the format for citizens band operators was three letters and four figures: *KTE9136.* Licenses issued since then use four letters and four figures: *KTEM1234.*

Shortwave stations, which operate with greater power than citizens band stations and on different frequencies, typically mix letters and figures: *K2LRX.*

See **channel**; **citizens band**; **radio station**; and **television station**.

call up (v.) **call-up** (n. and adj.)

Cambodia Use this rather than *Kampuchea* in datelines since the country continues to be known more widely by this name. In the body of stories *Kampuchea* may be used as long as it is identified as another name for *Cambodia.*

Cameroon Not *Camerouns* or *Cameroun.* See **geographic names**.

Camp Fire Boys and Girls The full name of the national organization formerly known as Camp Fire, Inc. Founded in 1910 as Camp Fire Girls, the name was changed to Camp Fire, Inc., in 1979, and again in 1993 to reflect the inclusion of boys. Headquarters is in Kansas City, Mo.

Both girls and boys are included in all levels of the organization. Boys and girls in kindergarten through second grades are *Starflights*. Children in third through fifth grades are *Adventure* club members. Children in sixth through eighth grades are *Discovery* members. Youths in ninth through 12th grades are *Horizon* members.

campaign manager Do not treat as a formal title. Always lowercase.

See **titles**.

Canada Montreal, Ottawa, Quebec and Toronto stand alone in datelines. For all other datelines, use the city name and the name of the province or territory spelled out.

The 10 provinces of Canada are Alberta, British Columbia, Manitoba, New Brunswick, Newfoundland and Labrador (but usually known as just Newfoundland), Nova Scotia, Ontario, Prince Edward Island, Quebec and Saskatchewan.

The three territories are the Yukon, the Northwest Territories, and Nunavut (created April 1, 1999).

The provinces have substantial autonomy from the federal government.

The territories are administered by the federal government, although residents of the territories do elect their own legislators and representatives to Parliament.

See **datelines**.

Canada goose Not *Canadian goose*.

Canadian Broadcasting Corp. *CBC* is acceptable in all references within contexts such as a television column. Otherwise, do not use *CBC* until second reference.

canal Capitalize as an integral part of a proper name: *the Suez Canal.*

Canal Zone Do not abbreviate. No longer used except when referring to the Panama Canal area during the time it was controlled by the United States, 1904-1979.

cancel, canceled, canceling, cancellation

cannon, canon A *cannon* is a weapon. See the **weapons** entry.

A *canon* is a law or rule, particularly of a church.

cannot

cant The distinctive stock words and phrases used by a particular sect or class.

See **dialect.**

can't hardly A double negative is implied. Better is: *can hardly.*

cantor See **Jewish congregations.**

Canuck This reference to a Canadian is sometimes considered a derogatory term. It should be avoided except when in quoted matter or in terms used in Canada, such as references to the hockey team, the *Vancouver Canucks.*

canvas, canvass *Canvas* is heavy cloth.

Canvass is a noun and a verb denoting a survey.

cape Capitalize as part of a proper name: *Cape Cod, Cape Hatteras.* Lowercase when standing alone.

Although local practice may call for capitalizing *the Cape* when the rest of the name is clearly understood, always use the full name on first reference in wire copy. On second reference in wire copy, either repeat the full name or use *the cape* in lowercase.

Cape Canaveral, Fla. Formerly Cape Kennedy. See **John F. Kennedy Space Center**.

capital The city where a seat of government is located. Do not capitalize.

When used in a financial sense, *capital* describes money, equipment or property used in a business by a person or corporation.

capitalization In general, avoid unnecessary capitals. Use a capital letter only if you can justify it by one of the principles listed here.

Many words and phrases, including special cases, are listed separately in this book. Entries that are capitalized without further comment should be capitalized in all uses.

If there is no relevant listing in this book for a particular word or phrase, consult Webster's New World Dictionary. Use lowercase if the dictionary lists it as an acceptable form for the sense in which the word is being used.

As used in this book, *capitalize* means to use uppercase for the first letter of a word. If additional capital letters are needed, they are called for by an example or a phrase such as use *all caps.*

Some basic principles:

PROPER NOUNS: Capitalize nouns that constitute the unique identification for a specific person, place, or thing: *John, Mary, America, Boston, England.*

Some words, such as the examples just given, are always proper nouns. Some common nouns receive proper noun status when they are used as the name of a particular entity: *General Electric, Gulf Oil.*

PROPER NAMES: Capitalize common nouns such as *party, river, street* and *west* when they are an integral part of the full name for a person, place or thing: *Democratic Party, Mississippi River, Fleet Street, West Virginia.*

Lowercase these common nouns when they stand alone in subsequent references: *the party, the river, the street.*

Lowercase the common noun elements of names in all plural uses: *the Democratic and Republican parties, Main and State streets, lakes Erie and Ontario.*

Among entries that provide additional guidelines are:

animals	historical periods
brand names	and events
building	holidays and
committee	holy days
congress	legislature
datelines	months
days of the week	monuments
directions and	nationalities and
regions	races
family names	nicknames
food	organizations and
foreign	institutions
governmental	planets
bodies	plants

foreign legislative bodies	police department
geographic names	religious references
governmental bodies	seasons
heavenly bodies	trademarks
	unions

POPULAR NAMES: Some places and events lack officially designated proper names but have popular names that are the effective equivalent: *the Combat Zone* (a section of downtown Boston), *the Main Line* (a group of Philadelphia suburbs), *the South Side* (of Chicago), *the Badlands* (of North Dakota), *the Street* (the financial community in the Wall Street area of New York).

The principle applies also to shortened versions of the proper names of one-of-a-kind events: *the Series* (for the World Series), *the Derby* (for the Kentucky Derby). This practice should not, however, be interpreted as a license to ignore the general practice of lowercasing the common noun elements of a name when they stand alone.

DERIVATIVES: Capitalize words that are derived from a proper noun and still depend on it for their meaning: *American, Christian, Christianity, English, French, Marxism, Shakespearean.*

Lowercase words that are derived from a proper noun but no longer depend on it for their meaning: *french fries, herculean, manhattan cocktail, malapropism, pasteurize, quixotic, venetian blind.*

SENTENCES: Capitalize the first word in a statement that stands as a sentence. See **sentences** and **parentheses**.

In poetry, capital letters are used for the first words of some phrases that would not be capitalized in prose. See **poetry**.

COMPOSITIONS: Capitalize the principal words in the names of books, movies, plays, poems, operas, songs, radio and television programs, works of art, etc. See **composition titles; magazine names;** and **newspaper names**.

TITLES: Capitalize formal titles when used immediately before a name. Lowercase formal titles when used alone or in constructions that set them off from a name by commas.

Use lowercase at all times for terms that are job descriptions rather than formal titles.

See **academic titles; courtesy titles; legislative titles; military titles; nobility titles; religious titles;** and **titles**.

ABBREVIATIONS: Capital letters apply in some cases. See the **abbreviations and acronyms** entry.

capitol Capitalize *U.S. Capitol* and *the Capitol* when referring to the building in Washington: *The meeting was held on Capitol Hill in the west wing of the Capitol.*

Follow the same practice when referring to state capitols: *The Virginia Capitol is in Richmond. Thomas Jefferson designed the Capitol of Virginia.*

captain See **military titles** for military and police usage.

Lowercase and spell out in such uses as *team captain Carl Yastrzemski.*

carat, caret, karat The weight of precious stones, especially diamonds, is expressed in *carats.* A carat is equal to 200 milligrams or about 3 grains.

A *caret* is a writer's and a proofreader's mark.

The proportion of pure gold used with an alloy is expressed in *karats*.

carbine See **weapons**.

cardinal See **Roman Catholic Church**.

cardinal numbers See **numerals**.

CARE Acceptable in all references for *Cooperative for American Relief Everywhere Inc.*

Headquarters is in Atlanta.

carefree

caretaker

Caribbean See **Western Hemisphere**.

carmaker, carmakers

car pool

carry-over (n. and adj.)

cash on delivery *c.o.d.* is preferred in all references.

caster, castor *Caster* is a roller.

Castor is the spelling for the oil and the bean from which it is derived.

catalog, cataloged, cataloger, cataloging, catalogist

Caterpillar A trademark for a brand of crawler tractor.

Use lowercase for the wormlike larva of various insects.

catholic, catholicism Use *Roman Catholic Church, Roman Catholic* or *Roman Catholicism* in the first references to those who believe that the pope, as bishop of Rome, has the ultimate authority in administering an earthly organization founded by Jesus Christ.

Most subsequent references may be condensed to *Catholic Church, Catholic* or *Catholicism. Roman Catholic* should continue to be used, however, if the context requires a distinction between Roman Catholics and members of other denominations who often describe themselves as Catholic. They include some high church Episcopalians (who often call themselves *Anglo-Catholics*), members of Eastern Orthodox churches, and members of some national Catholic churches that have broken with Rome. Among churches in this last category are the Polish National Catholic Church and the Lithuanian National Catholic Church.

Lowercase *catholic* where used in its generic sense of general or universal, meanings derived from a similar word in Greek.

Those who use *Catholic* in a religious sense are indicating their belief that they are members of a universal church that Jesus Christ left on Earth.

cats See **animals**.

CAT scan See **CT scan**.

cattle See **animals**.

Caucasian

cave in (v.) **cave-in** (n. and adj.)

CB See **citizens band radio**.

CBS Acceptable in all references for *CBS Inc.*, the former Columbia Broadcasting System.

Divisions include *CBS News*, *CBS Radio* and *CBS-TV*.

CD-ROM Acronym for a *compact disc* acting as a *read-only memory device*.

CD-ROM disc is redundant.

cease-fire, cease-fires (n. and adj.) The verb form is *cease fire*.

celebrant, celebrator Reserve *celebrant* for someone who conducts a religious rite: *He was the celebrant of the Mass.*

Use *celebrator* for someone having a good time: *The celebrators kept the party going until 3 a.m.*

cell phone Two words; an exception to Webster's.

cellophane Formerly a trademark, now a generic term.

Celsius Use this term rather than *centigrade* for the temperature scale that is part of the metric system.

The Celsius scale is named for Anders Celsius, a Swedish astronomer who designed it. In it, zero represents the freezing point of water, and 100 degrees is the boiling point at sea level.

To convert to Fahrenheit, multiply a Celsius temperature by 9, divide by 5 and add 32 (25 x 9 equals 225, divided by 5 equals 45, plus 32 equals 77 degrees Fahrenheit).

When giving a Celsius temperature, use these forms: *40 degrees Celsius* or *40 C* (note the space and no period after the capital *C*) if degrees and Celsius are clear from the context.

See **Fahrenheit** and **metric system** entries.

cement *Cement* is the powder mixed with water and sand or gravel to make *concrete*. The proper term is *concrete* (not *cement*) *pavement*, *blocks*, *driveways*, etc.

censer, censor, censure A *censer* is a container in which incense is burned.

To *censor* is to prohibit or restrict the use of something.

To *censure* is to condemn.

Centers for Disease Control and Prevention The centers, located in Atlanta, are the U.S. Public Health Service's national agencies for control of infectious and other preventable diseases. It works with state health departments to provide specialized services that they are unable to maintain on an everyday basis.

The normal form for first reference is the national *Centers for Disease Control and Prevention*. *CDC* is acceptable on second reference.

centi- A prefix denoting one-hundredth of a unit. Move a decimal point two places to the left in converting to the basic unit: *155.6 centimeters equals 1.556 meters*.

centigrade See **Celsius**.

centimeter One-hundredth of a meter.

There are 10 millimeters in a centimeter.

A centimeter is approximately the width of a large paper clip.

To convert to inches, multiply by .4 (5 centimeters x .4 equals 2 inches).

See **meter; metric system;** and **inch**.

Central America See **Western Hemisphere**.

Central Conference of American Rabbis See **Jewish Congregations**.

Central Intelligence Agency *CIA* is acceptable in all references.

The formal title for the individual who heads the agency is *director of central intelligence*. On first reference: *Director George Bush of the CIA, Director of Central Intelligence George Bush*, or *CIA Director George Bush*.

Central Standard Time (CST), Central Daylight Time (CDT) See **time zones**.

cents Spell out the word cents and lowercase, using numerals for amounts less than a dollar: *5 cents, 12 cents*. Use the $ sign and decimal system for larger amounts: *$1.01, $2.50*.

Numerals alone, with or without a decimal point as appropriate, may be used in tabular matter.

century Lowercase, spelling out numbers less than 10: *the first century, the 20th century*.

For proper names, follow the organization's practice: *20th Century Fox, Twentieth Century Fund, Twentieth Century Limited*.

Ceylon It is now *Sri Lanka*, which should be used in datelines and other references to the nation.

The people may be referred to as *Ceylonese* (n. or adj.) or *Sri Lankans*. The language is *Sinhalese*.

cha-cha

Chagas' disease After Charles Chagas, a Brazilian physician who identified the chronic wasting disease caused by the parasite that is carried by insects.

chain saw (two words)

chairman, chairwoman
Capitalize as a formal title before a name: *company Chairman Henry Ford, committee Chairwoman Margaret Chase Smith*.

Do not capitalize as a casual, temporary position: *meeting chairman Robert Jones*.

Do not use *chairperson* unless it is an organization's formal title for an office.

See **titles**.

chamber of deputies See **foreign legislative bodies**.

chancellor The translation to English for the first minister in the governments of Germany and Austria. Capitalize when used before a name.

See the **premier, prime minister** entry and **titles**.

changeable

changeover

change up (v.) change-up (n. and adj.)

channel Capitalize when used with a figure; lowercase elsewhere: *She turned to Channel*

3. No channel will broadcast the game.

Also: *the English Channel,* but the channel on second reference.

chapters Capitalize *chapter* when used with a numeral in reference to a section of a book or legal code. Always use Arabic figures: *Chapter 1, Chapter 20.*

Lowercase when standing alone.

character, reputation
Character refers to moral qualities.

Reputation refers to the way a person is regarded by others.

charismatic groups See **religious movements**.

Charleston, Charlestown, Charles Town *Charleston* is the name of the capital of West Virginia and a port city in South Carolina.

Charlestown is a section of Boston.

Charles Town is the name of a small city in West Virginia.

chauffeur

chauvinism, chauvinist
The words mean unreasoning devotion to one's race, sex, country, etc., with contempt for other races, sexes, countries, etc.

The terms come from Nicolas Chauvin, a soldier of Napoleon I, who was famous for his devotion to the lost cause.

check up (v.) **checkup** (n.)

Chemical Mace A trademark, usually shortened to *Mace,* for a brand of tear gas that is packaged in an aerosol canister and temporarily stuns its victims.

chess In stories, the names and pieces are spelled out, lowercase: *king, queen, bishop, pawn, knight, rook, kingside, queenside, white, black.*

Use the algebraic notation in providing tabular summaries.

In algebraic notation, the "ranks" are the horizontal rows of squares. The ranks take numbers, 1 to 8, beginning on white's side of the board.

The "files" are the vertical rows of squares. They take letters, a through h, beginning on white's left.

Thus, each square is identified by its file letter and rank number.

In the starting position, white's queen knight stands on *b1,* the queen on *d1,* the king on *e1;* black's queen knight stands on *b8,* the queen on *d8,* the king on *e8,* and so on.

Other features of the system follow:

—DESIGNATION OF PIECES: The major pieces are shown by a capital letter: *K* for king, *Q* for queen, *R* for rook, *B* for bishop and *N* for knight. No symbol is used for the pawn.

—MOVES BY PIECES: Shown by the letter of the piece (except for the pawn) and the destination square. For instance, *Bb5* means the bishop moves to square b5.

—MOVES BY PAWNS: Pawn moves are designated only by the name of the destination square. Thus, *e4* means the pawn on the e file moves to e4.

—CASTLING: It is written as *0-0* for the kingside and *0-0-0* for the queenside. *Kingside* is the side of the board (right half from white's point of view, left half from black's), on which each player's king starts. The other half is *queenside.*

—CAPTURES BY PIECES: A capture is recorded using an x after the letter for the capturing piece. For instance, if white's bishop captures the black pawn at the f6 square, it is written *Bxf6*.

—CAPTURES BY PAWNS: When a pawn captures a piece, the players name the file the pawn was on and the square where it made the capture. If white's pawn on a g file captured black's pawn on f6 square, the move would be *gxf6*. If black's pawn on an f file captured white's, it would be *fxg5*.

—CHECK: Use plus sign.

—AMBIGUITY: If more than one piece of the same type can move to a square, the rank number or file letter of the origination square is added. Thus, if a rook on d1 were to move to d4, but another rook also could move there, instead of Rd4 the move would be given as *R1d4*. If there are black knights on c6 and e6, and the one on e6 moves to d4, the move is given as *Ned4*.

The form, taken from a 1993 championship match:

	Short (White)	Karpov (Black)
1.	e4	c5
2.	Nf3	d6
3.	d4	cxd4
4.	Nxd4	Nf6
5.	Nc3	a6
6.	Bc4	e6
7.	Bb3	Nbd7
8.	f4	Nc5
9.	f5	Be7
10.	Qf3	0-0
11.	Be3	e5
12.	Nde2	b5
13.	Bd5	Rb8
14.	b4	Ncd7
15.	0-0	Nxd5
16.	Nxd5	Bb7
17.	Nec3	Nf6

18.	Rad1	Bxd5
19.	Nxd5	Nxd5
20.	Rxd5	Rc8
21.	Qg4	f6
22.	Rf3	Rxc2
23.	Rh3	Rf7
24.	Qh5	h6
25.	Qg6	Kf8
26.	Bxh6	gxh6
27.	Rxh6	Qb6+
28.	Rc5	Bd8
29.	Rh8+	Ke7
30.	Rh7	Rxh7
31.	Qxh7+	Kf8

Draw agreed.

Chevron Corp. Formerly Standard Oil Co. of California.

Chevy Not *Chevie* or *Chevvy*. This nickname for the *Chevrolet* should be used only in automobile features or in quoted matter.

Chicago The city in Illinois stands alone in datelines.

chief Capitalize as a formal title before a name: *She spoke to Police Chief Michael Codd. He spoke to Chief Michael Codd of the New York police.*

Lowercase when it is not a formal title: *union chief Walter Reuther.*

See **titles**.

chief justice Capitalize only as a formal title before a name: *Chief Justice Warren Burger.* The officeholder is the chief justice of the United States, not of the Supreme Court.

See **judge**.

Chile The nation.

chili, chilies The peppers.

chilly Moderately cold.

China When used alone, it refers to the mainland nation. Use it in datelines and other routine references.

Use *People's Republic of China, Communist China, mainland China* or *Red China* only in direct quotations or when needed to distinguish the mainland and its government from Taiwan.

For datelines on stories from the island of Taiwan, use the name of a community and *Taiwan*. In the body of a story, use *Nationalist China* or *Taiwan* for references to the government based on the island. Use the formal name of the government, the *Republic of China*, when required for legal precision.

Chinaman A patronizing term. Confine it to quoted matter.

Chinese names For most Chinese place names and personal names, use the official Chinese spelling system known as Pinyin: *Senior leader Deng Xiaoping, Beijing,* or *Zhejiang province.*

Note that the Chinese usually give the family name first (*Deng*) followed by the given name (*Xiaoping*). Second reference should be the family name only: *Deng.*

The Pinyin spelling system eliminates the hyphen or apostrophe previously used in many given names. Use the new spelling for *Mao Zedong* and *Zhou Enlai,* but keep the traditional American spelling for such historical figures as *Sun Yat-sen* and *Chiang Kai-shek.*

If the new Pinyin spelling of a proper noun is so radically different from the traditional American spelling that a reader might be confused, provide the Pinyin spelling followed by the traditional spelling in parentheses. For ex-

ample, the city of *Fuzhou* (*Foochow*). Or use a descriptive sentence: *Fuzhou is the capital of Fujian province, on China's eastern coast.*

Use the traditional American spellings for these place names: *China, Inner Mongolia, Shanghai, Tibet.*

Follow local spellings in stories dealing with Hong Kong and Taiwan.

Some Chinese have Westernized their names, putting their given names or the initials for them first: *P.Y. Chen, Jack Wang.* In general, follow an individual's preferred spelling.

Normally Chinese women do not take their husbands' surnames. Use the courtesy titles *Mrs., Miss,* or *Ms.* only when specifically requested. Never use *Madame* or *Mme.*

chip An integrated computer circuit.

chip-maker, chip-making Hyphenate as adjectives (but two words as nouns).

Christian Church (Disciples of Christ) The parentheses and the words they surround are part of the formal name.

The body owes its origins to an early 19th-century frontier movement to unify Christians.

The Disciples, led by Alexander Campbell in western Pennsylvania, and the Christians, led by Barton W. Stone in Kentucky, merged in 1832.

The local church is the basic organizational unit.

National policies are developed by the General Assembly, made up of representatives chosen by local churches and regional organizations.

The church lists more than 1 million members.

All members of the clergy may be referred to as *ministers. Pastor* applies if a minister leads a congregation.

On first reference, use *the Rev.* before the name of a man or woman. On second reference, use only the last name.

See **religious titles**.

Christian Science Church
See **Church of Christ, Scientist**.

Christmas, Christmas Day
Dec. 25. The federal legal holiday is observed on Friday if Dec. 25 falls on a Saturday, on Monday if it falls on a Sunday.

Never abbreviate *Christmas* to *Xmas* or any other form.

church Capitalize as part of the formal name of a building, a congregation or a denomination; lowercase in other uses: *St. Mary's Church, the Roman Catholic Church, the Catholic and Episcopal churches, a Roman Catholic church, a church.*

Lowercase in phrases where the church is used in an institutional sense: *She believes in the separation of church and state. The pope said the church opposes abortion.*

See **religious titles** and the entry for the denomination in question.

Churches of Christ
Approximately 18,000 independent congregations with a total U.S. membership of more than 2 million cooperate under this name. They sponsor numerous educational activities, primarily radio and television programs.

Each local church is autonomous and operates under a governing board of elders. The minister is an evangelist, addressed by members as *Brother.* The ministers do not use clergy titles. Do not precede their names by a title.

The churches do not regard themselves as a denomination. Rather, they stress a nondenominational effort to preach what they consider basic Bible teachings. The churches also teach that baptism is an essential part of the salvation process.

See **religious movements**.

churchgoer

Church of Christ, Scientist
This denomination was founded in 1879 by Mary Baker Eddy. Her teachings are contained in "Science and Health with Key to the Scriptures," which, along with the Bible, she ordained as the impersonal pastor of the church.

The Mother Church in Boston is the international headquarters. Its government provides for a board of directors, which transacts the business of the Mother Church.

A branch church, governed by its own democratically chosen board, is named First Church of Christ, Scientist, or Second Church, etc., according to the order of its establishment in a community.

The terms *Christian Science Church* or *Churches of Christ, Scientist,* are acceptable in all references to the denomination.

The word *Christian* is used because its teachings are based on the word and works of Jesus Christ. The word *Science* is used to reflect the concept that the laws of God are replicable and can be proved in healing sickness and sin.

The church is composed entirely of lay members and does not have clergy in the usual sense. Both men and women may serve as *readers*, *practitioners*, or *lecturers*.

The preferred form for these titles is to use a construction that sets them off from a name with commas. Capitalize them only when used as a formal title immediately before a name. Do not continue use of the title in subsequent references.

The terms *reverend* and *minister* are not applicable. Do not use *the Rev.* in any references.

See **religious titles**.

Church of England See **Anglican Communion.**

Church of Jesus Christ of Latter-day Saints, The Note
the capitalization and punctuation of *Latter-day*. *Mormon church*, *LDS church* or *the Latter-day Saints* can be used, but the official name is preferred in first reference in a story dealing primarily with church activities.

Members are referred to as *Latter-day Saints* or *Mormons*, the latter based on the church's sacred Book of Mormon.

The church is based on revelations that Joseph Smith said were brought to him in the 1820s by heavenly messengers.

Today, the church headquarters in Salt Lake City, Utah, directs more than 22,000 congregations with more than 10 million members worldwide.

Church hierarchy is composed of men known as general authorities. Among them, the policy-making body is the First Presidency, made up of a president and two or more counselors. It has final authority in all spiritual and worldly matters.

CLERGY: All worthy young men over the age of 12 are members of the priesthood. They can be ordained elders after age 18, usually after graduating from high school and before serving as missionaries. They may later become high priests, or bishops.

The only formal titles are *president* (for the head of the First Presidency), *bishop* (for members of the Presiding Bishopric and for local bishops) and *elder* (for other general authorities and church missionaries). Capitalize these formal titles before a name on first reference; use only the last name on second reference.

The terms *minister* or *the Rev.* are not used.

See **religious titles**.

SPLINTER GROUPS: The term *Mormon* is not properly applied to the other Latter Day Saints churches that resulted from the split after Smith's death.

The largest is the Reorganized Church of Jesus Christ of Latter Day Saints (note the lack of a hyphen and the capitalized *Day*), with headquarters in Independence, Mo. It has about 1,000 churches and 150,000 members.

CIA Acceptable in all references for *Central Intelligence Agency.*

cigarette

Cincinnati The city in Ohio stands alone in datelines.

CIO See **AFL-CIO.**

Citibank The former First National City Bank. The parent

holding company is Citicorp of New York.

cities and towns Capitalize them in all uses. See **datelines** for guidelines on when they should be followed by a state or a country name.

Capitalize official titles, including separate political entities such as *East St. Louis, Ill.,* or *West Palm Beach, Fla.*

The preferred form for the section of a city is lowercase: *the west end, northern Los Angeles.* But capitalize widely recognized names for the sections of a city: *South Side* (Chicago), *Lower East Side* (New York).

Spell out the names of cities unless in direct quotes: *A trip to Los Angeles,* but: *"We're going to L.A."*

See **city**.

citizen, resident, subject, national, native A *citizen* is a person who has acquired the full civil rights of a nation either by birth or naturalization. Cities and states in the United States do not confer citizenship. To avoid confusion, use *resident,* not *citizen,* in referring to inhabitants of states and cities.

Subject is the term used when the government is headed by a monarch or other sovereign.

National is applied to a person residing away from the nation of which he or she is a citizen, or to a person under the protection of a specified nation.

Native is the term denoting that an individual was born in a given location.

citizens band Without an apostrophe after the *s,* an exception to Webster's New World based on widespread practice.

CB is acceptable on second reference.

The term describes a group of radio frequencies set aside by the Federal Communications Commission for local use at low power by individuals or businesses.

Until summer 1976, the format for call letters was three letters and four figures: *KTE9136.* Licenses issued since then use four letters and four figures: *KTEM1234.*

city Capitalize *city* as part of a proper name: *Kansas City, New York City, Oklahoma City, Jefferson City.*

Lowercase elsewhere: *a Texas city; the city government; the city Board of Education;* and all *city of* phrases: *the city of Boston.*

Capitalize when part of a formal title before a name: *City Manager Francis McGrath.* Lowercase when not part of the formal title: *city Health Commissioner Frank Smith.*

See **city council** and **governmental bodies**.

city commission See the next entry.

city council Capitalize when part of a proper name: *the Boston City Council.*

Retain capitalization if the reference is to a specific council but the context does not require the city name:

BOSTON (AP) — The City Council ...

Lowercase in other uses: *the council, the Boston and New York city councils, a city council.*

Use the proper name if the body is not known as a city council: *the Miami City Commission, the City Commission, the commission; the Louisville Board of Alder-*

men, *the Board of Aldermen, the board.*

Use *city council* in a generic sense for plural references: *the Boston, Louisville and Miami city councils.*

city editor Capitalize as a formal title before a name. See **titles**.

city hall Capitalize with the name of a city, or without the name of a city if the reference is specific: *Boston City Hall, City Hall.*

Lowercase plural uses: *the Boston and New York city halls.*

Lowercase generic uses, including: *You can't fight city hall.*

citywide

civil cases, criminal cases A *civil case* is one in which an individual, business or agency of government seeks damages or relief from another individual, business or agency of government. Civil actions generally involve a charge that a contract has been breached or that someone has been wronged or injured.

A *criminal case* is one that the state or the federal government brings against an individual charged with committing a crime.

Civil War

claptrap

clean up (v.) **cleanup** (n. and adj.)

clear-cut (adj.)

clerical titles See **religious titles**.

Cleveland The city in Ohio stands alone in datelines.

clientele

cloak-and-dagger

Clorox A trademark for a brand of bleach.

closed shop A *closed shop* is an agreement between a union and an employer that requires workers to be members of a union before they may be employed.

A *union shop* requires workers to join a union within a specified period after they are employed.

An *agency shop* requires that the workers who do not want to join the union pay the union a fee instead of union dues.

A *guild shop*, a term often used when the union is The Newspaper Guild, is the same as a *union shop.*

See the **right-to-work** entry for an explanation of how some states prohibit contracts that require workers to join unions.

close-up (n. and adj.)

cloture Not *closure*, for the parliamentary procedure for closing debate.

Whenever practical, use a phrase such as closing debate or ending debate instead of the technical term.

CNN Acceptable in all references for the *Cable News Network.*

co- Retain the hyphen when forming nouns, adjectives and verbs that indicate occupation or status:

co-author	co-pilot
co-chairman	co-respondent (in a
co-defendant	divorce suit)

co-host co-signer
co-owner co-star
co-partner co-worker

(Several are exceptions to Webster's New World in the interests of consistency.)

Use no hyphen in other combinations:

coed cooperate
coeducation cooperative
coequal coordinate
coexist coordination
coexistence

Cooperate, coordinate and related words are exceptions to the rule that a hyphen is used if a prefix ends in a vowel and the word that follows begins with the same vowel.

Co. See **company**.

coast Lowercase when referring to the physical shoreline: *Atlantic coast, Pacific coast, east coast.*

Capitalize when referring to regions of the United States lying along such shorelines: *the Atlantic Coast states, a Gulf Coast city, the West Coast, the East Coast.*

Do not capitalize when referring to smaller regions: *the Virginia coast.*

Capitalize *the Coast* when standing alone only if the reference is to the West Coast.

coastal waters See **weather terms**.

coast guard Capitalize when referring to the U.S. force: *the U.S. Coast Guard, the Coast Guard, Coast Guard policy, the Guard.* Do not use the abbreviation *USCG.*

Use lowercase for similar forces of other nations.

This approach has been adopted for consistency, because many foreign nations do not use *coast guard* as the proper name.

See **military academies**.

Coast Guardsman Note spelling. Capitalize as a proper noun when referring to an individual in a U.S. Coast Guard unit: *He is a Coast Guardsman.*

Lowercase *guardsman* when it stands alone.

See **military titles**.

coastline

coattails

COBOL A computer programming language. Acronym for *Common Business-Oriented Language.* Use of COBOL on first reference is acceptable if identified as a programming language.

Coca-Cola, Coke Trademarks for a brand of cola drink.

cocaine The slang term *coke* should appear only in quoted matter.

Crack is a refined cocaine in crystalline rock form.

c.o.d. Acceptable in all references for *cash on delivery* or *collect on delivery.* (The use of lowercase is an exception to the first listing in Webster's New World.)

Cold War Capitalize when referring specifically to the post-World War II rivalry between the United States and the former Soviet Union. Use only in the historic sense.

collective nouns Nouns that denote a unit take singular verbs and pronouns: *class, committee, crowd, family, group, herd, jury, orchestra, team.*

Some usage examples: *The committee is meeting to set its agenda. The jury reached its verdict. A herd of cattle was sold.*

PLURAL IN FORM: Some words that are plural in form become collective nouns and take singular verbs when the group or quantity is regarded as a unit.

Right: *A thousand bushels is a good yield.* (A unit.)

Right: *A thousand bushels were created.* (Individual items.)

Right: *The data is sound.* (A unit.)

Right: *The data have been carefully collected.* (Individual items.)

collectors' item

college Capitalize when part of a proper name: *Dartmouth College.*

Consult special sections of the Webster's New World for lists of junior colleges, colleges and universities in the United States and Canadian colleges and universities.

See the **organizations and institutions** entry.

College of Cardinals See **Roman Catholic Church**.

collide, collision Two objects must be in motion before they can *collide.* An automobile cannot *collide* with a utility pole, for example.

colloquialisms The word describes the informal use of a language. It is not local or regional in nature, as dialect is.

Webster's New World Dictionary identifies many words as colloquial with the label *Colloq.* The label itself, the dictionary says, "does not indicate substandard or illiterate usage."

Many colloquial words and phrases characteristic of informal writing and conversation are acceptable in some contexts but out of place in others. Examples include *bum* and *phone.*

Other colloquial words normally should be avoided because they are substandard. Webster's New World notes, for example, that *ain't* is colloquial and not automatically illiterate or sub-standard usage. But it also notes that *ain't* is "a dialectal or substandard contraction." Thus it should not be used in news stories unless needed to illustrate substandard speech in writing.

See the **dialect** and **word selection** entries.

colon See the entry in the **Punctuation** chapter.

colonel See **military titles**.

colonial Capitalize *Colonial* as a proper adjective in all references to the *Colonies.* (See the next entry.)

colonies Capitalize only for the British dependencies that declared their independence in 1776, now known as the United States.

Colorado Abbrev.: *Colo.* See **state names**.

colorblind

colored In some societies, including the United States, the word is considered derogatory and should not be used.

In some countries of Africa, it is used to denote individuals of mixed racial ancestry. Whenever the word is used, place it in quotation marks and provide an explanation of its meaning.

Columbia Broadcasting System It no longer exists. See **CBS**.

Columbus Day Oct. 12. The federal legal holiday is the second Monday in October.

combat, combated, combating

comedian Use for both men and women.

comma See entry in **Punctuation** chapter.

commander See **military titles**.

commander in chief Capitalize only if used as a formal title before a name.
See **titles**.

commissioner Do not abbreviate. Capitalize when used as a formal title.
See **titles**.

commitment

committee Do not abbreviate. Capitalize when part of a formal name: *the House Appropriations Committee.*

Do not capitalize committee in shortened versions of long committee names: *the Special Senate Select Committee to Investigate Improper Labor-Management Practices,* for example, became *the rackets committee.*
See **subcommittee**.

commodity When used in a financial sense, the word describes the products of mining and agriculture before they have undergone extensive processing.

commonwealth A group of people united by their common interests.
See **state**.

Commonwealth of Independent States Founded Dec.
8, 1991, the federation is made up of 12 of the former republics of the U.S.S.R., or Soviet Union. Russia is the largest and richest. Three other former republics — Latvia, Lithuania and Estonia — became independent nations earlier in 1991. (The Soviet Union was formally dissolved in December 1991. Its last leader, Mikhail Gorbachev, resigned on Dec. 25, 1991.)

The republics (with adjective form in parentheses):

Armenia (Armenian); Azerbaijan (Azerbaijani); Belarus (Belarusian); Georgia (Georgian); Kazakstan (Kazak); Kyrgyzstan (Kyrgyz); Moldova (Moldovan); Russia (Russian); Tajikistan (Tajik); Turkmenistan (Turkmen); Ukraine (no the) (Ukrainian); Uzbekistan (Uzbek).

DATELINES: MOSCOW stands alone. Follow all other datelines with the name of the state. *ALMATY, Kazakstan.* (This spelling of Kazakstan is an exception to Webster's.)

BALTICS: Use the city and Lithuania, Latvia, or Estonia in datelines from these Baltic nations.

Commonwealth, the Formerly the British Commonwealth.
The members of this free association of sovereign states recognize the British sovereign as head of the Commonwealth. Some also

recognize the sovereign as head of their state; others do not.

The members are: Antigua and Barbuda, Australia, Bahamas, Bangladesh, Barbados, Belize, Botswana, Brunei, Cameroon, Canada, Cyprus, Dominica, Fiji, Gambia, Ghana, Grenada, Guyana, India, Jamaica, Kenya, Kiribati, Lesotho, Malawi, Malaysia, Maldives, Malta, Mauritius, Namibia, Nauru, New Zealand, Nigeria, Pakistan, Papua New Guinea, St. Kitts and Nevis, St. Lucia, St. Vincent and the Grenadines, Samoa, Seychelles, Sierra Leone, Singapore, Solomon Islands, South Africa, Sri Lanka, Swaziland, Tanzania, Tonga, Trinidad and Tobago, Tuvalu, Uganda, United Kingdom, Vanuatu, Western Samoa, Zambia and Zimbabwe.

Communicable Disease Center The former name of the *Centers for Disease Control and Prevention.* See entry under that name.

Communications Satellite Corp. See **Comsat Corp.**

Communications Workers of America The shortened form *Communications Workers union* is acceptable in all references.

Headquarters is in Washington.

communism, communist Lowercase, except in references to specific organizations: *the Communist Party of Russia.*

See the **political parties and philosophies** entry.

commutation See the **pardon, parole, probations** entry.

compact disc *CD* is acceptable on later references.

company, companies Use *Co.* or *Cos.* when a business uses either word at the end of its proper name: *Ford Motor Co., American Broadcasting Cos.* But: *Aluminum Company of America.*

If *company* or *companies* appears alone in second reference, spell the word out.

The forms for possessives: *Ford Motor Co.'s profits, American Broadcasting Cos.' profits.*

THEATRICAL: Spell out *company* in names of theatrical organizations: *the Martha Graham Dance Company.*

company (military) Capitalize only when part of a name: *Company B.* Do not abbreviate.

company names Consult the company or Standard & Poor's Register of Corporations if in doubt about a formal name. Do not, however, use a comma before Inc. or Ltd.

Generally, follow the spelling and capitalization preferred by the company: *iMac, eBay.* But capitalize the first letter if it begins a sentence.

Do not use all capital letter names unless the letters are individually pronounced: *CRX, USX.* Others should be uppercase and lowercase.

See the **organizations and institutions** entry.

compared to, compared with Use *compared to* when the intent is to assert, without the need for elaboration, that two or more items are similar: *She compared her work for women's rights* to Susan B. Anthony's campaign for women's suffrage.

Use *compared with* when juxtaposing two or more items to illustrate similarities and/or differences: *His time was 2:11:10, compared with 2:14 for his closest competitor.*

compatible

complacent, complaisant

Complacent means self-satisfied.

Complaisant means eager to please.

complement, compliment

Complement is a noun and a verb denoting completeness or the process of supplementing something: *The ship has a complement of 200 sailors and 20 officers. The tie complements his suit.*

Compliment is a noun or a verb that denotes praise or the expression of courtesy: *The captain complimented the sailors. She was flattered by the compliments on her outfit.*

complementary, complimentary

The husband and wife have complementary careers.

They received complimentary tickets to the show.

compose, comprise, constitute

Compose means to create or put together. It commonly is used in both the active and passive voices: *She composed a song. The United States is composed of 50 states. The zoo is composed of many animals.*

Comprise means to contain, to include all or embrace. It is best used only in the active voice, followed by a direct object: *The United States comprises 50 states. The jury comprises five men and seven women. The zoo comprises many animals.*

Constitute, in the sense of form or make up, may be the best word if neither *compose* nor *comprise* seems to fit: *Fifty states constitute the United States. Five men and seven women constitute the jury. A collection of animals can constitute a zoo.*

Use *include* when what follows is only part of the total: *The price includes breakfast. The zoo includes lions and tigers.*

composition titles

Apply the guidelines listed here to book titles, computer game titles (but not software titles), movie titles, opera titles, play titles, poem titles, song titles, television program titles, and the titles of lectures, speeches and works of art.

The guidelines, followed by a block of examples:

—Capitalize the principal words, including prepositions and conjunctions of four or more letters.

—Capitalize an article — *the, a, an* — or words of fewer than four letters if it is the first or last word in a title.

—Put quotation marks around the names of all such works except the Bible and books that are primarily catalogs of reference material. In addition to catalogs, this category includes almanacs, directories, dictionaries, encyclopedias, gazetteers, handbooks and similar publications.

—Translate a foreign title into English unless a work is known to the American public by its foreign name.

EXAMPLES: *"The Star-Spangled Banner," "The Rise and Fall of the Third Reich," "Gone With the Wind," "Of Mice and Men," "For*

Whom the Bell Tolls," "Time After Time," the NBC-TV "Today" program, the "CBS Evening News," "The Mary Tyler Moore Show." See **television program names** for further guidelines and examples.

Reference works: *Jane's All the World's Aircraft*; *Encyclopaedia Britannica*; *Webster's New World Dictionary of the American Language, Second Edition*.

Foreign works: *Rousseau's "War,"* not *Rousseau's "La Guerre."* But: *Leonardo da Vinci's "Mona Lisa," Mozart's "The Marriage of Figaro"* and *"The Magic Flute."* But: *"Die Walkuere"* and *"Gotterdammerung" from Wagner's "The Ring of the Nibelungen."*

compound adjectives See the hyphen entry in the Punctuation chapter.

comptroller, controller *Comptroller* generally is the accurate word for government financial officers.

The U.S. comptroller of the currency is an appointed official in the Treasury Department who is responsible for the chartering, supervising and liquidation of banks organized under the federal government's National Bank Act.

Controller generally is the proper word for financial officers of businesses and for other positions such as *air traffic controller*.

Capitalize *comptroller* and *controller* when used as the formal titles for financial officers. Use lowercase for *aircraft controller* and similar occupational applications of the word.

See **titles**.

computer terms See **Internet** section.

Comsat Corp. Formerly known as Communications Satellite Corp. Headquarters is in Bethesda, Md.

conclave A private or secret meeting. In the Roman Catholic Church it describes the private meeting of cardinals to elect a pope.

concrete See **cement**.

Confederate States of America The formal name of the states that seceded during the Civil War. The shortened form *the Confederacy* is acceptable in all references.

confess, confessed In some contexts the words may be erroneous.
See **admit**.

confirmation See **sacraments**.

Congo In datelines, give the name of the city followed by Congo:
KINSHASA, Congo (AP) —
In stories, *the Congo* or *Congo* as the construction of a sentence dictates. (Formerly Zaire.)
Do not confuse with Republic of Congo (capital, Brazzaville) to the west.

congress Capitalize *U.S. Congress* and *Congress* when referring to the U.S. Senate and House of Representatives. Although *Congress* sometimes is used as a substitute for the House, it properly is reserved for reference to both the Senate and House.

Capitalize *Congress* also if referring to a foreign body that uses the term, or its equivalent in a foreign language, as part of its formal name: *the Argentine Congress, the Congress.*

See **foreign legislative bodies**.

Lowercase when used as a synonym for *convention* or in second reference to an organization that uses the word as part of its formal name: *the Congress of Racial Equality, the congress.*

congressional Lowercase unless part of a proper name: *congressional salaries, the Congressional Quarterly, the Congressional Record.*

Congressional Directory
Use this as the reference source for questions about the federal government that are not covered by this stylebook.

congressional districts
Use figures and capitalize district when joined with a figure: *the 1st Congressional District, the 1st District.*

Lowercase *district* whenever it stands alone.

Congressional Record A
daily publication of the proceedings of Congress including a complete stenographic report of all remarks and debates.

congressman, congresswoman Use only in reference to
members of the U.S. House of Representatives.

See **legislative titles**.

Congress of Racial Equality *CORE* is acceptable on second
reference.

Headquarters is in New York.

Connecticut Abbrev.: *Conn.* See **state names**.

connote, denote *Connote* means to suggest or imply something beyond the explicit meaning: *To some people, the word marriage connotes too much restriction.*

Denote means to be explicit about the meaning: *The word demolish denotes destruction.*

Conrail This acronym is acceptable in all references to *Consolidated Rail Corp.* (The corporation originally used *ConRail*, but later changed to *Conrail*.)

A private, for-profit corporation, *Conrail* was set up by Congress as a monopoly in 1976 to reorganize and consolidate six bankrupt Northeast freight railroads — the Penn Central, the Erie Lackawanna, Reading, Central of New Jersey, Lehigh Valley, and Lehigh & Hudson River.

Philadelphia-based *Conrail* was sold to the public in 1987.

In 1999, CSX and Norfolk Southern completed their acquisition of *Conrail*, splitting the assets and sharing *Conrail* tracks and facilities in Detroit, Philadelphia and most of New Jersey. Norfolk Southern acquired 58 percent of *Conrail* and CSX 42 percent. Norfolk Southern, based in Norfolk, Va., operates a 21,600-mile rail system in 22 states, the District of Columbia, and Ontario, Canada. CSX, based in Richmond, Va., formed a 22,300-mile system serving 23 states, the District of Columbia, and Montreal and Ontario, Canada.

Do not confuse *Conrail* and *Amtrak* (see separate entry).

consensus

conservative See the **political parties and philosophies** entry.

Conservative Judaism See **Jewish congregations**.

constable Capitalize when used as a formal title before a name.
See **titles**.

constitute See the **compose, comprise, constitute** entry.

constitution Capitalize references to the U.S. Constitution, with or without the *U.S.* modifier: *The president said he supports the Constitution.*

When referring to constitutions of other nations or of states, capitalize only with the name of a nation or a state: *the French Constitution, the Massachusetts Constitution, the nation's constitution, the state constitution, the constitution.*

Lowercase in other uses: *the organization's constitution.*

Lowercase *constitutional* in all uses.

consul, consul general, consuls general Capitalize when used as a formal title before a noun.
See **titles**.

consulate A *consulate* is the residence of a consul in a foreign city. It handles the commercial affairs and personal needs of citizens of the appointing country.

Capitalize with the name of a nation; lowercase without it: *the French Consulate, the U.S. Consulate, the consulate.*

See **embassy** for the distinction between a consulate and an embassy.

consumer price index A measurement of changes in the retail prices of a constant marketbasket of goods and services. It is computed by comparing the cost of the marketbasket at a fixed time with its cost at subsequent or prior intervals.

Capitalize when referring to the U.S. index, issued monthly by the Bureau of Labor Statistics, an agency of the Labor Department.

The *U.S. Consumer Price Index* should not be referred to as a *cost-of-living index*, because it does not include the impact of income taxes and Social Security taxes on the cost of living, nor does it reflect changes in buying patterns that result from inflation. It is, however, the basis for computing cost-of-living raises in many union contracts.

The preferred form for second reference is *the index.* Confine *CPI* to quoted material.

Consumer Product Safety Commission

Contac A trademark for a brand of decongestant.

contagious

contemptible

continent The seven continents, in order of their land size: Asia, Africa, North America, South America, Europe, Antarctica and Australia.

Capitalize *the Continent* and *Continental* only when used as synonyms for Europe or European. Lowercase in other uses such as: *the continent of Europe, the European continent, the African and Asian continents.*

Continental Airlines Use this spelling of *Airlines*, which Continental has adopted for its public identity. Only its incorporation papers still read *Air Lines.*
Headquarters is in Houston.

Continental Divide The ridge along the Rocky Mountains that separates rivers flowing east from those that flow west.

continental shelf, continental slope Lowercase. The *shelf* is the part of a continent that is submerged in relatively shallow sea at gradually increasing depths, generally up to about 600 feet below sea level.
The *continental slope* begins at the point where the descent to the ocean bottom becomes very steep.

continual, continuous
Continual means a steady repetition, over and over again: *The merger has been the source of continual litigation.*
Continuous means uninterrupted, steady, unbroken: *All she saw ahead of her was a continuous stretch of desert.*

contractions Contractions reflect informal speech and writing. Webster's New World Dictionary includes many entries for contractions: *aren't* for *are not*, for example.
Avoid excessive use of contractions. Contractions listed in the dictionary are acceptable, however, in informal contexts where they reflect the way a phrase commonly appears in speech or writing.

See **colloquialisms; quotations in the news;** and **word selection**.

Contra, Contras Uppercase when used to describe Nicaraguan rebel groups.

contrasted to, contrasted with Use *contrasted to* when the intent is to assert, without the need for elaboration, that two items have opposite characteristics: *He contrasted the appearance of the house today to its ramshackle look last year.*
Use *contrasted with* when juxtaposing two or more items to illustrate similarities and/or differences: *He contrasted the Republican platform with the Democratic platform.*

control, controlled, controlling

controller See the **comptroller, controller** entry.

controversial An overused word; avoid it. See **noncontroversial**.

convention Capitalize as part of the name for a specific national or state political convention: *the Democratic National Convention, the Republican State Convention.*
Lowercase in other uses: *the national convention, the state convention, the convention, the annual convention of the American Medical Association.*

convict (v.) Follow with preposition *of*, not *for*: *He was convicted of murder.*

convince, persuade You may be *convinced that* something or *of* something. You must be *persuaded* to *do* something.

Right: *The robbers persuaded him to open the vault.*

Wrong: *The robbers convinced him to open the vault.*

Right: *The robbers convinced him that it was the right thing to do.*

Wrong: *The robbers persuaded him that it was the right thing to do.*

cookie, cookies

cooperate, cooperative

But *co-op* as a short term of *cooperative*, to distinguish it from *coop*, a cage for animals.

Cooperative for American Relief Everywhere See CARE.

coordinate, coordination

cop Be careful in the use of this colloquial term for *police officer*. It may be used in lighter stories and in casual, informal descriptions, but often is a derogatory term out of place in serious police stories.

copter Acceptable shortening of *helicopter*. But use it only as a noun or adjective. It is not a verb.

copy editor Seldom a formal title. See **titles**.

copyright (n., v. and adj.) *The disclosure was made in a copyright story.*

Use *copyrighted* only as the past tense of the verb: *He copyrighted the article.*

See **Copyright Guidelines** in Appendix.

co-respondent In a divorce suit.

Corn Belt The region in the north central Midwest where much corn and corn-fed livestock are raised. It extends from western Ohio to eastern Nebraska and northeastern Kansas.

Corp. See **corporation**.

corporal See **military titles**.

corporate names See **company names**.

corporation An entity that is treated as a person in the eyes of the law. It is able to own property, incur debts, sue and be sued.

Abbreviate *corporation* as *Corp.* when a company or government agency uses the word at the end of its name: *Gulf Oil Corp., the Federal Deposit Insurance Corp.*

Spell out *corporation* when it occurs elsewhere in a name: *the Corporation for Public Broadcasting.*

Spell out and lowercase *corporation* whenever it stands alone.

The form for possessives: *Gulf Oil Corp.'s profits.*

corps Capitalize when used with a word or a figure to form a proper name: *the Marine Corps, the Signal Corps, the 9th Corps.*

Capitalize when standing alone only if it is a shortened reference to *U.S. Marine Corps.*

The possessive form is *corps'* for both singular and plural: *one corps' location, two corps' assignments.*

corral, corralled, corralling

correctional facility, correctional institution See the **prison, jail** entry.

Corsica Use instead of *France* in datelines on stories from communities on this island.

Cortes The Spanish parliament. See **foreign legislative bodies.**

cosmonaut The applicable occupational term for astronauts of the former Soviet Union. Always use lowercase.
See **titles.**

cost of living The amount of money needed to pay taxes and to buy the goods and services deemed necessary to make up a given standard of living, taking into account changes that may occur in tastes and buying patterns.
The term often is treated incorrectly as a synonym for the *U.S. Consumer Price Index*, which does not take taxes into account and measures only price changes, keeping the quantities constant over time.
Hyphenate when used as a compound modifier: *The cost of living went up, but he did not receive a cost-of-living raise.*
See the **consumer price index** and **inflation** entries.

Cotton Belt The region in the South and Southwestern sections of the United States where much cotton is grown.

council, councilor, councilman, councilwoman A deliberative body and those who are members of it.
See the **counsel** entry and **legislative titles.**

Council of Economic Advisers A group of advisers who help the U.S. president prepare his annual economic report to Congress and recommend economic measures to him throughout the year.

counsel, counseled, counseling, counselor, counselor at law To *counsel* is to advise. A *counselor* is one who advises.
A *counselor at law* (no hyphens for consistency with *attorney at law*) is a lawyer. See **lawyer.**

count, countess See **nobility.**

counter- The rules in **prefixes** apply, but in general, no hyphen. Some examples:
counteract   counterproposal
countercharge   counterspy
counterfoil

countryside

county Capitalize when an integral part of a proper name: *Dade County, Nassau County, Suffolk County.*
Capitalize the full names of county governmental units: *the Dade County Commission, the Orange County Department of Social Services, the Suffolk County Legislature.*
Retain capitalization for the name of a county body if the proper noun is not needed in the context; lowercase the word *county* if it is used to distinguish an agency from state or federal counterparts: *the Board of Supervisors, the county Board of Supervisors; the Department of Social Services, the county Department of Social Services.* Lowercase *the*

board, *the department*, etc. whenever they stand alone.

Capitalize *county* if it is an integral part of a specific body's name even without the proper noun: *the County Commission, the County Legislature.* Lowercase *the commission, the legislature*, etc. when not preceded by the word *county*.

Capitalize as part of a formal title before a name: *County Manager John Smith.* Lowercase when it is not part of the formal title: *county Health Commissioner Frank Jones.*

Avoid *county of* phrases where possible, but when necessary, always lowercase: *the county of Westchester.*

Lowercase plural combinations: *Westchester and Rockland counties.*

Apply the same rules to similar terms such as *parish*.

See **governmental bodies**.

county court In some states, it is not a court but the administrative body of a county. In most cases, the *court* is presided over by a *county judge*, who is not a judge in the traditional sense but the chief administrative officer of the county.

The terms should be explained if they are not clear in the context.

Capitalize all references to a specific *county court*, and capitalize *county judge* when used as a formal title before a name. Do not use *judge* alone before a name except in direct quotations.

Examples:

SEVIERVILLE, Tenn. (AP) — A reluctant County Court approved a school budget today that calls for a 10 percent tax increase for property owners.

The county had been given an ultimatum by the state: Approve the budget or shut down the schools.

The chief administrative officer, County Judge Ray Reagan, said ...

coup d'etat The word *coup* usually is sufficient.

couple When used in the sense of two people, the word takes plural verbs and pronouns: *The couple were married Saturday and left Sunday on their honeymoon. They will return in two weeks.*

In the sense of a single unit, use a singular verb: *Each couple was asked to give $10.*

couple of The *of* is necessary. Never use *a couple tomatoes* or a similar phrase.

The phrase takes a plural verb in constructions such as: *A couple of tomatoes were stolen.*

course numbers Use Arabic numerals and capitalize the subject when used with a numeral: *History 6, Philosophy 209.*

court decisions Use figures and a hyphen: *The Supreme Court ruled 5-4, a 5-4 decision.* The word *to* is not needed, but use hyphens if it appears in quoted matter: *"The court ruled 5-to-4, the 5-to-4 decision."*

court districts See **court names**.

courtesy titles Refer to both men and women by first and last name: *Susan Smith* or *Robert Smith.* Use the courtesy titles *Mr., Miss, Ms.* or *Mrs.* only in direct quotations or in other special situations:

—When it is necessary to distinguish between two people who use the same last name, as in married couples or brothers and sisters, use a courtesy title for a woman if her preference is known, or identify her by first and last name.

—When a woman specifically requests it; for example, where a woman prefers to be known as *Mrs. Susan Smith* or *Ms. Susan Smith.*

In cases where a person's gender is not clear from the first name or from the story's context, indicate the gender by using *he* or *she* in subsequent reference.

courthouse Capitalize with the name of a jurisdiction: *the Cook County Courthouse, the U.S. Courthouse.* Lowercase in other uses: *the county courthouse, the courthouse, the federal courthouse.*

Court House (two words) is used in the proper names of some communities: *Appomattox Court House, Va.*

court-martial, court-martialed, courts-martial

court names Capitalize the full proper names of courts at all levels.

Retain capitalization if *U.S.* or a state name is dropped: *the U.S. Supreme Court, the Supreme Court, the state Superior Court, the Superior Court, Superior Court.*

For courts identified by a numeral: *2nd District Court, 8th U.S. Circuit Court of Appeals.*

For additional details on federal courts, see **judicial branch** and separate listings under **U.S.** and the court name.

See **judge** for guidelines on titles before the names of judges.

Court of St. James's Note the *'s.* The formal name for the royal court of the British sovereign. Derived from St. James's Palace, the former scene of royal receptions.

courtroom

cover up (v.) **cover-up** (n. and adj.) *He tried to cover up the scandal. He was prosecuted for the cover-up.*

crack up (v.) **crackup** (n. and adj.)

crawfish Not *crayfish.* An exception to Webster's New World based on the dominant spelling in Louisiana, where it is a popular delicacy.

criminal cases See the **civil cases, criminal cases** entry.

Crisco A trademark for a brand of vegetable shortening.

crisis, crises

crisscross

criterion, criteria

cross-examine, cross-examination

cross-eye (n.) **cross-eyed** (adj.)

cross fire

crossover (n. and adj.)

cross section (n.) **cross-section** (v.)

CRT Abbreviation for *cathode ray tube*. Do not use. *Display unit* is among the terms preferred.

CT scan *Computerized tomography*, a method of making multiple X-ray images of the body or parts of the body and using a computer to construct, from those images, cross-sectional views. (Formerly known as *CAT scan*.)

Cub Scouts See **Boy Scouts**.

cuckoo clock

cup Equal to 8 fluid ounces. The approximate metric equivalents are 240 milliliters or .24 of a liter.
To convert to liters, multiply by .24 (14 cups x .24 = 3.36 liters, or 3,360 milliliters).
See **liter**.

cupful, cupfuls Not *cupsful*.

curate See **religious titles**.

cure-all

Curia See **Roman Catholic Church**.

currency depreciation, currency devaluation A nation's money *depreciates* when its value falls in relation to the currency of other nations or in relation to its own prior value.
A nation's money is *devalued* when its value is reduced in relation to the currency of other nations, either deliberately by the government or through market forces.
When a nation devalues its currency, the goods it imports tend to become more expensive. Its exports tend to become less expensive in other nations and thus more competitive.
See **devaluations**.

curtain raiser

customs Capitalize *U.S. Customs Service*, or simply *the Customs Service*.
Lowercase elsewhere: *a customs official, a customs ruling, she went through customs*.

cut back (v.) **cutback** (n. and adj.) *He cut back spending. The cutback will require frugality.*

cut off (v.) **cutoff** (n. and adj.) *He cut off his son's allowance. The cutoff date for applications is Monday.*

cyclone See **weather terms**.

Cyclone A trademark for a brand of chain-link fence.

cynic, skeptic A *skeptic* is a doubter.
A *cynic* is a disbeliever.

czar Not *tsar*. It was a formal title only for the ruler of Russia and some other Slavic nations.
Lowercase in all other uses.

D

Dacron A trademark for a brand of polyester fiber.

DaimlerChrysler AG Merger of Chrysler Corp. and Daimler-Benz AG.

Dual headquarters in Auburn Hills, Mich., and Stuttgart, Germany.

dalai lama The traditional high priest of Lamaism, a form of Buddhism practiced in Tibet and Mongolia. *Dalai lama* is a title rather than a name, but it is all that is used when referring to the man. Capitalize *Dalai Lama* in references to the holder of the title, in keeping with the principles outlined in the **nobility** entry.

Dallas The city in Texas stands alone in datelines.

Dalles, The A city in Oregon.

dam Capitalize when part of a proper name: *Hoover Dam.*

damage, damages *Damage* is destruction: *Authorities said damage from the storm would total more than $1 billion.*

Damages are awarded by a court as compensation for injury, loss, etc.: *The woman received $25,000 in damages.*

dame See **nobility**.

damn it Use instead of *dammit*, but like other profanity it should be avoided unless there is a compelling reason.

See the **obscenities, profanities, vulgarities** entry.

dangling modifiers Avoid modifiers that do not refer clearly and logically to some word in the sentence.

Dangling: *Taking our seats, the game started.* (*Taking* does not refer to the subject, *game*, nor to any other word in the sentence.)

Correct: *Taking our seats, we watched the opening of the game.* (*Taking* refers to *we*, the subject of the sentence.)

Danish pastry

Dardanelles, the Not *the Dardanelles Strait.*

Dark Ages The period beginning with the sack of Rome in A.D. 476 and ending about the end of the 10th century. The term is derived from the idea that this period in Europe was characterized by intellectual stagnation, widespread ignorance and poverty.

dark horse

dash See entry in the **Punctuation** chapter.

data A plural noun, it normally takes plural verbs and pronouns.

See the **collective nouns** entry, however, for an example of when *data* may take singular verbs and pronouns.

database One word, in keeping with widespread usage. The collection of all data used and produced by a computer program.

data processing (n. and adj.) Do not hyphenate the adjective.

date line Two words for the imaginary line that separates one day from another.

See the **international date line** entry.

datelines Datelines on stories should contain a city name, entirely in capital letters, followed in most cases by the name of the state, county or territory where the city is located.

DOMESTIC DATELINES: A list of domestic cities that stand alone in datelines follows. The norms that influenced the selection were the population of the city, the population of its metropolitan region, the frequency of the city's appearance in the news, the uniqueness of its name, and experience that has shown the name to be almost synonymous with the state or nation where it is located.

No state with the following:

ATLANTA	MILWAUKEE
BALTIMORE	MINNEAPOLIS
BOSTON	NEW ORLEANS
CHICAGO	NEW YORK
CINCINNATI	OKLAHOMA CITY
CLEVELAND	PHILADELPHIA
DALLAS	PHOENIX
DENVER	PITTSBURGH
DETROIT	ST. LOUIS
HONOLULU	SALT LAKE CITY
HOUSTON	SAN ANTONIO
INDIANAPOLIS	SAN DIEGO
LAS VEGAS	SAN FRANCISCO
LOS ANGELES	SEATTLE
MIAMI	WASHINGTON

Also *HOLLYWOOD* when used instead of *LOS ANGELES* on stories about films and the film industry.

Stories from all other U.S. cities should have both the city and state name in the dateline, including *KANSAS CITY, Mo.*, and *KANSAS CITY, Kan.*

Spell out *Alaska, Hawaii, Idaho, Iowa, Maine, Ohio, Texas* and *Utah*. Abbreviate others as listed in this book under the full name of each state.

Use *Hawaii* on all cities outside Honolulu. Specify the island in the text if needed.

Follow the same practice for communities on islands within the boundaries of other states: *EDGARTOWN, Mass.*, for example, not *EDGARTOWN, Martha's Vineyard.*

REGIONAL CIRCUITS: On state wires, additional cities in a state or region may stand alone if requested by the newspapers served.

When this is done, provide a list to all offices in the region, to all newspapers affected and to New York headquarters.

U.S. POSSESSIONS: Apply the guidelines listed below in the ISLAND NATIONS AND TERRITORIES section and the OVERSEAS TERRITORIES section.

FOREIGN CITIES: These foreign locations stand alone in datelines:

BEIJING
BERLIN
DJIBOUTI
GENEVA
GIBRALTAR
GUATEMALA CITY
HAVANA
HONG KONG
JERUSALEM
KUWAIT
LONDON
LUXEMBOURG
MACAU

MEXICO CITY
MONACO
MONTREAL
MOSCOW
OTTAWA
PARIS
QUEBEC CITY
ROME
SAN MARINO
SINGAPORE
TOKYO
TORONTO
VATICAN CITY

In addition, use *UNITED NA-TIONS* alone, without a *N.Y.* designation, in stories from *U.N.* headquarters.

CANADIAN DATELINES: Datelines on stories from Canadian cities other than Montreal, Ottawa, Quebec City and Toronto should contain the name of the city in capital letters followed by the name of the province. Do not abbreviate any province or territory name.

COMMONWEALTH OF INDEPENDENT STATES: For cities in the former Soviet Union, datelines include city and republic name: *ALMATY, Kazakstan.*

OTHER FOREIGN NATIONS: Stories from other foreign cities that do not stand alone in datelines should contain the name of the country or territory (see the next section) spelled out.

SPELLING AND CHOICE OF NAMES: In most cases, the name of the nation in a dateline is the conventionally accepted short form of its official name: *Argentina,* for example, rather than *Republic of Argentina.* (If in doubt, look for an entry in this book. If none is found, follow Webster's New World Dictionary.)

Note these special cases:

—Instead of *United Kingdom,* use *England, Northern Ireland, Scotland* or *Wales.*

—For divided nations, use the commonly accepted names based on geographic distinctions: *North Korea, South Korea.*

—Use an article only with *El Salvador.* For all others, use just a country name — *Gambia, Netherlands, Philippines,* etc.

See **geographic names** for guidelines on spelling the names of foreign cities and nations not listed here or in separate entries.

ISLAND NATIONS AND TERRITORIES: When reporting from nations and territories that are made up primarily of islands but commonly are linked under one name, use the city name and the general name in the dateline. Identify an individual island, if needed, in the text:

Examples:

British Virgin Islands	Netherlands Antilles
Indonesia	Philippines

OVERSEAS TERRITORIES: Some overseas territories, colonies and other areas that are not independent nations commonly have accepted separate identities based on their geographic character or special status under treaties. In these cases, use the commonly accepted territory name after a city name in a dateline.

Examples:

Bermuda	Guam
Corsica	Martinique
Faeroe Islands	Puerto Rico
Greenland	Sardinia
Grenada	Sicily
Guadeloupe	Sikkim
Tibet	

WITHIN STORIES: In citing other cities within the body of a story:

—No further information is necessary if a city is in the same state as the datelined city in U.S. stories from abroad. Make an exception if confusion would result.

—Follow the city name with further identification in most cases where it is not in the same state or nation as the dateline city. The additional identification may be omitted, however, if no confusion would result — there is no need, for example, to refer to *Boston, Mass.*, in a story datelined *NEW YORK*.

—Provide a state or nation identification for the city if the story is undated. However, cities that stand alone in datelines may be used alone in undated stories if no confusion would result.

dateline selection A dateline should tell the reader that the AP obtained the basic information for the story in the datelined city.

Do not, for example, use a Washington dateline on a story written primarily from information that a newspaper reported under a Washington dateline. Use the home city of the newspaper instead.

This rule does not preclude the use of a story with a dateline different from the home city of a newspaper if it is from the general area served by the newspaper.

Use a foreign dateline only if the basic information in a story was obtained by a full- or part-time correspondent physically present in the datelined community.

If a radio broadcast monitored in another city was the source of information, use the dateline of the city where the monitoring took place and mention the fact in the story.

When a story has been assembled from sources in widely separated areas, use no dateline.

When a datelined story contains supplementary information obtained in another city, make that point clear in the context. Do not put parentheses around such material, however, unless the correspondent in the datelined community was cut off from incoming communications. Note the following examples:

—Material from another area was available in the datelined city:

LONDON (AP) — Prime Minister Wilson submitted his resignation today.

In Washington, a State Department spokesman said the change in government leadership would have no effect on negotiations involving the Common Market.

—Material from another area was not available to the correspondent in the dateline city because communications from the outside world were cut off:

PHNOM PENH, Cambodia (AP) — Khmer Rouge troops pushed into Phnom Penh today, barely hours after the United States ran down the Stars and Stripes and abandoned Cambodia to the Communists.

(In Washington, the State Department said Americans evacuated in a mass airlift had arrived safely aboard aircraft carriers and at bases in Thailand.)

dates Always use Arabic figures, without *st, nd, rd* or *th*. See **months** for examples and **punctuation** guidelines.

daughter-in-law, daughters-in-law

Daughters of the American Revolution *DAR* is acceptable on second reference.

Headquarters is in Washington.

daylight-saving time Not *savings*. Note the hyphen.

When linking the term with the name of a time zone, use only the word *daylight*: *Eastern Daylight Time, Pacific Daylight Time,* etc.

Lowercase *daylight-saving time* in all uses and *daylight time* whenever it stands alone.

A federal law, administered by the Transportation Department, specifies that daylight time applies from 2 a.m. on the first Sunday of April until 2 a.m. on the last Sunday of October in areas that do not specifically exempt themselves.

See **time zones**.

daylong

days of the week Capitalize them. Do not abbreviate, except when needed in a tabular format: *Sun, Mon, Tue, Wed, Thu, Fri, Sat* (three letters, without periods, to facilitate tabular composition).

See **time element**.

daytime

day to day, day-to-day Hyphenate when used as a compound modifier: *They have extended the contract on a day-to-day basis.*

D-Day June 6, 1944, the day the Allies invaded Europe in World War II.

DDT Preferred in all references for the insecticide *dichlorodiphenyltrichloroethane.*

de- See **foreign particles**.

deacon See the entry for the individual's denomination.

dead center

dead end (n.) **dead-end** (adj.) *She reached a dead end. He has a dead-end job.*

Dead Sea Scrolls

deaf See **disabled, handicapped, impaired**.

deaf-mute Avoid the term. The preferred form is to say that an individual cannot hear or speak. A *mute* person may be deaf or may be able to hear.

Do not use *deaf and dumb*.

dean Capitalize when used as a formal title before a name: *Dean John Jones, Deans John Jones and Susan Smith.*

Lowercase in other uses: *John Jones, dean of the college; the dean.*

dean's list Lowercase in all uses: *He is on the dean's list. She is a dean's list student.*

deathbed (n. and adj.)

decades Use Arabic figures to indicate decades of history. Use an apostrophe to indicate numerals that are left out; show plural by adding the letter *s*: *the 1890s, the '90s, the Gay '90s, the 1920s, the mid-1930s.*

See the **historical periods and events** entry.

December See **months**.

deci- A prefix denoting one-tenth of a unit. Move the decimal point one place to the left in converting to the basic unit: 15.5 decigrams = 1.55 grams.

decimal units Use a period and numerals to indicate decimal amounts. Decimalization should not exceed two places in textual material unless there are special circumstances.
See **fractions**.

Declaration of Independence Lowercase *the declaration* whenever it stands alone.

decorations See the **awards and decorations** entry.

Deepfreeze A trademark for a brand of home freezer.
If something is being postponed indefinitely, use two words: *The project is in the deep freeze.*

deep-sea (adj.)

Deep South Capitalize both words when referring to the region that consists of Alabama, Georgia, Louisiana, Mississippi and South Carolina.

deep water (n.) **deep-water** (adj.) *The creature swam in deep water. The ship needs a deep-water port.*

defendant

defense Do not use it as a verb.

defense attorney Always lowercase, never abbreviate.
See **attorney** and **titles**.

defense spending *Military spending* usually is the more precise term.

definitely Overused as a vague intensifier. Avoid it.

degree-day See **weather terms**.

degrees See **academic degrees**.

deity Lowercase. See **gods** and **religious references**.

dek- (before a vowel), **deka-** (before a consonant) A prefix denoting 10 units of a measure. Move the decimal point one place to the right to convert to the basic unit: 15.6 dekameters = 156 meters.

Delaware Abbrev.: *Del.* Only Rhode Island is smaller in area.
See **state names**.

delegate The formal title for members of the lower houses of some legislatures. Do not abbreviate. Capitalize only before their names. See **legislative titles**.
Always lowercase in other uses: *convention delegate Richard Henry Lee.*

Delta Air Lines Headquarters is in Atlanta.

demagogue, demagoguery Not *demagog.*

democrat, democratic, Democratic Party See the **political parties and philosophies** entry.

Democratic Governors' Conference Note the apostrophe.

Democratic National Committee On the second reference: *the national committee, the committee.*

Similarly: *Democratic State Committee, Democratic County Committee, Democratic City Committee, the state committee, the city committee, the committee.*

demolish, destroy Both mean to do away with something completely. Something cannot be partially *demolished* or *destroyed.* It is redundant to say *totally demolished* or *totally destroyed.*

denote See the **connote, denote** entry.

Denver The city in Colorado stands alone in datelines.

depart Follow it with a preposition: *He will depart from La Guardia. She will depart at 11:30 a.m.*

Do not drop the preposition as some airline dispatchers do.

Department of Agriculture; Department of Commerce; Department of Defense; Department of Education; Department of Energy (*DOE* acceptable on second reference); **Department of Health and Human Services** (formerly the Department of Health, Education and Welfare); **Department of Housing and Urban Development** (*HUD* acceptable on second reference); **Department of the Interior; Department of Justice; Department of Labor; Department of State; Department of Transportation** (*DOT* acceptable on second reference); **Department of the Treasury**.

Avoid acronyms when possible. A phrase such as *the depart-*

ment is preferable on second reference because it is more readable and avoids alphabet soup.

The *of* may be dropped and the title flopped while capitalization is retained: *the State Department.*

Lowercase *department* in plural uses, but capitalize the proper name element: *the departments of Labor and Justice.*

A shorthand reference to the proper name element also is capitalized: *Kissinger said, "State and Justice must resolve their differences."* But: *Henry Kissinger, the secretary of state.*

Lowercase *the department* whenever it stands alone.

Do not abbreviate *department* in any usage.

See **academic departments**.

dependent (n. and adj.) Not *dependant.*

depreciation The reduction in the value of capital goods due to wear and tear or obsolescence.

Estimated depreciation may be deducted from income each year as one of the costs of doing business.

depression Capitalize *Depression* and *the Great Depression* when referring to the worldwide economic hard times generally regarded as having begun with the stock market collapse of Oct. 28-29, 1929.

Lowercase in other uses: *the depression of the 1970s.*

depths See **dimensions**.

deputy Capitalize as a formal title before a name. See **titles**.

derogatory terms Do not use derogatory terms such as

krauts (for Germans) or *niggers* (for blacks) except in direct quotes, and then only when their use is an integral, essential part of the story.

See the **obscenities, profanities, vulgarities** entry and **word selection**.

-designate Hyphenate: *chairman-designate*. Capitalize only the first word if used as a formal title before a name.

See **titles**.

destroy See the **demolish, destroy** entry.

detective Do not abbreviate. Capitalize before a name only if it is a formal rank: *police Detective Frank Serpico, private detective Richard Diamond*.

See **titles**.

detente

detention center See the **prison, jail** entry.

Detroit The city in Michigan stands alone in datelines.

devaluations Devaluations occur when the value of a country's currency goes down in its relation to another currency. This may happen by government decree, or through market forces. Devaluations are expressed in percentages, but the normal method of figuring a percentage change won't work. Use the following rules:

Say currency A is quoted in a set of units to currency B. When currency A is devalued, 1) take the new exchange rate and subtract the old exchange rate, 2) divide the answer by the new exchange rate and 3) multiply the

answer by 100 to get the percentage devaluation.

Example:

9.5 (new rate) minus 6.3 (old rate) = 3.2

3.2 divided by 9.5 = 0.3368

0.3368 times 100 = 33.68421 (or 34 percent).

The ruble has been devalued against the dollar by 34 percent.

devil But capitalize *Satan*.

DEW line See **North Warning System**.

Dexedrine A trademark for a brand of appetite suppressant. It also may be called *dextroamphetamine sulfate*.

dialect The form of language peculiar to a region or a group, usually in matters of pronunciation or syntax. Dialect should be avoided, even in quoted matter, unless it is clearly pertinent to a story.

There are some words and phrases in everyone's vocabulary that are typical of a particular region or group. Quoting dialect, unless used carefully, implies substandard or illiterate usage.

When there is a compelling reason to use dialect, words or phrases are spelled phonetically, and apostrophes show missing letters and sounds: *"Din't ya yoosta live at Toidy-Toid Street and Sekun' Amya? Across from da moom pitchers?"*

See **colloquialisms; quotes in the news**; and **word selection**.

dialogue (n.)

diarrhea

Dictaphone A trademark for a brand of dictation recorder.

dictionaries For spelling, style and usage questions not covered in this stylebook, consult Webster's New World College Dictionary, Fourth Edition, published by IDG Books.

Use the first spelling listed in Webster's New World unless a specific exception is listed in this book.

If Webster's New World provides different spellings in separate entries (*tee shirt* and *T-shirt*, for example), use the spelling that is followed by a full definition (*T-shirt*).

If Webster's New World provides definitions under two different spellings for the same sense of a word, either use is acceptable. For example, *although* or *though*.

If there is no listing in either this book or Webster's New World, the backup dictionary, with more listings, is Webster's Third New International Dictionary, published by G. & C. Merriam Co. of Springfield, Mass.

Webster's New World is also the first reference for geographic names not covered in this stylebook. See **geographic names**.

die-hard (n. and adj.)

Diet The Japanese parliament. See **foreign legislative bodies**.

dietitian Not *dietician*.

different Takes the preposition *from*, not *than*.

differ from, differ with
To *differ from* means to be unlike.

To *differ with* means to disagree.

dilemma It means more than a problem. It implies a choice between two unattractive alternatives.

dimensions Use figures and spell out *inches, feet, yards*, etc., to indicate depth, height, length and width. Hyphenate adjectival forms before nouns.

EXAMPLES: *He is 5 feet 6 inches tall, the 5-foot-6-inch man, the 5-foot man, the basketball team signed a 7-footer.*

The car is 17 feet long, 6 feet wide and 5 feet high. The rug is 9 feet by 12 feet, the 9-by-12 rug.

The storm left 5 inches of snow.

Use an apostrophe to indicate feet and quote marks to indicate inches (5'6") only in very technical contexts.

Diners Club No apostrophe, in keeping with the practice the company has adopted for its public identity. Only its incorporation papers still read *Diners' Club*.

Headquarters is in New York.

diocese Capitalize as part of a proper name: *the Diocese of Rochester, the Rochester Diocese, the diocese*.

See **Episcopal Church** and **Roman Catholic Church**.

directions and regions In general, lowercase *north, south, northeast, northern*, etc., when they indicate compass direction; capitalize these words when they designate regions.

Some examples:

COMPASS DIRECTIONS: *He drove west. The cold front is moving east.*

REGIONS: *A storm system that developed in the Midwest is spreading eastward. It will bring showers to the East Coast by morning and to the entire Northeast by late in the day. High temperatures will prevail throughout the Western states.*

The North was victorious. The South will rise again. Settlers from the East went West in search of new lives. The customs of the East are different from those of the West. The Northeast depends on the Midwest for its food supply.

She has a Southern accent. He is a Northerner. Nations of the Orient are opening doors to Western businessmen. The candidate developed a Southern strategy. She is a Northern liberal.

The storm developed in the South Pacific. European leaders met to talk about supplies of oil from Southeast Asia.

WITH NAMES OF NATIONS: Lowercase unless they are part of a proper name or are used to designate a politically divided nation: *northern France, eastern Canada, the western United States.*

But: *Northern Ireland, South Korea.*

WITH STATES AND CITIES: The preferred form is to lowercase compass points only when they describe a section of a state or city: *western Texas, southern Atlanta.*

But capitalize compass points:
—When part of a proper name: *North Dakota, West Virginia.*
—When used in denoting widely known sections: *Southern California, the South Side of Chicago, the Lower East Side of New York.* If in doubt, use lowercase.

IN FORMING PROPER NAMES: When combining with another common noun to form the name for a region or location: *the North Woods, the South Pole, the Far East, the Middle East, the West Coast* (the entire region, not the coastline itself — see **coast**), *the Eastern Shore* (see separate entry), *the Western Hemisphere.*

director The former title for the individuals who head the Federal Bureau of Investigation and the Central Intelligence Agency. Capitalize when used immediately before their names or those of others for whom director is a formal title: *FBI Director J. Edgar Hoover.*

Most uses of *director*, however, involve an occupational description not capitalized in any use: *company director Joseph Warren.*
See **titles**.

dis- The rules in prefixes apply, but in general, no hyphen. Some examples:
dismember   disservice
dissemble   dissuade

disabled, handicapped, impaired In general do not describe an individual as *disabled* or *handicapped* unless it is clearly pertinent to a story. If such a description must be used, make it clear what the handicap is and how much the person's physical or mental performance is affected.

Some terms include:
disabled A general term used for a physical or cognitive condition that substantially limits one or more of the major daily life activities.

handicap It should be avoided in describing a disability.

blind Describes a person with complete loss of sight. For others use terms such as *visually impaired* or *person with low vision*.

deaf Describes a person with total hearing loss. For others use *partial hearing loss* or *partially deaf*. Avoid using *deaf-mute*. Do not use *deaf and dumb*.

mute Describes a person who physically cannot speak. Others with speaking difficulties are *speech impaired*.

wheelchair-user People use wheelchairs for independent mobility. Do not use *confined to a wheelchair*, or *wheelchair-bound*. If a wheelchair is needed, say why.

disc Use this spelling except for computer-related references: *laserdisc*, *videodisc*, but *hard disk*.
See **disk**.

disc jockey *DJ* is acceptable on second reference in a column or other special context. Use announcer in other contexts.

discreet, discrete *Discreet* means prudent, circumspect: *"I'm afraid I was not very discreet,"* she wrote.

Discrete means detached, separate: *There are four discrete sounds from a quadraphonic system.*

diseases Do not capitalize *arthritis, emphysema, leukemia, migraine, pneumonia*, etc.

When a disease is known by the name of a person identified with it, capitalize only the individual's name: *Bright's disease, Parkinson's disease*, etc.

disinterested, uninterested *Disinterested* means impartial, which is usually the better word to convey the thought.

Uninterested means that someone lacks interest.

disk Use this spelling, not *disc*, for the thin, flat plate on which computer data can be stored. Do not use as an abbreviation for *diskette*.
See **disc**.

diskette A generic term that means *floppy disk*. Not synonymous with *disk*.

dispel, dispelled, dispelling

disposable personal income The income that a person retains after deductions for income taxes, Social Security taxes, property taxes and for other payments such as fines and penalties to various levels of government.

Disposall A trademark for a type of mechanical garbage disposer.

dissociate Not *disassociate*.

distances Use figures for 10 and above, spell out one through nine: *He walked four miles.*

Distant Early Warning Line The *DEW line* was deactivated in 1985. See **North Warning System**.

district Always spell it out. Use a figure and capitalize *district* when forming a proper name: *the 2nd District.*

district attorney Do not abbreviate. Capitalize when used as a formal title before a name: *District Attorney Hamilton Burger.*

Use *DA* (no periods) only in quoted matter.

See **titles**.

district court See **court names** and **U.S. District Court**.

District of Columbia Abbreviate as *D.C.* when the context requires that it be used in conjunction with *Washington*. Spell out when used alone.

The district, rather than *D.C.*, should be used in subsequent references.

ditto marks They can be made with quotation marks, but their use in newspapers, even in tabular material, is confusing. Don't use them.

dive, dived, diving Not *dove* for the past tense.

divided nations See **datelines** and entries under the names of these nations.

dividend See entry in **Business Guidelines**.

division See the **organizations and institutions** entry; **military units**; and **political divisions**.

divorcee The fact that a woman has been divorced should be mentioned only if a similar story about a man would mention his marital status.

When the woman's marital status is relevant, it seldom belongs in the lead. Avoid stories that begin: *A 35-year-old divorcee ...*

The preferred form is to say in the body of the story that a woman is divorced.

Dixie cup A trademark for a paper drinking cup.

doctor Use *Dr.* in first reference as a formal title before the name of an individual who holds a doctor of dental surgery, doctor of medicine, doctor of osteopathy, or doctor of podiatric medicine degree: *Dr. Jonas Salk*.

The form *Dr.*, or *Drs.*, in a plural construction, applies to all first-reference uses before a name, including direct quotations.

If appropriate in the context, *Dr.* also may be used on first reference before the names of individuals who hold other types of doctoral degrees. However, because the public frequently identifies *Dr.* only with physicians, care should be taken to assure that the individual's specialty is stated in first or second reference. The only exception would be a story in which the context left no doubt that the person was a dentist, psychologist, chemist, historian, etc.

In some instances it also is necessary to specify that an individual identified as *Dr.* is a physician. One frequent case is a story reporting on joint research by physicians, biologists, etc.

Do not use *Dr.* before the names of individuals who hold only honorary doctorates.

Do not continue the use of *Dr.* in subsequent references.

See **academic degrees**; **courtesy titles**; and **religious titles**.

dogs See **animals**.

dollars Always lowercase. Use figures and the $ sign in all except casual references or amounts without a figure: *The book cost $4. Dad, please give me a dollar. Dollars are flowing overseas.*

For specified amounts, the word takes a singular verb: *He said $500,000 is what they want.*

For amounts of more than $1 million, use the $ and numerals up to two decimal places. Do not link the numerals and the word by a hyphen: *It is worth $4.35 million. It is worth exactly $4,351,242. He proposed a $300 billion budget.*

The form for amounts less than $1 million: *$4, $25, $500, $1,000, $650,000.*

See **cents.**

domino, dominoes

door to door, door-to-door
Hyphenate when used as a compound modifier: *He is a door-to-door salesman.*

But: *He went from door to door.*

DOS An acronym for *disk operating system.* Spell out.

double-faced

doughnut Not *donut.*

Dow Jones & Co. The company publishes The Wall Street Journal and Barron's National Business and Financial Weekly. It also operates the Dow Jones News Service.

For stock market watchers, it provides the Dow Jones industrial average, the Dow Jones transportation average, the Dow Jones utility average, and the Dow Jones composite average.

Headquarters is in New York.

down- The rules in **prefixes** apply, but in general, no hyphen. Some examples:

downgrade	downtown

-down Follow Webster's New World. Some examples, all nouns and/or adjectives:

breakdown	rundown
countdown	sit-down

All are two words when used as verbs.

Down East Use only in reference to Maine.

downstate Lowercase unless part of a proper name: *downstate Illinois.* But: *the Downstate Medical Center.*

Down syndrome Not *Down's,* for the genetic, chromosomal disorder first reported in 1866 by Dr. J. Langdon Down.

Down Under Australia, New Zealand and environs.

Dr. See **doctor.**

draft beer Not *draught beer.*

drama See **composition titles.**

Dramamine A trademark for a brand of motion sickness remedy.

Drambuie A trademark for a brand of Scottish liqueur.

dressing room

Dripolator A trademark for a brand of drip coffee maker.

drive See **addresses.**

drive-in (n.)

drop out (v.) dropout (n.)

drought

drowned, was drowned If a person suffocates in water or

other fluid, the proper statement is that the individual *drowned*. To say that someone *was drowned* implies that another person caused the death by holding the victim's head under the water.

Dr Pepper A trademark (no period after Dr) for a brand of soft drink.

Headquarters is in Dallas.

drugs Because the word drugs has come to be used as a synonym for narcotics in recent years, *medicine* is frequently the better word to specify that an individual is taking medication.

drunk, drunken *Drunk* is the spelling of the adjective used after a form of the verb *to be: He was drunk.*

Drunken is the spelling of the adjective used before nouns: *a drunken driver, drunken driving.*

drunkenness

duel A contest between two people. Three people cannot duel.

duffel Not *duffle*.

duke, duchess See **nobility**.

Dumpster Trademark for a large metal trash bin.

Use trash bin or trash container instead.

Dunkirk Use this spelling rather than *Dunkerque*, in keeping with widespread practice.

du Pont, E.I. Note the spelling of the name of the U.S. industrialist born in France. Use *du Pont* on second reference.

The company named after him is *E.I. du Pont de Nemours & Co.*

of Wilmington, Del. Capitalize the shortened form *DuPont* (no space, capital P) in keeping with company practice. The shortened form is acceptable in all references.

See **foreign particles**.

dust storm See **weather terms**.

Dutch oven, Dutch treat, Dutch uncle

dyed-in-the-wool (adj.)

dyeing, dying *Dyeing* refers to changing colors.

Dying refers to death.

E

each Takes a singular verb.

each other, one another
Two people look at *each other*.

More than two look at *one another*.

Either phrase may be used when the number is indefinite: *We help each other. We help one another.*

earl, countess See **nobility**.

earmark

earth Generally lowercase; capitalize when used as the proper name of the planet. *She is down to earth. How does the pattern apply to Mars, Jupiter, Earth, the sun and the moon? The astronauts returned to Earth. He hopes to move heaven and earth.*

See **planets**.

earthquakes Hundreds of earthquakes occur each year. Most are so small they cannot be felt.

The best source for information on major earthquakes is the National Earthquake Information Service operated by the U.S. Geological Survey in Golden, Colo.

Earthquake magnitudes are measures of earthquake size calculated from ground motion recorded on seismographs. The Richter scale, named for Dr.

Charles F. Richter, is no longer widely used.

Magnitudes are usually reported simply as *magnitude 6.7*, for example, without specifying the scale being used. The various scales differ only slightly from one another.

In the first hours after a quake, earthquake size should be reported as a *preliminary magnitude of 6.7*, for example. Early estimates are often revised, and it can be several days before seismologists calculate a final figure.

Magnitudes are measured on several different scales. The most commonly used measure is the *moment magnitude*, related to the area of the fault on which an earthquake occurs, and the amount the ground slips.

The magnitude scale being used should be specified only when necessary. An example would be when two centers are reporting different magnitudes because they are using different scales.

With each scale, every increase of one number, say from 5.5 to 6.5, means that the quake's magnitude is 10 times as great. Theoretically, there is no upper limit to the scales.

A quake of magnitude 2.5 to 3 is the smallest generally felt by people.

—Magnitude 4: The quake can cause moderate damage.

—Magnitude 5: The quake can cause considerable damage.

—Magnitude 6: The quake can cause severe damage.

—Magnitude 7: A major earthquake, capable of widespread, heavy damage.

—Magnitude 8: An earthquake capable of tremendous damage.

NOTABLE QUAKES: Earthquakes noted for both their magnitude and the amount of damage they caused include:

—Shensi province of China, January 1556: Killed 830,000 people, the largest number of fatalities on record from an earthquake.

—Tokyo and Yokohama, Japan, September 1923: Magnitude later computed as 8.3. The quake and subsequent fires destroyed most of both cities, killing an estimated 200,000 people. Until the China quake of 1976, this was the highest fatality toll in the 20th century.

—San Francisco, April 1906: Moment magnitude later computed as 7.9. The quake and subsequent fire were blamed for an estimated 700 deaths.

—Alaska, March 1964: Magnitude 7.5. Killed 114 people.

—Guatemala, February 1976: Magnitude 7.5. Authorities reported more than 234,000 deaths.

—Hopeh province of northern China, July 28, 1976: Magnitude 8.0. A government document later said 655,237 people were killed and 779,000 injured. The fatality total was second only to the toll in the Shensi quake of 1556.

—Mexico, Sept. 19, 1985: A quake registered at 8.1 left 9,500 people dead.

—Kobe, Japan, Jan. 17, 1995: A 7.2 magnitude quake killed nearly 5,300 people in collapsed buildings and fires.

OTHER TERMS: The word *temblor* (not *tremblor*) is a synonym for earthquake.

The word *epicenter* refers to the point on the Earth's surface above the underground center, or focus, of an earthquake.

east, eastern See the **directions and regions** entry.

Easter In the computation used by the Latin Rite of the Roman Catholic Church and by Protestant churches, it falls on the first Sunday after the first full moon that occurs on or after March 21. If the full moon falls on a Sunday, Easter is the next Sunday.

Easter may fall, therefore, between March 22 and April 25 inclusive.

Eastern Europe No longer a separate political unit, but can be used in specific references to the region. Use only in historic sense. (Also *Western Europe*.)

Eastern Hemisphere The half of the Earth made up primarily of Africa, Asia, Australia and Europe.

Eastern Orthodox churches The term applies to a group of churches that have roots in the earliest days of Christianity and do not recognize papal authority over their activities.

Churches in this tradition were part of the undivided Christendom that existed until the Great Schism of 1054. At that time, many of the churches in the western half of the old Roman Empire accorded the bishop of

Rome supremacy over other bishops. The result was a split between eastern and western churches.

The autonomous churches that constitute Eastern Orthodoxy are organized along mostly national lines. They recognize the patriarch of Constantinople (modern-day Istanbul) as their leader. He convenes councils, but his authority is otherwise that of a "first among equals."

Eastern orthodox churches today count about 200 million members. They include the Greek Orthodox Church and the Russian Orthodox Church.

In the United States, organizational lines are based on the national backgrounds of various ethnic groups. The largest is the Greek Orthodox Archdiocese of America, with about 2 million members. Next is the Orthodox Church in America, with about 1 million members, including people of Bulgarian, Romanian, Russian and Syrian descent.

The churches have their own disciplines on matters such as married clergy — a married man may be ordained, but a priest may not marry after ordination.

Some of these churches call the archbishop who leads them a *metropolitan*, others use the term *patriarch*. He normally heads the principal archdiocese within a nation. Working with him are other archbishops, bishops, priests and deacons.

Archbishops and bishops frequently follow a monastic tradition in which they are known only by a first name. When no last name is used, repeat the title before the sole name in subsequent references.

Some forms: *Metropolitan Theodosius, archbishop of Wash-ington and metropolitan of America and Canada.* On second reference: *Metropolitan Theodosius. Archbishop* may be replaced by *the Most Rev.* on first reference. *Bishop* may be replaced by *the Rt. Rev.* on first reference.

Use *the Rev.* before the name of a priest on first reference.

See **religious titles**.

Eastern Rite churches The term applies to a group of Catholic churches that are organized along ethnic lines traceable to the churches established during the earliest days of Christianity.

These churches accept the authority of the pope, but they have considerable autonomy in ritual and questions of discipline such as married clergy — a married man may be ordained, but marriage is not permitted after ordination.

Worldwide membership totals more than 10 million.

Among the churches of the Eastern Rite are the Antiochean-Maronite, Armenian Catholic, Byzantine-Byelorussian, Byzantine-Russian, Byzantine-Ruthenian, Byzantine-Ukrainian and Chaldean Catholic.

See **Roman Catholic Church**.

Eastern Shore A region on the east side of Chesapeake Bay, including parts of Maryland and Virginia.

Eastern Shore is not a synonym for *East Coast*.

Eastern Standard Time (EST), Eastern Daylight Time (EDT) See **time zones**.

easygoing

ecology The study of the relationship between organisms and their surroundings. It is not synonymous with *environment*.

Right: *The laboratory is studying the ecology of man and the desert.*

Wrong: *Even so simple an undertaking as maintaining a lawn affects ecology.* (Use *environment* instead.)

Ecstasy Capitalize (no quote marks) this and other synthetic drug names.

Ecuadorean

editor Capitalize *editor* before a name only when it is an official corporate or organizational title. Do not capitalize as a job description.
See **titles**.

editorial, news In references to a newspaper, reserve *news* for the news department, its employees and news articles. Reserve *editorial* for the department that prepares the editorial page, its employees and articles that appear on the editorial page.

editor in chief Follow the style of the publication, but in general, no hyphen. Capitalize when used as a formal title before a name: *Editor in Chief Horace Greeley.*
See **titles**.

effect See the **affect, effect** entry.

Eglin Air Force Base, Fla. Not *Elgin.*

either Use it to mean one or the other, not both.

Right: *She said to use either door.*

Wrong: *There were lions on either side of the door.*

Right: *There were lions on each side of the door. There were lions on both sides of the door.*

either...or, neither...nor The nouns that follow these words do not constitute a compound subject; they are alternate subjects and require a verb that agrees with the nearer subject:

Neither they nor he is going. Neither he nor they are going.

El Al Israel Airlines. An *El Al airliner* is acceptable in any reference.

Headquarters in Tel Aviv.

elder For its use in religious contexts, see the entry for an individual's denomination.

elderly Use this word carefully and sparingly.

It is appropriate in generic phrases that do not refer to specific individuals: *concern for the elderly, a home for the elderly,* etc.

If the intent is to show that an individual's faculties have deteriorated, cite a graphic example and give attribution for it.

Apply the same principle to terms such as *senior citizen.*

-elect Always hyphenate and lowercase: *President-elect Reagan.*

Election Day The first Tuesday after the first Monday in November.

election returns Use figures, with commas every three digits starting at the right and counting left. Use the word *to* (not a hyphen) in separating different totals listed together: *Jimmy Carter defeated Gerald Ford 40,827,292 to 39,146,157 in 1976* (this is the actual final figure).

Use the word *votes* if there is any possibility that the figures could be confused with a ratio: *Nixon defeated McGovern 16 votes to 3 votes in Dixville Notch.*

Do not attempt to create adjectival forms such as *the 40,827,292-39,146,157 vote.*

See **vote tabulations**.

Electoral College But *electoral vote(s).*

electrocardiogram *EKG* is acceptable on second reference.

ellipsis See entry in **Punctuation** chapter.

El Salvador The use of the article in the name of the nation helps to distinguish it from its capital, *San Salvador.*

Use *Salvadoran(s)* in references to citizens of the nation.

e-mail Short form of *electronic mail.* Many e-mail or Internet addresses use symbols such as the at symbol (@), or the tilde (~) that cannot be transmitted correctly in some member computing systems. When needed, spell them out and provide an explanatory editor's note.

(Also *e-commerce, e-business.*)

embargo See the **boycott, embargo** entry.

embargo times See **release times**.

embarrass, embarrassing, embarrassed, embarrassment

embassy An *embassy* is the official residence of an ambassador in a foreign country and the office that handles the political relations of one nation with another.

A *consulate,* the residence of a consul in a foreign city, handles the commercial affairs and personal needs of citizens of the appointing country.

Capitalize with the name of a nation; lowercase without it: *the French Embassy, the U.S. Embassy, the embassy.*

emcee, emceed, emceeing A colloquial verb and noun best avoided. A phrase such as: *He was the master of ceremonies* is preferred.

emeritus This word often is added to formal titles to denote that individuals who have retired retain their rank or title.

When used, place *emeritus* after the formal title, in keeping with the general practice of academic institutions: *Professor Emeritus Samuel Eliot Morison, Dean Emeritus Courtney C. Brown, Publisher Emeritus Barnard L. Colby.*

Or: *Samuel Eliot Morison, professor emeritus of history; Courtney C. Brown, dean emeritus of the faculty of business; Barnard L. Colby, publisher emeritus.*

emigrate, immigrate One who leaves a country *emigrates* from it.

One who comes into a country *immigrates.*

The same principle holds for *emigrant* and *immigrant.*

Emmy, Emmys The annual awards by the Academy of Television Arts & Sciences (for prime-time programming; based in Los

Angeles) and the National Academy of Television Arts and Sciences (for daytime, news and sports; based in New York).

Empirin A trademark for a brand of aspirin compound.

employee Not *employe*.

empty-handed

enact See the **adopt, approve, enact, pass** entry.

encyclopedia But follow the spelling of formal names: *Encyclopaedia Britannica*.

Energy Research and Development Administration It no longer exists. Its functions were transferred in 1977 to the Department of Energy.

enforce But *reinforce*.

engine, motor An *engine* develops its own power, usually through internal combustion or the pressure of air, steam or water passing over vanes attached to a wheel: *an airplane engine, an automobile engine, a jet engine, a missile engine, a steam engine, a turbine engine.*

A *motor* receives power from an outside source: *an electric motor, a hydraulic motor.*

England London stands alone in datelines. Use *England* after the names of other English communities in datelines.

See **datelines** and **United Kingdom**.

English muffin, English setter

Enovid A trademark for a brand of birth control pill. It also may be called *norethynodrel with mestranol.*

enquire, enquiry The preferred words are *inquire, inquiry*.

enroll, enrolled, enrolling

en route Always two words.

ensign See **military titles**.

ensure, insure Use *ensure* to mean guarantee: *Steps were taken to ensure accuracy.*

Use *insure* for references to insurance: *The policy insures his life.*

entitled Use it to mean a right to do or have something. Do not use it to mean titled.

Right: *She was entitled to the promotion.*

Right: *The book was titled "Gone With the Wind."*

enumerations See examples in the **dash** and **periods** entries in the **Punctuation** chapter.

envelop Other verb forms: *enveloping, enveloped*. But: *envelope* (n.)

environment See **ecology**.

Environmental Protection Agency *EPA* is acceptable on second reference.

envoy Not a formal title. Lowercase.

See **titles**.

epicenter The point on the Earth's surface above the underground center, or focus, of an earthquake.

See **earthquakes**.

epidemiology

Episcopal, Episcopalian

Episcopal is the adjective form; use *Episcopalian* only as a noun referring to a member of the Episcopal Church: *She is an Episcopalian.* But: *She is an Episcopal priest.*

Capitalize *Episcopal* when referring to the Episcopal Church. Use lowercase when the reference is simply to a body governed by bishops.

Episcopal Church

Acceptable in all references for the *Protestant Episcopal Church in the United States of America*, the U.S. national church that is a member of the Anglican Communion.

The church is governed nationally by two bodies — the permanent Executive Council and the General Convention, which meets every three years.

After the council, the principal organizational units are, in descending order of size, provinces, dioceses or missionary districts, local parishes and local missions.

The National Council is composed of bishops, priests, laymen and laywomen. One bishop is designated the leader and holds the formal title of presiding bishop.

The General Convention has final authority in matters of policy and doctrine. All acts must pass both of its houses — the House of Bishops and the House of Deputies. The latter is composed of an equal number of clergy and lay delegates from each diocese.

A province is composed of several dioceses. Each has a provincial synod made up of a house of bishops and a house of deputies. The synod's primary duty is to coordinate the work of the church in its area.

Within a diocese, a bishop is the principal official. He is helped by the Diocesan Convention, which consists of all the clergy in the diocese and lay representatives from each parish.

The parish or local church is governed by a vestry, composed of the pastor and lay members elected by the congregation.

The clergy consists of bishops, priests, deacons and brothers. A priest who heads a parish is described as a *rector* rather than a pastor.

For first reference to bishops, use *Bishop* before the individual's name: *Bishop John M. Allin.* An acceptable alternative in referring to U.S. bishops is *the Rt. Rev.* The designation *the Most Rev.* is used before the names of the archbishops of Canterbury and York.

For first references, use *the Rev.* before the name of a priest, *Deacon* before the name of a deacon.

See **Anglican Communion** and **religious titles**.

epoch See the **historical periods and events** entry.

equal An adjective without comparative forms.

When people speak of a *more equal* distribution of wealth, what is meant is *more equitable*.

equal, equaled, equaling

Equal Employment Opportunity Commission

EEOC is acceptable on second reference.

equally as Do not use the words together; one is sufficient.

Omit the *equally* shown here in parentheses: *She was (equally) as wise as Marilyn.*

Omit the *as* shown here in parentheses: *She and Marilyn were equally (as) liberal.*

Equal Rights Amendment *ERA* is acceptable on second reference.

Ratification required approval by three-fourths (38) of the 50 states by June 30, 1982. Ratification failed when only 35 states had approved the amendment by the deadline. The original deadline was March 22, 1979, but was extended by Congress.

The text:

Section 1. Equality of rights under the law shall not be denied or abridged by the United States or by any state on account of sex.

Section 2. The Congress shall have the power to enforce, by appropriate legislation, the provisions of this article.

Section 3. This amendment shall take effect two years after the date of ratification.

equal time, fairness doctrine *Equal time* applies to the Federal Communications Commission regulation that requires a radio or television station to provide a candidate for political office with air time equal to any time that an opponent receives beyond the coverage of news events.

If a station broadcasts material that takes a stand on an issue, the FCC's *fairness doctrine* may require it to give advocates of a different position an opportunity to respond.

equator Always lowercase.

equitable See **equal**.

ERA Acceptable in all references to baseball's *earned run average*.

Acceptable on second reference for *Equal Rights Amendment*.

eras See the **historical periods and events** entry.

escalator Formerly a trademark, now a generic term.

escalator clause A clause in a contract providing for increases or decreases in wages, prices, etc., based on fluctuations in the cost of living, production, expenses, etc.

Eskimo, Eskimos Some, especially in northern Canada, use the term *Inuit* for these native peoples of northern North America. Follow the preference of those involved in the story.

espresso The coffee is *espresso*, not *expresso*.

essential clauses, nonessential clauses These terms are used in this book instead of *restrictive clause* and *nonrestrictive clause* to convey the distinction between the two in a more easily remembered manner.

Both types of clauses provide additional information about a word or phrase in the sentence.

The difference between them is that the *essential clause* cannot be eliminated without changing the meaning of the sentence — it so *restricts* the meaning of the word or phrase that its absence would lead to a substantially different interpretation of what the author meant.

The *nonessential clause*, however, can be eliminated without altering the basic meaning of the sentence — it does not *restrict* the meaning so significantly that its absence would radically alter the author's thought.

PUNCTUATION: An essential clause must not be set off from the rest of a sentence by commas. A nonessential clause must be set off by commas.

The presence or absence of commas provides the reader with critical information about the writer's intended meaning. Note the following examples:

—*Reporters who do not read the Stylebook should not criticize their editors.* (The writer is saying that only one class of reporters, those who do not read the Stylebook, should not criticize their editors. If the *who ... Stylebook* phrase were deleted, the meaning of the sentence would be changed substantially.)

—*Reporters, who do not read the Stylebook, should not criticize their editors.* (The writer is saying that all reporters should not criticize their editors. If the *who ... Stylebook* phrase were deleted, this meaning would not be changed.)

USE OF WHO, THAT, WHICH: When an essential or nonessential clause refers to a human being or animal with a name, it should be introduced by *who* or *whom*. (See the **who, whom** entry.) Do not use commas if the clause is essential to the meaning; use them if it is not.

That is the preferred pronoun to introduce essential clauses that refer to an inanimate object or an animal without a name. *Which* is the only acceptable pronoun to introduce a nonessential clause that refers to an inanimate object or an animal without a name.

The pronoun *which* occasionally may be substituted for *that* in the introduction of an essential clause that refers to an inanimate object or an animal without a name. In general, this use of *which* should appear only when *that* is used as a conjunction to introduce another clause in the same sentence: *He said Monday that the part of the army which suffered severe casualties needs reinforcement.*

See **that (conjunction)** for guidelines on the use of that as a conjunction.

essential phrases, nonessential phrases These

terms are used in this book instead of *restrictive phrase* and *nonrestrictive phrase* to convey the distinction between the two in a more easily remembered manner.

The underlying concept is the one that also applies to clauses:

An *essential phrase* is a word or group of words critical to the reader's understanding of what the author had in mind.

A *nonessential phrase* provides more information about something. Although the information may be helpful to the reader's comprehension, the reader would not be misled if the information were not there.

PUNCTUATION: Do not set an essential phrase off from the rest of a sentence by commas:

We saw the award-winning movie "One Flew Over the Cuckoo's Nest." (No comma, because many movies have won awards, and without the name of the movie the reader would not know which movie was meant.)

They ate dinner with their daughter Julie. (Because they have more than one daughter, the inclusion of Julie's name is critical if the reader is to know which daughter is meant.)

Set off nonessential phrases by commas:

We saw the 1975 winner in the Academy Award competition for best picture, "One Flew Over the Cuckoo's Nest." (Only one movie won the award. The name is informative, but even without the name no other movie could be meant.)

They ate dinner with their daughter Julie and her husband, David. (Julie has only one husband. If the phrase read *and her husband David*, it would suggest that she had more than one husband.)

The company chairman, Henry Ford II, spoke. (In the context, only one person could be meant.)

Indian corn, or maize, was harvested. (*Maize* provides the reader with the name of the corn, but its absence would not change the meaning of the sentence.)

DESCRIPTIVE WORDS: Do not confuse punctuation rules for nonessential clauses with the correct punctuation when a nonessential word is used as a descriptive adjective. The distinguishing clue often is the lack of an article or pronoun:

Right: *Julie and husband Jeff went shopping. Julie and her husband, Jeff, went shopping.*

Right: *Company Chairman Henry Ford II made the announcement. The company chairman, Henry Ford II, made the announcement.*

Eurasian Of European and Asian descent.

euro The common currency of 12 of the 15 European Union nations.

Austria, Belgium, Finland, France, Germany, Ireland, Italy, Luxembourg, Netherlands, Portugal and Spain adopted the euro as of Jan. 1, 1999; Greece officially joined them Jan. 1, 2001. Britain, Denmark and Sweden chose not to adopt the currency.

The Vatican also adopted the euro as its official currency.

Euro bank notes and coins go into circulation in 2002.

European Community See **European Union**.

European Union *The European Union,* based in Brussels, Belgium, was created by the Treaty on European Union signed in February 1992 and took effect Nov. 1, 1993. It is an outgrowth of the 1958 European Economic Community, which itself was formed out of the 1952 European Coal and Steel Community. The six founding members of the *European Union* are France, Germany, Italy, Netherlands, Belgium, and Luxembourg. Other members are Denmark, Greece, Ireland, Portugal, Spain and the United Kingdom, with Austria, Sweden and Finland joining as of Jan. 1, 1995.

evangelical See **religious movements**.

Evangelical Friends Alliance See **Quakers**.

evangelism See **religious movements**.

evangelist Capitalize only in reference to the men credited with writing the Gospels: *The four Evangelists were Matthew, Mark, Luke and John.*

In lowercase, it means a preacher who makes a profession of seeking conversions.

eve Capitalize when used after the name of a holiday: *New Year's Eve, Christmas Eve.* But: *the eve of Christmas.*

even-steven Not *even-stephen.*

every day (adv.) **everyday** (adj.) *She goes to work every day. He wears everyday shoes.*

every one, everyone Two words when it means each individual item: *Every one of the clues was worthless.*

One word when used as a pronoun meaning all persons: *Everyone wants his life to be happy.* (Note that *everyone* takes singular verbs and pronouns.)

ex- Use no hyphen for words that use *ex-* in the sense of *out of*:
excommunicate   expropriate
Hyphenate when using *ex-* in the sense of *former*:
ex-convict   ex-president
Do not capitalize *ex-* when attached to a formal title before a name: *ex-President Nixon.* The prefix modifies the entire term: *ex-New York Gov. Nelson Rockefeller*; not *New York ex-Gov.*
Usually *former* is better.

exaggerate

Excedrin A trademark for a brand of aspirin compound.

except See the **accept, except** entry.

exclamation point See entry in **Punctuation** chapter.

execute To *execute* a person is to kill him in compliance with a military order or judicial decision.

See the **assassin, killer, murderer** entry and the **homicide, murder, manslaughter** entry.

executive branch Always lowercase.

executive director Capitalize before a name only if it is a formal corporate or organizational title.

See **titles**.

Executive Mansion Capitalize only in references to the White House.

Executive Protective Service It is now the *Secret Service Uniformed Division.*

See **Secret Service**.

executor Use for both men and women.

Not a formal title. Always lowercase.

See **titles**.

exorcise, exorcism Not *exorcize.*

expel, expelled, expelling

Explorers See **Boy Scouts**.

Export-Import Bank of the United States *Export-Import Bank* is acceptable in all references; *Ex-Im Bank* is acceptable on second reference.

Headquarters is in Washington.

extol, extolled, extolling

extra- Do not use a hyphen when *extra* means *outside of* unless the prefix is followed by a word beginning with *a* or a capitalized word:

extralegal	extraterrestrial
extramarital	extraterritorial

But:

extra-alimentary	extra-Britannic

Follow *extra-* with a hyphen when it is part of a compound modifier describing a condition beyond the usual size, extent or degree:

extra-base hit	extra-large book
extra-dry drink	extra-mild taste

extrasensory perception
ESP is acceptable on second reference.

extreme unction See **sacraments**.

Exxon Mobil Corp. Energy corporation formed from the 1999 merger of Exxon and Mobil, both formerly part of Standard Oil.

Headquarters is in Irving, Texas, with exploration, production and chemical operations based in Houston.

eye, eyed, eyeing

eyestrain

eye to eye, eye-to-eye
Hyphenate when used as a compound modifier: *an eye-to-eye confrontation.*

eyewitness

F

face to face When a story says two people meet for discussions, talks or debate, it is unnecessary to say they met *face to face.*

fact-finding (adj.)

Faeroe Islands Use in datelines after a community name in stories from this group of Danish islands in the northern Atlantic Ocean between Iceland and the Shetland Islands.

Fahrenheit The temperature scale commonly used in the United States.

The scale is named for Gabriel Daniel Fahrenheit, a German physicist who designed it. In it, the freezing point of water is 32 degrees and the boiling point is 212 degrees.

To convert to Celsius, subtract 32 from Fahrenheit figure, multiply by 5 and divide by 9 (77 - 32 = 45, times 5 = 225, divided by 9 = 25 degrees Celsius.)

In cases that require mention of the scale, use these forms: *86 degrees Fahrenheit* or *86 F* (note the space and no period after the *F*) if degrees and Fahrenheit are clear from the context.

See **Celsius** and **Kelvin.**

For guidelines on when Celsius temperatures should be used, see **metric system** entry.

TEMPERATURE CONVERSIONS

Following is a temperature conversion table. Celsius temperatures have been rounded to the nearest whole number.

F	C	F	C	F	C
-26	-32	19	-7	64	18
-24	-31	21	-6	66	19
-22	-30	23	-5	68	20
-20	-29	25	-4	70	21
-18	-28	27	-3	72	22
-17	-27	28	-2	73	23
-15	-26	30	-1	75	24
-13	-25	32	0	77	25
-11	-24	34	1	79	26
-9	-23	36	2	81	27
-8	-22	37	3	82	28
-6	-21	39	4	84	29
-4	-20	41	5	86	30
-2	-19	43	6	88	31
0	-18	45	7	90	32
1	-17	46	8	91	33
3	-16	48	9	93	34
5	-15	50	10	95	35
7	-14	52	11	97	36
9	-13	54	12	99	37
10	-12	55	13	100	38
12	-11	57	14	102	39
14	-10	59	15	104	40
16	-9	61	16	106	41
18	-8	63	17	108	42

fairness doctrine See the **equal time, fairness doctrine** entry.

fall See **seasons.**

fallout (n.)

false titles Often derived from occupational titles or other labels.

Always lowercase. See **titles**.

family names Capitalize words denoting family relationships only when they precede the name of a person or when they stand unmodified as a substitute for a person's name: *I wrote to Grandfather Smith. I wrote Mother a letter. I wrote my mother a letter.*

Fannie Mae A publicly held company traded on the New York Stock Exchange to help provide money for home mortgages, primarily conventional mortgages, by buying residential mortgages for its investment portfolio and packaging pools of mortgages from lenders.

The nickname *Fannie Mae* is acceptable, but somewhere in the story the company should be identified as the *Federal National Mortgage Association.*

Fannie May A trademark for a brand of candy.

Far East The easternmost portions of the continent of Asia: China, Japan, North and South Korea, Taiwan, Hong Kong and the eastern portions of Russia.

Confine *Far East* to this restricted sense. Use the *Far East and Southeast Asia* when referring to a wider portion of eastern Asia.

See the **Asian subcontinent** and **Southeast Asia** entries.

far-flung (adj.)

far-off (adj.)

far-ranging (adj.)

farsighted When used in a medical sense, it means that a person can see objects at a distance but has difficulty seeing materials at close range.

farther, further Farther refers to physical distance: *He walked farther into the woods.*

Further refers to an extension of time or degree: *She will look further into the mystery.*

Far West For the U.S. region, generally west of the Rocky Mountains.

fascism, fascist See the **political parties and philosophies** entry.

father Use *the Rev.* in first reference before the names of Episcopal, orthodox and Roman Catholic priests. Use *Father* before a name only in direct quotations.

See **religious titles**.

father-in-law, fathers-in-law

Father's Day The third Sunday in June.

Father Time

fax (n.) or (v.) Acceptable as short version of facsimile or facsimile machine in all uses.

faze, phase *Faze* means to embarrass or disturb: *The snub did not faze her.*

Phase denotes an aspect or stage: *They will phase in a new system.*

FBI Acceptable in all references for *Federal Bureau of Investigation.*

feather bedding, featherbedding *Feather bedding* is a mattress stuffed with feathers.

Featherbedding is the practice of requiring an employer to hire more workers than needed to handle a job.

features They are not exempt from normal style rules. See **special contexts** for guidelines on some limited exceptions.

February See **months**.

federal Use a capital letter for the architectural style and for corporate or governmental bodies that use the word as part of their formal names: *Federal Express, the Federal Trade Commission.* (See separate entries for governmental agencies.)

Lowercase when used as an adjective to distinguish something from state, county, city, town or private entities: *federal assistance, federal court, the federal government, a federal judge.*

Also: *federal District Court* (but *U.S. District Court* is preferred) and *federal Judge Ann Aldrich* (but *U.S. District Judge Ann Aldrich* is preferred).

Federal Aviation Administration *FAA* is acceptable on second reference.

Federal Bureau of Investigation *FBI* is acceptable in all references. To avoid alphabet soup, however, use *the bureau* in some references.

Federal Communications Commission *FCC* is acceptable on second reference.

federal court Always lowercase.

The preferred form for first reference is to use the proper name of the court. See entries under **U.S.** and the court name.

Do not create nonexistent entities such as *Manhattan Federal Court.* Instead, use *a federal court in Manhattan.*

See **judicial branch**.

Federal Crop Insurance Corp. Do not abbreviate.

Federal Deposit Insurance Corp. *FDIC* is acceptable on second reference.

Federal Emergency Management Agency *FEMA* is acceptable on second reference.

Federal Energy Regulatory Commission This agency replaced the Federal Power Commission in 1977. It regulates interstate natural gas and electricity transactions.

FERC is acceptable on second reference, but *the agency* or *the commission* is preferred.

Federal Farm Credit Board Do not abbreviate.

Federal Highway Administration Reserve the *FHA* abbreviation for the *Federal Housing Administration.*

Federal Home Loan Bank Board Do not abbreviate.

Federal Home Mortgage Corp. See **Freddie Mac** entry.

Federal Housing Administration *FHA* is acceptable on second reference.

federal legal holidays See the **holidays and holy days** entry.

Federal Mediation and Conciliation Service Do not abbreviate. Use *the service* on second reference.

Federal National Mortgage Association See **Fannie Mae** entry.

Federal Power Commission It no longer exists. See **Federal Energy Regulatory Commission**.

Federal Register This publication, issued every workday, is the legal medium for recording and communicating the rules and regulations established by the executive branch of the federal government.

Individuals or corporations cannot be held legally responsible for compliance with a regulation unless it has been published in the Register.

In addition, executive agencies are required to publish in advance some types of proposed regulations.

Federal Reserve System, Federal Reserve Board On second reference, use the *Federal Reserve, the Reserve, the Fed, the system* or *the board*.

Also: *the Federal Reserve Bank of New York* (*Boston*, etc.), *the bank*.

Federal Trade Commission *FTC* is acceptable on second reference.

felony, misdemeanor A *felony* is a serious crime. A *misdemeanor* is a minor offense against the law.

A fuller definition of what constitutes a felony or misdemeanor depends on the governmental jurisdiction involved.

At the federal level, a *misdemeanor* is a crime that carries a potential penalty of no more than a year in jail. A *felony* is a crime that carries a potential penalty of more than a year in prison. Often, however, a statute gives a judge options such as imposing a fine or probation in addition to or instead of a jail or prison sentence.

A *felon* is a person who has been convicted of a *felony*, regardless of whether the individual actually spends time in confinement or is given probation or a fine instead.

See the **prison, jail** entry.

Ferris wheel

ferryboat

fertility rate As calculated by the federal government, it is the number of live births per 1,000 females age 15 through 44 years.

fewer, less In general, use *fewer* for individual items, *less* for bulk or quantity.

Wrong: *The trend is toward more machines and less people.* (People in this sense refers to individuals.)

Wrong: *She was fewer than 60 years old.* (Years in this sense refers to a period of time, not individual years.)

Right: *Fewer than 10 applicants called.* (Individuals.)

Right: *I had less than $50 in my pocket.* (An amount.) But: *I had fewer than 50 $1 bills in my pocket.* (Individual items.)

fiance (man) **fiancee** (woman)

Fiberglas Note the single *s*. A

trademark for fiberglass or glass fiber.

field house

figuratively, literally *Figuratively* means in an analogous sense, but not in the exact sense. *He bled them white.*

Literally means in an exact sense, do not use it figuratively.

Wrong: *He literally bled them white.* (Unless the blood was drained from their bodies.)

figure The symbol for a number: *the figure 5.*
See **numerals**.

filibuster To *filibuster* is to make long speeches to obstruct the passage of legislation.

A legislator who used such methods also is a *filibuster*, not a *filibusterer*.

Filipinos The people of the Philippines.

film ratings See **movie ratings**.

financial editor Capitalize only as formal title before a name. See **titles**.

firearms See **weapons**.

fire department See the **governmental bodies** entry for the basic rules on capitalization.

See **titles** and **military titles** for guidelines on titles.

firefighter, fireman The preferred term to describe a person who fights fire is *firefighter*.

One meaning of *fireman* is a person who tends fires in a furnace. *Fireman* is also an acceptable synonym for *firefighter*.

firm A business partnership is correctly referred to as a *firm. He joined a law firm.*

Do not use *firm* in references to an incorporated business entity. Use *the company* or *the corporation* instead.

first degree, first-degree Hyphenate when used as a compound modifier: *It was murder in the first degree. He was convicted of first-degree murder.*

first family Always lowercase.

first lady Not a formal title. Do not capitalize, even when used before the name of a chief of state's wife.
See **titles**.

first quarter, first-quarter Hyphenate when used as a compound modifier: *He scored in the first quarter. The team took the lead on his first-quarter goal.*

fiscal, monetary *Fiscal* applies to budgetary matters.

Monetary applies to money supply.

fiscal year The 12-month period that a corporation or governmental body uses for bookkeeping purposes.

The federal government's fiscal year starts three months ahead of the calendar year — fiscal 1987, for example, ran from Oct. 1, 1986, to Sept. 30, 1987.

fitful It means restless, not a condition of being fit.

fjord

flack, flak *Flack* is slang for press agent.

Flak is a type of anti-aircraft fire, hence figuratively a barrage of criticism.

flagpole, flagship

flail, flay To *flail* is to swing the arms widely.

To *flay* is, literally, to strip off the skin by whipping. Figuratively, *to flay* means to tongue-lash a person.

flair, flare *Flair* is conspicuous talent.

Flare is a verb meaning to blaze with sudden, bright light or to burst out in anger. It is also a noun meaning a flame.

flak See the **flack, flak** entry.

flare up (v.) **flare-up** (n.) See the **flair, flare** entry.

flash flood See **weather terms**.

flaunt, flout To *flaunt* is to make an ostentatious or defiant display: *She flaunted her intelligence.*

To *flout* is to show contempt for: *He flouts the law.*

flautist The preferred word is *flutist.*

fleet Use figures and capitalize *fleet* when forming a proper name: *the 6th Fleet.*

Lowercase *fleet* whenever it stands alone.

flier, flyer *Flier* is the preferred term for an aviator or a handbill.

Flyer is the proper name of some trains and buses: *The Western Flyer.*

flimflam, flimflammed

flip-flop

floods, flood stage See **weather terms**.

floodwaters

floor leader Treat it as a job description, lowercased, rather than a formal title: *Republican floor leader John Smith.*

Do not use when a formal title such as *majority leader, minority leader* or *whip* would be the accurate description.

See the **legislative titles** and **titles** entries.

floppy disk Use *diskette.*

Florida Abbrev.: *Fla.* See **state names**.

Florida Keys A chain of small islands extending southwest from the southern tip of mainland Florida.

Cities, or the islands themselves, are followed by *Fla.* in datelines:
KEY WEST, Fla. (AP) —

flounder, founder A *flounder* is a fish; to *flounder* is to move clumsily or jerkily, to flop about: *The fish floundered on land.*

To *founder* is to bog down, become disabled or sink: *The ship floundered in the heavy seas for hours, then foundered.*

flout See the **flaunt, flout** entry.

flowers See **plants**.

fluid ounce Equal to 1.8 cubic inches, two tablespoons or six teaspoons. The metric equivalent is approximately 30 milliliters.

To convert to milliliters, multiply by 30 (3 ounces x 30 equals 90 milliliters).

See **liter**.

fluorescent

flush To become red in the face. See **livid**.

flutist The preferred term, rather than *flautist*.

flyer See the **flier, flyer** entry.

FM Acceptable in all references for the *frequency modulation* system of radio transmission.

f.o.b. Acceptable on first reference for free on board. The concept should be explained, however, in contexts not addressed to business-oriented audiences: The seller agrees to put an item on a truck, ship, etc., at no charge, but the transportation costs must be paid by the buyer.

-fold No hyphen:

twofold   fourfold

folk singer, folk song

following The word usually is a noun, verb or adjective: *He has a large following. He is following his conscience. The following statement was made.*

Although Webster's New World records its use as a preposition, the preferred word is *after*: *He spoke after dinner.* Not: *He spoke following dinner.*

follow up (v.) follow-up

(n. and adj.)

food Most food names are lowercase: *apples, cheese, peanut butter.*

Capitalize brand names and trademarks: *Roquefort cheese, Tabasco sauce.*

Most proper nouns or adjectives are capitalized when they occur in a food name: *Boston brown bread, Russian dressing, Swiss cheese, Waldorf salad.*

Lowercase is used, however, when the food does not depend on the proper noun or adjective for its meaning: *french fries, graham crackers, manhattan cocktail.*

If a question arises, check the separate entries in this book. If there is no entry, follow Webster's New World. Use lowercase if the dictionary lists it as an acceptable form for the sense in which the word is used.

The same principles apply to foreign names for foods: *mousse de saumon* (salmon mousse), *pomme de terre* (literally, "apple of the earth" — for potato), *salade Russe* (Russian salad).

Food and Agriculture Organization Not *Agricultural*.

FAO is acceptable on second reference to this U.N. agency.

Food and Drug Administration *FDA* is acceptable on second reference.

foot The basic unit of length in the measuring system that has been used in the United States. Its origin was a calculation that this was the length of the average human foot.

The metric equivalent is exactly 30.48 centimeters, which may be rounded to 30 centimeters for most comparisons.

For most conversions to centimeters, it is adequate to multiply 30 (5 feet x 30 equals 150 centimeters). For more exact figures, multiply by 30.48 (5 feet x 30.48 equals 152.4 centimeters).

To convert to meters, multiply by .3 (5 feet x .3 equals 1.5 meters).

See **centimeter, meter;** and **dimensions.**

foot-and-mouth disease

forbear, forebear *To forbear* is to avoid or shun.

A *forebear* is an ancestor.

forbid, forbade, forbidding

forcible rape A redundancy that usually should be avoided. It may be used, however, in stories dealing with both rape and statutory rape, which does not necessarily involve the use of force.

Ford Motor Co. Use *Ford*, not *FMC*, on second reference.

Headquarters is in Dearborn, Mich.

fore- The rules in prefixes apply, but in general, no hyphen. Some examples:

forebrain	foregoing
forefather	foretooth

There are three nautical exceptions, based on long-standing practice:

fore-topgallant	fore-topsail
fore-topmast	

forecast Use *forecast* also for the past tense, not *forecasted*.

See **weather terms.**

forego, forgo *To forego* means to go before, as in *foregone conclusion.*

To forgo means to abstain from.

foreign governmental bodies
Capitalize the names of the specific foreign governmental agencies and departments, either with the name of the nation or without it if clear in the context: *French Foreign Ministry, the Foreign Ministry.*

Lowercase *the ministry* or a similar term when standing alone.

foreign legislative bodies
In general, capitalize the proper name of a specific legislative body abroad, whether using the name in a foreign language or an English equivalent.

The most frequent names in use are *congress, national assembly* and *parliament.*

GENERIC USES: Lowercase *parliament* or a similar term only when used generically to describe a body for which the foreign name is being given: *the Diet, Japan's parliament.*

PLURALS: Lowercase *parliament* and similar terms in plural constructions: *the parliaments of England and France, the English and French parliaments.*

INDIVIDUAL HOUSES: The principle applies also to individual houses of the nation's legislature, just as *Senate* and *House* are capitalized in the United States:

ROME (AP) — New leaders have taken control in the Chamber of Deputies.

Lowercase *assembly* when used as a shortened reference to national assembly.

In many countries, *national assembly* is the name of a unicameral legislative body. In some, such as France, it is the name for the lower house of a legislative body known by some other name such as *parliament*.

foreign money Generally, amounts of foreign money mentioned in news stories should be converted to dollars. If it is necessary to mention the foreign amount, provide the dollar equivalent in parentheses.

The basic monetary units of nations are listed in Webster's New World Dictionary under "Monetary Units of All Nations." Do not use the exchange rates listed in the dictionary. Instead, use, as appropriate, the official exchange rates, which change from day to day on the world's markets.

foreign names For foreign place names, use the primary spelling in Webster's New World Dictionary. If it has no entry, follow the National Geographic Atlas of the World.

For personal names, follow the individual's preference for an English spelling if it can be determined. Otherwise:

—Use the nearest phonetic equivalent in English if one exists: *Alexander Solzhenitsyn*, for example, rather than *Aleksandr*, the spelling that would result from a transliteration of the Russian letters into the English alphabet.

If a name has no close phonetic equivalent in English, express it with an English spelling that approximates the sound in the original language: *Anwar Sadat*.

For additional guidelines, see **Arabic names; Chinese names; Portuguese names; Russian names; Spanish names**.

foreign particles Lower-case particles such as *de, la*, and *von* when part of a given name: *Charles de Gaulle, Baron Manfred von Richthofen.*

Capitalize the particles only when the last name starts a sentence: *De Gaulle spoke to von Richthofen.*

foreign words Some foreign words and abbreviations have been accepted universally into the English language: *bon voyage; versus, vs.; et cetera, etc.* They may be used without explanation if they are clear in the context.

Many foreign words and their abbreviations are not understood universally, although they may be used in special applications such as medical or legal terminology. If such a word or phrase is needed in a story, place it in quotation marks and provide an explanation: *"ad astra per aspera," a Latin phrase meaning "to the stars through difficulty."*

foreman, forewoman Seldom a formal title.

formal titles See **titles**.

former Always lowercase. But retain capitalization for a formal title used immediately before a name: *former President Nixon.*

Formica A trademark for a brand of laminated plastic.

Formosa See **Taiwan**.

Formosa Strait Not *the straits of Taiwan.*

formula, formulas Use figures in writing formulas, as illustrated in the entries on metric units.

forsake, forsook, forsaken

fort Do not abbreviate, for cities or for military installations.
In datelines for cities:
FORT LAUDERDALE, Fla. (AP) —
In datelines for military installations:
FORT BRAGG, N.C. (AP) —

fortnight The expression two weeks is preferred.

FORTRAN A computer programming language. Acronym for *Formula Translation*. Use of acronym on first reference is acceptable if it is identified as a programming language.

fortuneteller, fortunetelling

forty, forty-niner '49er is acceptable.

forward Not *forwards*.

foul, fowl *Foul* means offensive, out of line.
A *fowl* is a bird, especially the larger domestic birds used as food: chickens, ducks, turkeys.

founder See the **flounder, founder** entry.

4x4 *Four-wheel drive* is preferred, unless *4x4* is part of the car model's proper name.

four-flush (stud poker)

Four-H Club *4-H Club* is preferred. Members are *4-H'ers*.

four-star general

Fourth Estate Capitalize when used as a collective name for journalism and journalists.
The description is attributed to Edmund Burke, who is reported to have called the reporters' gallery in Parliament a "Fourth Estate."
The three estates of early English society were the Lords Spiritual (the clergy), the Lords Temporal (the nobility) and the Commons (the bourgeoisie).

Fourth of July, July Fourth Also *Independence Day*.
The federal legal holiday is observed on Friday if July 4 falls on a Saturday, on Monday if it falls on a Sunday.

fractions Spell out amounts less than 1 in stories, using hyphens between the words: *two-thirds, four-fifths, seven-sixteenths*, etc.
Use figures for precise amounts larger than 1, converting to decimals whenever practical.
Fractions are preferred, however, in stories about stocks. See **stock market prices**.
When using fractional characters, remember that most newspaper type fonts can set only 1/8, 1/4, 3/8, 1/2, 5/8, 3/4 and 7/8 as one unit; use *1 1/2, 2 5/8*, etc. with no space between the figure and the fraction. Other fractions require a hyphen and individual figures, with a space between the whole number and the fraction: *1 3-16, 2 1-3, 5 9-10*.
In tabular material, use figures exclusively, converting to decimals if the amounts involve extensive use of fractions that cannot be expressed as a single character.
See **percentages**.

fragment, fragmentary *Fragment* describes a piece or pieces broken from the whole:

She sang a fragment of the song.

Fragmentary describes disconnected and incomplete parts: *Early returns were fragmentary.*

frame up (v.) frame-up (n.)

frankfurters They were first called hot dogs in 1906 when a cartoonist, T.A. "Tad" Dorgan, showed a dachshund inside an elongated bun.

fraternal organizations and service clubs

Capitalize the proper names: *American Legion, Lions Club, Independent Order of Odd Fellows, Rotary Club.*

Capitalize also words describing membership: *He is a Legionnaire, a Lion, an Odd Fellow, an Optimist and a Rotarian.* See **American Legion** for the rationale on *Legionnaire.*

Capitalize the formal titles of officeholders when used before a name.

See **titles.**

Freddie Mac A government-chartered organization formed to help provide money for home mortgages by buying mortgages from lenders such as banks and repackaging them as investment securities.

Freddie Mac, a publicly held company traded on the New York Stock Exchange, packages conventional mortgages as well as FHA mortgages.

The nickname *Freddie Mac* is acceptable, but somewhere in the story the company should be identified as the *Federal Home Mortgage Corp.*

free-for-all (n. and adj.)

free-lance (v. and adj.)

The noun: *free-lancer.*

free on board See f.o.b.

freewheeling

Free World An imprecise description. Use only in quoted matter.

freeze-dry, freeze-dried, freeze-drying

freezing drizzle, freezing rain

See **weather terms.**

French Canadian, French Canadians

Without a hyphen. An exception to the normal practice in describing a dual ethnic heritage.

French Foreign Legion Retain capitalization if shortened to the Foreign Legion.

Lowercase *the legion* and *legionnaires.* Unlike the situation with the American Legion, the French Foreign Legion is a group of active soldiers.

french fries

See **capitalization** and **food.**

frequency modulation FM is acceptable in all references.

Friday

See **days of the week.**

Friends General Conference, Friends United Meeting

See **Quakers.**

Frigidaire A trademark for a brand of refrigerator.

Frisbee A trademark for a plastic disc thrown as a toy. Use *Frisbee disc* for the trademarked version and *flying disc* for other generic versions.

front line (n.) **front-line** (adj.)

front page (n.) **front-page** (adj.)

front-runner

frost See **weather terms**.

fruits See **food**.

fulfill, fulfilled, fulfilling

full- Hyphenate when used to form compound modifiers:

full-dress   full-page
full-fledged   full-scale
full-length

See the listings that follow and Webster's New World Dictionary for the spelling of other combinations.

full house (poker)

full time, full-time Hyphenate when used as a compound modifier: *He works full time. She has a full-time job.*

fulsome It means disgustingly excessive. Do not use it to mean lavish or profuse.

fundamentalist See **religious movements**.

fund raising, fund-raising, fund-raiser *Fund raising is difficult. They planned a fund-raising campaign. A fund-raiser was hired.*

funnel cloud See **weather terms**.

furlough

further See the **farther, further** entry.

fuselage

fusillade

G

G The general audience rating. See **movie ratings**.

gage, gauge A *gage* is security or a pledge.

A *gauge* is a measuring device.

Gauge is also a term used to designate the size of shotguns. See **weapons**.

gaiety

gale See **weather terms**.

gallon Equal to 128 fluid ounces. The metric equivalent is approximately 3.8 liters.

To convert to liters, multiply by 3.8 (3 gallons x 3.8 = 11.4 liters).

See **imperial gallon; liter;** and **metric system**.

Gallup Poll Prepared by the Gallup Organization, Princeton, N.J. The separate Gallup Youth Survey is prepared by the George H. Gallup International Institute.

game plan

gamut, gantlet, gauntlet A *gamut* is a scale of notes or any complete range or extent.

A *gantlet* is a flogging ordeal, literally or figuratively.

A *gauntlet* is a glove. *To throw down the gauntlet* means to issue a challenge. *To take up the gauntlet* means to accept a challenge.

gamy, gamier, gamiest

garnish, garnishee *Garnish* means to adorn or decorate.

As a verb, *garnishee* (*garnisheed, garnisheeing*) means to attach a debtor's property or wages to satisfy a debt. As a noun, it identifies the individual whose property was attached.

gauge See the **gage, gauge** entry.

gay Acceptable as popular synonym for both male and female homosexuals (n. and adj.), although it is generally associated with males, while *lesbian* is the more common term for female homosexuals. Avoid references to gay, homosexual or alternative "lifestyle."

general, general of the air force, general of the army See **military titles**.

General Accounting Office The *General Accounting Office* is a nonpartisan congressional agency that audits federal programs.

GAO is acceptable on second reference.

general assembly See **legislature** for its treatment as the name of a state's legislative body.

Capitalize when it is the formal name for the ruling or consultative body of an organization: *the General Assembly of the World Council of Churches.*

General Assembly (U.N.)

General Assembly may be used on the first reference in a story under a United Nations dateline.

Use *U.N. General Assembly* in other first references, *the General Assembly* or *the assembly* in subsequent references.

general court Part of the official proper name for the legislatures in Massachusetts and New Hampshire. Capitalize specific references with or without the state name: *the Massachusetts General Court, the General Court.*

In keeping with the accepted practice, however, *Legislature* may be used instead and treated as a proper name. See **legislature**.

Lowercase *legislature* in a generic use such as: *The General Court is the legislature in Massachusetts.*

General Electric Co. *GE* is

acceptable on second reference.

Headquarters is in Fairfield, Conn.

general manager Capitalize only as a formal title before a name.

See **titles**.

General Motors Corp. *GM*

is acceptable on second reference.

Headquarters is in Detroit.

General Services Administration *GSA* is acceptable on

second reference.

genie Not *jinni,* the spelling under which Webster's New World gives the definition.

gentile Generally, any person not a Jew; often, specifically a Christian. But to Mormons it is anyone not a Mormon.

gentleman Do not use as a synonym for *man.* See **lady**.

genus, species In scientific or biological names, capitalize the first, or generic, Latin name for the class of plant or animal and lowercase the species that follows: *Homo sapiens, Tyrannosaurus rex.*

geographic names The basic guidelines:

DOMESTIC: The authority for spelling place names in the 50 states and territories is the U.S. Postal Service Directory of Post Offices, with two exceptions:

—Do not use the postal abbreviations for state names. For acceptable abbreviations, see entries in this book under each state's name. See **state names** for rules on when the abbreviations may be used.

—Abbreviate *Saint* as *St.* (But abbreviate *Sault Sainte Marie* as *Sault Ste. Marie.*)

FOREIGN: The first source for the spelling of all foreign place names is Webster's New World Dictionary as follows:

—Use the first-listed spelling if an entry gives more than one.

—If the dictionary provides different spellings in separate entries, use the spelling that is followed by a full description of the location.

If the dictionary does not have

an entry, use the first-listed spelling in the National Geographic Atlas of the World.

NEW NAMES: Follow the styles adopted by the United Nations and the U.S. Board on Geographic Names on new cities, new independent nations and nations that change their names.

DATELINES: See the **datelines** entry.

CAPITALIZATION: Capitalize common nouns when they form an integral part of a proper name, but lowercase them when they stand alone: *Pennsylvania Avenue, the avenue; the Philippine Islands, the islands; the Mississippi River, the river.*

Lowercase common nouns that are not a part of a specific name: *the Pacific islands, the Swiss mountains, Zhejiang province.*

For additional guidelines, see **addresses**; **capitalization**; the **directions and regions** entry; and **island**.

Georgia Abbrev.: *Ga.* See **state names**.

German measles Also known as *rubella*.

Germany *East Germany* and *West Germany* were reunited as of Oct. 3, 1990. *Berlin* stands alone in datelines.

getaway (n.)

get-together (n.)

ghetto, ghettos Do not use indiscriminately as a synonym for the sections of cities inhabited by minorities or the poor. *Ghetto* has

a connotation that government decree has forced people to live in a certain area.

In most cases, *section, district, slum area* or *quarter* is the more accurate word. Sometimes a place name alone has connotations that make it best: *Harlem, Watts*.

GI, GIs *Soldier* is preferred unless the story contains the term in quoted matter or involves a subject such as the *GI Bill of Rights*.

gibe, jibe To *gibe* means to taunt or sneer: *They gibed him about his mistakes.*

Jibe means to shift direction or, colloquially, to agree: *They jibed their ship across the wind. Their stories didn't jibe.*

Gibraltar, Strait of Not *Straits*. The entrance to the Mediterranean from the Atlantic Ocean. The British colony on the peninsula that juts into the strait stands alone in datelines as *GIBRALTAR*.

giga- A prefix denoting 1 billion units of a measure. Move a decimal point nine places to the right, adding zeros if necessary, to convert to the basic unit: 5.5 gigatons = 5,500,000,000 tons.

girl Applicable until 18th birthday is reached. Use *woman* or *young woman* afterward.

girlfriend, boyfriend

Girl Scouts The full name of the national organization is *Girl Scouts of the United States of America*. Headquarters is in New York.

Girls 6 through 8 are *Brownie Girl Scouts* or *Brownies*. Girls 9

through 11 are *Junior Girl Scouts* or *Juniors*. Girls 12 through 14 are *Cadette Girl Scouts* or *Cadettes*. Girls 15 through 17 are *Senior Girl Scouts* or *Seniors*.
See **Boy Scouts**.

glamour One of the few *our* endings still used in American writing. But the adjective is *glamorous*.

globe-trotter, globe-trotting But the proper name of the basketball team is the *Harlem Globetrotters*.

GMT For *Greenwich Mean Time*. See **time zones**.

gobbledygook

go-between (n.)

godchild, goddaughter Also: *godfather, godliness, godmother, godsend, godson, godspeed*. Always lowercase.

gods and goddesses Capitalize *God* in references to the deity of all monotheistic religions. Capitalize all noun references to the deity: *God the Father, Holy Ghost, Holy Spirit*, etc. Lowercase personal pronouns: *he, him, thee, thou*.
Lowercase *gods* and *goddesses* in references to the deities of polytheistic religions.
Lowercase *god, gods* and *goddesses* in references to false gods: *He made money his god.*
See **religious references**.

go-go

good, well *Good* is an adjective that means something is as it should be or is better than average.

When used as an adjective, *well* means suitable, proper, healthy. When used as an adverb, *well* means in a satisfactory manner or skillfully.
Good should not be used as an adverb. It does not lose its status as an adjective in a sentence such as *I feel good*. Such a statement is the idiomatic equivalent of *I am in good health*. An alternative, *I feel well*, could be interpreted as meaning that your sense of touch was good.
See the **bad, badly** entry and **well**.

goodbye Not *goodby*.

Good Conduct Medal

Good Friday The Friday before Easter.

good will (n.) **goodwill** (adj.)

GOP See **Grand Old Party**.

Gospel(s), gospel Capitalize when referring to any or all of the first four books of the New Testament: *the Gospel of St. John, the Gospels.*
Lowercase in other references: *She is a famous gospel singer.*

gourmand, gourmet A *gourmand* is a person who likes good food and tends to eat to excess; a glutton.
A *gourmet* is a person who likes fine food and is an excellent judge of food and drink.

government Always lowercase, never abbreviate: *the federal government, the state government, the U.S. government.*

government, junta, regime

A *government* is an established system of political administration: *the U.S. government.*

A *junta* is a group or council that often rules after a coup: *A military junta controls the nation.* A junta becomes a government after it establishes a system of political administration.

The word *regime* is a synonym for *political system*: *a democratic regime, an authoritarian regime.* Do not use *regime* to mean government or junta. For example, use *the Franco government* in referring to the government of Spain under Francisco Franco, not *Franco regime.* But: *The Franco government was an authoritarian regime.*

An *administration* consists of officials who make up the executive branch of a government: *the Reagan administration.*

governmental bodies

Follow these guidelines:

FULL NAME: Capitalize the full proper names of governmental agencies, departments, and offices: *The U.S. Department of State, the Georgia Department of Human Resources, the Boston City Council, the Chicago Fire Department.*

WITHOUT JURISDICTION: Retain capitalization in referring to a specific body if the dateline or context makes the name of the nation, state, county, city, etc. unnecessary: *The Department of State* (in a story from Washington), *the Department of Human Resources* or *the state Department of Human Resources* (in a story from Georgia), *the City Council* (in a story from Boston), *the Fire Department* or *the city Fire Department* (in a story from Chicago).

Lowercase further condensations of the name: *the department, the council,* etc.

For additional guidance see **assembly; city council; committee; congress; legislature; house of representatives; senate; Supreme Court of the United States;** and **supreme courts of the states.**

FLIP-FLOPPED NAMES: Retain capital names for the name of a governmental body if its formal name is flopped to delete the word *of*: *the State Department, the Human Resources Department.*

GENERIC EQUIVALENTS: If a generic term has become the equivalent of a proper name in popular use, treat it as a proper name: *Walpole State Prison,* for example, even though the proper name is the *Massachusetts Correctional Institute-Walpole.*

For additional examples, see **legislature; police department;** and the **prison, jail** entry.

PLURALS, NONSPECIFIC REFERENCES: All words that are capitalized when part of a proper name should be lowercased when they are used in the plural or do not refer to a specific, existing body. Some examples:

All states except Nebraska have a state senate. The town does not have a fire department. The bill requires city councils to provide matching funds. The president will address the lower houses of the New York and New Jersey legislatures.

FOREIGN BODIES: The same principles apply. See **foreign governmental bodies** and **foreign legislative bodies.**

governor Capitalize and abbreviate as *Gov.* or *Govs.* when used as a formal title before one or more names in regular text. Capitalize and spell out when used as a formal title before one or more names in direct quotations.

Lowercase and spell out in all other uses.

See the next entry and **titles**.

governor general, governors general The formal title for the British sovereign's representatives in Canada and elsewhere.

Do not abbreviate in any use.

grade, grader Hyphenate both the noun forms (*first-grader, second-grader, 10th-grader*, etc.) and the adjectival forms (*a fourth-grade pupil, a 12th-grade pupil*).

graduate (v.) *Graduate* is correctly used in the active voice: *She graduated from the university.*

It is correct, but unnecessary, to use the passive voice: *He was graduated from the university.*

Do not, however, drop *from*: *John Adams graduated from Harvard.* Not: *John Adams graduated Harvard.*

graham, graham crackers The crackers are made from a finely ground whole-wheat flour named for Sylvester Graham, a U.S. dietary reformer.

grain The smallest unit in the system of weights that has been used in the United States. It originally was defined as the weight of 1 grain of wheat.

It takes 437.5 grains to make an ounce. There are 7,000 grains to a pound.

See **ounce (weight)** and **pound**.

gram The basic unit of weight in the metric system. It is the weight of 1 cubic centimeter of water at 4 degrees Celsius.

A gram is roughly equivalent to the weight of a paper clip, or approximately one-twenty-eighth of an ounce.

To convert to ounces, multiply by .035 (86 grams x .035 equals 3 ounces).

See **metric system**.

grammar

granddad, granddaughter Also: *grandfather, grandmother, grandson.*

grand jury Always lowercase: *a Los Angeles County grand jury, the grand jury.*

This style has been adopted because, unlike the case with city council and similar governmental units, a jurisdiction frequently has more than one grand jury session.

Grand Old Party *GOP* is acceptable as a second-reference synonym for *Republican Party* without first spelling out *Grand Old Party.*

grant-in-aid, grants-in-aid

gray Not grey. But: *greyhound.*

great- Hyphenate *great-grandfather, great-great-grandmother*, etc.

Use *great grandfather* only if the intended meaning is that the grandfather was a great man.

Great Atlantic & Pacific Tea Co. Inc. *A&P* is acceptable in all references.

Headquarters is in Montvale, N.J.

Great Britain It consists of England, Scotland and Wales, but not Northern Ireland.

Britain is acceptable in all references.

See **United Kingdom**.

Great Depression See **Depression**.

greater Capitalize when used to define a community and its surrounding region: *Greater Boston.*

Great Lakes The five, from the largest to the smallest: Lake Superior, Lake Huron, Lake Michigan, Lake Erie, Lake Ontario.

Great Plains Capitalize *Great Plains* or *the Plains* when referring to the U.S. prairie lands that extend from North Dakota to Texas and from the Missouri River to the Rocky Mountains.

Use *northern Plains, southwestern Plains*, etc., when referring to a portion of the region.

Greek Orthodox Archdiocese of America See **Eastern Orthodox churches**.

Greek Orthodox Church See **Eastern Orthodox churches**.

Green Revolution The substantial increase in agricultural yields that resulted from the development of new varieties of grains.

Greenwich Mean Time (GMT) See **time zones** and **meridians**.

gringo See the **nationalities and races** entry.

grisly, grizzly *Grisly* is horrifying, repugnant.

Grizzly means grayish or is a short form for *grizzly bear.*

grits Ground hominy. The word normally takes plural verbs and pronouns: *Grits are to country ham what Yorkshire pudding is to roast beef.*

gross domestic product The sum of all goods and services produced within U.S. borders, it is calculated quarterly by the Commerce Department.

Lowercase in all uses, but *GDP* is acceptable in later references.

Groundhog Day Feb. 2.

groundskeeper

groundswell

group Takes singular verbs and pronouns: *The group is reviewing its position.*

grown-up (n. and adj.)

G-string

Guadalupe (Mexico)

Guadeloupe (West Indies)

Guam Use in datelines after the name of a community. See **datelines**.

guarantee Preferred to *guaranty*, except in proper names.

guard Usually a job description, not a formal title. See **titles**.

guardsman See **National Guard** and **Coast Guardsman**.

Guatemala City Stands alone in datelines.

gubernatorial

guerrilla Unorthodox soldiers and their tactics.

guest Do not use as a verb except in quoted matter. (An exception to a use recorded by Webster's New World.)

Guild, The See **Newspaper Guild, The**.

Guinness Book of Records

Gulf Coast Capitalize when referring to the region of the United States lying along the Gulf of Mexico.
See **coast**.

Gulf Oil Corp. Headquarters is in Pittsburgh.

Gulf Stream But the racetrack is *Gulfstream Park*.

gunbattle, gunboat, gunfight, gunfire, gunpoint, gunpowder

gung-ho A colloquialism to be used sparingly.

guns See **weapons**.

guru

gypsy, gypsies Capitalize references to the wandering Caucasoid people found throughout the world.
Lowercase when used generically to mean one who is constantly on the move: *I plan to become a gypsy. She hailed a gypsy cab.*

gypsy moth

H

habeas corpus A writ ordering a person in custody to be brought before a court. It places the burden of proof on those detaining the person to justify the detention.

When *habeas corpus* is used in a story, define it.

Hades But lowercase *hell*.

Hague, The In datelines: *THE HAGUE, Netherlands (AP) —* In text: *The Hague*.

half It is not necessary to use the preposition *of*: *half the time* is correct, but *half of the time* is not wrong.

half- Follow Webster's New World Dictionary. Hyphenate if not listed there.

Some frequently used words without a hyphen:

halfback	halftone
halfhearted	halftrack

Also: *halftime*, an exception to the dictionary in keeping with widespread practice in sports copy.

Some frequently used combinations that are two words without a hyphen:

half brother	half size
half dollar	half sole (n.)
half note	half tide

Some frequently used combinations that include a hyphen:

half-baked	half-life
half-blood	half-moon
half-cocked	half-sole (v.)
half-hour	half-truth

half-mast, half-staff On ships and at naval stations ashore, flags are flown at *half-mast*.

Elsewhere ashore, flags are flown at *half-staff*.

hallelujah

Halley's comet After Edmund Halley, an English astronomer who predicted the comet's appearance once every 75 years, last seen in 1985-86.

Halloween

halo, halos

handicapped See **disabled, handicapped, impaired**.

handmade

hand-picked

hands off, hands-off Hyphenate when used as a compound modifier: *He kept his hands off the matter. He follows a hands-off policy.*

hand to hand, hand-to-hand, hand to mouth, hand-to-mouth Hyphenate when used as compound modifiers: *The cup was passed from* *hand to hand. They live a hand-to-mouth existence.*

hang, hanged, hung One *hangs* a picture, a criminal or oneself.

For past tense or the passive, use *hanged* when referring to executions or suicides, *hung* for other actions.

hangar, hanger A *hangar* is a building.

A *hanger* is used for clothes.

hangover

hanky-panky

Hanukkah The Jewish Festival of Lights, an eight-day commemoration of rededication of the Temple by the Maccabees after their victory over the Syrians.

Usually occurs in December but sometimes falls in late November.

harass, harassment

harebrained An offensive term; do not use.

harelip Avoid. *Cleft lip* is preferred.

Harper's Magazine Not to be confused with Harper's Bazaar.

Harris Poll Prepared by Harris Interactive of New York.

Havana The city in Cuba stands alone in datelines.

Hawaii Do not abbreviate. Residents are *Hawaiians*, technically natives of Polynesian descent.

The state comprises 132 is-

lands about 2,400 miles southwest of San Francisco. Collectively, they are the *Hawaiian Islands*.

The largest island in land area is Hawaii. Honolulu and Pearl Harbor are on Oahu, where more than 80 percent of the state's residents live.

Honolulu stands alone in datelines. Use *Hawaii* after all other cities in datelines, specifying the island in the text, if needed.

See **datelines** and **state names**.

Hawaiian Airlines Headquarters is in Honolulu.

Hawaii Standard Time The time zone used in Hawaii. There is no daylight time in Hawaii.

H-bomb Use *hydrogen bomb* unless a direct quotation is involved.

he, him, his, thee, thou Personal pronouns referring to the deity are lowercase.

See **deity**.

headlong

head-on (adj., adv.)

headquarters May take a singular or a plural verb.

Do not use *headquarter* as a verb.

health care Two words.

hearing examiner See **administrative law judge**.

hearsay

heaven

heavenly bodies Capitalize the proper names of planets,

stars, constellations, etc.: *Mars, Arcturus, the Big Dipper, Aries.* See **earth**.

For comets, capitalize only the proper noun element of the name: *Halley's comet.*

Lowercase sun and moon, but capitalize them if their Greek or Latin names are used: *Helios, Luna.*

Lowercase nouns and adjectives derived from the proper names of planets and other heavenly bodies: *jovian, lunar, martian, solar, venusian.*

hect- (before a vowel), **hecto-** (before a consonant) A prefix denoting 100 units of a measure. Move a decimal point two places to the right, adding zeros if necessary, to convert to the basic unit: 5.5 hectometers = 550 meters.

hectare A unit of surface measure in the metric system equal to 100 ares or 10,000 square meters.

A hectare is equal to 2.47 acres, 107,639.1 square feet or 11,959.9 square yards.

To convert to acres, multiply by 2.47 (5 hectares x 2.47 = 12.35 acres).

See **are** and **metric system**.

heights See **dimensions**.

heliport

hell But capitalize *Hades*.

helter-skelter

hemisphere Capitalize *Northern Hemisphere, Western Hemisphere,* etc.

Lowercase *hemisphere* in other uses: *the Eastern and Western hemispheres, the hemisphere.*

hemorrhage

hemorrhoid

her Do not use this pronoun in reference to nations or ships, except in quoted matter.

Use *it* instead.

here The word is frequently redundant, particularly in the lead of a datelined story. Use only if there is some specific need to stress that the event being reported took place in the community.

If the location must be stressed in the body of the story, repeat the name of the datelined community, both for the reader's convenience and to avoid problems if the story is topped with a different dateline.

Her Majesty Capitalize when it appears in quotations or is appropriate before a name as the long form of a formal title.

For other purposes, use the woman's name or *the queen.*

See **nobility**.

heroin The narcotic, originally a trademark.

hertz This term, the same in singular or plural, has been adopted as the international unit of frequency equal to one cycle per second.

In contexts where it would not be understood by most readers, it should be followed by a parenthetical explanation: *15,400 hertz (cycles per second).*

Do not abbreviate.

hideaway

hi-fi

high-tech

highway designations

Use these forms, as appropriate in the context, for highways identified by number: *U.S. Highway 1, U.S. Route 1, U.S. 1, state Route 34, Route 34, Interstate Highway 495, Interstate 495.* On second reference only for *Interstate: I-495.*

When a letter is appended to a number, capitalize it but do not use a hyphen: *Route 1A.*

See **addresses**.

highway patrol

Capitalize if used in the formal name of a police agency: *the Kansas Highway Patrol, the Highway Patrol.* Lowercase *highway patrolman* in all uses.

See **state police**.

hike

People take *hikes* through the woods, but they *increase* prices.

Hindu, Hinduism

The dominant religion of India. It has about 470 million followers making it the world's third largest religion after Christianity and Islam. There are more than 300,000 followers in North America.

The basic teaching is that the soul never dies, but is reborn each time the body dies. The soul may be reborn in either human or animal form. The following rule is that of karma and states that no matter how small the action or thought of an individual it will affect how the soul will be reborn in the next generation. The cycle of death and rebirth continues until a soul reaches spiritual perfection. At that point the soul is united in total enlightenment and peace with the supreme being and the cycle is ended.

There are a number of gods and goddesses, all of whom are different focuses of the one supreme being. The primary gods are Brahma, Vishnu, called the preserver, and Siva, the destroyer. Vishnu has had important human incarnations as Krishna and Rama. The primary goddess is Devi, who is also known as Durga, Kali, Sarasvati, Lakshimi and other names. She represents in her forms either motherhood and good fortune or destruction. There are thousands of other deities and saints which also may receive prayers and offerings.

Hindus also believe that animals have souls and many are worshiped as gods. There are thousands of sects and organization runs from virtually none to very strict depending on the group. There is no formal clergy.

Hiroshima

On Aug. 6, 1945, this Japanese city and military base were the targets of the first atomic bomb dropped as a weapon. The explosion had the force of 20,000 tons (20 kilotons) of TNT. It destroyed more than four square miles and killed or injured 160,000 people.

his, her

Do not presume maleness in constructing a sentence, but use the pronoun *his* when an indefinite antecedent may be male or female: *A reporter attempts to protect his sources.* (Not *his or her* sources, but note the use of the word *reporter* rather than *newsman.*)

Frequently, however, the best choice is a slight revision of the sentence: *Reporters attempt to protect their sources.*

His Majesty

Capitalize when it appears in quotations or is appropriate before a name as the long form of a formal title.

For other purposes, use the man's name or *king*.

See **nobility**.

Hispanic The preferred term for those whose ethnic origin is in a Spanish-speaking country. *Latino* is acceptable for *Hispanics* who prefer that term. Use a more specific identification when possible, such as *Cuban, Puerto Rican* or *Mexican-American* or the name of an indigenous group in a Latin American country. Avoid *Chicano* as a synonym for *Mexican-American*. Refer to people of Brazilian and Portuguese origin as such, not as *Hispanic*.

Hispaniola The island shared by the Dominican Republic and Haiti.

See **Western Hemisphere**.

historic, historical A *historic* event is an important occurrence, one that stands out in history.

Any occurrence in the past is a *historical* event.

historical periods and events Capitalize the names of widely recognized epochs in anthropology, archaeology, geology and history: *the Bronze Age, the Dark Ages, the Middle Ages, the Pliocene Epoch*.

Capitalize also widely recognized popular names for the periods and events: *the Atomic Age, the Boston Tea Party, the Civil War, the Exodus* (of the Israelites from Egypt), *the Great Depression, Prohibition*.

Lowercase *century*: *the 18th century*.

Capitalize only the proper nouns or adjectives in general descriptions of a period: *ancient Greece, classical Rome, the Victorian era, the fall of Rome*.

For additional guidance, see separate entries in this book for many epochs, events and historical periods. If this book has no entry, follow the capitalization in Webster's New World Dictionary, using lowercase if the dictionary lists it as an acceptable form for the sense in which the word is used.

history Avoid the redundant *past history*.

hit and run (v.) **hit-and-run** (n. and adj.) *The coach told him to hit and run. He scored on a hit-and-run. She was struck by a hit-and-run driver.*

hitchhike, hitchhiker

HIV See **AIDS** entry.

hocus-pocus

hodgepodge

Hodgkin's disease After Dr. Thomas Hodgkin, the English physician who first described the disease of the lymph nodes.

ho-hum

hold up (v.) **holdup** (n. and adj.)

holidays and holy days Capitalize them: *New Year's Eve, New Year's Day, Groundhog Day, Easter, Hanukkah*, etc.

The legal holidays in federal law are New Year's, Martin Luther King Jr. Day, Washington's Birthday, Memorial Day, Independence Day, Labor Day, Columbus Day, Veterans Day, Thanksgiving and Christmas. See individual entries for the official dates and when they are observed if they fall on a weekend.

The designation of a day as a federal legal holiday means that federal employees receive the day off or are paid overtime if they must work. Other requirements that may apply to holidays generally are left to the states. Many follow the federal lead in designating a holiday, but they are not required to do so.

Hollywood Stands alone in datelines when used instead of *Los Angeles* on stories about films and the film industry.

Holocaine A trademark for a type of local anesthetic.

Holy Communion See **sacraments**.

Holy Father The preferred form is to use *the pope* or *the pontiff*, or to give the individual's name.

Use *Holy Father* in direct quotations or special contexts where a particular literary effect is desired.

holy orders See **sacraments**.

Holy See The headquarters of the Roman Catholic Church in Vatican City.

Holy Spirit Now preferred over *Holy Ghost* in most usage.

Holy Week The week before Easter.

homemade

home page (two words)

hometown See **comma** in **Punctuation** section for guidelines on how to list a hometown after an individual's name.

homicide, murder, manslaughter *Homicide* is a legal term for slaying or killing.

Murder is malicious, premeditated homicide. Some states define certain homicides as murder if the killing occurs in the course of armed robbery, rape, etc.

Manslaughter is homicide without malice or premeditation.

A person should not be described as a *murderer* until convicted of the charge.

Unless authorities say premeditation was obvious, do not say that a victim *was murdered* until someone has been convicted in court. Instead, say that a victim *was killed* or *slain*.

See **execute** and the **assassin, killer, murderer** entry.

Hong Kong Stands alone in datelines.

Honolulu The city in Hawaii stands alone in datelines. It is on the island of Oahu.

See **Hawaii**.

honorary degrees All references to honorary degrees should specify that the degree was honorary.

Do not use *Dr.* before the name of an individual whose only doctorate is honorary.

honorary titles See **nobility**.

hoof-and-mouth disease Use *foot-and-mouth disease*.

hooky Not *hookey*.

hopefully It means in a hopeful manner. Do not use it to mean it is hoped, let us or we hope.

Right: *It is hoped that we will complete our work in June.*

Right: *We hope that we will complete our work in June.*

Wrong as a way to express the thought in the previous two sentences: *Hopefully, we will complete our work in June.*

horsepower

horse races Capitalize their formal names: *Kentucky Derby, Preakness, Belmont Stakes*, etc.

horses' names Capitalize. See **animals**.

host Do not use it as a verb. (Exception to a usage recorded in Webster's New World.)

hotel Capitalize as part of the proper name for a specific hotel: *the Waldorf-Astoria Hotel.*

Lowercase when standing alone or used in an indefinite reference to one hotel in a chain: *The city has a Sheraton hotel.*

Hotel and Restaurant Employees and Bartenders International Union The shortened forms *Hotel and Restaurant Employees union* and *Bartenders union* acceptable in all references.

Headquarters in Cincinnati.

hot line The circuit linking the United States and Russia. Lowercase.

household, housing unit In the sense used by the Census Bureau, a *household* is made up of all occupants of a *housing unit.* A household may contain more than one family or may be used by one person.

A *housing unit*, as defined by the bureau, is a group of rooms or single room occupied by people who do not live and eat with any other person in the structure. It must have either direct access from the outside or through a common hall, or have a kitchen or cooking equipment for the exclusive use of the occupants.

House of Commons, House of Lords The two houses of the British Parliament.

On second reference: *Commons* or *the Commons, Lords* or *the Lords.*

house of delegates See the next entry.

house of representatives Capitalize when referring to a specific governmental body: *the U.S. House of Representatives, the Massachusetts House of Representatives.*

Capitalize shortened references that delete the words *of Representatives*: *the U.S. House, the Massachusetts House.*

Retain capitalization if *U.S.* or the name of a state is dropped but the reference is to a specific body.

BOSTON (AP) — The House has adjourned for the year.

Lowercase plural uses: *the Massachusetts and Rhode Island houses.*

Apply the same principle to similar legislative bodies such as *the Virginia House of Delegates.*

See the **organizations and institutions** entry for guidelines on how to handle the term when it is used by a nongovernmental body.

housing unit See the

household, housing unit entry.

Houston The city in Texas stands alone in datelines.

howitzer See **weapons**.

human, human being *Human* is preferred, but either is acceptable.

hurly-burly

hurricane Capitalize hurricane when it is part of the name that weather forecasters assign to a storm: *Hurricane Hazel.*

But use *it* and *its* — not *she, her* or *hers* or *he, him* or *his* — in pronoun references.

And do not use the presence of a woman's name as an excuse to attribute sexist images of women's behavior to a storm. Avoid, for example, such sentences as: *The fickle Hazel teased the Louisiana coast.*

See **weather terms**.

husband, widower Use *husband*, not *widower*, in referring to the spouse of a woman who dies.

hush-hush

Hyannis Port, Mass.

hydro- The rules in **prefixes** apply, but in general, no hyphen. Some examples:

hydroelectric   hydrophobia

hyper- The rules in **prefixes** apply, but in general, no hyphen. Some examples:

hyperactive   hypercritical

hyphen See entry in **Punctuation** chapter.

I

Iberia Air Lines of Spain
An *Iberia airliner* is acceptable in
any reference.
Headquarters is in Madrid.

IBM Acceptable as first refer-
ence for *International Business
Machines*.
Headquarters is in Armonk,
N.Y.

ICBM, ICBMs Acceptable on
first reference for *intercontinental
ballistic missile(s)*, but the term
should be defined in the body of a
story.
Avoid the redundant *ICBM
missiles*.

ice age Lowercase, because it
denotes not a single period but
any of a series of cold periods
marked by glaciation alternating
with periods of relative warmth.
Capitalize the proper nouns in
the names of individual ice ages,
such as the *Wisconsin ice age*.
The most recent series of ice
ages happened during the *Pleis-
tocene* epoch, which began about
1.6 million years ago. During that
time, glaciers sometimes covered
much of North America and
northwestern Europe.
The present epoch, the
Holocene or *Recent*, began about
10,000 years ago, when the continental glaciers had retreated to
Antarctica and Greenland.

Icelandair Headquarters is
in Reykjavik, Iceland.

ice storm See **weather
terms**.

Idaho Do not abbreviate. See
state names.

illegal Use *illegal* only to
mean a violation of the law. Be
especially careful in labor-management disputes, where one side
often calls an action by the other
side illegal. Usually it is a charge
that a contract or rule, not a law,
has been violated.

Illinois Abbrev.: *Ill.* See **state
names**.

illusion See the **allusion, illusion** entry.

imam Lowercase when describing the leader of a prayer in
a Muslim mosque. Capitalize before a name when used as the formal title for a Muslim leader or
ruler.
See **religious titles**.

immigrate See the **emigrate, immigrate** entry.

**impassable, impassible,
impassive** *Impassable* means
that passage is impossible: *The
bridge was impassable.*

Impassible and *impassive* describe lack of sensitivity to pain or suffering. Webster's New World notes, however, that *impassible* suggests an inability to be affected, while *impassive* implies only that no reaction was noticeable: *She was impassive throughout the ordeal.*

impeachment The constitutional process accusing an elected official of a crime in an attempt to remove the official from office. Do not use as a synonym for convicted or removed from office.

impel, impelled, impelling

imperial gallon The standard British gallon, equal to 277.42 cubic inches or about 1.2 U.S. gallons.

The metric equivalent is approximately 4.5 liters.

See **liter**.

imperial quart One-fourth of an imperial gallon.

implausible

imply, infer Writers or speakers *imply* in the words they use.

A listener or reader *infers* something from the words.

impostor Not *imposter*.

impromptu It means without preparation or advance thought.

in, into *In* indicates location: *He was in the room.*

Into indicates motion: *She walked into the room.*

"in" When employed to indicate that something is in vogue, use quotation marks only if followed by a noun: *It was the "in" thing to do. Raccoon coats are in again.*

in- No hyphen when it means *not*:

inaccurate	insufferable

Often solid in other cases:

inbound	infighting
indoor	inpatient (n., adj.)
infield	

A few combinations take a hyphen, however:

in-depth	in-house
in-group	in-law

Follow Webster's New World when in doubt.

-in Precede with a hyphen:

break-in	walk-in
cave-in	write-in

inasmuch as

Inauguration Day Capitalize only when referring to the total collection of events that include inauguration of a U.S. president; lowercase in other uses: *Inauguration Day is Jan. 20. The inauguration day for the change has not been set.*

Inc. See **incorporated**.

inch Equal to one-twelfth of a foot.

The metric equivalent is exactly 2.54 centimeters.

To convert to centimeters, multiply by 2.54 (6 inches x 2.54 equals 15.24 centimeters).

See **centimeter**; **foot**; and **dimensions**.

inches per second A rating used for the speed of tape recorders.

The abbreviation *ips* (no periods) is acceptable on first reference in specialized contexts such as a records column; otherwise do not use *ips* until second reference.

include Use *include* to introduce a series when the items that follow are only part of the total: *The price includes breakfast. The zoo includes lions and tigers.*

Use *comprise* when the full list on individual elements is given: *The zoo comprises 100 types of animals, including lions and tigers.*

See the **compose, comprise, constitute** entry.

incorporated Abbreviate and capitalize as Inc. when used as part of a corporate name. It usually is not needed, but when it is used, do not set off with commas: *J.C. Penney Co. Inc. announced...*

See **company names**.

incorporator Do not capitalize when used before a name.

See **titles**.

incredible, incredulous *Incredible* means unbelievable. *Incredulous* means skeptical.

incur, incurred, incurring

Independence Day *July Fourth* or *Fourth of July* also are acceptable.

The federal legal holiday is observed on Friday if July 4 falls on a Saturday, on Monday if it falls on a Sunday.

index, indexes

Index of Leading Economic Indicators A composite of 10 economic measurements that was developed to help forecast likely shifts in the U.S. economy as a whole.

It is compiled by the Conference Board, a private business-sponsored research group.

Indiana Abbrev.: *Ind.* See **state names**.

Indianapolis The city in Indiana stands alone in datelines.

Indian Ocean See **oceans**.

Indians *American Indian* is the preferred term for those in the United States. Where possible, be precise and use the name of the tribe: *He is a Navajo commissioner. Native American* is acceptable in quotations and names of organizations.

In news stories about American Indians, such words as *wampum, warpath, powwow, tepee, brave, squaw,* etc., can be disparaging and offensive. Be careful and certain of their usage.

indict Use *indict* only in connection with the legal process of bringing charges against an individual or corporation.

To avoid any suggestion that someone is being judged before a trial, do not use phrases such as *indicted for killing* or *indicted for bribery.* Instead, use *indicted on a charge of killing* or *indicted on a bribery charge.*

For guidelines on related words, see the entries under **accuse; allege;** and **arrest**.

indiscreet, indiscrete *Indiscreet* means lacking prudence. Its noun form is *indiscretion.*

Indiscrete means not separated into distinct parts. Its noun form is *indiscreteness.*

indiscriminate, indiscriminately

indispensable

indo- Usually hyphenated and capitalized:

Indo-Aryan	Indo-Hittite
Indo-German	Indo-Iranian

But: *Indochina.*

Indochina Formerly French Indochina, now divided into Cambodia, Laos and Vietnam.

Indochinese peninsula

Located here are the nations of Cambodia, Laos, Myanmar, Thailand and Vietnam.

Indonesia Use after the name of a community in datelines on stories from this nation.

Specify an individual island, if needed, in the text.

indoor (adj.) **indoors** (adv.) *He plays indoor tennis. He went indoors.*

infant Applicable to children through 12 months old.

infantile paralysis The preferred term is *polio.*

inflation A sustained increase in prices. The result is a decrease in the purchasing power of money.

There are two basic types of inflation:

—*Cost-push inflation occurs* when rising costs are the chief reason for the increased prices.

—*Demand-pull inflation* occurs when the amount of money available exceeds the amount of goods and services available for sale.

infra- The rules in prefixes apply, but in general, no hyphen. Some examples:

infrared	infrastructure

initials Use periods and no space when an individual uses initials instead of a first name: *H.L. Mencken.*

This format has been adopted to assure that in typesetting the initials are set on the same line.

Do not give a name with a single initial (*J. Jones*) unless it is the individual's preference or a first name cannot be learned.

See **middle initials**.

injuries They are *suffered*, not *sustained* or *received.*

in-law

Inner Light See **Quakers**.

innocent Use *innocent*, rather than *not guilty*, in describing a defendant's plea or a jury's verdict, to guard against the word *not* being dropped inadvertently.

innocuous

innuendo

inoculate

input Do not use as a verb in describing the introduction of data into a computer.

inquire, inquiry Not *enquire, enquiry.*

insignia Same form for singular and plural.

insofar as

in spite of *Despite* means the same thing and is shorter.

intelligence quotient *IQ* is acceptable in all references.

inter- The rules in **prefixes** apply, but in general, no hyphen. Some examples:

inter-American   interstate
interracial

intercontinental ballistic missile See **ICBM, ICBMs**.

Internal Revenue Service
IRS is acceptable on second reference.

Capitalize also *Internal Revenue*, but lowercase *the revenue service*.

International Association of Machinists and Aerospace Workers The shortened form *Machinists* union is acceptable in all references.

Headquarters is in Washington.

International Bank for Reconstruction and Development *World Bank* is acceptable in all references.

Headquarters is in Washington.

International Brotherhood of Electrical Workers
Use the full name on first reference to avoid confusion with the United Electrical, Radio and Machine Workers of America.

IBEW is acceptable on second reference.

Headquarters is in Washington.

International Brotherhood of Painters and Allied Trades of the United States and Canada The shortened

form *Painters union* is acceptable in all references.

Headquarters is in Washington.

International Brotherhood of Teamsters, Chauffeurs, Warehousemen and Helpers of America The shortened form *Teamsters union* is acceptable in all references.

Capitalize *Teamsters* and *the Teamsters* in references to the union or its members.

Lowercase *teamster* when no specific reference to the union is intended.

Headquarters is in Washington.

International Court of Justice The principal judicial organ of the United Nations, established at The Hague in 1945.

The court is not open to individuals. It has jurisdiction over all matters specifically provided for either in the U.N. charter or in treaties and conventions in force. It also has jurisdiction over cases referred to it by U.N. members and by nonmembers such as Switzerland that subscribe to the court statute.

The court serves as the suc cessor to the Permanent Court of International Justice of the League of Nations, which also was known as the World Court.

On second reference use *international court* or *world court* in lowercase. Do not abbreviate.

International Criminal Police Organization *Interpol* is acceptable in all references.

Headquarters is in Paris.

international date line
The imaginary line drawn north and south through the Pacific

Ocean, largely along the 180th meridian.

By international agreement, when it is 12:01 a.m. Sunday just west of the line, it is 12:01 a.m. Saturday just east of it.

See **time zones**.

International Labor Organization *ILO* is acceptable on second reference.

Headquarters is in Geneva.

International Longshore and Warehouse Union *ILWU* is acceptable on second reference.

Headquarters is in San Francisco.

International Longshoremen's Association *ILA* is acceptable on second reference.

Headquarters is in New York.

International Monetary Fund *IMF* is acceptable on second reference.

Headquarters is in Washington.

International Telecommunications Satellite Organization *Intelsat* is acceptable on first reference, but the body of the story should identify it as the shortened form of the full name.

(The original name was International Telecommunications Satellite Consortium.)

Headquarters is in Washington.

International Union, United Automobile, Aerospace and Agricultural Implement Workers of America This is the full, formal name for the union known more commonly as the *United Auto Workers*.

See the entry that begins **United Automobile**.

Internet See special section on next page.

Interpol Acceptable in all references for *International Criminal Police Organization*.

intra- The rules in **prefixes** apply, but in general, no hyphen. Some examples:

intramural   intrastate

intranet A private computer network within an organization. Lowercase.

IOU, IOUs

Iowa Do not abbreviate. See **state names**.

ips See **inches per second**.

IQ Acceptable in all references for **intelligence quotient**.

Iran The nation formerly called Persia. It is not an Arab country.

The people are *Iranians*, not *Persians* or *Irani*.

For the language, use *Persian*, the word widely accepted outside Iran. Inside Iran, the language is called *Farsi*.

Iraq The Arab nation coinciding roughly with ancient Mesopotamia.

Its people are *Iraqis*. The dialect of Arabic is *Iraqi*.

Ireland Acceptable in most references to the independent nation known formally as the Irish Republic.

Use *Irish Republic* when a distinction must be made between this nation and *Northern Ireland*, a part of the United Kingdom.

Internet A decentralized, worldwide network of computers that can communicate with each other. In later references, *the Net* is acceptable.

Be acutely aware of the potential dangers of using information from *Internet* and e-mail sources. All such electronic information — from computer disk data to e-mail to material posted on the *Internet* — falls into the "tangible form" category that is subject to copyright protection as well as libel guidelines.

Use care, too, in copying online jargon and abbreviated forms, unless they are generally understood.

Internet addresses include e-mail addresses and Web site designations. Follow the spelling and capitalization of the Web site owner. If an *Internet* address falls at the end of a sentence, use a period. (If an address breaks between lines, split it directly before a slash or a dot that is part of the address, without an inserted hyphen.) Although in some cases it may not be necessary, use the *http://* protocol at the start of a Web address, as well as other starts, such as *ftp://*.

When a story mentions a specific Web site or Web service, include the Internet address, the URL, within the text. This is essential information for the reader.

Add *Internet* addresses (URLs) to the end of a story when they provide additional information, but aren't specifically referred to in a story.

An example:

PASADENA, Calif. (AP) -- NASA abandoned any real hope Tuesday for the missing-in-action Mars Polar Lander and promised to investigate every aspect of the failed mission and delay future expeditions to the Red Planet if necessary.

The last, best chance to make radio contact with the spacecraft yielded only silence early Tuesday. A somber Richard Cook, the spacecraft's operations manager at NASA's Jet Propulsion Laboratory, said the flight team had "played its last ace." ...

On the Net: NASA Mars site: http://marslander.jpl.nasa.gov
UCLA site on experiments aboard the mission: http://mars.ucla.edu

Avoid URLs that are particularly lengthy and complicated, unless essential to guide the reader to a particular document.

Some symbols in *Internet* addresses, such as the "at" sign and the tilde, result in garbles in some newspaper computers. Spell them out instead and provide an explanatory note. (See **Nontransmitting Symbols** in the **Filing Practices** section.)

Some commonly used *Internet*, computer and telecommunications terms:

Adobe Acrobat A file reader that decodes documents to the portable document format.

applet Small programs that can be downloaded quickly and used by computers with a World Wide Web browser.

ASCII An acronym for *American Standard Code for Information Interchange.* A numeric code used to represent the letters of the Roman alphabet, numbers and punctuation marks. Use of the acronym on first reference is acceptable if it is identified as a code.

baud Commonly, a unit for measuring the speed of data transmission by computer; actually the switching speed of a line or number of transitions made per second.

bit Acceptable in all references as an acronym for *binary digit.* Actual data take the form of electrical impulses. These can be thought of as either on or off or 1 and 0. The pulses are bits.

byte A computer "word" made up of bits. The most common size *byte* contains eight bits, or binary digits.

browser Software that enables personal computer users to navigate the World Wide Web and to perform various operations once they are linked with a site. The two most often used are Netscape Navigator and Microsoft Internet Explorer.

CD-ROM For a *compact disc* acting as a *read-only memory* device.
CD-ROM disc is redundant.

cell phone Two words; an exception to Webster's.

chat room A World Wide Web site that enables computer users to message each other in an online conversation.

cookie Term for special information about an individual computer user, stored in a file on a hard drive, and usually accessed by a server when the user connects to a Web site.

cyberspace A term popularized by William Gibson in the novel "Neuromancer" to refer to the digital world of computer networks. It has spawned numerous words with *cyber-* prefixes, but try to avoid most of these cutesy coinages. When the combining form is used, follow the general rule for prefixes and do not use a hyphen before a word starting with a consonant.

database

DNS Acronym for the *domain name system*, an international network of *Internet* domain servers, names and addresses.

domain name Internet address used for locating Web sites, e-mail systems and other online features, listed at the right of the @ sign in the address. The system has a hierarchical structure, with each section separated by a period. The name to the right of the final period is the top-level domain name, or suffix, defining the type of entity, such as *.com* (for commerce, the most common suffix); *.net* (primarily for network service providers); *.org* (organizations); *.edu* (reserved for educational institutions); *.gov* (reserved for U.S. government); *.mil* (reserved for U.S. military); *.int* (reserved for organizations established by international treaty); *.arpa* (reserved for Internet infrastructure functions). In addition, 244 countries and territories have two-letter country codes, such as *.us* for the United States and *.fr* for France.

The U.S. Commerce Department is in charge of adding top-level names, although it has delegated that function to the Internet Corporation for Assigned Names and Numbers, or ICANN, a nonprofit organization based in Marina del Rey, Calif.

DSL Acronym for *digital subscriber line*, for high-speed access to the Internet over the telephone network.

dot-com As an informal adjective describing companies that do business mainly on the *Internet*.

download To copy a file from one computer to another.

dpi Dots per inch, a measure of print and screen resolution.

DVD Acronym for *digital video disk* (or *digital versatile disk*), similar to CD-ROMs, but able to hold more music, video or data.

Easter eggs A hidden "surprise" in a program or on a

Web site, as an extra level of a computer game or a message.

e-mail Electronic mail or message. Also *e-book, e-business, e-commerce, e-shopping*. (The lowercase prefix is an exception to Webster's preference.)

emoticon A typographical cartoon or symbol generally used to indicate mood or appearance, as :-) and often looked at sideways. Also known as *smileys*.

end user, end-user Two words as a noun, hyphenated as an adjective.

FAQ Acronym for *frequently asked questions*, a format often used to summarize information on the *Internet*. Spell it out in copy.

freeware Free software.

FTP *File transfer protocol*, a common procedure for transferring files on the *Internet*. The acronym is acceptable in second reference.

GIF Acronym for *graphics interchange format*, a compression format for images. The acronym is acceptable in copy, but it should be explained somewhere in the story. Use lowercase in a file name.

hacker In common usage, the term has evolved to mean one who uses computer skills to unlawfully penetrate proprietary computer systems.

home page The "front" page of a particular Web site.

HTML For *hypertext markup language*. (Lowercase in Web addresses.)

HTTP For *hypertext transfer protocol*. (Lowercase in Web addresses.)

hyperlink A link from one part of an *Internet* page to another page, as a restaurant home page with a link to its menu.

hypertext A system of linking electronic documents.

intranet A private network inside a company or organization, only for internal use.

IP address *Internet* protocol address, a numeric address given to a computer connected to the *Internet*.

IT Acronym for *information technology*; spell it out.

Java A trademark of Sun Microsystems Inc. for a computer programming language that can be run across the *Internet*.

JavaScript A scripting language, developed by Netscape, designed to run inside Web pages.

JPEG, JPG Acronyms for *joint photographic experts group*, one of two common types of image compression mechanisms used on the World Wide Web (along with *GIF*).

kilobyte A unit of measurement for digital data storage. In the metric system, a *kilobyte* is 1,000 bytes; in computer binary terms, it is 1,024 bytes. Thus, 64KB means 64 times 1,024 bytes, or 65,536 bytes (not 64,000). Abbrev. *KB*. (Similarly, *MB* for megabytes, *GB* for gigabytes.) Note no space when used with numerals: *a 400KB file*.
Use *Kb* in abbreviations for kilobits and *Kbps* for kilobits per second.

listserv A software program for setting up and maintaining discussion groups through e-mail.

login, logon, logoff

megabyte A unit of storage capacity in computer systems, loosely 1 million bytes. Abbrev.: *MB*.

megahertz A measure of the speed of a computer processor. Abbrev.: *MHz*.

online One word in all cases for the computer connection term.

plug-in A smaller add-on computer program that works in conjunction with a larger application, such as a browser.

PDF *Portable document format*, a file format for the Adobe Acrobat reader.

Pentium processor A type of computer processor made by Intel Corp. Use Roman numerals in describing versions of this processor: *Pentium III*.

portal A starting point for searching the Web, often offering services of its own.

protocol A specification, such as *http*, that defines how computers will talk to each other.

RAM Acronym for *random access memory*, the "working memory" of a computer into which programs can be introduced and then executed.

ROM Acronym for *read-only memory*, a storage chip that cannot be reprogrammed by the computer user. Spell out.

search engine A service that allows a user to find a Web site by typing in the topic.

server The computer that is host to a Web site.

screen saver Two words.

shareware Software programs that may be tried without cost, but require a registration fee if used.

source code A set of instructions or tags in a programming language, generally used to build Web pages. (There is no plural form.)

URL *Uniform Resource Locator*, an *Internet* address. An example:
http://politics.ap.org/states/mi.html
http: is the protocol, or method of transfer.
// indicates a computer name follows.
politics is the server.

ap.org is the domain.
/states is the folder.
/mi.html indicates a file (*.html* is the file type).
The URL should always be the last line on a story; other under-dash material, such as a list of contributors to the story, goes above the *URL*.

Usenet A worldwide system of discussion areas called *newsgroups*.

World Wide Web A global system of linking documents, images, sounds and other files across the *Internet*. It is generally credited as the concept of researcher Tim Berners-Lee who developed the first practical system in 1989 at the European Laboratory for Particle Physics (Conseil Europeen pour la Recherche Nucleaire, or CERN).
The shorter *the Web* is acceptable. Also, *Web site* (an exception to Webster's preference), *Web page*. But *webcast*, *webmaster*.

whois A means of looking up names in a remote database, to find the "who" behind the domain name.

workstation One word.

XML For *extensible markup language*, used to sort, search and format information.

INTERNET SEARCH TIPS

Welcome to the Internet

Imagine a library with more than a billion books, all scattered across the floor in no discernible order — and no card catalog.

Welcome to the World Wide Web.

There are some very valuable items in the midst of this mess, but they're not always so easy to find. That's what makes the Web one of the most useful and one of the most frustrating weapons in the journalists' research arsenal.

Picking the Right Search Engine

Guiding you through this clutter are two basic tools: *search engines* and *subject directories*.

Search engines use a computer program (often called a spider, because it "crawls" across the Web) to compile databases of Web pages and then index them by content. *Metasearch engines* are programs that can search several of these indexes simultaneously.

Subject directories are organized collections of Web sites, generally chosen by human editors, and organized into categories. General-interest directories like Yahoo! try to cover the whole Web, while more specialized subject directories like FindLaw limit themselves to particular topics.

It's important to pick the right tool for the job. In general, search engines provide more quantity and subject directories more quality in their listings. Search engines are good for obscure topics or specific pieces of information (for example, the text of the Americans with Disabilities Act). Subject directories are good for giving you a broader overview (for example, community programs geared to help the disabled).

Keep in mind, however, that both are limited. They cover only a fraction of the Web, they're often out of date, and they miss mounds of information, particularly the contents of databases and PDF (portable document format) files. A good search engine or subject directory may be able to tell you that the FAA keeps records of all aviation accidents, but it can't tell you whether those records include a November 1997 crash near Barrow, Alaska.

Formulating a Search

Once you've found your search tool, you need to compose a search query. Choosing the right keywords is critical.

• Choose keywords as specific as possible. The surest way to produce a useless search is to use overly general keywords, such as "budget" or "nuclear energy." Nouns make the best keywords.

- Look for uncommon words that identify your topic and your topic only. Unusual proper or technical names are always good. Avoid ambiguous words or words with dual meanings.
- Use several keywords at a time, or better yet, use phrases. Searching for the phrase "time zone," for example, is better than searching for the words "time" and "zone" separately. For even better results, use two or three different phrases.
- Don't assume that everyone knows how to spell correctly. Use variant spellings and common misspellings ("enviroment," for example), particularly when dealing with a difficult word or name. If available, use the wildcard option to cover alternative spellings. Use synonyms, too. You might find with "physician" what you didn't find with "doctor."
- Use logical operators like AND, OR and NOT. "Apples AND Oranges" will find only sites that contain both words; "Apples OR Oranges" will find sites that have either; and "Apples NOT Oranges" will find only sites that do have apples but don't have oranges. Syntax varies from search engine to search engine, so check the help page if you're not sure how to structure these queries.

Refining a Search

Your first search often won't be your last. If you don't find what you need in the first 40 or so results, you need to refine your search and try again.

To narrow your search, add another keyword or two, or turn a couple of keywords into a phrase. Change an "OR" to an "AND." Pick a specific area of your topic rather than the topic itself. Pick the name of a main player in the story — particularly if it's an unusual name. Or, rather than searching for what you want, try to think instead of who might have the information, then search for that person or organization.

If your first effort, on the other hand, produces too few hits, widen your search. Choose more common words. Drop a keyword or two. Change an "AND" to an "OR." Use more synonyms or variant spellings.

Advanced Searching

Take advantage of advanced search options.

Some sites allow a "proximity operator" such as NEAR, which will find words close to each other, but not necessarily next to each other. Others permit wildcards, which act like the blank square in Scrabble: for example, 'psych*' will find psychology, psychoanalysis, and psychosomatic.

Most search engines allow you to restrict your search to specific domains (such as ".gov" for government sites, for example), or to specific elements of the page, such as photos, titles, or links.

Using Caution

Do not mistake the Web for an encyclopedia, and the search engine for a table of contents. The Web is a sprawling databank that's about one-quarter wheat and three-quarters chaff. Any information you find should be assessed with the same care that you use for everything else. In particular, check these points:

• Who is sponsoring the page? Is the author identifiable? You should avoid anonymous pages just as you avoid anonymous sources.

• Is there contact information in case you want to follow up? One way to check who owns a page is the Whois query at www.networksolutions.com/cgi-bin/whois/whois.

• Is the domain type (.edu or .gov, for example) appropriate for the information provided? Web sites set up by professional groups are generally more reliable than personal home pages.

• The source for the information on the page should be clearly stated, whether original or borrowed. Is it a primary or secondary source? Can it be checked somewhere else?

• Based on what you know, how accurate does the information seem? If there's something on the site that you know is incorrect, it's likely there are errors elsewhere.

• Are there any obvious signs of bias? One possible clue: The type of sites that this site links to.

• Is the page current? If it hasn't been updated lately, the information may be outdated. Right-click on the page and choose "View Info"; that often includes the date when the page was last modified.

Search Engine URLs

• *yahoo.com*
• *altavista.com*
• *hotbot.com*
• *google.com*
• *askjeeves.com*
• *dogpile.com*

Irish coffee Brewed coffee containing Irish whiskey, topped with cream or whipped cream.

Irish International Airlines The preferred name is *Aer Lingus*.

Headquarters is in Dublin, Ireland.

Irish Republican Army An outlawed paramilitary group committed to overthrowing Northern Ireland and its links with Britain. Its formal name is Provisional IRA. It was founded in 1969 with the aim of abolishing Northern Ireland as a predominantly British Protestant state. Its members claim direct lineage to the old IRA, which wrested the predominantly Catholic rest of Ireland from British control following a 1919-21 rebellion.

IRA is acceptable, but *Irish Republican Army* should be spelled out somewhere in the story.

Sinn Fein (pronounced "shin fane") is a legal political party that is linked with the *IRA*, but not technically a wing of it.

Iron Curtain

irregardless A double negative. *Regardless* is correct.

Islam Followers are called Muslims. Their holy book is the Quran, which according to Islamic belief was revealed by Allah (God) to the prophet Mohammed in the seventh century in Mecca and Medina. Their place of worship is a mosque. Their weekly holy day, equivalent of the Christian sabbath, is Friday.

It is the religion of about 850 million people in the world. Although Arabic is the language of the Quran and Muslim prayers,

not all Arabs are Muslims and not all Muslims are Arabs. Most of the world's Muslims live in a wide belt that stretches halfway around the world: across West Africa and North Africa, through the Arab countries of the Middle East and on to Turkey, Iran, Afghanistan, Pakistan and other Asian countries, parts of the former Soviet Union and western China, to Indonesia and the southern Philippines.

There are two major divisions in Islam:

—*Sunni* The biggest single sect in Islam, comprising about 85 percent of all Muslims. Nations with Sunni majorities include Egypt, Saudi Arabia and most other Arab nations, as well as non-Arab Turkey and Afghanistan. Most Palestinian Muslims and most West African Muslims are Sunnis.

The Saudis sometimes are referred to as Wahhabi Muslims. This is a subgroup within the Sunni branch of Islam.

—*Shiite* The second-largest sect, after the Sunni. Iran, home of militant Islamic fundamentalism, is the only nation with an overwhelming Shiite majority. Iraq, Lebanon and Bahrain have large Shiite communities, in proportion to their overall populations.

(The schism between Sunni and Shiite stems from the very early days of Islam and arguments over Mohammed's successors as caliph, the spiritual and temporal leader of Muslims. The Shiites wanted the caliphate to descend through Ali, Mohammed's son-in-law. Ali eventually became the fourth caliph, but he was murdered; Ali's son al-Hussein was massacred with his fighters at Karbala, in what is now Iraq. Shiites considered the later caliphs to be usurpers. The Sunnis no longer have a caliph.)

Titles for the clergy vary from sect to sect and from country to country, but these are the most common:

Grand Mufti — The highest authority in Quranic law and interpretation, a title used mostly by Sunnis.

Sheik — Used by most clergymen in the same manner that *the Rev.* is used as a Christian clerical title, especially common among Sunnis. (Not all sheiks are clergymen. *Sheik* can also be a secular title of respect or nobility)

Ayatollah — Used by Shiites, especially in Iran, to denote senior clergymen, such as *Ayatollah Ruhollah Khomeini.*

Hojatoleslam — A rank below ayatollah.

Mullah — Lower level clergy.

Imam — Used by some sects as a title for the prayer leader at a mosque. Among the Shiites, it usually has a more exalted connotation.

The adjective is *Islamic.*

See **Muslims** and **Nation of Islam**.

island Capitalize *island* or *islands* as part of a proper name: *Prince Edward Island, the Hawaiian Islands.*

Lowercase *island* and *islands* when they stand alone or when the reference is to the islands in a given area: *the Pacific islands.*

Lowercase all *island of* constructions: *the island of Nantucket.*

U.S. DATELINES: For communities on islands within the boundaries of the United States, use the community name and the state name:

EDGARTOWN, Mass. (AP) —

Honolulu stands alone, however.

DATELINES ABROAD: If an island has an identity of its own (*Bermuda, Prince Edward Island, Puerto Rico, Sardinia, Taiwan,* etc.) use the community name and the island name:

HAMILTON, Bermuda (AP) —

Havana, Hong Kong, Macau and *Singapore* stand alone, however.

If the island is part of a chain, use the community name and the name of the chain:

MANILA, Philippines (AP) —

Identify the name of the island in the text if relevant: *Manila is on the island of Luzon.*

For additional guidelines, see **datelines**.

it Use this pronoun, rather than *she*, in references to nations and ships.

italic Type face cannot be sent through AP computers. (It is used in this book only to indicate style examples and in using a word as a word.)

See **words as words**.

it's, its *It's* is a contraction for *it is* or *it has: It's up to you. It's been a long time.*

Its is the possessive form of the neuter pronoun: *The company lost its assets.*

IUD Acceptable on second reference for *intrauterine device.*

Ivy League Brown University, Columbia University, Cornell University, Dartmouth College, Harvard University, Princeton University, the University of Pennsylvania and Yale University.

Jacuzzi Trademark for a brand of whirlpool products. Generic terms are whirlpool bath or whirlpool spa.

jail Not interchangeable with *prison*. See the **prison, jail** entry.

Jamaica rum Not *Jamaican rum*.

Jane's All the World's Aircraft, Jane's Fighting Ships The reference sources for questions about aircraft and military ships not covered in this book.

The reference for nonmilitary ships is Lloyd's Register of Shipping.

January See **months**.

Japan Airlines *JAL* is acceptable on second reference.

Headquarters is in Tokyo.

Japan Current A warm current flowing from the Philippine Sea east of Taiwan and northeast past Japan.

jargon The special vocabulary and idioms of a particular class or occupational group.

In general, avoid jargon. When it is appropriate in a special context, include an explanation of any words likely to be unfamiliar to most readers.

See **dialect** and **word selection**.

Jaws of Life Trademark name for the tool used to pry open parts of a vehicle to free those trapped inside.

Jaycees Members of the U.S. Junior Chamber of Commerce, affiliated with the worldwide body, Junior Chamber International.

See the **fraternal organizations and service clubs** and **Junior Chamber of Commerce** entries.

J.C. Penney Co. Inc. Headquarters is in Plano, Texas.

jeep, Jeep Lowercase the military vehicle.

Capitalize if referring to the rugged, four-wheel drive civilian vehicle so trademarked.

Jehovah's Witnesses The denomination was founded in Pittsburgh in 1872 by Charles Taze Russell, a former Congregationalist layman.

Witnesses do most of their work through three legal corporations: the Watch Tower Bible and Tract Society of Pennsylvania, the Watchtower Bible and Tract Society of New York Inc., and, in England, the International Bible Students Association. A governing body consisting largely of the principal officers of the corporations oversees the denomination.

U.S. membership is listed at more than 900,000.

Jehovah's Witnesses believe that they adhere to the oldest religion on Earth, the worship of Almighty God revealed in the Bible as Jehovah.

They regard civil authority as necessary and obey it "as long as its laws do not contradict God's law." Witnesses refuse to bear arms, salute the flag or participate in secular government.

They refuse blood transfusions as being against the Bible, citing the section of Leviticus that reads: "Whatsoever man...eats any manner of blood, I will cut him off from among his people."

There are no formal titles, but there are three levels of ministry: *publishers* (baptized members who do evangelistic work), *regular pioneers*, who devote greater time to activities, and *special pioneers* (full-time workers).

Jell-O A trademark for a brand of gelatin dessert.

Jerusalem Stands alone in datelines.

Jesus The central figure of Christianity, he also may be called *Jesus Christ* or *Christ*.

Personal pronouns referring to him are lowercase.

jet, jetliner, jet plane See **aircraft terms**.

Jet Ski A registered trademark of Kawasaki for a type of personal watercraft.

Jew Use for men and women. Do not use *Jewess*.

Jewish congregations A Jewish congregation is autonomous. No synods, assemblies or hierarchies control the activities of an individual synagogue.

In the United States, there are three major expressions of Judaism:

1. Orthodox Judaism. Most of its congregations are represented nationally by the Union of Orthodox Jewish Congregations of America. Most of its rabbis are members of the Rabbinical Council of America.

2. Reform Judaism. Its national representatives are the Union of American Hebrew Congregations and the Central Conference of American Rabbis.

3. Conservative Judaism. Its national representatives are the United Synagogue of Conservative Judaism and the Rabbinical Assembly.

The American Jewish Year Book estimates 5.7 million U.S. Jews as of 1997, including ethnic Jews who do not practice Judaism. Conservative and Reform are the largest U.S. branches of Judaism, well exceeding the Orthodox and the very small Reconstructionist branches.

Jews generally believe that a divine kingdom will be established on Earth, opening a messianic era that will be marked by peace and bliss. They also believe that they have a mandate from God to work toward this kingdom.

The only formal titles in use are *rabbi*, for the spiritual leader of a congregation, and *cantor*, for the individual who leads the congregation in song. Capitalize these titles before an individual's full name on first reference. On second reference, use only the last name.

See **religious titles** and **Zionism**.

Jewish holy days See separate listings for **Hanukkah, Passover, Purim, Rosh Hashana, Shavuot, Sukkot** and **Yom Kippur.**

The High Holy Days are Rosh Hashana and Yom Kippur. All Jewish holy days and the Jewish Sabbath start at sunset before the day marked on most calendars.

jibe See the **gibe, jibe** entry.

job descriptions Always lowercase. See **titles.**

John F. Kennedy Space Center Located in Cape Canaveral, Fla., it is the National Aeronautics and Space Administration's principal launch site for manned spacecraft.

Kennedy Space Center is acceptable in all references.

For datelines on launch stories:

CAPE CANAVERAL, Fla. (AP) —

See **Lyndon B. Johnson Space Center.**

Johns Hopkins University No apostrophes.

Joint Chiefs of Staff Also: *the Joint Chiefs.* But lowercase *the chiefs* or *the chiefs of staff.*

Jr. See the **junior, senior** entry.

judge Capitalize before a name when it is the formal title for an individual who presides in a court of law. Do not continue to use the title in second reference.

Do not use *court* as part of the title unless confusion would result without it:

—No *court* in the title: *U.S. District Judge John Sirica, District Judge John Sirica, federal Judge John Sirica, Judge John Sirica, U.S. Circuit Judge Homer Thornberry, appellate Judge John Blair.*

—*Court* needed in the title: *Juvenile Court Judge John Jones, Criminal Court Judge John Jones, Superior Court Judge Robert Harrison, state Supreme Court Judge William Cushing.*

When the formal title *chief judge* is relevant, put the court name after the judge's name: *Chief Judge John Sirica of the U.S. District Court in Washington, D.C.; Chief Judge Clement F. Haynsworth Jr. of the 4th U.S. Circuit Court of Appeals.*

Do not pile up long court names before the name of a judge. Make it *Judge John Smith of Allegheny County Common Pleas Court.* Not: *Allegheny County Common Pleas Court Judge John Smith.*

Lowercase *judge* as an occupational designation in phrases such as *beauty contest judge Bert Parks.*

See **administrative law judge; court names; judicial branch;** and **justice.**

judge advocate The plural: *judge advocates.* Also: *judge advocate general, judge advocates general.*

Capitalize as a formal title before a name.

See **titles.**

judgment Not *judgement.*

judicial branch Always lowercase.

The federal court system that exists today as the outgrowth of Article 3 of the Constitution is composed of the Supreme Court of the United States, the U.S. Court of Appeals, U.S. District Courts, and the U.S. Customs Court. There are also four district judges for U.S. territories.

The U.S. Tax Court and the U.S. Court of Military Appeals are not part of the judicial branch as such.

For more detail on all federal courts, see separate entries under the names listed here.

Judicial Conference of the United States

This rule-making body for the courts of the judicial branch meets twice a year. Its 25 members are the chief justice, the chief judges of the 11 circuit courts, one district judge from each of the circuits, and the chief judges of the U.S. Court of Claims and the U.S. Court of Customs and Patent Appeals.

Day-to-day functions are handled by the Administrative Office of U.S. Courts.

jukebox

July See **months**.

jumbo jet

Any very large jet plane, including the Boeing 747, the DC-10, the L-1011 and the C-5A.

June See **months**.

junior, senior

Abbreviate as *Jr.* and *Sr.* only with full names of persons or animals. Do not precede by a comma: *Joseph P. Kennedy Jr.*

The notation *II* or *2nd* may be used if it is the individual's pref-

erence. Note, however, that *II* and *2nd* are not necessarily the equivalent of *junior* — they often are used by a grandson or nephew.

If necessary to distinguish between father and son in second reference, use the *elder Smith* or the *younger Smith*.

See **names**.

Junior Chamber of Commerce

A volunteer organization of young men and women involved in civic service and leadership training.

Members are called *Jaycees*.

U.S. headquarters is in Tulsa, Okla.; international headquarters in Coral Gables, Fla.

See **Jaycees**.

junta See the **government, junta, regime** entry.

jury

The word takes singular verbs and pronouns: *The jury has been sequestered until it reaches a verdict.*

Do not use awkward phrases such as *seven-man, five-woman jury.* Make it: *a jury of seven men and five women.*

Do not capitalize: *a U.S. District Court jury, a federal jury, a Massachusetts Superior Court jury, a Los Angeles County grand jury.*

See **grand jury**.

justice

Capitalize before a name when it is the formal title. It is the formal title for members of the U.S. Supreme Court and for jurists on some state courts. In such cases, do not use *judge* in first or subsequent references.

See **judge**; **Supreme Court of the United States**; and **titles**.

justice of the peace Capitalize as a formal title before a name. Do not abbreviate.

See **titles**.

juvenile delinquent Juveniles may be declared delinquents in many states for anti-social behavior or for breaking the law. In some states, laws prohibit publishing or broadcasting the names of juvenile delinquents.

Follow the local practice unless there is a compelling reason to the contrary. Consult with the General Desk if you believe such an exception is warranted.

K

K Use *K* in references to modem transmission speeds, in keeping with standard usage: *a 56K modem* (no space after numeral).

The abbreviation should not be used to mean 1,000 or $1,000.

Kansas Abbrev.: *Kan.* See **state names**.

Kansas City Use *KANSAS CITY, Kan.,* or *KANSAS CITY, Mo.,* in datelines to avoid confusion between the two.

karat See the **carat, caret, karat** entry.

Kelvin scale A scale of temperature based on, but different from, the Celsius scale. It is used primarily in science to record very high and very low temperatures. The Kelvin scale starts at zero and indicates the total absence of heat (absolute zero).

Zero on the Kelvin scale is equal to minus 273.15 degrees Celsius and minus 459.67 degrees Fahrenheit.

The freezing point of water is 273.16 degrees Kelvin. The boiling point of water is 373.16 degrees Kelvin.

To convert from Celsius to Kelvin, add 273.15 to the Celsius temperature.

See **Celsius** and **Fahrenheit**.

Kennedy Space Center See **John F. Kennedy Space Center**.

Kentucky Abbrev.: *Ky.* Legally a commonwealth, not a state. See **state** and **state names**.

kerosene Formerly a trade mark, now a generic term.

ketchup Not *catchup* or *catsup*.

keynote address Also: *keynote speech*.

Keystone Kops

KGB Acceptable on first reference, but the story should contain a phrase identifying it as the former Russian secret police and intelligence agency.

The initials stand for the Russian words meaning *Committee for State Security*.

kibbutz An Israeli collective settlement.

The plural is *kibbutzim*.

kidnap, kidnapped, kidnapping, kidnapper

kids Use *children* unless you are talking about goats, or the use of *kids* as an informal synonym for *children* is appropriate in the context.

killer See the **assassin, killer, murderer** entry.

kilo- A prefix denoting 1,000 units of a measure. Move a decimal point three places to the right, adding zeros if necessary, to convert to the basic unit: 10.5 kilograms equals 10,500 grams.

kilocycles The new term is *kilohertz.*

kilogram The metric term for 1,000 grams.

A kilogram is equal to approximately 2.2 pounds or 35 ounces.

To convert to pounds, multiply by 2.2 (9 kilograms x 2.2 equals 19.8 pounds).

See **gram; metric system**; and **pound.**

kilohertz Equals 1,000 hertz (1,000 cycles per second), replacing *kilocycles* as the correct term in applications such as broadcast frequencies.

kilometer The metric term for 1,000 meters. (Abbrev.: *km.*)

A kilometer is equal to approximately 3,281 feet, or five-eighths (0.62) of a mile.

To convert to miles, multiply by 0.62 (5 kilometers x 0.62 equals 3.1 miles).

See **meter; metric system**; and **miles.**

kiloton, kilotonnage A unit used to measure the power of nuclear explosions. One kiloton has the explosive force of 1,000 tons of TNT.

The atomic bomb dropped Aug. 6, 1945, on Hiroshima, Japan, in the first use of the bomb as a weapon had an explosive force of 20 kilotons.

A *megaton* has the force of a million tons of TNT. A *gigaton* has the force of a billion tons of TNT.

kilowatt-hour The amount of electrical energy consumed when 1,000 watts are used for one hour.

The abbreviation *kwh* is acceptable on second reference.

kindergarten

king Capitalize only when used before the name of royalty: *King George VI.* Continue in subsequent references that use the king's given name: *King George*, not *George.*

Lowercase *king* when it stands alone.

Capitalize in plural uses before names: *Kings George and Edward.*

Lowercase in phrases such as *chess king Bobby Fischer.*

See **nobility** and **titles.**

Kitty Litter A brand of absorbent material used in cat litter boxes. Use a generic term such as *cat box litter.*

Klan in America See **Ku Klux Klan.**

Kleenex A trademark for a brand of facial tissue.

KLM Royal Dutch Airlines A *KLM airliner* is acceptable in any reference.

Headquarters is in Amsterdam, Netherlands.

Kmart No hyphen, no space, lowercase *m.* Headquarters is in Troy, Mich.

Knesset The Israeli parliament. See **foreign legislative bodies.**

knickknack

knight See **nobility**.

Knights of Columbus *K. of C.* or *the Knights* may be used on second reference.

See the **fraternal organizations and service clubs** entry.

knot A knot is 1 nautical mile (6,076.10 feet) per hour. It is redundant to say *knots per hour*.

To convert knots into approximate statute miles per hour, multiply knots by 1.15.

Always use figures: *Winds were at 7 to 9 knots; a 10-knot wind.*

See **nautical mile**.

know-how

Kodak A trademark for cameras and other photographic products made by Eastman Kodak Co. of Rochester, N.Y.

Koran See **Quran**.

Korean names North Korean names are generally three separate words, each starting with a capital letter: *Kim Il Sung.* South Korean names are three words with the second two names hyphenated and a lowercase letter after the hyphen: *Kim Young-sam.*

In all cases, the family name comes first.

Korean War But lowercase *Korean conflict.*

kosher Always lowercase.

kowtow

Kriss Kringle Not *Kris.*

kudos It means credit or praise for an achievement.

The word is singular and takes singular verbs.

Ku Klux Klan There are a number of separate organizations known as the *Klan in America.*

Some of them do not use the full name *Ku Klux Klan,* but each may be called that, and the *KKK* initials may be used for any of them on second reference.

The two largest Klan organizations are the National Knights of the Ku Klux Klan, based at Stone Mountain, Ga., and the United Klans of America, based at Tuscaloosa, Ala.

An Imperial Board, composed of leaders from the various groups, meets occasionally to coordinate activities.

Capitalize formal titles before a name: *Imperial Wizard James R. Venable, Grand Dragon Dale Reusch.* Members are *Klansmen.*

Kuomintang The Chinese Nationalist political party. Do not follow with the word *party. Tang* means party.

Kuril Islands Use in datelines after a community name in stories from these islands. Name an individual island, if needed, in the text.

Explain in the text that a small portion of the archipelago is claimed by Japan but most are part of Russia.

Kuwait Stands alone in datelines.

Kwanzaa A seven-day celebration, based on African festivals, from Dec. 26 through Jan. 1. The name comes from the Swahili for "first fruits."

L

la See **foreign particles**.

Labor Day The first Monday in September.

Laborers' International Union of North America The shortened form *Laborers' union* is acceptable in all references.
Headquarters is in Washington.

Labor Party Not *labour*, even if British.

Labrador The mainland portion of the Canadian province of Newfoundland.
Use *Newfoundland* in datelines after the name of a community. Specify in the text that it is in Labrador.

Ladies' Home Journal

lady Do not use as a synonym for *woman*. *Lady* may be used when it is a courtesy title or when a specific reference to fine manners is appropriate without patronizing overtones.
See **nobility**.

lager (beer)

lake Capitalize as part of a proper name: *Lake Erie, Canandaigua Lake, the Finger Lakes.*

Lowercase in plural uses: *lakes Erie and Ontario; Canandaigua and Seneca lakes.*

lamebrain

lame duck (n.) **lame-duck** (adj.)

Land Rover No hyphen. A trademark for a brand of all-terrain vehicle.

languages Capitalize the proper names of languages and dialects: *Aramaic, Cajun, English, Gullah, Persian, Serbo-Croatian, Yiddish.*

lanolin Formerly a trademark, now a generic term.

larceny See the **burglary, larceny, robbery, theft** entry.

last Avoid the use of last as a synonym for latest if it might imply finality. *The last time it rained, I forgot my umbrella,* is acceptable. But: *The last announcement was made at noon today* may leave the reader wondering whether the announcement was the final announcement, or whether others are to follow.
The word *last* is not necessary to convey the notion of most recent when the name of a month or day is used:
Preferred: *It happened*

Wednesday. It happened in April.
Correct, but redundant: *It happened last Wednesday.*

But: *It happened last week. It happened last month.*

Lastex A trademark for a type of elastic yarn.

Last Supper

late Do not use it to describe someone's actions while alive.

Wrong: *Only the late senator opposed this bill.* (The senator was not dead at that time.)

latex A resin-based substance used in making elastic materials and paints.

Latin America See **Western Hemisphere**.

Latin Rite See **Roman Catholic Church**.

latitude and longitude

Latitude, the distance north or south of the equator, is designated by parallels. *Longitude,* the distance east or west of Greenwich, England, is designated by meridians.

Use these forms to express degrees of latitude and longitude: *New York City lies at 40 degrees 45 minutes north latitude and 74 degrees 0 minutes west longitude; New York City lies south of the 41st parallel north and along the 74th meridian west.*

Latter Day Saints, Latter-day Saints See Church of Jesus Christ of Latter-day Saints.

Laundromat A trademark for a coin-operated laundry.

Law Enforcement Assistance Administration *LEAA* is acceptable on second reference.

laws Capitalize legislative acts but not bills: *the Taft-Hartley Act, the Kennedy bill.*

lawsuit *Civil lawsuit* is redundant.

lawyer A generic term for all members of the bar.

An *attorney* is someone legally appointed or empowered to act for another, usually, but not always, a lawyer. An *attorney at law* is a lawyer.

A *barrister* is an English lawyer who is specially trained and appears exclusively as a trial lawyer in higher courts. He is retained by a solicitor, not directly by the client. There is no equivalent term in the United States.

Counselor, when used in a legal sense, means a person who conducts a case in court, usually, but not always, a lawyer. A *counselor at law* is a lawyer. *Counsel* frequently is used collectively for a group of counselors.

A *solicitor* in England is a lawyer who performs legal services for the public. A solicitor appears in lower courts but does not have the right to appear in higher courts, which are reserved to barristers.

A *solicitor* in the United States is a lawyer employed by a governmental body. *Solicitor* is generally a job description, but in some agencies it is a formal title.

Solicitor general is the formal title for a chief law officer (where there is no attorney general) or for the chief assistant to the law officer (when there is an attorney general). Capitalize when used before a name.

Do not use *lawyer* as a formal title.

See the **attorney, lawyer** entry and **titles**.

lay, lie The action word is *lay*. It takes a direct object. *Laid* is the form for its past tense and its past participle. Its present participle is *laying*.

Lie indicates a state of reclining along a horizontal plane. It does not take a direct object. Its past tense is *lay*. Its past participle is *lain*. Its present participle is *lying*.

When *lie* means to make an untrue statement, the verb forms are *lie, lied, lying*.

Some examples:

PRESENT OR FUTURE TENSES:

Right: *I will lay the book on the table. The prosecutor tried to lay the blame on him.*

Wrong: *He lays on the beach all day. I will lay down.*

Right: *He lies on the beach all day. I will lie down.*

IN THE PAST TENSE:

Right: *I laid the book on the table. The prosecutor has laid the blame on him.*

Right: *He lay on the beach all day. He has lain on the beach all day. I lay down. I have lain down.*

WITH THE PRESENT PARTICIPLE:

Right: *I am laying the book on the table. The prosecutor is laying the blame on him.*

Right: *He is lying on the beach. I am lying down.*

Leaning Tower of Pisa

leatherneck Lowercase this nickname for a member of the U.S. Marine Corps. It is derived from the leather lining that was formerly part of the collar on the Marine uniform.

lectern, podium, pulpit, rostrum A speaker stands *behind a lectern, on a podium* or *rostrum,* or *in the pulpit.*

lecturer A formal title in the Christian Science Church. An occupational description in other uses.

lectures Capitalize and use quotation marks for their formal titles, as described in **composition titles**.

left hand (n.) **left-handed** (adj.) **left-hander** (n.)

leftist, ultra-leftist In general, avoid these terms in favor of a more precise description of an individual's political philosophy.

As popularly used today, particularly abroad, *leftist* often applies to someone who is merely liberal or believes in a form of democratic socialism.

Ultra-leftist suggests an individual who subscribes to a communist view or one holding that liberal or socialist change cannot come within the present form of government.

See **radical** and the **rightist, ultra-rightist** entry.

left wing (n.) But: *left-wing* (adj.), *left-winger* (n.).

legal holiday See the **holidays and holy days** entry.

legerdemain

legion, legionnaire See **American Legion** and **French Foreign legion**.

Legionnaires' disease The disease takes its name from an outbreak at the Pennsylvania American Legion convention held at the Bellevue-Stratford Hotel in Philadelphia in July 1976. Thirty-four people died — 29 Legionnaires or family members and five other people who had been near the hotel. The disease was diagnosed for the first time after 221 people contracted the illness in Philadelphia.

The bacterium believed to be responsible is found in soil and grows in water, such as air-conditioning ducts, storage tanks and rivers.

The Centers for Disease Control and Prevention in Atlanta estimates that 25,000 people a year in the United States get the disease, whose pneumonialike symptoms begin in two to three days after exposure.

legislative titles

FIRST REFERENCE FORM: Use *Rep.*, *Reps.*, *Sen.* and *Sens.* as formal titles before one or more names in regular text. Spell out and capitalize these titles before one or more names in a direct quotation. Spell out and lowercase *representative* and *senator* in other uses.

Spell out other legislative titles in all uses. Capitalize formal titles such as *assemblyman, assemblywoman, city councilor, delegate,* etc., when they are used before a name. Lowercase in other uses.

Add *U.S.* or state before a title only if necessary to avoid confusion: *U.S. Sen. Nancy Kassebaum spoke with state Sen. Hugh Carter.*

FIRST REFERENCE PRACTICE: The use of a title such as *Rep.* or *Sen.* in first reference is normal in most stories. It is not mandatory, however, provided an individual's title is given later in the story.

Deletion of the title on first reference is frequently appropriate, for example, when an individual has become well known: *Barry Goldwater endorsed President Ford today. The Arizona senator said he believes the president deserves another term.*

SECOND REFERENCE: Do not use legislative titles before a name on second reference unless they are part of a direct quotation.

CONGRESSMAN, CONGRESSWOMAN: *Rep.* and *U.S. Rep.* are the preferred first-reference forms when a formal title is used before the name of a U.S. House member. The words *congressman* or *congresswoman,* in lowercase, may be used in subsequent references that do not use an individual's name, just as senator is used in references to members of the Senate.

Congressman and *congresswoman* should appear as capitalized formal titles before a name only in direct quotation.

ORGANIZATIONAL TITLES: Capitalize titles for formal, organizational offices within a legislative body when they are used before a name: *Speaker Thomas P. O'Neill, Majority Leader Robert C. Byrd, Minority Leader John J. Rhodes, Democratic Whip James C. Wright, Chairman John J. Sparkman of the Senate Foreign Relations Committee, President Pro Tem John C. Stennis.*

See party **affiliation** and **titles**.

legislature Capitalize when preceded by the name of a state: *the Kansas Legislature.*

Retain capitalization when the state name is dropped but the reference is specifically to that state's legislature:

TOPEKA, Kan. (AP) — Both houses of the Legislature adjourned today.

Capitalize *legislature* in subsequent specific references and in such constructions as: *the 100th Legislature, the state Legislature.*

Although the word *legislature* is not part of the formal, proper name for the lawmaking bodies in many states, it commonly is used that way and should be treated as such in any story that does not use the formal name.

If a given context or local practice calls for the use of a formal name such as *Missouri General Assembly*, retain the capital letters if the name of the state can be dropped, but lowercase the word *assembly* if it stands alone. Lowercase *legislature* if a story uses it in a subsequent reference to a body identified as a general assembly.

Lowercase *legislature* when used generically: *No legislature has approved the amendment.*

Use *legislature* in lowercase for all plural references: *The Arkansas and Colorado legislatures are considering the amendment.*

In 49 states the separate bodies are a senate and a *house* or *assembly.* The *Nebraska Legislature* is a unicameral body.

See **assembly; general assembly; governmental bodies; house of representatives;** and **senate.**

Lent The period from Ash Wednesday through Holy Saturday, the day before Easter. The 40-day Lenten period for penance, suggested by Christ's 40 days in the desert, does not include the six Sundays between Ash Wednesday and Easter.

See **Easter** for the method of computing when Easter occurs.

lesbian, lesbianism Lowercase in references to homosexual women, except in names of organizations.

less See the **fewer, less** entry.

-less No hyphen before this suffix:

childless   waterless
tailless

let up (v.) **letup** (n. and adj.)

Levi's A trademark for a brand of jeans.

liaison

liberal, liberalism See the **political parties and philosophies** entry.

lie See the **lay, lie** entry.

lie in state Only people who are entitled to a state funeral may formally lie in state. In the United States, this occurs in the rotunda in the Capitol.

Those entitled to a state funeral are a president, a former president, a president-elect or any other person designated by the president.

Members of Congress may lie in state, and a number have done so. The decision is either house's to make, although the formal process normally begins with a request from the president.

Those entitled to an official funeral, but not to lie in state, are the vice president, the chief justice, Cabinet members and other government officials when designated by the president.

lieutenant See **military titles.**

lieutenant governor Capitalize and abbreviate as *Lt. Gov.* or *Lt. Govs.* when used as a formal title before one or more names in regular text. Capitalize and spell out when used as a formal title before one or more names in direct quotations.

Lowercase and spell out in all other uses.

See **titles.**

Life Saver, Life Savers Trademarks for a brand of roll candy.

life-size

lifestyle

lifetime

lift off (v.) **liftoff** (n. and adj.)

light, lighted, lighting Do not use *lit* as the past tense form.

lightning The electrical discharge.

light-year The distance that light travels in one year at the rate of 186,282 miles per second. It works out to about 5.88 trillion miles (5,878,612,800,000 miles).

likable Not *likeable.*

like, as

Use *like* as a preposition to compare nouns and pronouns. It requires an object: *Jim blocks like a pro.*

The conjunction *as* is the correct word to introduce clauses: *Jim blocks the linebacker as he should.*

like- Follow with a hyphen when used as a prefix meaning similar to:

like-minded   like-natured

No hyphen in words that have meanings of their own:

likelihood   likewise
likeness

-like Do not precede this suffix by a hyphen unless the letter *l* would be tripled:

bill-like   lifelike
businesslike   shell-like

limousine

linage, lineage *Linage* is the number of lines.

Lineage is ancestry or descent.

Lincoln's Birthday Capitalize *birthday* in references to the holiday.

Lincoln was born Feb. 12. His birthday is not a federal legal holiday.

line numbers Use figures and lowercase the word line in naming individual lines of a text: *line 1, line 9.* But: *the first line, the 10th line.*

linoleum Formerly a trademark, now a generic term.

Linotype A trademark for a brand of typesetting machine that casts an entire line of type in one bar or slug.

lion's share The term comes

from an Aesop fable in which the lion took all the spoils of a joint hunt.

Use it to mean the whole of something, or the best and biggest portion.

Do not use it to mean majority.

liter The basic unit of volume in the metric system. It is defined as the volume occupied by 1 kilogram of distilled water at 4 degrees Celsius. It works out to a total of 1,000 cubic centimeters (1 cubic decimeter).

It takes 1,000 milliliters to make a liter.

A liter is equal to approximately 34 fluid ounces or 1.06 liquid quarts. A liter equals .91 of a dry quart. The metric system makes no distinction between dry volume and liquid volume.

To convert to liquid quarts, multiply by 1.06 (4 liters x 1.06 equals 4.24 liquid quarts).

To convert to dry quarts, multiply by .91 (4 liters x .91 equals 3.64 dry quarts).

To convert to liquid gallons, multiply by .26 (8 liters x .26 equals 2.08 gallons).

See **gallon**; **kilogram**; **metric system**; **quart (dry)**; and **quart (liquid)**.

literally See the **figuratively, literally** entry.

literature See **composition titles**.

Little League, Little League Baseball The official name of the worldwide youth baseball and softball organization and its affiliated local leagues.

livable Not *liveable*.

livid It is not a synonym for *fiery, bright, crimson, red* or *flaming*. If a person turns *livid* with rage, his face becomes ashen or pale. It can mean *blue, bluish gray, gray, dull white, dull purple* or *grayish black*.

Lloyds Bank International Ltd. A prominent bank with headquarters in London.

Lloyd's of London A prominent group of insurance companies with headquarters in London.

Lloyd's Register of Shipping The reference source for questions about nonmilitary ships not covered in this book.

It is published by Lloyd's Register of Shipping Trust Corp. Ltd. in London.

local Avoid the irrelevant use of the word.

Irrelevant: *The injured were taken to a local hospital.*

Better: *The injured were taken to a hospital.*

local of a union Always use a figure and capitalize *local* when giving the name of a union subdivision: *Local 222 of The Newspaper Guild.*

Lowercase *local* standing alone in plural uses: *The local will vote Tuesday. He spoke to locals 2, 4 and 10.*

Lockheed Martin Corp. (No hyphen.) Headquarters is in Bethesda, Md.

lodges See the **fraternal organizations and service clubs** entry.

London The city in England stands alone in datelines.

long distance, long-distance Always a hyphen in reference to telephone calls: *We keep in touch by long-distance. He called long-distance. She took the long-distance call.*

In other uses, hyphenate only when used as a compound modifier: *She traveled a long distance. She made a long-distance trip.*

longitude See the **latitude and longitude** entry.

longshoreman Capitalize *longshoreman* only if the intended meaning is that the individual is a member of the International Longshore and Warehouse Union or the International Longshoremen's Association.

long term, long-term Hyphenate when used as a compound modifier: *We will win in the long term. He has a long-term assignment.*

long time, longtime *They have known each other a long time. They are longtime partners.*

long ton Also known as a *British ton.* Equal to 2,240 pounds. See **ton.**

Lord's Supper See **sacraments.**

Los Angeles The city in California stands alone in datelines.
Confine *L.A.* to quoted matter.

LOT Polish Airlines Headquarters is in Warsaw, Poland.

Louisiana Abbrev.: *La.* See **state names.**

Low Countries Belgium, Luxembourg and Netherlands.

lowercase One word (n., v., adj.) when referring to the absence of capital letters. Originally from printers' practice.

LSD Acceptable in all references for *lysergic acid diethylamide.*

Lt. Gov. See **lieutenant governor.**

Lucite A trademark for an acrylic plastic.

Lufthansa German Airlines A *Lufthansa airliner* is acceptable in any reference.
Headquarters is in Cologne, Germany.

Lutheran churches The basic unit of government in Lutheran practice is the congregation. It normally is administered by a council, headed either by the senior pastor or a lay person elected from the membership of the council. The council customarily consists of a congregation's clergy and elected lay people.

The three major Lutheran bodies in the United States merged on Jan. 1, 1988, into a new organization, the Evangelical Lutheran Church in America, with about 5.3 million members in more than 11,000 congregations.

The Lutheran Church in America was the largest and most geographically spread of the three and was formed in 1962 from a merger of four bodies with Danish, Finnish, German and Swedish backgrounds. It merged with the American Lutheran Church, a mostly Midwestern group formed in 1960 through a merger of four bodies with Danish, German and Norwegian backgrounds, and the relatively small west-central Association of Evangelical Lutheran Churches.

The Lutheran Church-Missouri Synod, founded in 1847, has 2.6 million members and is a separate and distinct body.

Lutheran teachings go back to Martin Luther, a 16th-century Roman Catholic priest whose objections to elements of Roman Catholic practice began the movement known as the Protestant Reformation.

Members of the clergy are known as *ministers. Pastor* applies if a minister leads a congregation.

On first reference, use *the Rev.* before the name of a man or woman. On second reference, use only the last name.

See **religious titles**.

Luxembourg Stands alone in datelines.

-ly Do not use a hyphen between adverbs ending in *-ly* and adjectives they modify: *an easily remembered rule, a badly damaged island, a fully informed woman.*

See the compound modifiers section of the **hyphen** entry.

Lyndon B. Johnson Space Center Formerly the Manned Spacecraft Center. Located in Houston, it is the National Aeronautics and Space Administration's principal control and training center for manned spaceflight.

Johnson Space Center is acceptable in all references.

In datelines:

SPACE CENTER, Houston (AP) —

See **John F. Kennedy Space Center**.

Macau Stands alone in datelines. (Spelling is an exception to Webster's New World.)

Mace A trademark, shortened from *Chemical Mace*, for a brand of tear gas that is packaged in an aerosol canister and temporarily stuns its victims.

machine gun (n.) But: *machine-gun* (v. and adj.), *machine-gunner*.
See **weapons**.

Mach number Named for Ernst Mach, an Austrian physicist, the figure represents the ratio of the speed of an object to the speed of sound in the surrounding medium, such as air, through which the object is moving.
A rule of thumb for speed of sound is approximately 750 miles per hour at sea level and approximately 660 miles per hour at 30,000 feet above sea level.
A body traveling at *Mach 1* would be traveling at the speed of sound. *Mach 2* would equal twice the speed of sound.

Mafia Lowercase as a synonym for organized crime. (A cap *M* can be used when referring to the secret society of criminals.)

magazine names Capitalize the name but do not place it in quotes. Lowercase magazine unless it is part of the publication's formal title: *Harper's Magazine, Newsweek magazine, Time magazine*.
Check the masthead if in doubt.

magistrate Capitalize when used as a formal title before a name. See **titles**.

Magna Carta Not Magna Charta. The charter the English barons forced King John of England to grant at Runnymede in June 1215. It guaranteed certain civil and political liberties.

Mailgram A trademark for a telegram sent to a post office near the recipient's address and delivered to the address by a letter carrier.

mailman *Letter carrier* or *postal worker* is preferable because many women hold this job.

Maine Do not abbreviate. See **state names**.

mainland China See **China**.

major See **military titles**.

majority, plurality *Majority* means more than half of an amount.

Plurality means more than the next highest number.

COMPUTING MAJORITY: To describe how large a majority is, take the figure that is more than half and subtract everything else from it: If 100,000 votes were cast in an election and one candidate received 60,000 while opponents received 40,000, the winner would have a *majority* of 20,000 votes.

COMPUTING PLURALITY: To describe how large a plurality is, take the highest number and subtract from it the next highest number: If, in the election example above, the second-place finisher had 25,000 votes, the winner's *plurality* would be 35,000 votes.

Suppose, however, that no candidate in this example had a majority. If the first-place finisher had 40,000 votes and the second-place finisher had 30,000, for example, the leader's *plurality* would be 10,000 votes.

USAGE: When *majority* and *plurality* are used alone, they take singular verbs and pronouns: *The majority has made its decision.*

If a plural word follows an *of* construction, the decision on whether to use a singular or plural verb depends on the sense of the sentence: *A majority of two votes is not adequate to control the committee. The majority of the houses on the block were destroyed.*

majority leader Capitalize when used as a formal title before a name: *Majority Leader Richard Gephardt.* Lowercase elsewhere.
See **legislative titles** and **titles**.

make up (v.) **makeup** (n., adj.)

malarkey Not *malarky.*

Maldives Use this official name with a community name in a dateline. The body of the story should note that the nation frequently is called the *Maldive Islands.*

Mallorca Use instead of Spain in datelines on stories from communities on this island.

man, mankind Either may be used when both men and women are involved and no other term is convenient. In these cases, do not use duplicate phrases such as *a man or a woman* or *mankind and womankind.*
Frequently the best choice is a substitute such as *humanity, a person* or *an individual.*
See **women**.

manageable

manager Capitalize when used as a formal title before a name: *General Manager Dick O'Connell.*
Do not capitalize in job descriptions such as *equipment manager John Smith.*
See **titles**.

managing editor Capitalize when used as a formal title before a name.
See **titles**.

Manitoba A province of central Canada. Do not abbreviate.
See **datelines**.

manslaughter See the **homicide, murder, manslaughter** entry.

mantel, mantle A *mantel* is a shelf. A *mantle* is a cloak.

Maoism (Maoist) The communist philosophy and policies of Mao Tse-tung. See the **political parties and philosophies** entry.

March See **months**.

Mardi Gras Literally *fat Tuesday*, the term describes a day of merrymaking on the Tuesday before Ash Wednesday.

In New Orleans and many Roman Catholic countries, the Tuesday celebration is preceded by a week or more of parades and parties.

marijuana Not *marihuana*.

Marines Capitalize when referring to U.S. forces: *the U.S. Marines, the Marines, the Marine Corps, Marine regulations.* Do not use the abbreviation *USMC*.

Capitalize *Marine* when referring to an individual in a Marine Corps unit: *He is a Marine.*

Maritime Provinces The Canadian provinces of Nova Scotia, New Brunswick and Prince Edward Island.

marketbasket, marketplace

marquess, marchioness, marquis, marquise See **nobility**.

marshal, marshaled, marshaling, Marshall *Marshal* is the spelling for both the verb and the noun: *Marilyn will marshal her forces. Erwin Rommel was a field marshal.*

Marshall is used in proper names: *George C. Marshall, John Marshall, the Marshall Islands.*

Marshall Islands Named for John Marshall, a British explorer.

In datelines, give the name of a city and *Marshall Islands*. List the name of an individual island in the text.

Martin Luther King Jr. Day Federal holiday honoring Martin Luther King Jr., who was born Jan. 15, 1929, is on the third Monday in January. It was first celebrated in 1986.

Marxism (Marxist) The system of thought developed by Karl Marx and Friedrich Engels. See the **political parties and philosophies** entry.

Maryland Abbrev.: *Md.* See **state names**.

Mason-Dixon Line The boundary line between Pennsylvania and Maryland, generally regarded as separating the North from the South. (Named for 18th-century surveyors Charles Mason and Jeremiah Dixon, the line later was extended to West Virginia.)

Masonite A trademark for a brand of hardboard.

Mass It is *celebrated*, not *said*. Always capitalize when referring to the ceremony, but lowercase any preceding adjectives: *high Mass, low Mass, requiem Mass.*

In Eastern Orthodox churches the correct term is *Divine Liturgy*. See **Roman Catholic Church**.

Massachusetts Abbrev.: *Mass.* Legally a commonwealth, not a state.

See **state** and **state names**.

master of arts, master of science A *master's degree* or a *master's* is acceptable in any reference.
See **academic degrees**.

matrimony See **sacraments**.

maturity In a financial sense, the date on which a bond, debenture or note must be repaid.
See **loan terminology** in Business Guidelines.

May See **months**.

May Day, mayday *May Day* is May 1, often observed as a festive or political holiday.
Mayday is the international distress signal, from the French *m'aidez*, a reflexive verb meaning "help me."

mayors' conference See **U.S. Conference of Mayors**.

MC For *master of ceremonies*, but only in quoted matter. See **emcee**.

McDonnell Douglas Corp. Headquarters is in St. Louis.

M.D. A word such as *physician* or *surgeon* is preferred.
See **doctor** and **academic titles**.

meager

mean See the **average, mean, median, norm** entry.

Medal of Freedom It is now the *Presidential Medal of Freedom*. See entry under that name.

Medal of Honor The nation's highest military honor, awarded by Congress for risk of life in combat beyond the call of duty. Use *Medal of Honor recipient* or a synonym, but not *winner*.
There is no *Congressional Medal of Honor*.

Medfly Mediterranean fruit fly. The capital *M* is an exception to Webster's.

media In the sense of mass communication, such as magazines, newspapers, the news services, radio and television, the word is plural: *The news media are resisting attempts to limit their freedom.*

median See the **average, mean, median, norm** entry.

mediate See the **arbitrate, mediate** entry.

Medicaid A federal-state program that helps pay for health care for the needy, aged, blind and disabled, and for low-income families with children.
A state determines eligibility and which health services are covered. The federal government reimburses a percentage of the state's expenditures.

Medicare The federal health care insurance program for people aged 65 and over, and for the disabled. Eligibility is based mainly on eligibility for Social Security.
Medicare helps pay charges for hospitalization, for stays in skilled nursing facilities, for physician's charges and for some associated health costs. There are limitations on the length of stay and type of care.

In Canada, *Medicare* refers to the nation's national health insurance program.

medicine See the **drugs, medicine** entry.

medieval

mega- A prefix denoting 1 million units of a measure. Move the decimal point six places to the right, adding zeros if necessary, to convert to the basic unit: 5.5 megatons = 5,500,000 tons.

melee

Melkite Church See **Eastern Rite churches**.

memento, mementos

memo, memos

memorandum, memorandums

Memorial Day Formerly May 30. The federal legal holiday is the last Monday in May.

menage a trois

menswear Not *men's wear*.

Mercedes-Benz Note hyphen in this division of Daimler-Chrysler.

merchant marine Lowercase in referring to the ships of a nation used in commerce. Capitalize only in references to the organization the Merchant Marine or the U.S. Merchant Marine Academy. Members are *merchant mariners* or *merchant crewmen*, but not marines.

Mercurochrome A trademark for a brand of antiseptic for wounds.

meridians Use numerals and lowercase to identify the imaginary locater lines that ring the globe from north to south through the poles. They are measured in units of 0 to 180 degrees east and west of the *prime meridian*, which runs through Greenwich, England.

Examples: *33rd meridian* (if location east or west of Greenwich is obvious), *1st meridian west, 100th meridian.*

See the **latitude and longitude** entry.

merry-go-round

messiah Capitalize in religious uses. Lowercase when used generically to mean a liberator.

meter The basic unit of length in the metric system.

It is equal to approximately 39.37 inches, which may be rounded off to 39.5 inches in most comparisons.

It takes 100 centimeters to make a meter.

It takes 1,000 meters to make a kilometer.

To convert to inches, multiply by 39.37 (5 meters x 39.37 = 196.85 inches).

To convert to yards, multiply by 1.1 (5 meters x 1.1 = 5.5 yards).

See **inch; metric system;** and **yards**.

Methodist churches The term *Methodist* originated as a nickname applied to a group of 18th century Oxford University students known for their methodical application to Scripture study and prayer.

The principal Methodist body in the United States is the United Methodist Church, which also has some member conferences outside the United States. It was formed in 1968 by the merger of the Methodist Church and the Evangelical United Brethren Church. It has about 10 million members.

The government of the United Methodist Church follows a stratified pattern from the General Conference through several intermediate conferences down to the local congregation.

The General Conference, which meets every four years, has final authority in all matters. Its members, half lay and half clergy, are elected by the annual conferences.

A Methodist bishop presides over a "church area," which may embrace one or more annual conferences. Bishops have extensive administrative powers, including the authority to place, transfer and remove local church pastors, usually in consultation with district superintendents.

Districts in each conference are responsible for promotion of mission work, support of colleges, hospitals and publications, and examination of candidates for the ministry.

Members of a congregation form a charge conference. It elects officers to a board that assists the pastor.

Methodism in the United States also includes three major black denominations: the African Methodist Episcopal Church, the African Methodist Episcopal Zion Church and the Christian Methodist Episcopal Church.

Methodists believe in the Trinity and the humanity and divinity of Christ. There are two sacraments, baptism and the Lord's Supper.

Ordained individuals are known as *bishops* and *ministers*. *Pastor* applies if a minister leads a congregation.

For first references to bishops use the word: *Bishop W. Kenneth Goodson of Richmond, Va.*

For first reference to ministers, use *the Rev.* before the name of a man or woman. On second reference, use only the last name.

See **religious titles**.

metric system In general, metric terms should be included in a story when they are relevant.

There are no hard-and-fast rules on when they are relevant, but the following two guidelines have been developed to cover questions likely to arise as metric measurements gain increased acceptance in the United States:

—Use metric terms when they are the primary form in which the source of a story has provided statistics. Follow the metric units with equivalents in the terms more widely known in the United States. Normally, the equivalent should be in parentheses after the metric figure. A general statement such as: *A kilometer equals about five-eighths of a mile*, would be acceptable, however, to avoid repeated use of parenthetical equivalents in a story that uses kilometers many times.

—Provide metric equivalents for traditional forms if a metric unit has become widely known. As speedometers with kilometer markings become more prevalent, for example, a story about speed limits might list miles per hour and provide kilometers per hour in parentheses.

CONVERSION FORMULAS: A conversion table follows. To avoid the need for long strings of figures, prefixes are added to the metric units to denote fractional elements or large multiples. The prefixes are: *pico-* (one-trillionth), *nano-* (one-billionth), *micro-* (one-millionth), *milli-* (one-thousandth), *centi-* (one-hundreth), *deci-* (one-tenth), *deka-* (10 units), *hecto-* (100 units), *kilo-* (1,000 units), *mega-* (1 million units), *giga-* (1 billion units), *tera-* (1 trillion units). Entries for each prefix show how to convert a unit preceded by the prefix to the basic unit.

In addition, separate entries for **gram, meter, liter, Celsius** and other frequently used metric units define them and give examples of how to convert them to equivalents in the terminology that has been used in the United States.

Similarly, entries for **pound, inch, quart, Fahrenheit**, etc., contain examples of how to convert these terms to metric forms.

ABBREVIATIONS: The abbreviation *mm* for millimeter is acceptable in references to film widths (*8 mm film*) and weapons

METRIC CONVERSION CHART

INTO METRIC

If You Know	Multiply By	To get
LENGTH		
inches	2.54	centimeters
foot	30	centimeters
yards	0.91	meters
miles	1.6	kilometers
AREA		
sq. inches	6.5	sq. centimeters
sq. feet	0.09	sq. meters
sq. yards	0.8	sq. meters
sq. miles	2.6	sq. kilometers
acres	0.4	hectares
MASS (Weight)		
ounces	28	grams
pounds	0.45	kilograms
short ton	0.9	metric ton
VOLUME		
teaspoons	5	milliliters
tablespoons	15	milliliters
fluid ounces	30	milliliters
cups	0.24	liters
pints	0.47	liters
quarts	0.95	liters
gallons	3.8	liters
cubic feet	0.03	cubic meters
cubic yards	0.76	cubic meters
TEMPERATURE		
Fahrenheit	Subtract 32 then multiply by 5/9ths	Celsius

OUT OF METRIC

If You Know	Multiply By	To get
LENGTH		
millimeters	0.04	inches
centimeters	0.4	inches
meters	3.3	feet
kilometers	0.62	miles
AREA		
sq. centimeters	0.16	sq. inches
sq. meters	1.2	sq. yards
sq. kilometers	0.4	sq. miles
hectares	2.47	acres
MASS (Weight)		
grams	0.035	ounces
kilograms	2.2	pounds
metric tons	1.1	short tons
VOLUME		
milliliters	0.03	fluid ounces
liters	2.1	pints
liters	1.06	quarts
liters	0.26	gallons
cubic meters	35	cubic feet
cubic meters	1.3	cubic yards
TEMPERATURE		
Celsius	Multiply by 9/5ths, then add 32	Fahrenheit

(*a 105 mm cannon*). (Note space between numeral and abbreviation.)

Do not otherwise use metric abbreviations in news copy.

The principal abbreviations, for reference in the event they are used by a source, are: *g* (gram), *kg* (kilogram), *t* (metric ton), *m* (meter), *cm* (centimeter), *km* (kilometer), *mm* (millimeter), *L* (liter, capital *L* to avoid confusion with the figure *1*) and *mL* (milliliter).

metric ton Equal to approximately 2,204.62 pounds. See **ton**.

Metro-Goldwyn-Mayer Inc. *MGM* is acceptable in all references.

Headquarters is in Santa Monica, Calif.

Mexico City The city in Mexico stands alone in datelines.

Miami The city in Florida stands alone in datelines.

Michigan Abbrev.: *Mich.* See **state names**.

micro- A prefix denoting one-millionth of a unit.

Move the decimal point six places to the left in converting to the basic unit: 2,999,888.5 microseconds = 2.9998885 seconds.

mid- No hyphen unless a capitalized word follows:

mid-America	midsemester
mid-Atlantic	midterm

But use a hyphen when *mid-* precedes a figure: *mid-30s*.

Middle Ages A.D. 476 to approximately A.D. 1450.

Middle Atlantic States As defined by the U.S. Census Bureau, they are New Jersey, New York and Pennsylvania.

Less formal references often consider Delaware part of the group. See **Northeast region**.

middle class, middle-class *He is a member of the middle class. She has middle-class values.*

Middle East The term applies to southwest Asia west of Pakistan and Afghanistan (Iran, Iraq, Israel, Kuwait, Jordan, Lebanon, Oman, Qatar, Saudi Arabia, South Yemen, Syria, Turkey, United Arab Emirates and Yemen), northeastern Africa (Egypt and Sudan), and the island of Cyprus.

Popular usage once distinguished between the *Near East* (the westerly nations in the listing) and the *Middle East* (the easterly nations), but the two terms now overlap, with current practice favoring *Middle East* for both areas.

Use *Middle East* unless *Near East* is used by a source in a story.

Mideast is also acceptable, but *Middle East* is preferred.

middle initials In general, use them. They are an integral part of a person's name.

Particular care should be taken to include middle initials in stories where they help identify a specific individual. Examples include casualty lists and stories naming the accused in a crime.

A middle initial may be dropped if a person does not use one or is publicly known without it: *Mickey Mantle* (not *Mickey C.*), *the Rev. Billy Graham* (not *Billy F.*). See **names**.

middleman

middle names Use them only with people who are publicly known that way (*James Earl Jones*), or to prevent confusion with people of the same name.

See **middle initials; names.**

Middle West Definitions vary, but the term generally applies to the 12 states that the U.S. Census Bureau includes in the North Central region. See **North Central region.**

The shortened form *Midwest* is acceptable in all references.

The forms for adjectives are *Middle Western, Midwestern.*

See the **directions and regions** entry.

midnight Do not put a *12* in front of it. It is part of the day that is ending, not the one that is beginning.

midshipman See **military academies.**

MiG The *i* in this designation for a type of Russian fighter is lowercase because it is the Russian word for *and*. The initials are from the last names of the designers, Arten Mikoyan and Mikhail Gurevich.

The forms: *MiG-19, MiG-21s.* See **aircraft names.**

mile Also called a statute mile, it equals 5,280 feet.

The metric equivalent is approximately 1.6 kilometers.

To convert to kilometers, multiply by 1.6 (5 miles x 1.6 equals 8 kilometers).

See **foot; kilometer; knot;** and **nautical mile.**

Use figures for amounts under 10 in dimensions, formulas and speeds: *The farm measures 5 miles by 4 miles. The car slowed*

to 7 mph. The new model gets 4 miles more per gallon.

Spell out below 10 in distances: *He drove four miles.*

miles per gallon The abbreviation *mpg* is acceptable on second reference.

miles per hour The abbreviation *mph* (no periods) is acceptable in all references.

military academies Capitalize *U.S. Air Force Academy, U.S. Coast Guard Academy, U.S. Military Academy, U.S. Naval Academy.* Retain capitalization if the *U.S.* is dropped: *the Air Force Academy,* etc.

Lowercase *academy* whenever it stands alone.

Cadet is the proper title on first reference for men and women enrolled at the Army, Air Force and Coast Guard academies. *Midshipman* is the proper title for men and women enrolled at the Naval Academy.

Use the appropriate title on first reference. On second reference, use only the last name.

military titles Capitalize a military rank when used as a formal title before an individual's name.

See the lists that follow to determine whether the title should be spelled out or abbreviated in regular text. Spell out any title used before a name in a direct quotation.

On first reference, use the appropriate title before the full name of a member of the military.

In subsequent references, do not continue using the title before a name. Use only the last name.

Spell out and lowercase a title when it is substituted for a name: *Gen. John J. Pershing arrived today. An aide said the general would review the troops.*

In some cases, it may be necessary to explain the significance of a title: *Army Sgt. Maj. John Jones described the attack. Jones, who holds the Army's highest rank for enlistees, said it was unprovoked.*

In addition to the ranks listed on the next page, each service has ratings such as *machinist, radarman, torpedoman,* etc., that are job descriptions. Do not use any of these designations as a title on first reference. If one is used before a name in a subsequent reference, do not capitalize or abbreviate it.

ABBREVIATIONS: The abbreviations, with the highest ranks listed first:

MILITARY TITLES

Rank	*Usage before a name*

ARMY

Commissioned Officers

general	Gen.
lieutenant general	Lt. Gen.
major general	Maj. Gen.
brigadier general	Brig. Gen.
colonel	Col.
lieutenant colonel	Lt. Col.
major	Maj.
captain	Capt.
first lieutenant	1st Lt.
second lieutenant	2nd Lt.

Warrant Officers

chief warrant officer	Chief Warrant Officer
warrant officer	Warrant Officer

Enlisted Personnel

sergeant major of the Army	Sgt. Maj. of the Army
command sergeant major	Command Sgt. Maj.
sergeant major	Sgt. Maj.
first sergeant	1st Sgt.
master sergeant	Master Sgt.

sergeant first class	Sgt. 1st Class
staff sergeant	Staff Sgt.
sergeant	Sgt.
corporal	Cpl.
specialist	Spc.
private first class	Pfc.
private	Pvt.

NAVY, COAST GUARD

Commissioned Officers

admiral	Adm.
vice admiral	Vice Adm.
rear admiral upper half	Rear Adm.
rear admiral lower half	Rear Adm.
captain	Capt.
commander	Cmdr.
lieutenant commander	Lt. Cmdr.
lieutenant	Lt.
lieutenant junior grade	Lt. j.g.
ensign	Ensign

Warrant Officers

chief warrant officer	Chief Warrant Officer
warrant officer	Warrant Officer

Enlisted Personnel

master chief petty officer of the Navy	Master Chief Petty Officer of the Navy
senior chief petty officer	Senior Chief Petty Officer
chief petty officer	Chief Petty Officer
petty officer first class	Petty Officer 1st Class
petty officer second class	Petty Officer 2nd Class
petty officer third class	Petty Officer 3rd Class
seaman	Seaman
seaman apprentice	Seaman Apprentice
seaman recruit	Seaman Recruit

MARINE CORPS

Ranks and abbreviations for commissioned officers are the same as those in the Army. Warrant officer ratings follow the same system used in the Navy. There are no specialist ratings.

Others

sergeant major of the Marine Corp.	Sgt. Maj. of the Marine Corps
master gunnery sergeant	Master Gunnery Sgt.
master sergeant	Master Sgt.
first sergeant	1st Sgt.
gunnery sergeant	Gunnery Sgt.
staff sergeant	Staff Sgt.
sergeant	Sgt.
corporal	Cpl.
lance corporal	Lance Cpl.
private first class	Pfc.
private	Pvt.

AIR FORCE

Ranks and abbreviations for commissioned officers are the same as those in the Army.

Enlisted Designations

chief master sergeant of the Air Force	Chief Master Sgt. of the Air Force
chief master sergeant	Chief Master Sgt.
senior master sergeant	Senior Master Sgt.
master sergeant	Master Sgt.
technical sergeant	Tech. Sgt.
staff sergeant	Staff Sgt.
senior airman	Senior Airman
airman first class	Airman 1st Class
airman	Airman
airman basic	Airman

PLURALS: Add *s* to the principal element in the title: *Majs. John Jones and Robert Smith; Maj. Gens. John Jones and Robert Smith; Spcs. John Jones and Robert Smith.*

RETIRED OFFICERS: A military rank may be used in first reference before the name of an officer who has retired if it is relevant to a story. Do not, however, use the military abbreviation *Ret.*

Instead, use *retired* just as *former* would be used before the title of a civilian: *They invited retired Army Gen. John Smith.*

FIREFIGHTERS, POLICE OFFICERS: Use the abbreviations listed here when a military-style title is used before the name of a firefighter or police officer outside a direct quotation. Add *police* or *fire* before the title if needed for clarity: *police Sgt. William Smith, fire Capt. David Jones.*

Spell out titles such as *detective* that are not used in the armed forces.

military units Use Arabic figures and capitalize the key words when linked with the figures: *1st Infantry Division* (or *the 1st Division*), *5th Battalion, 395th Field Artillery, 7th Fleet.*

But: *the division, the battalion, the artillery, the fleet.*

millennium

milli- A prefix denoting one-thousandth of a unit. Move the decimal three places to the left in converting to the basic unit: 1,567.5 millimeters equals 1.5675 meters.

milligram One-thousandth of a gram.

Equal to approximately one-twenty-eight-thousandth of an ounce.

To convert to ounces, multiply by 0.000035 (140 milligrams x 0.000035 equals 0.0049 ounces).

See **metric system**.

milliliter One-thousandth of a liter.

Equal to approximately one-fifth of a teaspoon.

Thirty milliliters equals 1 fluid ounce.

To convert to teaspoons, multiply by 0.2 (5 milliliters x 0.2 equals 1 teaspoon).

See **liter** and **metric system**.

millimeter One-thousandth of a meter.

It takes 10 millimeters to make a centimeter.

A millimeter is roughly equal to the thickness of a paper clip.

To convert to inches, multiply by .04 (5 millimeters x .04 is 0.2 of an inch).

May be abbreviated as *mm* when used with a numeral in first or subsequent references to film or weapons: *35 mm film, 105 mm artillery piece.* (Note space after numeral.)

See **meter**; **metric system**; and **inch**.

millions, billions Use figures with *million* or *billion* in all except casual uses: *I'd like to make a billion dollars.* But: *The nation has 1 million citizens. I need $7 billion.*

Do not go beyond two decimal places. *7.51 million people, $256 billion, 7,542,500 people, $2,565,750,000.* Decimals are preferred where practical: *1.5 million.* Not: *1 1/2 million.*

Do not mix *millions* and *billions* in the same figure: *2.6 billion.* Not: *2 billion 600 million.*

Do not drop the word *million* or *billion* in the first figure of a range: *He is worth from $2 million to $4 million.* Not: *$2 to $4 million,* unless you really mean $2.

Note that a hyphen is not used to join the figures and the word *million* or *billion,* even in this type of phrase: *The president submitted a $300 billion budget.*

milquetoast Not *milk toast* when referring to a shrinking, apologetic person. Derived from Caspar Milquetoast, a character in a comic strip by Harold T. Webster.

Milwaukee The city in Wisconsin stands alone in datelines.

mimeograph Formerly a trademark, now a generic term.

mini- The rules in prefixes apply, but in general, no hyphen. Some examples:

miniseries   miniskirt
minivan

minister It is not a formal title. Do not use it before the name of a member of the clergy.

See **religious titles** and the entry for an individual's denomination.

ministry See **foreign governmental bodies**.

Minneapolis The city in Minnesota stands alone in datelines.

Minnesota Abbrev.: *Minn.* See **state names**.

Minnesota Mining and Manufacturing Preferred use is *3M* for this company headquartered in Maplewood, Minn. Its products are known under the names *3M* and *Scotch*.

minority leader Treat the same as *majority leader.* See that entry and **legislative titles**.

minuscule Not *miniscule.*

minus sign Use a hyphen, not a dash, but use the word *minus* if there is any danger of confusion.

Use a word, not a minus sign, to indicate temperatures below zero: *minus 10* or *5 below zero.*

mips Acronym for *million instructions per second*. Spell out on first reference.

MIRV, MIRVs Acceptable on first reference for *multiple independently targetable re-entry vehicle(s)*.

Explain in the text that a *MIRV* is an intercontinental ballistic missile with several warheads, each of which can be directed to a different target.

misdemeanor See the **felony, misdemeanor** entry.

mishap A minor misfortune. People are not killed in *mishaps*.

Miss See **courtesy titles**.

missile names Use Arabic figures and capitalize the proper name but not the word *missile*: *Pershing 2 missile*.

See **ABM**; **ICBM**; **MIRV**; and **SAM**.

Mississippi Abbrev.: *Miss.* See **state names**.

Missouri Abbrev.: *Mo.* See **state names**.

mix up (v.) **mix-up** (n. and adj.)

Mobil Corp. See **Exxon Mobil**.

mock-up (n.)

model numbers See **serial numbers**.

modem Modulator/demodulator.

Monaco After the Vatican, the world's smallest state.

The *Monaco* section stands alone in datelines. The other two sections, *La Condamine* and *Monte Carlo*, are followed by *Monaco*:
    MONTE CARLO, Monaco (AP) —

Monday See **days of the week**.

Monday morning quarterback One who second-guesses.

M-1, M-14 See **weapons**.

monetary See the **fiscal, monetary** entry.

monetary units See **cents; dollars;** and **pounds**.

moneymaker

monsignor See **Roman Catholic Church**.

Montana Abbrev.: *Mont.* See **state names**.

Montessori method After Maria Montessori, a system of training young children. It emphasizes training of the senses and guidance to encourage self-education.

monthlong

months Capitalize the names of months in all uses. When a month is used with a specific date, abbreviate only *Jan., Feb., Aug., Sept., Oct., Nov.* and *Dec.* Spell out when using alone, or with a year alone.

When a phrase lists only a month and a year, do not separate the year with commas. When a phrase refers to a month, day and year, set off the year with commas.

EXAMPLES: *January 1972 was a cold month. Jan. 2 was the coldest day of the month. His birthday is May 8. Feb. 14, 1987, was the target date.*

In tabular material, use these three-letter forms without a period: *Jan, Feb, Mar, Apr, May, Jun, Jul, Aug, Sep, Oct, Nov, Dec.*

See **dates** and **years**.

Montreal The city in Canada stands alone in datelines.

monuments Capitalize the popular names of monuments and similar public attractions: *Lincoln Memorial, Statue of Liberty, Washington Monument, Leaning Tower of Pisa,* etc.

moon Lowercase. See **heavenly bodies**.

mo-ped Hyphen is an exception to Webster's.

mop up (v.) **mop-up** (n. and adj.)

Moral Majority Not *the* Moral Majority.

more than See **over**.

Mormon church Acceptable in references to *The Church of Jesus Christ of Latter-day Saints,* but the official name is preferred in first reference in a story dealing primarily with church activities.

See the entry under the formal name.

Moscow The city in Russia stands alone in datelines.

Moslem(s) The preferred term to describe adherents of Islam is *Muslim(s).*

mosquito, mosquitoes

mother-in-law, mothers-in-law

Mother Nature

Mother's Day The second Sunday in May.

motor See the **engine, motor** entry.

mount Spell out in all uses, including the names of communities and of mountains: *Mount Clemens, Mich.; Mount Everest.*

mountains Capitalize as part of a proper name: *Appalachian Mountains, Ozark Mountains, Rocky Mountains.*

Or simply: *the Appalachians, the Ozarks, the Rockies.*

Mountain Standard Time (MST), Mountain Daylight Time (MDT) See **time zones**.

Mountain States As defined by the U.S. Census Bureau, the eight are Arizona, Colorado, Idaho, Montana, Nevada, New Mexico, Utah and Wyoming.

movie ratings The ratings used by the Motion Picture Association of America are:

G — *General audiences.* All ages admitted.

PG — *Parental guidance suggested.* Some material may not be suitable for children.

PG-13 — Special *parental guidance* strongly suggested for children under 13. Some material may be inappropriate for young children.

R — *Restricted.* Under 17 requires accompanying parent or adult guardian.

NC-17 — No one under 17 admitted.

When the ratings are used in news stories or reviews, use these forms as appropriate: *the movie has an R rating, an R-rated movie, the movie is R-rated.*

movie titles See **composition titles**.

mph Acceptable in all references for *miles per hour* or *miles an hour.*

Mr., Mrs. The plural of *Mr.* is *Messrs.;* the plural of *Mrs.* is *Mmes.*

These abbreviated spellings apply in all uses, including direct quotations.

See **courtesy titles** for guidelines on when to use Mr. and Mrs.

Ms. This is the spelling and punctuation for all uses of the courtesy title, including direct quotations.

There is no plural. If several women who prefer *Ms.* must be listed in a series, repeat *Ms.* before each name.

See **courtesy titles** for guidelines on when to use *Ms.*

Muhammad The prophet and founder of the Islamic religion. Use other spellings only if preferred by a specific person for his own name or in a title or the name of an organization.

multi- The rules in prefixes apply, but in general, no hyphen. Some examples:

multicolored	multimillion
multilateral	multimillionaire

Multigraph A trademark for a brand of dictating machine.

Multilith A trademark for a brand of duplicating machine.

murder See the **homicide, murder, manslaughter** entry.

murderer See the **assassin, killer, murderer** entry.

Murphy's law The law is: *If something can go wrong, it will.*

music Capitalize, but do not use quotation marks, on descriptive titles for orchestral works: *Bach's Suite No. 1 for Orchestra; Beethoven's Serenade for Flute, Violin and Viola.* If the instrumentation is not part of the title but is added for explanatory purposes, the names of the instruments are lowercased: *Mozart's Sinfonia Concertante in E flat major* (the common title) *for violin and viola.* If in doubt, lowercase the names of the instruments.

Use quotation marks for non-musical terms in a title: *Beethoven's "Eroica" Symphony.* If the work has a special full title, all of it is quoted: *"Symphonie Fantastique," "Rhapsody in Blue."*

In subsequent references, lowercase *symphony, concerto,* etc.

musket See **weapons**.

Muslims The preferred term to describe adherents of Islam.

A *Black Muslim* is a member of a predominantly black Islamic sect in the United States. However, the term is considered derogatory by members of the sect, who call themselves *Muslims.*

Mutual Broadcasting System Inc. *Mutual Radio* is acceptable in all references. Use *Mutual,* not *MBS,* in subsequent references.

Muzak A trademark for a type of recorded background music.

N

n. See **nouns**.

naive

names In general, people are entitled to be known however they want to be known, as long as their identities are clear.

When an individual elects to change the name by which he has been known, such as Cassius Clay's transition to Muhammad Ali, provide both names in stories until the new name is known by the public. After that, use only the new name unless there is a specific reason for including the earlier identification.

See the **junior, senior** entry and the entries under **middle initials**; **nicknames**; and **sex changes**.

nano- A prefix denoting one-billionth of a unit. Move the decimal point nine places to the left in converting to the basic unit: 2,999,888,777.5 nanoseconds equals 2.9998887775 seconds.

naphtha See the **oil** entry.

narrow-minded

Nation of Islam The nationalist religious movement traces its origins in 1930 to W.D. Fard, also known as Wali Fard, who called for racial separation. Elijah Muhammad took over the leader-ship in 1934, holding the post until his death in 1975. A son, Warith (Wallace) Dean Muhammad, succeeded to the leadership and pointed the movement toward integration and traditional Islam. Louis Farrakhan led a militant faction into a separatist movement in 1976.

The Nation of Islam does not release membership figures, but published estimates have ranged from 10,000 to more than 20,000.

Use the title *minister* on first reference to clergymen: *Minister Louis Farrakhan.*

national See the **citizen, resident, subject, national, native** entry.

National Aeronautics and Space Administration *NASA* is acceptable on first reference.

If *NASA* is used in first reference to avoid a cumbersome lead, mention the full name later.

national anthem Lowercase. But: *"The Star-Spangled Banner."*

National Association for the Advancement of Colored People *NAACP* is acceptable on first reference to avoid a cumbersome lead, but provide the full name in the body of the story.

Headquarters is in Baltimore.

National Association of Letter Carriers The shortened form *Letter Carriers union* is acceptable in all references.

Headquarters is in Washington.

National Baptist Convention of America See **Baptist churches**.

National Baptist Convention U.S.A. Inc. See **Baptist churches**.

National Broadcasting Co. See **NBC**.

national chairman Capitalize when used before the name of the individual who heads a political party: *Democratic National Chairman Kenneth M. Curtis*.

National Conference of Catholic Bishops See **Roman Catholic Church**.

National Council of the Churches of Christ in the U.S.A. This interdenominational, cooperative body includes most major Protestant and Eastern Orthodox denominations in the United States.

The shortened form *National Council of Churches* is acceptable in all references.

Headquarters is in New York.

See **World Council of Churches**.

National Education Association *NEA* is acceptable on second reference.

Headquarters is in Washington.

National FFA Organization Formerly the Future Farmers of America. *FFA* is acceptable

on second reference.

Headquarters is in Alexandria, Va.

National Governors' Association Note the apostrophe. Represents the governors of the 50 states and five territories.

Its office is in Washington.

national guard Capitalize when referring to U.S. or state-level forces: *the National Guard, the Guard, the Iowa National Guard, Iowa's National Guard, National Guard troops*.

Use lowercase for the forces of other nations.

National Guardsman Note spelling. Capitalize as a proper noun when referring to an individual in a federal or state National Guard unit: *He is a National Guardsman.*

Lowercase *guardsman* when it stands alone.

See **military titles**.

National Hurricane Center See **weather terms**.

National Institutes of Health This agency within the Department of Health and Human Services is the principal biomedical research arm of the federal government.

Its agencies are: National Cancer Institute; National Center for Research Resources; National Eye Institute; National Human Genome Research Institute; National Heart, Lung and Blood Institute; National Institute on Aging; National Institute on Alcohol Abuse and Alcoholism; National Institute of Allergy and Infectious Diseases; National Institute of Arthritis and Musculoskeletal and Skin Diseases; National Institute of Child Health and Human Development; National Institute on Drug Abuse; National Institute on Deafness and Other Communication Disorders; National Institute of Diabetes and Digestive and Kidney Diseases; National Institute of Dental Research; National Institute of Environmental Health Sciences; National Institute of General Medical Sciences; National Institute of Mental Health; National Institute of Neurological Disorders and Stroke; National Institute of Nursing Research; National Library of Medicine; Office of Alternative Medicine; Office of Medical Applications of Research; Office of Research on Women's Health; National Institutes of Health Clinical Center; Center for Scientific Review; Center for Information Technology.

All the agencies are in Bethesda, Md., except the National Institute of Environmental Health Sciences, which is in Research Triangle Park, N.C.

nationalist Lowercase when referring to a partisan of a country. Capitalize only when referring to alignment with a political party for which this is the proper name.

See the **political parties and philosophies** entry.

Nationalist China See **China**.

nationalities and races
Capitalize the proper names of nationalities, peoples, races, tribes, etc.: *Arab, Arabic, African, American, Caucasian, Cherokee, Chinese* (both singular and plural), *Eskimo* (plural *Eskimos*), *French Canadian, Gypsy* (*Gypsies*), *Japanese* (singular and plural), *Jew, Jewish, Latin, Negro*

(*Negroes*), *Nordic, Sioux, Swede,* etc.

Lowercase *black* (noun or adjective), *white, red, mulatto,* etc. See **colored**.

See **race** for guidelines on when racial identification is pertinent in a story.

Lowercase derogatory terms such as *honky* and *nigger.* Use them only in direct quotes when essential to the story and flag the contents in an editor's note.

National Labor Relations Board *NLRB* is acceptable on second reference.

National League of Cities
Its members are the governments of cities with 30,000 or more residents, and some state and municipal leagues.

It is separate from the U.S. Conference of Mayors, whose membership is limited to mayors of cities with 30,000 or more residents. The organizations often engage in joint projects, however.

The office is in Washington.

National Organization for Women Not *of. NOW* is acceptable on second reference.

Headquarters is in Washington.

National Rifle Association *NRA* is acceptable on second reference.

Headquarters is in Washington.

National Weather Service
No longer the U.S. Weather Bureau. *The weather service* (lowercase) may be used in any reference.

See **weather terms**.

nationwide

native See the **citizen, resident, subject, national, native** entry.

NATO Acceptable in all references for the *North Atlantic Treaty Organization*, but use it sparingly. A phrase such as *the alliance* is less burdensome to the reader.

Naugahyde A trademark for a brand of simulated leather.

nautical mile It equals 1 minute of arc of a great circle or 6,076.11549 feet, or 1,852 meters. To convert to approximate statute miles (5,280 feet), multiply the number of nautical miles by 1.15.
See **knot**.

naval, navel *Naval* pertains to a navy.
A *navel* is a bellybutton.
A *navel orange* is a seedless orange, so named because it has a small depression, like a navel.

naval station Capitalize only as part of a proper name: *Norfolk Naval Station*.

navy Capitalize when referring to U.S. forces: *the U.S. Navy, the Navy, Navy policy.* Do not use the abbreviation *USN*.
Lowercase when referring to the naval forces of other nations: *the British navy.*
This approach has been adopted for consistency, because many foreign nations do not use *navy* as the proper name.
See **military academies** and **military titles**.

Nazi, Nazism Derived from the German for the National Socialist German Workers' Party, the fascist political party founded

in 1919 and abolished in 1945. Under Adolf Hitler, it seized control of Germany in 1933.
See the **political parties and philosophies** entry.

NBC Acceptable in all references to the *National Broadcasting Co.*
Divisions are *NBC News, NBC Radio* and *NBC-TV*.

NCR Corp. Formerly National Cash Register Co.
Headquarters is in Dayton, Ohio.

NC-17 The movie rating that denotes individuals under 17 are not admitted. (Previously, an *X rating*.)

Near East There is no longer a substantial distinction between this term and *Middle East*.
See the **Middle East** entry.

nearsighted When used in a medical sense, it means an individual can see well at close range but has difficulty seeing objects at a distance.

Nebraska Abbrev.: *Neb*. See **state names**.

negligee

neither...nor See the **either...or, neither...nor** entry.

Netherlands In datelines, give the name of the community followed by *Netherlands*:
AMSTERDAM, Netherlands (AP) —
In stories: *the Netherlands* or *Netherlands* as the construction of a sentence dictates.

Netherlands Antilles In datelines, give the name of the

community followed by *Netherlands Antilles*. Do not abbreviate.

Identify an individual island, if needed, in the text.

net income, net profit See **profit terminology** in the Business Guidelines and Style section.

neutron weapon A small warhead designed to be mounted on a Lance missile or fired from an 8-inch gun. It produces twice the deadly radiation of older, tactical nuclear warheads but less than one-tenth as much explosive power, heat and fallout. This means the warhead can kill people while causing little damage to buildings and other structures.

It is not a *bomb*. It is a *weapon* or a *warhead*.

If *neutron bomb* is used in a direct quote, explain in a subsequent paragraph that the warhead would be fired on a missile or from artillery and not dropped, like a bomb, from a plane.

The weapon officially is known as an *enhanced radiation weapon.*

Nevada Abbrev.: *Nev.* See **state names**.

New Brunswick One of the three Maritime Provinces of Canada. Do not abbreviate.

See **datelines**.

New England Connecticut, Maine, Massachusetts, New Hampshire, Rhode Island and Vermont.

Newfoundland This Canadian province comprises the island of Newfoundland and the mainland section known as Labrador. Do not abbreviate.

In datelines, use Newfoundland after the names of all cities and towns. Specify in the text whether the community is on the island or in Labrador.

See **datelines**.

New Hampshire Abbrev.: *N.H.* See **state names**.

New Jersey Abbrev.: *N.J.* See **state names**.

New Mexico Abbrev.: *N.M.* See **state names**.

New Orleans The city in Louisiana stands alone in datelines.

New South The era that began in the South in the 1960s with a thriving economy and the election of state officials who advocated the abolition of racial segregation.

Old South applies to the South before the Civil War.

Newspaper Association of America Formerly the American Newspaper Publishers Association. *NAA* is acceptable in second reference. Also *the newspaper association, the association.*

Headquarters is in Reston, Va.

Newspaper Guild, The Formerly the American Newspaper Guild, it is a union for newspaper and news service employees, generally those in the news and business departments.

On second reference: *the Guild.*

Headquarters is in Washington.

newspaper names Capitalize *the* in a newspaper's name if that is the way the publication prefers to be known. Do not place name in quotes.

Lowercase *the* before newspaper names if a story mentions several papers, some of which use *the* as part of the name and some of which do not.

Where location is needed but is not part of the official name, use parentheses: *The Huntsville (Ala.) Times.*

Consult the International Year Book published by Editor & Publisher to determine whether a two-name combination is hyphenated.

newsstand

New Testament See **Bible**.

New World The Western Hemisphere.

New Year's, New Year's Day, New Year's Eve But: *What will the new year bring?*

The federal legal holiday is observed on Friday if Jan. 1 falls on a Saturday, on Monday if it falls on a Sunday.

New York Abbrev.: *N.Y.* Use *New York state* when a distinction must be made between state and city. See **state names**.

New York City Use *NEW YORK* in datelines, not the name of an individual community or borough such as *Flushing* or *Queens.*

Identify the borough in the body of the story if pertinent.

New York Stock Exchange *NYSE* is acceptable on second reference as an adjective. Use *the stock exchange* or *the exchange* for other second references.

Capitalize the nickname *Big Board* when used.

nicknames A nickname should be used in place of a person's given name in news stories only when it is the way the individual prefers to be known: *Jimmy Carter.*

When a nickname is inserted into the identification of an individual, use quotation marks: *Sen. Henry M. "Scoop" Jackson.* Also: *Jackson is known as "Scoop."*

In sports stories and sports columns, commonly used nicknames may be substituted for a first name without the use of quotation marks: *Woody Hayes, Bear Bryant, Catfish Hunter, Bubba Smith,* etc. But in sports stories where the given name is used, and in all news stories: *Paul "Bear" Bryant.*

Capitalize without quotation marks such terms as *Sunshine State, the Old Dominion, Motown, the Magic City, Old Hickory, Old Glory, Galloping Ghost.*

See **names**.

nightclub

nighttime

nitpicking

nitty-gritty

No. Use as the abbreviation for *number* in conjunction with a figure to indicate position or rank: *No. 1 man, No. 3 choice.*

Do not use in street addresses, with this exception: *No. 10 Downing St.,* the residence of Britain's prime minister.

Do not use in the names of schools: *Public School 19.*

Nobel Prize, Nobel Prizes The five established under terms of the will of Alfred Nobel are: Nobel Peace Prize, Nobel Prize in chemistry, Nobel Prize in literature, Nobel Prize in physics, Nobel Prize in physiology or medicine. (Note the capitalization styles.)

The Nobel Memorial Prize in Economic Sciences is not a Nobel Prize in the same sense. The Central Bank of Sweden established it in 1968 as a memorial to Alfred Nobel. References to this prize should include the word *Memorial* to help make this distinction. Explain the status of the prize in the story when appropriate.

Nobel Prize award ceremonies are held on Dec. 10, the anniversary of Alfred Nobel's death in 1896. The award ceremony for peace is in Oslo and the other ceremonies are in Stockholm.

Capitalize prize in references that do not mention the category: *He is a Nobel Prize winner. She is a Nobel Prize-winning scientist.*

Lowercase *prize* when not linked with the word Nobel: *The peace prize was awarded Monday.*

nobility References to members of the nobility in nations that have a system of rank present special problems because nobles frequently are known by their titles rather than their given or family names. Their titles, in effect, become their names.

The guidelines here relate to Britain's nobility. Adapt them as appropriate to members of nobility in other nations.

Orders of rank among British nobility begin with the royal family. The term *royalty* is reserved for the families of living and deceased sovereigns.

Next, in descending order, are dukes, marquesses (also called marquises), earls, viscounts and barons. Many hold inherited titles; others have been raised to the nobility by the sovereign for their lifetimes. Occasionally the sovereign raises an individual to the nobility and makes the title inheritable by the person's heirs, but the practice is increasingly rare.

Sovereigns also confer honorary titles, which do not make an individual a member of the nobility. The principal designations, in descending order, are baronet and knight.

In general, the guidelines in **courtesy titles** and **titles** apply. However, honorary titles and titles of nobility are capitalized when they serve as an alternate name.

Some guidelines and examples:

ROYALTY: Capitalize *king, queen, prince* and *princess* when they are used directly before one or more names; lowercase when they stand alone:

Queen Elizabeth II, Queen Elizabeth II of the United Kingdom of Great Britain and Northern Ireland, the queen. Kings George and Edward. Queen Mother Elizabeth, the queen mother.

Also capitalize a longer form of the sovereign's title when its use is appropriate in a story or it is being quoted: *Her Majesty Queen Elizabeth.*

Use *Prince* or *Princess* before the names of a sovereign's children: *Princess Anne, the princess.*

The male heir to the throne normally is designated *Prince of Wales*, and the title becomes, in common usage, an alternate name. Capitalize when used: *The queen invested her eldest son as Prince of Wales. Prince Charles is now the Prince of Wales. The prince is a bachelor. Charles, Prince of Wales, was married today. His wife is known as the Princess of Wales.*

DUKE: The full title — *Duke of Wellington*, for example — is an alternate name, capitalized in all uses. Lowercase duke when it stands alone.

The designation *Arthur, Duke of Wellington*, is appropriate in some cases, but never *Duke Arthur* or *Lord Arthur.*

The wife of a *duke* is a *duchess: the Duchess of Wellington, the duchess,* but never *Duchess Diana* or *Lady Diana.*

A duke normally also has a lesser title. It is commonly used for his eldest son if he has one. Use the courtesy titles *Lord* or *Lady* before the first names of a duke's children.

Some examples:

Lady Jane Wellesley, only daughter of the eighth Duke of Wellington, has been linked romantically with Prince Charles, heir to the British throne. The eldest of Lady Jane's four brothers is Arthur Charles, the Marquess Douro. The Wellingtons, whose family name is Wellesley, are not of royal blood. However, they rank among the nation's most famous aristocrats thanks to the first duke, the victor at Waterloo.

MARQUESS, MARQUIS, EARL, VISCOUNT, BARON: The full titles serve as alternate names and should be capitalized. Frequently, however, the holder of such a title is identified as a lord: *The Marquess of Bath*, for example, more commonly is known as *Lord Bath.*

Use *Lady* before the name of a woman married to a man who holds one of these titles. The wife of a marquess is a marchioness, the wife of a marquis is a marquise, the wife of an earl is a countess (earl is the British equivalent of count), the wife of a viscount is a viscountess, the wife of a baron is a baroness.

Use *Lord* or *Lady* before the first names of the children of a marquess.

Use *Lady* before the first name of an earl's daughter.

The Honorable often appears before the names of sons of earls, viscounts and barons who do not have titles. Their names should stand alone in news stories, however.

The Honorable also appears frequently before the names of unmarried daughters of viscounts and barons. In news stories, however, use a full name on first reference, a last name preceded by *Miss* on second.

Some examples:

Queen Elizabeth gave her sister's husband, Antony Armstrong-Jones, the title Earl of Snowdon. Their son, David, is the Viscount Linley. They also have a daughter, Lady Sarah Armstrong-Jones. Lord Snowdon, a photographer, was known as Antony Armstrong-Jones before he received his title.

BARONET, KNIGHT: Use *Sir* before a name if appropriate in the context; otherwise follow routine practice for names: *Sir Harold Wilson* on first reference, *Sir Harold* (not *Sir Wilson*) on second. Or: *Prime Minister Harold Wilson* on first reference, *Wilson* on second.

Do not use both an honorary title and a title of authority such as *prime minister* before a name.

Use *Lady* before the name of the wife of a baronet or knight.

For a woman who has received an honor in her own right, use *Dame* before her name if it is the way she is known or it is appropriate in the context: *Dame Margot Fonteyn* on first reference, *Dame Margot* on second.

nobody

noisome, noisy *Noisome* means offensive, noxious.
Noisy means clamorous.

nolo contendere The literal meaning is, "I do not wish to contend." Terms such as *no contest* or *no-contest plea* are acceptable in all references.

When a defendant in a criminal case enters this plea, it means that he is not admitting guilt but is stating that he will offer no defense. The person is then subject to being judged guilty and punished as if he had pleaded guilty or had been convicted. The principal difference is that the defendant retains the option of denying the same charge in another legal proceeding.

no man's land

non- The rules of **prefixes** apply, but in general no hyphen when forming a compound that does not have special meaning and can be understood if *not* is used before the base word. Use a hyphen, however, before proper nouns or in awkward combinations, such as *non-nuclear*. Follow Webster's New World Dictionary.

nonaligned nations A political rather than economic or geographic term used primarily during the Cold War. Although nonaligned nations do not belong to Western or Eastern military alliances or blocs, they profess not to be neutral, like Switzerland, but activist alternatives.

Do not confuse *nonaligned*

with *Third World*, although some Third World nations may belong to the nonaligned group.

See the **Third World** entry.

noncontroversial All issues are controversial. A *noncontroversial issue* is impossible. A *controversial issue* is redundant.

none It usually means no single one. When used in this sense, it always takes singular verbs and pronouns: *None of the seats was in its right place.*

Use a plural verb only if the sense is no two or no amount: *None of the consultants agree on the same approach. None of the taxes have been paid.*

nonrestrictive clauses See **essential clauses, nonessential clauses**.

noon Do not put a *12* in front of it.

See **midnight** and **times**.

no one

norm See the **average, mean, median, norm** entry.

north, northern, northeast, northwest See the **directions and regions** entry.

North America See **Western Hemisphere**.

North Atlantic Treaty Organization *NATO* is acceptable in all references, but use it sparingly. A phrase such as *the alliance* is less burdensome to the reader.

North Carolina Abbrev.: *N.C.* See **state names**.

North Central region As defined by the U.S. Census Bureau, the 12-state region is broken into eastern and western divisions.

The five *East North Central* states are Indiana, Illinois, Michigan, Ohio and Wisconsin.

The seven *West North Central* states are Iowa, Kansas, Minnesota, Missouri, Nebraska, North Dakota and South Dakota.

See **Northeast region; South;** and **West** for the bureau's other regional breakdowns.

North Dakota Abbrev.: *N.D.* See **state names.**

Northeast region As defined by the U.S. Census Bureau, the nine-state region is broken into two divisions — the *New England* states and the *Middle Atlantic* states.

Connecticut, Maine, Massachusetts, New Hampshire, Rhode Island and Vermont are the *New England* states.

New Jersey, New York and Pennsylvania are classified as the *Middle Atlantic* states.

See **North Central region; South;** and **West** for the bureau's other regional breakdowns.

Northern Ireland Use *Northern Ireland* after the names of all communities in datelines.

See **datelines** and **United Kingdom.**

Northrop Grumman Corp. Formerly Grumman Corp. Headquarters is in Los Angeles.

North Slope The portion of Alaska north of Brooks Range, a string of mountains extending across the northern part of the state.

North Warning System A system of long-range radar stations along the 70th parallel in North America. Previous system, known as the Distant Early Warning (DEW) line, was deactivated in 1985.

Northwest Airlines Headquarters is in Eagan, Minn.

Northwest Territories A territorial section of Canada. Do not abbreviate. Use in datelines after the names of all cities and towns in the territory.

See **Canada.**

nouns The abbreviation *n.* is used in this book to identify the spelling of the noun forms of words frequently misspelled.

Nova Scotia One of the three Maritime Provinces of Canada. Do not abbreviate.

See **datelines.**

November See **months.**

Novocain A trademark for a drug used as a local anesthetic. It also may be called *procaine.*

nowadays Not *nowdays.*

Nuclear Regulatory Commission This commission has taken over the regulatory functions previously performed by the Atomic Energy Commission.

NRC is acceptable on second reference, but *the agency* or *the commission* is preferred.

nuclear terminology In reporting on nuclear energy, include the definitions of appropriate terms, especially those related to radiation.

core The part of a nuclear reactor that contains its fissionable fuel. In a reactor core, atoms of fuel, such as uranium, are split. This releases energy in the form of heat which, in turn, is used to boil water for steam. The steam powers a turbine, and the turbine drives a generator to produce electricity.

fission The splitting of the nucleus of an atom, releasing energy.

meltdown The worst possible nuclear accident in which the reactor core overheats to such a degree that the fuel melts. If the fuel penetrates its protective housing, radioactive materials will be released into the environment.

rad The standard unit of measurement for absorbed radiation. A *millirad* is a thousandth of a rad. There is considerable debate among scientists whether there is any safe level of absorption.

radiation Invisible particles or waves given off by radioactive material, such as uranium. Radiation can damage or kill body cells, resulting in latent cancers, genetic damage or death.

rem The standard unit of measurement of absorbed radiation in living tissue, adjusted for different kinds of radiation so that 1 rem of any radiation will produce the same biological effect. A millirem is a thousandth of a rem.

A diagnostic chest X-ray involves between 20 millirems and 30 millirems of radiation. Each American, on average, receives 100 millirems to 200 millirems of radiation a year from natural "background" sources, such as cosmic rays, and man-made sources, such as diagnostic X-rays. There is considerable debate among scientists over the safety of repeated low doses of radiation.

roentgen The standard measure of X-ray exposure.

uranium A metallic, radioactive element used as fuel in nuclear reactors.

numerals A numeral is a figure, letter, word or group of words expressing a number.

Roman numerals use the letters *I, V, X, L, C, D* and *M*. Use Roman numerals for wars and to show personal sequence for animals and people: *World War II, Native Dancer II, King George VI, Pope John XXIII*. See **Roman numerals**.

Arabic numerals use the figures *1, 2, 3, 4, 5, 6, 7, 8, 9* and *0*. Use Arabic forms unless Roman numerals are specifically required. See **Arabic numerals**.

The figures *1, 2, 10, 101*, etc. and the corresponding words — *one, two, ten, one hundred one*, etc. — are called cardinal numbers. The term ordinal number applies to *1st, 2nd, 10th, 101st, first, second, tenth, one hundred first*, etc.

Follow these guidelines in using numerals:

LARGE NUMBERS: When large numbers must be spelled out, use a hyphen to connect a word ending in y to another word; do not use commas between other separate words that are part of one number: *twenty; thirty; twenty-one; thirty-one; one hundred forty-three; one thousand one hundred fifty-five; one million two hundred seventy-six thousand five hundred eighty-seven.*

SENTENCE START: Spell out a numeral at the beginning of a sentence. If necessary, recast the sentence. There is one exception — a numeral that identifies a calendar year.
Wrong: *993 freshmen entered the college last year.*
Right: *Last year 993 freshmen entered the college.*
Right: *1976 was a very good year.*

CASUAL USES: Spell out casual expressions:
A thousand times no! Thanks a million. He walked a quarter of a mile.

PROPER NAMES: Use words or numerals according to an organization's practice: *3M, Twentieth Century Fund, Big Ten.*

FRACTIONS: See the **fractions** entry.

DECIMALS: See the **decimal units** entry.

FIGURES OR WORDS?
For ordinals:
—Spell out *first* through *ninth* when they indicate sequence in time or location: *first base, the First Amendment, he was first in line.* Starting with *10th* use figures.
—Use *1st, 2nd, 3rd, 4th,* etc. when the sequence has been assigned in forming names. The principal examples are geographic, military and political designations such as *1st Ward, 7th Fleet* and *1st Sgt.* See examples in the separate entries listed below.
For cardinal numbers, consult the following separate entries:

act numbers	**latitude and**
addresses	**longitude**
ages	mile
aircraft names	millions, billions
amendments to	monetary units
the Constitution	No.
betting odds	page numbers
century	parallels
channel	percentages
chapters	political divisions
congressional	proportions
districts	ratios
course numbers	recipes
court decisions	room numbers
court names	route numbers
dates	scene numbers
decades	serial numbers
decimal units	sizes
dimensions	spacecraft
district	designations
earthquakes	speeds
election returns	telephone
fleet	temperatures
formula	times
fractions	weights
handicaps (sports)	years
highway	
designations	

SOME PUNCTUATION AND USAGE EXAMPLES:
—*Act 1, Scene 2*
—*a 5-year-old girl*
—*DC-10 but 747B*
—*a 5-4 court decision*
—*2nd District Court*
—*the 1980s, the '80s*
—*the House voted 230-205.* (Fewer than 1,000 votes.)
—*Jimmy Carter defeated Gerald Ford 40,827,292 to 39,146,157.* (More than 1,000 votes.)
—*Carter defeated Ford 10 votes to 2 votes in Little Junction.* (To avoid confusion with ratio.)
—*5 cents, $1.05, $650,000, $2.45 million*
—*No. 3 choice,* but *Public School 3*
—*0.6 percent, 1 percent, 6.5 percent*
—*a pay increase of 12 percent to 15 percent.* Or: *a pay increase of between 12 percent and 15 percent*
Also: *from $12 million to $14*

million
    —*a ratio of 2-to-1, a 2-1 ratio*
    —*a 4-3 score*
    —*(350) 262-4600*
    —*minus 10, zero, 60 degrees*

OTHER USES: For uses not covered by these listings: Spell out whole numbers below 10, use figures for 10 and above. Typical examples: *They had three sons and two daughters. They had a fleet of 10 station wagons and two buses.*

IN A SERIES: Apply the appropriate guidelines: *They had 10 dogs, six cats and 97 hamsters. They had four four-room houses, 10 three-room houses and 12 10-room houses.*

nuns See **sister**.

Nuremberg Use this spelling for the city in Germany, instead of Nuernberg, in keeping with widespread practice.

nylon Not a trademark.

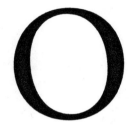

oasis, oases

obscenities, profanities, vulgarities Do not use them in stories unless they are part of direct quotations and there is a compelling reason for them.

When a profanity, obscenity or vulgarity is used, flag the story at the top:
Eds: Note contents of 4th graf.

Then confine the offending language, in quotation marks, to a separate paragraph that can be deleted easily by editors who do not want it.

In reporting profanity that normally would use the words *damn* or *god*, lowercase *god* and use the following forms: *damn, damn it, goddamn it.* Do not, however, change the offending words to euphemisms. Do not, for example, change *damn it* to *darn it.*

If a full quote that contains profanity, obscenity or vulgarity cannot be dropped but there is no compelling reason for the offensive language, replace letters of an offensive word with a hyphen.

When the subject matter of a story may be considered offensive, but the story does not contain quoted profanity, obscenities or vulgarities, flag the story at the top:
Editors: The contents may be offensive to some readers.

For guidelines on racial or ethnic slurs, see the **nationalities and races** entry.

Occident, Occidental Capitalize when referring to Europe, the Western Hemisphere or an inhabitant of these regions.

Occidental Petroleum Corp. Headquarters is in Los Angeles.

Occupational Safety and Health Administration *OSHA* is acceptable on second reference.

occupational titles They are always lowercase. See **titles.**

occur, occurred, occurring Also: *occurrence.*

oceangoing

ocean The five, from the largest to the smallest: Pacific Ocean, Atlantic Ocean, Indian Ocean, Antarctic Ocean, Arctic Ocean.

Lowercase *ocean* standing alone or in plural uses: *the ocean, the Atlantic and Pacific oceans.*

October See **months.**

odd- Follow with a hyphen:
odd-looking   odd-numbered
See **betting odds.**

oddsmaker

off-, -off Follow Webster's New World Dictionary. Hyphenate if not listed there.

Some commonly used combinations with a hyphen:

off-color	off-white
off-peak	send-off
off-season	stop-off

Some combinations without a hyphen:

cutoff	offside
liftoff	offstage
offhand	playoff
offset	standoff
offshore	takeoff

off-Broadway, off-off-Broadway
See the **Broadway, off-Broadway, off-off-Broadway** entry.

office Capitalize *office* when it is part of an agency's formal name: *Office of Management and Budget.*

Lowercase all other uses, including phrases such as: *the office of the attorney general, the* *U.S. attorney's office.* See **Oval Office.**

officeholder

off of The *of* is unnecessary: *He fell off the bed.* Not: *He fell off of the bed.*

Ohio Do not abbreviate. See **state names.**

oil In shipping, oil and oil products normally are measured by the ton. For news stories, convert these tonnage figures to gallons.

There are 42 gallons to each barrel of oil. The number of barrels per ton varies, depending on the type of oil product.

To convert tonnage to gallons:
—Determine the type of oil.
—Consult the table below to find out how many barrels per ton for that type of oil.
—Multiply the number of tons by the number of barrels per ton. The result is the number of bar-

---

OIL EQUIVALENCY TABLE

Type of Product	Barrels Per Short Ton (2,000 lbs.)	Barrels Per Metric Ton (2,204.6 lbs.)	Barrels Per Long Ton (2,240 lbs.)
crude oil, foreign	6.349	6.998	7.111
crude oil, domestic	6.770	7.463	7.582
gasoline and naphtha	7.721	8.511	8.648
kerosene	7.053	7.775	7.900
distillate fuel oil	6.580	7.253	7.369
residual fuel oil	6.041	6.660	6.766
lubricating oil	6.349	6.998	7.111
lubricating grease	6.665	7.346	7.464
wax	7.134	7.864	7.990
asphalt	5.540	6.106	6.205
coke	4.990	5.500	5.589
road oil	5.900	6.503	6.608
jelly and petrolatum	6.665	7.346	7.464
liquefied pet. gas	10.526	11.603	11.789
Gilsonite	5.515	6.080	6.177

rels in the shipment.

—Multiply the number of barrels by 42. The result is the number of gallons.

EXAMPLE: A tanker spills 20,000 metric tons of foreign crude petroleum. The table shows 6.998 barrels of foreign crude petroleum per metric ton. Multiply 6.998 x 20,000 equals 139,960 barrels. Multiply 139,960 x 42 is 5,878,320 gallons.

TABLE: The table on the previous page is based on figures supplied by the American Petroleum Institute.

OK, OK'd, OK'ing, OKs Do not use *okay*.

Oklahoma Abbrev.: *Okla.* See **state names**.

Oklahoma City Stands alone in datelines.

Old City of Jerusalem The walled part of the city.

Old South The South before the Civil War. See **New South**.

Old Testament See **Bible**.

old-time, old-timer, old times

Old West The American West as it was being settled in the 19th century.

Old World The Eastern Hemisphere: Asia, Europe, Africa. The term also may be an allusion to European culture and customs.

Olympic Airways Headquarters is in Athens, Greece.

Olympics Capitalize all references to the international athletic contests: *the Olympics, the Winter Olympics, the Olympic Games, an Olympic-size pool*, but lowercase *the games* when used alone.

An Olympic-size pool is 50 meters long by 25 meters wide.

Lowercase other uses: *a beer-drinking olympics*.

on Do not use *on* before a date or day of the week when its absence would not lead to confusion: *The meeting will be held Monday. He will be inaugurated Jan. 20.*

Use *on* to avoid an awkward juxtaposition of a date and a proper name: *John met Mary on Monday. He told Reagan on Thursday that the bill was doomed.*

Use *on* also to avoid any suggestion that a date is the object of a transitive verb: *The House killed on Tuesday a bid to raise taxes. The Senate postponed on Wednesday its consideration of a bill to reduce import duties.*

one- Hyphenate when used in writing fractions:

one-half   one-third

Use phrases such as *a half* or *a third* if precision is not intended.

See **fractions**.

one another See the **each other, one another** entry.

one person, one vote The adjective form: *one-person, one-vote. He supports the principle of one person, one vote. The one-man, one-vote rule.*

Supreme Court rulings all use the phrase *one person, one vote*, not *one man, one vote*.

one-sided

one time, one-time *He did it one time. He is a one-time winner. She is a one-time friend.*

Ontario This Canadian province is the nation's first in total population and second to Quebec in area. Do not abbreviate.
See **datelines**.

operas See **composition titles**.

opinion polls See the **polls and surveys** entry.

opossum The only North American marsupial. No apostrophe is needed to indicate missing letters in a phrase such as *playing possum.*

oral, verbal, written Use oral to refer to spoken words: *He gave an oral promise.*
Use *written* to refer to words committed to paper: *We had a written agreement.*
Use *verbal* to compare words with some other form of communication: *His tears revealed the sentiments that his poor verbal skills could not express.*

ordinal numbers See **numerals**.

Oregon Abbrev.: *Ore.* See **state names**.

Oreo A trademark for a brand of chocolate sandwich cookie held together by a white filling.
The use of the word by blacks indicates belief that another black is "black outside but white inside."

Organization of American States *OAS* is acceptable on second reference. Headquarters is in Washington.

Organization of Petroleum Exporting Countries Use the full name for most first references. *OPEC* may be used on first reference in business oriented copy, but the body of the story should identify it as the shortened form of the name.
The 11 OPEC members: Algeria, Indonesia, Iran, Iraq, Kuwait, Libya, Nigeria, Qatar, Saudi Arabia, United Arab Emirates, Venezuela.
Headquarters is in Vienna, Austria.

organizations and institutions Capitalize the full names of organizations and institutions: *the American Medical Association; First Presbyterian Church; General Motors Corp.; Harvard University, Harvard University Medical School; the Procrastinators Club; the Society of Professional Journalists.*
Retain capitalization if *Co., Corp.* or a similar word is deleted from the full proper name: *General Motors.* See **company**; **corporation**; and **incorporated**.

SUBSIDIARIES: Capitalize the names of major subdivisions: *the Pontiac Motor Division of General Motors.*

INTERNAL ELEMENTS: Use lowercase for internal elements of an organization when they have names that are widely used generic terms: *the board of directors of General Motors, the board of trustees of Columbia University, the history department of Harvard University, the sports department of the Daily Citizen-Leader.*

Capitalize internal elements of an organization when they have names that are not widely used generic terms: *the General Assembly of the World Council of Churches, the House of Delegates of the American Medical Association, the House of Bishops and House of Deputies of the Episcopal Church.*

FLIP-FLOPPED NAMES: Retain capital letters when commonly accepted practice flops a name to delete the word of: *College of the Holy Cross, Holy Cross College; Harvard School of Dental Medicine, Harvard Dental School.*

Do not, however, flop formal names that are known to the public with the word of: *Massachusetts Institute of Technology,* for example, not *Massachusetts Technology Institute.*

ABBREVIATIONS AND ACRONYMS: Some organizations and institutions are widely recognized by their abbreviations: *Alcoa, GOP, NAACP, NATO.* For guidelines on when such abbreviations may be used, see the individual listings and the entries under **abbreviations and acronyms** and **second reference.**

Orient, Oriental Capitalize when referring to the Far East nations of Asia and nearby islands. Asian is the preferred term for an inhabitant of these regions.

Also: *Oriental rug, Oriental cuisine.*

Orlon A trademark for a form of acrylic fiber similar to nylon.

orthodox Capitalize when referring to membership in or the activities of an Eastern Orthodox church. See **Eastern Orthodox**

Churches.

Capitalize also in phrases such as *Orthodox Judaism* or *Orthodox Jew.* See **Jewish congregations.**

Do not describe a member of an Eastern Orthodox church as a *Protestant.* Use a phrase such as *Orthodox Christian* instead.

Lowercase *orthodox* in nonreligious uses: *an orthodox procedure.*

Orthodox Church in America See **Eastern Orthodox churches.**

Oscar, Oscars See **Academy Awards.**

oscillating theory See **big-bang theory.**

Ottawa The capital of Canada stands alone in datelines.

Ouija A trademark for a board used in seances.

ounce (dry) Units of dry volume are not customarily carried to this level.

See **pint (dry).**

ounce (liquid) See **fluid ounce.**

ounce (weight) It is defined as 437.5 grains.

The metric equivalent is approximately 28 grams.

To convert to grams, multiply by 28 (5 ounces x 28 = 140 grams).

See **grain** and **gram.**

out- Follow Webster's New World. Hyphenate if not listed there.

Some frequently used words:

outargue	outpost
outbox	output

outdated	outscore
outfield	outstrip
outfox	outtalk
outpatient (n., adj.)	

-out Follow Webster's New World. Hyphenate nouns and adjectives not listed there.

Some frequently used words (all nouns):

cop-out	hide-out
fade-out	pullout
fallout	walkout
flameout	washout

Two words for verbs:

fade out	walk out
hide out	wash out
pull out	

Outer Banks The sandy islands along the North Carolina coast.

out of bounds But as a modifier: *out-of-bounds. The ball went out of bounds. He took an out-of-bounds pass.*

out of court, out-of-court *They settled out of court. He accepted an out-of-court settlement.*

Oval Office The White House office of the president.

over It generally refers to spatial relationships: *The plane flew over the city.*

Over can, at times, be used with numerals: *She is over 30. I paid over $200 for this suit.* But *more than* may be better: *Their salaries went up more than $20 a week.* Let your ear be your guide.

over- Follow Webster's New World. A hyphen seldom is used. Some frequently used words:

overbuy	overrate
overexert	override

See the **overall** entry.

-over Follow Webster's New World Dictionary. Hyphenate if not listed there.

Some frequently used words (all are nouns, some also are used as adjectives):

carry-over	stopover
holdover	walkover
takeover	

Use two words when any of these occurs as a verb.

See **suffixes**.

overall A single word in adjectival and adverbial use: *Overall, the Democrats succeeded. Overall policy.*

The word for the garment is *overalls.*

owner Not a formal title. Always lowercase: *Atlanta Braves owner Ted Turner.*

Oyez Not *oyes.* The cry of court and public officials to command silence.

Ozark Mountains Or simply: *the Ozarks.*

P

Pablum A trademark for a soft, bland food for infants.

In lowercase, *pablum* means any over-simplified or bland writing or idea.

pacemaker Formerly a trademark, now a generic term for a device that electronically helps a person's heart maintain a steady beat.

Pacific Ocean See **oceans.**

Pacific Standard Time (PST), Pacific Daylight Time (PDT) See **time zones.**

page numbers Use figures and capitalize *page* when used with a figure. When a letter is appended to the figure, capitalize it but do not use a hyphen: *Page 1, Page 10, Page 20A.*

One exception: *It's a Page One story.*

paintings See **composition titles.**

palate, palette, pallet *Palate* is the roof of the mouth.

A *palette* is an artist's paint board.

A *pallet* is a bed.

Palestine Liberation Organization Not *Palestinian. PLO* is acceptable in all references.

pan- Prefix meaning "all" takes no hyphen when combined with a common noun:

panchromatic   pantheism

Most combinations with *pan-* are proper nouns, however, and both *pan-* and the proper name it is combined with are capitalized:

Pan-African   Pan-Asiatic
Pan-American

Panama City Use *PANAMA CITY, Fla.,* or *PANAMA CITY, Panama,* in datelines to avoid confusion between the two.

pantsuit Not *pants suit.*

pantyhose

papal nuncio Do not confuse with an *apostolic delegate.* See the **apostolic delegate, papal nuncio** entry.

Pap test (or **smear**) After George Papanicolaou, the U.S. anatomist who developed this test for cervical and uterine cancer.

parallel, paralleled, paralleling

parallels Use figures and lowercase to identify the imaginary locater lines that ring the globe from east to west. They are measured in units of 0 to 90 degrees north or south of the equator.

Examples: *4th parallel north, 89th parallel south,* or, if location north or south of the equator is obvious: *19th parallel.*

See the **latitude and longitude** entry.

pardon, parole, probation The terms often are confused, but each has a specific meaning. Do not use them interchangeably.

A *pardon* forgives and releases a person from further punishment. It is granted by a chief of state or a governor. By itself, it does not expunge a record of conviction, if one exists, and it does not by itself restore civil rights.

A *general pardon,* usually for political offenses, is called *amnesty.*

Parole is the release of a prisoner before the sentence has expired, on condition of good behavior. It is granted by a parole board, part of the executive branch of government, and can be revoked only by the board.

Probation is the suspension of sentence for a person convicted, but not yet imprisoned, on condition of good behavior. It is imposed and revoked only by a judge.

parentheses See the entry in the **Punctuation** chapter.

parent-teacher association *PTA* is acceptable in all references. Capitalize when part of a proper name: *the Franklin School Parent-Teacher Association* or *the Parent-Teacher Association of the Franklin School.*

pari-mutuel

Paris The city in France stands alone in datelines.

parish Capitalize as part of the formal name for a church congregation or a governmental jurisdiction: *St. John's Parish, Jefferson Parish.*

Lowercase standing alone or in plural combinations: *the parish, St. John's and St. Mary's parishes, Jefferson and Plaquemines parishes.*

See **county** for additional guidelines on governmental jurisdictions.

parishioner Note spelling for this member of a parish, an adminstrative district of various churches, particularly Roman Catholic and Anglican churches. Do not use for Judaism or non-hierarchal Protestant denominations.

Parkinson's disease After James Parkinson, the English physician who described this degenerative disease of later life.

Parkinson's law After C. Northcote Parkinson, the British economist who came to the satirical conclusion that work expands to fill the time allotted to it.

parliament See **foreign legislative bodies**.

parliamentary Lowercase unless part of a proper name.

parole See the **pardon, parole, probation** entry.

partial quotes See **quotation marks** in the **Punctuation** chapter.

particles See **foreign particles**.

part time, part-time Hyphenate when used as a compound modifier: *She works part time. She has a part-time job.*

party See the **political parties and philosophies** entry.

party affiliation Let relevance be the guide in determining whether to include a political figure's party affiliation in a story.

Party affiliation is pointless in some stories, such as an account of a governor accepting a button from a poster child.

It will occur naturally in many political stories.

For stories between these extremes, include party affiliation if readers need it for understanding or are likely to be curious about what it is.

GENERAL FORMS: When party designation is given, use any of these approaches as logical in constructing a story:
—*Democratic Sen. Hubert Humphrey of Minnesota said...*
—*Sen. Hubert Humphrey, D-Minn., said...*
—*Sen. Hubert Humphrey also spoke. The Minnesota Democrat said...*
—*Rep. Morris Udall of Arizona is seeking the Democratic presidential nomination.* Not: *Rep. Morris Udall, D-Ariz., is seeking the Democratic...*

In stories about party meetings, such as a report on the Republican National Convention, no specific reference to party affiliation is necessary unless an individual is not a member of the party in question.

SHORT-FORM PUNCTUATION: Set short forms such as *D-Minn.* off from a name by commas, as illustrated above.

Use the abbreviations listed in the entries for each state. (No abbreviations for *Alaska, Hawaii, Idaho, Iowa, Maine, Ohio, Texas* and *Utah.*)

Use *R-* for Republicans, *D-* for Democrats, and three-letter combinations for other affiliations: *Sen. James Buckley, R-Con-N.Y., spoke with Sen. Harry Byrd, D-Ind-Va.*

FORM FOR U.S. HOUSE MEMBERS: The normal practice for U.S. House members is to identify them by party and state. In contexts where state affiliation is clear and home city is relevant, such as a state election roundup, identify representatives by party and city: *U.S. Reps. Thomas P. O'Neill Jr., D-Cambridge, and Margaret Heckler, R-Wellesley.* If this option is used, be consistent throughout the story.

FORM FOR STATE LEGISLATORS: Short-form listings showing party and home city are appropriate in state wire stories. For trunk wire stories, the normal practice is to say that the individual is a *Republican* or *Democrat.* Use a short-form listing only if the legislator's home city is relevant.

See **legislative titles**.

pass See the **adopt, approve, enact, pass** entry.

passenger lists When providing a list of victims in a disaster, arrange names alphabetically according to last name, include street addresses if available, and use a paragraph for each name:
Jones, Joseph, 260 Town St., Sample, N.Y.
Williams, Susan, 780 Main St., Example, N.J.

passenger mile One passenger carried one mile, or its equivalent, such as two passengers carried one-half mile.

passer-by, passers-by

Passover The weeklong Jewish commemoration of the deliverance of the ancient Hebrews from slavery in Egypt. Occurs in March or April.

pasteurize

pastor See **religious titles** and the entry for the individual's denomination.

patriarch Lowercase when describing someone of great age and dignity.

Capitalize as a formal title before a name in some religious uses. See **Eastern Orthodox churches; religious titles;** and **Roman Catholic Church**.

patrol, patrolled, patrolling

patrolman, patrolwoman Capitalize before a name only if the word is a formal title. In some cities, the formal title is *police officer*.

See **titles**.

payload

peacekeeping

peacemaker, peacemaking

peace offering

peacetime

peacock It applies only to the male. The female is a *peahen*.

Both are *peafowl*.

peck A unit of dry measure equal to 8 dry quarts or one-fourth of a bushel.

The metric equivalent is approximately 8.8 liters.

To convert to liters, multiply by 8.8 (5 pecks x 8.8 = 44 liters). See **liter**.

pedal, peddle When riding a bicycle or similar vehicle, you *pedal* it.

When selling something, you may *peddle* it.

peddler

pell-mell

penance See **sacraments**.

peninsula Capitalize as part of a proper name: *the Florida Peninsula, the Upper Peninsula of Michigan.*

penitentiary See the **prison, jail** entry.

Pennsylvania Abbrev.: *Pa.* Legally a commonwealth, not a state.

See **state** and **state names**.

Pennsylvania Dutch The individuals are of German descent. The word *Dutch* is a corruption of *Deutsch*, the German word for "German."

penny-wise See **-wise**. Also: *pound-foolish*.

Pentecost The seventh Sunday after Easter.

Pentecostalism See **religious movements**.

people, persons Use *person*

when speaking of an individual: *One person waited for the bus.*

The word *people* is preferred to persons in all plural uses. For example: *Thousands of people attended the fair. What will people say? There were 17 people in the room.*

Persons should be used only when it is in a direct quote or part of a title as in *Bureau of Missing Persons.*

People also is a collective noun that takes a plural verb when used to refer to a single race or nation: *The American people are united.* In this sense, the plural is *peoples*: *The peoples of Africa speak many languages.*

people's Use this possessive form when the word occurs in the formal name of a nation: *the People's Republic of China.*

Use this form also in such phrases as *the people's desire for freedom.*

Pepsi, Pepsi Cola Trademarks for a brand of cola soft drink.

Pepsico Inc. Formerly the Pepsi-Cola Co.

Headquarters is in Purchase, N.Y.

percent One word. It takes a singular verb when standing alone or when a singular word follows an *of* construction: *The teacher said 60 percent was a failing grade. He said 50 percent of the membership was there.*

It takes a plural verb when a plural word follows an *of* construction: *He said 50 percent of the members were there.*

percentages Use figures: *1 percent, 2.5 percent* (use deci-

mals, not fractions), *10 percent.*

For amounts less than 1 percent, precede the decimal with a zero: *The cost of living rose 0.6 percent.*

Repeat *percent* with each individual figure: *He said 10 percent to 30 percent of the electorate may not vote.*

periods See the entry in the **Punctuation** chapter.

perk A shortened form of *perquisite*, often used by legislators to describe fringe benefits. In the state of New York, legislators also use the word *lulu* to describe the benefits they receive in lieu of pay.

When either word is used, define it.

permissible

Persian Gulf Use this long-established name for the body of water off the southern coast of Iran.

Some Arab nations call it the *Arabian Gulf.* Use *Arabian Gulf* only in direct quotations and explain in the text that the body of water is more commonly known as the *Persian Gulf.*

personifications Capitalize them: *Grim Reaper, John Barleycorn, Mother Nature, Old Man Winter, Sol,* etc.

persons See the **people, persons** entry.

-persons Do not use coined words such as *chairperson* or *spokesperson* in regular text.

Instead, use *chairman* or *spokesman* if referring to a man or the office in general. Use *chairwoman* or *spokeswoman* if referring to a woman. Or, if applicable, use a neutral word such as *leader* or *representative*.

Use *chairperson* or similar coinage only in direct quotations or when it is the formal description for an office.

persuade See the **convince, persuade** entry.

Peter Principle It is: Employees are promoted until they reach their level of incompetence.

From the book by Laurence J. Peter.

petty officer See **military titles**.

PG, PG-13 The *parental guidance* ratings. See **movie ratings**.

phase See the **faze, phase** entry.

Ph.D., Ph.D.s The preferred form is to say a person *holds a doctorate* and name the individual's area of specialty.

See **academic degrees** and **doctor**.

phenomenon, phenomena

Philadelphia The city in Pennsylvania stands alone in datelines.

Philippines In datelines, give the name of a city or town followed by *Philippines*:
MANILA, Philippines (AP) —
Specify the name of an individual island, if needed, in the text.

In stories: *the Philippines* or *the Philippine Islands* as the construction of a sentence dictates.

The people are *Filipinos*. The language is *Pilipino*.

Photostat A trademark for a type of photocopy.

piano, pianos

pica A unit of measure in printing, equal to a fraction less than one-sixth of an inch.

A pica contains 12 points.

picket, pickets, picketed, picket line *Picket* is both the verb and the noun. Do not use *picketer*.

picnic, picnicked, picnicking, picnicker

pico- A prefix denoting one-trillionth of a unit. Move the decimal point 12 places to the left in converting to the basic unit: 2,999,888,777,666.5 picoseconds equals 2.9998887776665 seconds.

pigeon

pigeonhole (n. and v.)

Pikes Peak No apostrophe. After Zebulon Montgomery Pike, a U.S. general and explorer. The 14,110-foot peak is in the Rockies of central Colorado.

pile up (v.) **pileup** (n., adj.)

pill Do not capitalize in references to oral contraceptives. Use *birth control pill* on first reference if necessary for clarity.

pilot Not a formal title. Do not capitalize before a name. See **titles**.

pingpong A synonym for *table tennis*.

The trademark name is *Ping-Pong*.

pint (dry) Equal to 33.6 cubic inches, or one-half of a dry quart.

The metric equivalent is approximately .55 of a liter.

To convert to liters, multiply by .55 (5 dry pints x .55 is 2.75 liters).

See **liter** and **quart (dry)**.

pint (liquid) Equal to 16 fluid ounces, or two cups.

The approximate metric equivalents are 470 milliliters or .47 of a liter.

To convert to liters, multiply by .47 (4 pints x .47 is 1.88 liters).

See **liter**.

Pinyin The official Chinese spelling system.

See **Chinese names**.

pipeline

Pittsburgh The city in Pennsylvania stands alone in datelines.

The spelling is *Pittsburg* (no *h*) for communities in California, Illinois, Kansas, New Hampshire, Oklahoma and Texas.

plains See **Great Plains**.

planets Capitalize the proper names of planets: *Jupiter, Mars, Mercury, Neptune, Pluto, Saturn, Uranus, Venus*.

Capitalize *earth* when used as the proper name of our planet: *The astronauts returned to Earth.*

Lowercase nouns and adjectives derived from the proper names of planets and other heavenly bodies: *martian, jovian, lunar, solar, venusian*.

See **earth** and **heavenly bodies**.

planning Avoid the redundant *future planning*.

plants In general, lowercase the names of plants, but capitalize proper nouns or adjectives that occur in a name.

Some examples: *tree, fir, white fir, Douglas fir; Scotch pine; clover, white clover, white Dutch clover.*

If a botanical name is used, capitalize the first word; lowercase others: *pine tree (Pinus), red cedar (Juniperus virginiana), blue azalea (Callicarpa americana), Kentucky coffee tree (Gymnocladus dioica).*

Plastic Wood A trademark for a brand of wood-filler compound.

play titles See **composition titles**.

plead, pleaded, pleading Do not use the colloquial past tense form, *pled*.

Plexiglas Note the single *s*. A trademark for plastic glass.

plow Not *plough*.

plurality See the **majority, plurality** entry.

plurals Follow these guidelines in forming and using plural words:

MOST WORDS: Add *s*: *boys, girls, ships, villages*.

WORDS ENDING IN CH, S, SH, SS, X and Z: Add *es*: *churches, lenses, parishes, glasses, boxes, buzzes.* (*Monarchs* is an exception.)

WORDS ENDING IN IS: Change *is* to *es*: *oases, parentheses, theses*.

WORDS ENDING IN Y: If *y* is preceded by a consonant or *qu*, change *y* to *i* and add *es*: *armies, cities, navies, soliloquies*. (See PROPER NAMES below for an exception.)

Otherwise add *s*: *donkeys, monkeys*.

WORDS ENDING IN O: If *o* is preceded by a consonant, most plurals require *es*: *buffaloes, dominoes, echoes, heroes, potatoes*. But there are exceptions: *pianos*. See individual entries in this book for many of these exceptions.

WORDS ENDINGS IN F: In general, change *f* to *v* and add *es*: *leaves, selves*. (*Roof, roofs* is an exception.)

LATIN ENDINGS: Latin-root words ending in *us* change *us* to *i*: *alumnus, alumni*.

Most ending in *a* change to *ae*: *alumna, alumnae* (*formula, formulas* is an exception).

Most ending in *um* add *s*: *memorandums, referendums, stadiums*. Among those that still use the Latin ending: *addenda, curricula, media*.

Use the plural that Webster's New World lists as most common for a particular sense of word.

FORM CHANGE: *man, men; child, children; foot, feet; mouse, mice*; etc.

Caution: When *s* is used with any of these words it indicates possession and must be preceded by an apostrophe: *men's, children's*, etc.

WORDS THE SAME IN SINGULAR AND PLURAL: *corps, chassis, deer, moose, sheep*, etc.

The sense in a particular sentence is conveyed by the use of a singular or plural verb.

WORDS PLURAL IN FORM, SINGULAR IN MEANING: Some take singular verbs: *measles, mumps, news*.

Others take plural verbs: *grits, scissors*.

COMPOUND WORDS: Those written solid add *s* at the end: *cupfuls, handfuls, tablespoonfuls*.

For those that involve separate words or words linked by a hyphen, make the most significant word plural:

—Significant word first: *adjutants general, aides-de-camp, attorneys general, courts-martial, daughters-in-law, passers-by, postmasters general, presidents-elect, secretaries general, sergeants major*.

—Significant word in the middle: *assistant attorneys general, deputy chiefs of staff*.

—Significant word last: *assistant attorneys, assistant corporation counsels, deputy sheriffs, lieutenant colonels, major generals*.

WORDS AS WORDS: Do not use *'s*: *His speech had too many "ifs," "ands" and "buts."* (Exception to Webster's New World.)

PROPER NAMES: Most ending in *es* or *s* or *z* add *es*: *Charleses, Joneses, Gonzalezes*.

Most ending in *y* add *s* even if preceded by a consonant: *the Duffys, the Kennedys, the two Kansas Citys*. Exceptions include *Alleghenies* and *Rockies*.

For others, add *s*: *the Carters, the McCoys, the Mondales*.

FIGURES: Add *s*: *The custom began in the 1920s. The airline has two 727s. Temperatures will be in the low 20s. There were five size 7s.*

(No apostrophes, an exception to Webster's New World guideline under "apostrophe.")

SINGLE LETTERS: Use *'s*: *Mind your p's and q's. He learned the three R's and brought home a report card with four A's and two B's. The Oakland A's won the pennant.*

MULTIPLE LETTERS: Add *s*: *She knows her ABCs. I gave him five IOUs. Four VIPs were there.*

PROBLEMS, DOUBTS: Separate entries in this book give plurals for troublesome words and guidance on whether certain words should be used with singular or plural verbs and pronouns. See also **collective nouns** and **possessives**.

For questions not covered by this book, use the plural that Webster's New World lists as most common for a particular sense of a word.

Note also the guidelines that the dictionary provides under its "plural" entry.

p.m., a.m. Lowercase, with periods. Avoid the redundant *10 p.m. tonight.*

pocket veto Occurs only when Congress has adjourned. If Congress is in session, a bill that remains on the president's desk for 10 days becomes law without his signature. If Congress adjourns, however, a bill that fails to get his signature within 10 days is vetoed.

Many states have similar procedures, but the precise requirements vary.

podium See the **lectern, podium, pulpit, rostrum** entry.

poetic license It is valid for poetry, not news or feature stories.

See **colloquialisms** and **special contexts**.

poetry See **composition titles** for guidelines on the names of poems.

Capitalize the first word in a line of poetry unless the author deliberately has used lowercase for a special effect. Do not, however, capitalize the first word on indented lines that must be created simply because the writer's line is too long for the available printing width.

poinsettia Note the *ia*.

point Do not abbreviate. Capitalize as part of a proper name: *Point Pleasant*.

point (printing) As a unit of measure in printing, a *point* equals a fraction less than a seventy-second of an inch. A pica contains 12 *points*.

See **pica**.

point-blank

Polaroid A trademark for Polaroid Land instant-picture cameras and for transparent material containing embedded crystals capable of polarizing light.

police department In communities where this is the formal name, capitalize *police department* with or without the name of the community: *the Los Angeles Police Department, the Police Department*.

If a police agency has some

other formal name such as *Division of Police*, use that name if it is the way the department is known to the public. If the story uses *police department* as a generic term for such an agency, put *police department* in lowercase.

If a police agency with an unusual formal name is known to the public as a *police department*, treat *police department* as the name, capitalizing it with or without the name of the community. Use the formal name only if there is a special reason in the story.

If the proper name cannot be determined for some reason, such as the need to write about a police agency from a distance, treat *police department* as the proper name, capitalizing it with or without the name of the community.

Lowercase *police department* in plural uses: *the Los Angeles and San Francisco police departments*.

Lowercase *the department* whenever it stands alone.

police titles See **military titles** and **titles**.

policy-maker (n.) **policy-making** (n. and adj.)

polio The preferred term for *poliomyelitis* and *infantile paralysis*.

Politburo Acceptable in all references for the *Political Bureau of the Communist Party*.

political divisions Use Arabic figures and capitalize the accompanying word when used with the figures: *1st Ward, 10th Ward, 3rd Precinct, 22nd Precinct, the ward, the precinct.*

political parties and

philosophies Capitalize both the name of the party and the word *party* if it is customarily used as part of the organization's proper name: *the Democratic Party, the Republican Party.*

Capitalize *Communist, Conservative, Democrat, Liberal, Republican, Socialist*, etc., when they refer to a specific party or its members. Lowercase these words when they refer to political philosophy (see examples below).

Lowercase the name of a philosophy in noun and adjective forms unless it is the derivative of a proper name: *communism, communist; fascism, fascist.* But: *Marxism, Marxist; Nazism, Nazi.*

EXAMPLES: *John Adams was a Federalist, but a man who subscribed to his philosophy today would be described as a federalist. The liberal Republican senator and his Conservative Party colleague said they believe that democracy and communism are incompatible. The Communist said he is basically a socialist who has reservations about Marxism.*

See **convention** and **party affiliation**.

politicking

politics Usually it takes a plural verb: *My politics are my own business.*

As a study or science, it takes a singular verb: *Politics is a demanding profession.*

polls and surveys Stories based on public opinion polls must include the basic information for an intelligent evaluation of the results. Such stories must be carefully worded to avoid exaggerating the meaning of the poll results.

Information that should be in every story based on a poll includes the answers to these questions:

1. Who did the poll? (The place to start is the polling firm, political campaign or other group that conducted the poll.)

2. How many people were interviewed? How were they selected? (Only polls based on a scientific sample of a population can be used as a reliable and accurate measure of that population's opinions. Polls based on interviews on street corners, calling a 900-number or mailing coupons back from magazines may be good entertainment, but such polls have no validity. They should be avoided. In such unscientific pseudo-polls, the opinions come from people who "select themselves" to participate. If such polls are reported for entertainment value, they must never be portrayed as accurately reflecting public opinion and their failings must be highlighted.)

3. Who was interviewed? (A valid poll reflects only the opinions of the population that was sampled. A poll of business executives can only represent the views of business executives, not of all adults. Many political polls are based on interviews only with registered voters, since registration is usually required for voting. Close to the election, polls may be based only on "likely voters." If "likely voters" are used as the base, ask the pollster how that group was identified.)

4. How was the poll conducted — by telephone or in people's homes?

5. When was the poll taken? (Opinions can change quickly, especially in response to events.)

6. Who paid for the poll? (Be wary of polls paid for by candidates or interest groups. The release of poll results is often a campaign tactic or publicity ploy. Any reporting of such polls must highlight the poll's sponsor and the potential for bias from such sponsorship.)

7. What are the sampling error margins for the poll and for subgroups mentioned in the story? (Sampling error margins should be provided by the polling organization. The error margins vary inversely with the sample size: the fewer people interviewed, the larger the sampling error. If the opinions of a subgroup — women, for example — are important to the story, the sampling error for that subgroup should be included. The subgroup error margins are always larger than the margin for the entire poll.)

8. What questions were asked and in what order? (Small differences in question wording can cause big differences in results. The exact texts of the question need not be in every poll story unless it is crucial or controversial.)

When writing and editing poll stories, here are areas for close attention:

—Do not exaggerate the poll results. A difficult situation arises with pre-election polls in deciding when to write that the poll says one candidate is leading another. The rules are: If the margin between the candidates is more than twice the sampling error margin, then the poll says one candidate is leading. If the margin is less than the sampling error margin, the poll says that the race is close, that the candidates are "about even." If the margin is more than the sampling error, but less than twice the sampling error, then one candidate can be said to be "apparently leading" or "slightly ahead" in the race.

—Comparisons with other polls are often newsworthy. Earlier poll results can show changes in public opinion. Be careful comparing polls from different polling organizations. Different poll techniques can cause differing results.

—Sampling error is not the only source of error in a poll, but it is one that can be quantified. Question wording, interviewer skill and computer processing are all sources of error in surveys.

—No matter how good the poll, no matter how wide the margin, the poll does not say one candidate will win an election. Polls can be wrong and the voters can change their minds before they cast their ballots.

pom-pom, pompom *Pompom* is sometimes used to describe a rapid firing automatic weapon. Define the word if it must be used.

A *pompom* (also sometimes spelled *pompon*) is a large ball of crepe paper or fluffed cloth, often waved by cheerleaders or atop a hat. It is also a flower that appears on some varieties of chrysanthemums.

pontiff Not a formal title. Always lowercase.

pooh-pooh

pope Capitalize when used as a formal title before a name; lowercase in all other uses: *Pope Paul spoke to the crowd. At the close of his address, the pope gave his blessing.*
See **Roman Catholic Church**

and **titles**.

Popsicle A trademark for a brand of flavored ice on a stick.

popular names See **capitalization**.

pore, pour The verb *pore* means to gaze intently or steadily: *She pored over her books.*

The verb *pour* means to flow in a continuous stream: *It poured rain. He poured the coffee.*

port, starboard Nautical for left and right. Port is left. Starboard is right. Change to *left* or *right* unless in direct quotes.

Portuguese names The family names of both the father and mother usually are considered part of a person's full name. In everyday use, customs sometimes vary with individuals and countries.

The normal sequence is given name, mother's family name, father's family name: *Maria Santos Ferreira.*

On second reference, use only the father's family name (*Ferreira*), unless the individual prefers or is widely known by a multiple last name (*Ferreira Castro*).

Some Portuguese use an *e* (for *and*) between the two names: *Joao Canto e Castro.* This would not be split on second reference, but would be *Canto e Castro.*

When a surname is preceded by *da, do, dos,* or *das,* include it in the second reference. *Jorge da Costa,* for example, would be *Da Costa* on second reference.

A married woman adds her husband's surname to the end of hers. If *Maria Santos Ferreira* married *Joao Costa da Silva,* her full name would be *Maria Ferreira da Silva.*

Occasionally, a woman may choose not to take her husband's surname for personal reasons or because the mother's family has an aristocratic or famous surname. Use both surnames if the individual's choice is not known.

possessives Follow these guidelines:

PLURAL NOUNS NOT ENDING IN S: Add 's: *the alumni's contributions, women's rights.*

PLURAL NOUNS ENDING IN S: Add only an apostrophe: *the churches' needs, the girls' toys, the horses' food, the ships' wake, states' rights, the VIPs' entrance.*

NOUNS PLURAL IN FORM, SINGULAR IN MEANING: Add only an apostrophe: *mathematics' rules, measles' effects.* (But see INANIMATE OBJECTS below.)

Apply the same principle when a plural word occurs in the formal name of a singular entity: *General Motors' profits, the United States' wealth.*

NOUNS THE SAME IN SINGULAR AND PLURAL: Treat them the same as plurals, even if the meaning is singular: *one corps' location, the two deer's tracks, the lone moose's antlers.*

SINGULAR NOUNS NOT ENDING IN S: Add 's: *the church's needs, the girl's toys, the horse's food, the ship's route, the VIP's seat.*

Some style guides say that singular nouns ending in *s* sounds such as *ce, x,* and *z* may take either the apostrophe alone or 's. See SPECIAL EXPRES-

SIONS, but otherwise, for consistency and ease in remembering a rule, always use 's if the word does not end in the letter *s*: *Butz's policies, the fox's den, the justice's verdict, Marx's theories, the prince's life, Xerox's profits.*

SINGULAR COMMON NOUNS ENDING IN S: Add 's unless the next word begins with *s*: *the hostess's invitation, the hostess' seat; the witness's answer, the witness' story.*

SINGULAR PROPER NAMES ENDING IN S: Use only an apostrophe: *Achilles' heel, Agnes' book, Ceres' rites, Descartes' theories, Dickens' novels, Euripides' dramas, Hercules' labors, Jesus' life, Jules' seat, Kansas' schools, Moses' law, Socrates' life, Tennessee Williams' plays, Xerxes' armies.*

SPECIAL EXPRESSIONS: The following exceptions to the general rule for words not ending in *s* apply to words that end in an *s* sound and are followed by a word that begins with *s*: *for appearance' sake, for conscience' sake, for goodness' sake.* Use 's otherwise: *the appearance's cost, my conscience's voice.*

PRONOUNS: Personal interrogative and relative pronouns have separate forms for the possessive. None involve an apostrophe: *mine, ours, your, yours, his, hers, its, theirs, whose.*

Caution: If you are using an apostrophe with a pronoun, always double-check to be sure that the meaning calls for a contraction: *you're, it's, there's, who's.*

Follow the rules listed above in forming the possessives of other pronouns: *another's idea, others' plans, someone's guess.*

COMPOUND WORDS: Applying the rules above, add an apostrophe or *'s* to the word closest to the object possessed: *the major general's decision, the major generals' decisions, the attorney general's request, the attorneys general's request.* See the **plurals entry** for guidelines on forming the plurals of these words.

Also: *anyone else's attitude, John Adams Jr.'s father, Benjamin Franklin of Pennsylvania's motion.* Whenever practical, however, recast the phrase to avoid ambiguity: *the motion by Benjamin Franklin of Pennsylvania.*

JOINT POSSESSION, INDIVIDUAL POSSESSION: Use a possessive form after only the last word if ownership is joint: *Fred and Sylvia's apartment, Fred and Sylvia's stocks.*

Use a possessive form after both words if the objects are individually owned: *Fred's and Sylvia's books.*

DESCRIPTIVE PHRASES: Do not add an apostrophe to a word ending in *s* when it is used primarily in a descriptive sense: *citizens band radio, a Cincinnati Reds infielder, a teachers college, a Teamsters request, a writers guide.*

Memory Aid: The apostrophe usually is not used if *for* or *by* rather than *of* would be appropriate in the longer form: *a radio band for citizens, a college for teachers, a guide for writers, a request by the Teamsters.*

An *'s* is required, however, when a term involves a plural word that does not end in *s*: *a children's hospital, a people's re-*

public, *the Young Men's Christian Association.*

DESCRIPTIVE NAMES: Some governmental, corporate and institutional organizations with a descriptive word in their names use an apostrophe; some do not. Follow the user's practice: *Actors' Equity, Diners Club, the Ladies' Home Journal, the National Governors' Association.* See separate entries for these and similar names frequently in the news.

QUASI POSSESSIVES: Follow the rules above in composing the possessive form of words that occur in such phrases as *a day's pay, two weeks' vacation, three days' work, your money's worth.*

Frequently, however, a hyphenated form is clearer: *a two-week vacation, a three-day job.*

DOUBLE POSSESSIVE: Two conditions must apply for a double possessive — a phrase such as *a friend of John's* — to occur: 1. The word after *of* must refer to an animate object, and 2. The word before *of* must involve only a portion of the animate object's possessions.

Otherwise, do not use the possessive form of the word after *of*: *The friends of John Adams mourned his death.* (All the friends were involved.) *He is a friend of the college.* (Not *college's,* because college is inanimate.)

Memory Aid: This construction occurs most often, and quite naturally, with the possessive forms of personal pronouns: *He is a friend of mine.*

INANIMATE OBJECTS: There is no blanket rule against creating a possessive form for an inanimate object, particularly if the object is treated in a personified sense. See some of the earlier examples, and note these: *death's call, the wind's murmur.*

In general, however, avoid excessive personalization of inanimate objects, and give preference to an *of* construction when it fits the makeup of the sentence. For example, the earlier references to *mathematics' rules* and *measles' effects* would better be phrased: *the rules of mathematics, the effects of measles.*

post- Follow Webster's New World. Hyphenate if not listed there.

Some words without a hyphen:

postdate	postnuptial
postdoctoral	postoperative
postelection	postscript
postgraduate	postwar

Some words that use a hyphen:

post-bellum	post-mortem

post office It may be used but it is no longer capitalized because the agency is now the *U.S. Postal Service.*

Use lowercase in referring to an individual office: *I went to the post office.*

potato, potatoes

pothole

pound (monetary) The English pound sign is not used. Convert the figures to dollars in most cases. Use a figure and spell out *pounds* if the actual figure is relevant.

pound (weight) Equal to 16 ounces. The metric equivalent is approximately 454 grams, or .45 kilograms.

To convert to kilograms, multiply the number of pounds by .45 (20 pounds x .45 equals 9 kilograms).

See **gram** and **kilogram**.

pour See the **pore, pour** entry.

poverty level An income level judged inadequate to provide a family or individual with the essentials of life. The figure for the United States is adjusted regularly to reflect changes in the Consumer Price Index.

practitioner See **Church of Christ, Scientist**.

pre- The rules in **prefixes** apply. The following examples of exceptions to first-listed spellings in Webster's New World are based on the general rule that a hyphen is used if a prefix ends in a vowel and the word that follows begins with the same vowel:

pre-election	pre-establish
pre-eminent	pre-exist
pre-empt	

Otherwise, follow Webster's New World, hyphenating if not listed there. Some examples:

prearrange	prehistoric
precondition	preignition
precook	prejudge
predate	premarital
predecease	prenatal
predispose	pretax
preflight	pretest
preheat	prewar

Some hyphenated coinage, not listed in the dictionary:

pre-convention	pre-dawn

preacher A job description, not a formal religious title. Do not capitalize.

See **titles** and **religious titles**.

precincts See **political divisions**.

predominant, predomi-

nantly Use these primary spellings listed in Webster's New World for the adjectival and adverbial forms. Do not use the alternates it records, *predominate* and *predominately.*

The verb form, however, is *predominate.*

prefixes See separate listings for commonly used prefixes.

Generally do not hyphenate when using a prefix with a word starting with a consonant.

Three rules are constant, although they yield some exceptions to first-listed spellings in Webster's New World Dictionary:

—Except for *cooperate* and *coordinate*, use a hyphen if the prefix ends in a vowel and the word that follows begins with the same vowel.

—Use a hyphen if the word that follows is capitalized.

—Use a hyphen to join doubled prefixes: *sub-subparagraph.*

premier, prime minister These two titles often are used interchangeably in translating to English the title of an individual who is the first minister in a national government that has a council of ministers.

Prime minister is the correct title throughout the Commonwealth, formerly the British Commonwealth. See **Commonwealth** for a list of members.

Prime minister is the best or traditional translation from most other languages. For consistency, use it throughout the rest of the world with these exceptions:

—Use *chancellor* in Austria and Germany.

—Follow the practice of a nation if there is a specific preference that varies from this general practice.

Premier is also the correct title for the individuals who lead the provincial governments in Canada and Australia.

See **titles**.

premiere A first performance.

Presbyterian churches
There are four levels of authority in Presbyterian practice — individual congregations, presbyteries, synods and a general assembly.

Congregations are led by a pastor, who provides guidance in spiritual matters, and by a session, composed of ruling elders chosen by the congregation to represent the members in matters of government and discipline.

A presbytery is composed of all the ministers and an equal number of ruling elders, including at least one from each congregation, in a given district. Although the next two levels are technically higher, the presbytery has the authority to rule on many types of material and spiritual questions.

Presbyteries unite to form a synod, whose members are elected by the presbyteries. A synod generally meets once a year to decide matters such as the creation of new presbyteries and to pass judgment on appeals and complaints that do not affect the doctrine or constitution of the church.

A general assembly, composed of delegations of pastors and ruling elders from each presbytery, meets yearly to decide issues of doctrine and discipline within a Presbyterian body. It also may create new synods, divide old ones and correspond with general assemblies of other Presbyterian bodies.

The northern and southern branches of Presbyterianism merged in 1983 to become the Presbyterian Church (U.S.A.). Its membership totals 3 million. Formerly, Presbyterianism in the United States was concentrated in two bodies. The principal body in the North was the United Presbyterian Church in the United States of America. The Presbyterian Church in the United States was the principal Southern body.

Presbyterians believe in the Trinity and the humanity and divinity of Christ. Baptism, which may be administered to children, and the Lord's Supper are the only sacraments.

All Presbyterian clergymen may be described as *ministers*. *Pastor* applies if a minister leads a congregation.

On first reference, use *the Rev.* before the name of a man or woman. On second reference, use only the last name.

See **religious titles**.

presently Use it to mean *in a little while* or *shortly*, but not to mean *now*.

presidency Always lowercase.

president Capitalize president only as a formal title before one or more names: *President Reagan, Presidents Ford and Carter.*

Lowercase in all other uses: *The president said today. He is running for president. Lincoln was president during the Civil War.*
See **titles**.

FIRST NAMES: In most cases, the first name of a current or former U.S. president is not neces-

sary on first reference. Use first names when necessary to avoid confusion: *President Andrew Johnson, President Lyndon Johnson.* First names also may be used for literary effect, or in feature or personality contexts.

For presidents of other nations and of organizations and institutions, capitalize president as a formal title before a full name: *President Josip Broz Tito of Yugoslavia* (not: *President Tito* on first reference), *President John Smith of Acme Corp.*

On second reference, use only the last name.

presidential Lowercase unless part of a proper name.

Presidential Medal of Freedom This is the nation's highest civilian honor. It is given by the president, on the recommendation of the Distinguished Civilian Service Board, for "exceptionally meritorious contribution to the security of the United States or other significant public or private endeavors."

Until 1963 it was known as the Medal of Freedom.

Presidents Day Not adopted by the federal government as the official name of the Washington's Birthday holiday. However, some federal agencies, states and local governments use the term.

presiding officer Always lowercase.

press conference News conference is preferred.

press secretary Seldom a formal title. For consistency, always use lowercase, even when used before an individual's name.

(The formal title for the person who serves a U.S. president in this capacity is *assistant to the president for press relations*.)
See **titles**.

pretense, pretext A *pretext* is something that is put forward to conceal a truth: *He was discharged for tardiness, but the reason given was only a pretext for general incompetence.*

A *pretense* is a false show, a more overt act intended to conceal personal feelings: *My profuse compliments were all pretense.*

priest A vocational description, not a formal title. Do not capitalize.
See **religious titles** and the entries for the **Roman Catholic Church** and **Episcopal Church**.

prima-facie (adj.)

primary Do not capitalize: *the New Hampshire primary, the Democratic primary, the primary.*

primary day Use lowercase for any of the days set aside for balloting in a primary.

prime meridian See **meridians**.

prime minister See the **premier, prime minister** entry.

prime rate The interest rate that commercial banks charge on loans to their borrowers with the best credit ratings.

Fluctuations in the prime rate seldom have an immediate impact on consumer loan rates. Over the long term, however, consistent increases (or decreases) in the prime rate can lead to increases (or decreases) in the interest rates for mortgages and all types of personal loans.

prince, princess Capitalize when used as a royal title before a name; lowercase when used alone: *Prince Charles, the prince.*
See **nobility**.

Prince Edward Island One of the three Maritime Provinces of Canada. Do not abbreviate.
See **datelines**.

principal, principle *Principal* is a noun and adjective meaning someone or something first in rank, authority, importance or degree: *She is the school principal. He was the principal player in the trade. Money is the principal problem.*

Principle is a noun that means a fundamental truth, law, doctrine or motivating force: *They fought for the principle of self-determination.*

prior to *Before* is less stilted for most uses. *Prior to* is appropriate, however, when a notion of requirement is involved: *The fee must be paid prior to the examination.*

prison, jail Do not use the two words interchangeably.

DEFINITIONS: *Prison* is a generic term that may be applied to the maximum security institutions often known as *penitentiaries* and to the medium security facilities often called *correctional institutions* or *reformatories*. All such facilities confine people serving sentences for felonies.

A *jail* is a facility normally used to confine people serving sentences for misdemeanors, persons awaiting trial or sentencing on either felony or misdemeanor charges, and persons confined for civil matters such as failure to pay alimony and other types of contempt of court.

See the **felony, misdemeanor** entry.

The guidelines for capitalization:

PRISONS: Many states have given elaborate formal names to their prisons. They should be capitalized when used, but commonly accepted substitutes should also be capitalized as if they were proper names. For example, use either *Massachusetts Correctional Institution-Walpole* or *Walpole State Prison* for the maximum security institution in Massachusetts.

Do not, however, construct a substitute when the formal name is commonly accepted: It is the *Colorado State Penitentiary*, for example, not *Colorado State Prison*.

On second reference, any of the following may be used, all in lowercase: *the state prison, the prison, the state penitentiary, the penitentiary.*

Use lowercase for all plural constructions: *the Colorado and Kansas state penitentiaries.*

JAILS: Capitalize *jail* when linked with the name of the jurisdiction: *Los Angeles County Jail.* Lowercase *county jail, city jail* and *jail* when they stand alone.

FEDERAL INSTITUTIONS: Maximum security institutions are known as *penitentiaries: the U.S. Penitentiary at Lewisburg* or *Lewisburg Penitentiary* on first reference; *the federal penitentiary* or *the penitentiary* on second reference.

Medium security institutions include the word *federal* as part of their formal names: *the Federal Correctional Institution at Danbury, Conn.* On second reference: *the correctional institution, the federal prison, the prison.*

Most federal facilities used to house people awaiting trial or serving sentences of a year or less have the proper name *Federal Detention Center.* The term *Metropolitan Correctional Center* is being adopted for some new installations. On second reference: *the detention center, the correctional center.*

prisoner(s) of war *POW(s)* is acceptable on second reference.

Hyphenate when used as a compound modifier: *a prisoner-of-war trial.*

private See **military titles**.

privilege, privileged

pro- Use a hyphen when coining words that denote support for something. Some examples:

pro-labor   pro-business
pro-peace   pro-war

No hyphen when *pro* is used in other senses: *produce, profile, pronoun,* etc.

probation See the **pardon, parole, probation** entry.

Procter & Gamble Co. *P&G* is acceptable on second reference.

Headquarters is in Cincinnati.

profanity See the **obscenities, profanities, vulgarities** entry.

professor Never abbreviate. Lowercase before a name. Do not continue in second reference unless part of a quotation.

See **academic titles** and **titles**.

profit-sharing (n. and adj.) The hyphen for the noun is an exception to Webster's New World.

Prohibition Capitalize when referring to the period that began when the 18th Amendment to the Constitution prohibited the manufacture, sale or transportation of alcoholic liquors.

The amendment was declared ratified Jan. 29, 1919, and took effect Jan. 16, 1920. It was repealed by the 21st Amendment, which took effect Dec. 5, 1933, the day it was declared ratified.

pronouncers When necessary to use a *pronouncer*, put it in parentheses immediately following the word or name. The syllable to be stressed should be in caps with an apostrophe: *Ayatollah Khomeini (koh-MAY'-nee)*.

Here are the basic sounds represented by AP phonetic symbols:

Vowels	Consonants
a — apple, bat	g — got, beg
ah — father, hot	j — gem, job
ar — far, harm	k — cap, keep
aw — law, long	ch — chair
ay — ace, fate	s — see
e — bed	sh — shut
ehr — merry	y — yes
ee — see, tea	z — zoom
i — pin, middle	zh — mirage
oh — go, oval	kh — guttural "k"
oo — food, two	
or — for, torn	
ow — cow	
oy — boy	
u — foot, put	
uh — puff	
ur — burden, curl	
y, eye — ice, time	

propeller

proper nouns See **capitalization**.

prophecy (n.) **prophesy** (v.)

proportions Always use figures: *2 parts powder to 6 parts water*.

proposition Do not abbreviate. Capitalize when used with a figure in describing a ballot question: *He is uncommitted on Proposition 15.*

prosecutor Capitalize before a name when it is the formal title. In most cases, however, the formal title is a term such as *attorney general, state's attorney* or *U.S. attorney*. If so, use the formal title on first reference.

Lowercase *prosecutor* if used before a name on a subsequent reference, generally to help the reader distinguish between prosecutor and defense attorney without having to look back to the start of the story.

See **titles**.

prostate gland Not *prostrate*.

Protestant, Protestantism Capitalize these words when they refer either to denominations formed as a result of the break from the Roman Catholic Church in the 16th century or to the members of these denominations.

Church groups covered by the term include Anglican, Baptist, Congregational, Methodist, Lutheran, Presbyterian and Quaker denominations. See separate entries for each.

Protestant is not generally applied to Christian Scientists, Jehovah's Witnesses or Mormons.

Do not use *Protestant* to describe a member of an Eastern Orthodox church. Use a phrase such as *Orthodox Christian* instead.

See **religious movements**.

Protestant Episcopal Church See **Episcopal Church**.

protester Not *protestor*.

prove, proved, proving Use *proven* only as an adjective: *a proven remedy*.

provinces Names of provinces are set off from community names by commas, just as the names of U.S. states are set off from city names: *They went to Halifax, Nova Scotia, on their vacation.*

Do not capitalize province: *They visited the province of Nova Scotia. The earthquake struck Shensi province.*

See **datelines**.

proviso, provisos

provost marshal The plural: *provost marshals*.

PTA See **parent-teacher association**.

PT boat It stands for *patrol torpedo boat*.

Public Broadcasting Service It is not a network, but an association of public television stations organized to buy and distribute programs selected by a vote of the members.

PBS is acceptable on first reference only within contexts such as a television column. Otherwise, do not use *PBS* until second reference.

public schools Use figures and capitalize *public school* when used with a figure: *Public School 3, Public School 10.*

If a school has a commemorative name: *Benjamin Franklin School.*

publisher Capitalize when used as a formal title before an individual's name: *Publisher Isaiah Thomas of the Massachusetts Spy.*

See **titles**.

Puerto Rico Do not abbreviate. See **datelines**.

Pulitzer Prizes These yearly awards for outstanding work in journalism and the arts were endowed by the late Joseph Pulitzer, publisher of the old New York World, and first given in 1917. They are awarded by the trustees of Columbia University on recommendation of an advisory board.

Capitalize *Pulitzer Prize*, but lowercase the categories: *Pulitzer Prize for public service, Pulitzer Prize for fiction*, etc.

Also: *She is a Pulitzer Prize winner. He is a Pulitzer Prize-winning author.*

pull back (v.) **pullback** (n.)

pull out (v.) **pullout** (n.)

pulpit See the **lectern, podium, pulpit, rostrum** entry.

punctuation Think of it as a courtesy to your readers, designed to help them understand a story.

Inevitably, a mandate of this scope involves gray areas. For this reason, the punctuation entries in this book refer to guidelines rather than rules. Guidelines should not be treated casually, however.

See **Punctuation** chapter for separate entries under: **ampersand; apostrophe; brackets;**

colon; comma; dash; ellipsis; exclamation mark; hyphen; parentheses; period; question mark; quotation marks; and **semicolon.**

pupil, student Use *pupil* for children in kindergarten through eighth grade.

Student or *pupil* is acceptable for grades nine through 12.

Use *student* for college and beyond.

Purim The Jewish Feast of Lots, commemorating Esther's deliverance of the Jews in Persia from a massacre plotted by Haman. Occurs in February or March.

push-button (n., adj.)

push up (v.) **push-up** (n., adj.)

put out (v.) **putout** (n.)

pygmy Capitalize only when referring specifically to any of several races of unusually small African or Asian peoples.

Pyrex A trademark for a brand of oven glassware.

Q-and-A format See **question mark** in **Punctuation** chapter.

Qantas Airways Headquarters is in Sydney, Australia.

QE2 Acceptable on second reference for the ocean liner Queen Elizabeth 2.

(But use a Roman numeral for the monarch: *Queen Elizabeth II.*)

Q-Tips A trademark for a brand of cotton swabs.

Quaalude A trade name for a drug containing methaqualone. Not synonymous with illegal drugs containing methaqualone.

Quakers This informal name may be used in all references to members of the *Religious Society of Friends*, but always include the full name in a story dealing primarily with Quaker activities.

The denomination originated with George Fox, an Englishman who objected to Anglican emphasis on ceremony. In the 1640s, he said he heard a voice that opened the way for him to develop a personal relationship with Christ, described as the Inner Light, a term based on the Gospel description of Christ as the "true light."

Brought to court for opposing the established church, Fox tangled with a judge who derided him as a "quaker" in reference to his agitation over religious matters.

The basic unit of Quaker organization is the weekly meeting, which corresponds to the congregation in other churches.

Various yearly meetings form larger associations that assemble at intervals of a year or more. The largest is the Friends United Meeting. Its 15 yearly meeting members represent about half the Friends in the world.

Others include the Evangelical Friends Alliance and the Friends General Conference. Members of the conference include some yearly meetings that also are affiliated with the Friends United Meeting.

Overall, Friends count about 120,000 members in the United States and Canada and a total of 200,000 worldwide.

Fox taught that the Inner Light emancipates a person from adherence to any creed, ecclesiastical authority or ritual forms.

There is no recognized ranking of clergy over lay people. However, there are meeting officers, called *elders* or *ministers*. Many Quaker ministers, particularly in the Midwest and West, use *the Rev.* before their names and describe themselves as *pastors*.

Capitalize *elder, minister* or *pastor* when used as a formal title before a name. Use *the Rev.* before a name on first reference if it is a minister's practice. On second reference, use only the last name.

See **religious titles**.

quakes See **earthquakes**.

quart (dry) Equal in volume to 67.2 cubic inches. The metric equivalent is approximately 1.1 liters.

To convert to liters, multiply by 1.1 (5 dry quarts x 1.1 is 5.5 liters).

See **liter**.

quart (liquid) Equal in volume to 57.75 cubic inches. Also equal to 32 fluid ounces.

The approximate metric equivalents are 950 milliliters or .95 of a liter.

To convert to liters, multiply by .95 (4 quarts x .95 is 3.8 liters).

See **liter**.

quasar Acceptable in all references for a *quasi-stellar astronomical object*, often a radio source. Most astronomers consider quasars the most distant objects observable in the heavens.

Quebec The city in Canada stands alone in datelines.

Use *Quebec City* in the body of a story if the city must be distinguished from the province.

Do not abbreviate any reference to the province of Quebec, Canada's largest in area and second largest in population.

See **datelines**.

queen Capitalize only when used before the name of royalty: *Queen Elizabeth II*. Continue in second references that use the queen's given name: *Queen Elizabeth*.

Lowercase *queen* when it stands alone.

Capitalize in plural uses: *Queens Elizabeth and Victoria*.

See **nobility** and **titles**.

queen mother A widowed queen who is mother of the reigning monarch. See **nobility**.

question mark See entry in **Punctuation** chapter.

questionnaire

quick-witted

quotation marks See entry in **Punctuation** chapter.

quotations in the news
Never alter quotations even to correct minor grammatical errors or word usage. Casual minor tongue slips may be removed by using ellipses but even that should be done with extreme caution. If there is a question about a quote, either don't use it or ask the speaker to clarify.

If a person is unavailable for comment, detail attempts to reach that person. (*Smith was out of the country on business; Jones did not return phone messages left at the office.*)

Do not routinely use abnormal spellings such as *gonna* in attempts to convey regional dialects or mispronunciations. Such spellings are appropriate when relevant or help to convey a desired touch in a feature.

FULL vs. PARTIAL QUOTES: In general, avoid fragmentary

quotes. If a speaker's words are clear and concise, favor the full quote. If cumbersome language can be paraphrased fairly, use an indirect construction, reserving quotation marks for sensitive or controversial passages that must be identified specifically as coming from the speaker.

CONTEXT: Remember that you can misquote someone by giving a startling remark without its modifying passage or qualifiers. The manner of delivery sometimes is part of the context. Reporting a smile or a deprecatory gesture may be as important as conveying the words themselves.

OFFENSIVE LANGUAGE: See the **obscenities, profanities, vulgarities** entry.

PUNCTUATION: See the **quotation marks** entry in the **Punctuation** chapter.

Quran The preferred spelling for the Muslim holy book. Use the spelling *Koran* only if preferred by a specific organization or in a specific title or name.

R

R The *restricted* rating. See **movie ratings**.

rabbi See **Jewish congregations**.

Rabbinical Assembly See **Jewish congregations**.

Rabbinical Council of America See **Jewish congregations**.

raccoon

race Identification by race is pertinent:

—In biographical and announcement stories, particularly when they involve a feat or appointment that has not routinely been associated with members of a particular race.

—When it provides the reader with a substantial insight into conflicting emotions known or likely to be involved in a demonstration or similar event.

In some stories that involve a conflict, it is equally important to specify that an issue cuts across racial lines. If, for example, a demonstration by supporters of busing to achieve racial balance in schools includes a substantial number of whites, that fact should be noted.

Do not use racially derogatory terms unless they are part of a quotation that is essential to the story.

See the **obscenities, profanities, vulgarities** entry and the **nationalities and races** entry.

rack, wrack The noun *rack* applies to various types of framework; the verb *rack* means to arrange on a rack, to torture, trouble or torment: *He was placed on the rack. She racked her brain.*

The noun *wrack* means ruin or destruction, and generally is confined to the phrase *wrack and ruin.*

The verb *wrack* has substantially the same meaning as the verb *rack*, the latter being preferred.

racket Not *racquet*, for the light bat used in tennis and badminton.

radar A lowercase acronym for *radio detection and ranging.*

radical In general, avoid this description in favor of a more precise definition of an individual's political views.

When used, it suggests that an individual believes change must be made by tearing up the roots or foundation of the present order.

Although *radical* often is applied to individuals who hold strong socialist or communist views, it also is applied at times to individuals who believe an existing form of government must be replaced by a more authoritarian or militaristic one.

See the **leftist, ultra-leftist** and **rightist, ultra-rightist** entries.

radio Capitalize and use before a name to indicate an official voice of the government: *Radio Moscow.*

Lowercase and place after the name when indicating only that the information was obtained from broadcasts in a city. *Havana radio,* for example, is the form used in referring to reports that are broadcast on various stations in the Cuban capital.

radio station The call letters alone are frequently adequate, but when this phrase is needed, use lowercase: *radio station WHEC.*

See **call letters.**

railroads Capitalize when part of a name: *the Illinois Central Gulf Railroad.*

Railroad companies vary the spellings of their names, using *Railroad, Rail Road, Railway,* etc. Consult the Official Railway Guide-Freight Service and the Official Railway Guide-Passenger Service for official spellings.

Use *the railroad* for all lines in second references.

Use *railroads* in lowercase for all plurals: *the Penn Central and Santa Fe railroads.*

See **Amtrak** and **Conrail.**

rainstorm See **weather terms.**

raised, reared Only humans may be *reared.*

All living things, including humans, may be *raised.*

RAM See **Internet** section.

Ramadan The Muslim holy month, a period of daily fasting from sunrise to sunset, ending with the Islamic holiday of Eid al-Fitr.

ranges The form: *$12 million to $14 million.* Not: *$12 to $14 million.*

rank and file (n.) The adjective form: *rank-and-file.*

rarely It means seldom. *Rarely ever* is redundant, but *rarely if ever* often is the appropriate phrase.

ratios Use figures and hyphens: *the ratio was 2-to-1, a ratio of 2-to-1, a 2-1 ratio.* As illustrated, the word *to* should be omitted when the numbers precede the word *ratio.*

Always use the word *ratio* or a phrase such as *a 2-1 majority* to avoid confusion with actual figures.

ravage, ravish *To ravage* is to wreak great destruction or devastation: *Union troops ravaged Atlanta.*

To ravish is to abduct, rape or carry away with emotion: *Soldiers ravished the women.*

Although both words connote an element of violence, they are not interchangeable. Buildings and towns cannot be *ravished.*

rayon Not a trademark.

re- The rules in **prefixes**

apply. The following examples of exceptions to first-listed spellings in Webster's New World are based on the general rule that a hyphen is used if a prefix ends in a vowel and the word that follows begins with the same vowel:

re-elect	re-enlist
re-election	re-enter
re-emerge	re-entry
re-employ	re-equip
re-enact	re-establish
re-engage	re-examine

For many other words, the sense is the governing factor:

recover (regain)	re-cover (cover again)
reform (improve)	re-form (form again)
resign (quit)	re-sign (sign again)

Otherwise, follow Webster's New World. Use a hyphen for words not listed there unless the hyphen would distort the sense.

reader See **Church of Christ, Scientist.**

Realtor The term *real estate agent* is preferred. Use *Realtor* only if there is a reason to indicate that the individual is a member of the National Association of Realtors.
See **service marks.**

reared See **raised, reared** entry.

rebut, refute *Rebut* means to argue to the contrary: *He rebutted his opponent's statement.*
Refute connotes success in argument and almost always implies an editorial judgment. Instead, use *deny, dispute, rebut* or *respond to.*

recipes Always use figures. See **fractions.**
Do not use abbreviations. Spell out *teaspoon, tablespoon,* etc.

See the **food** entry for guidelines on when to capitalize the names of foods.

recision The preferred spelling is *rescission.*

reconnaissance

Reconstruction The process of reorganizing the Southern states after the Civil War.

record Avoid the redundant *new record.*

rector See **religious titles.**

recur, recurred, recurring Not *reoccur.*

Red Capitalize when used as a political, geographic or military term: *the Red army.*

Red China See **China.**

red-haired, redhead, redheaded All are acceptable for a person with red hair.
Redhead also is used colloquially to describe a type of North American diving duck.

red-handed (adj. and adv.)

red-hot

redneck From the characteristic sunburned neck acquired in the fields by farm laborers. It refers to poor, white rural residents of the South and often is a derogatory term.

re-elect, re-election

refer See the **allude, refer** entry.

referable

reference works Capitalize their proper names.

Do not use quotation marks around the names of books that are primarily catalogs of reference material. In addition to catalogs, this category includes almanacs, directories, dictionaries, encyclopedias, gazetteers, handbooks and similar publications.

EXAMPLES: *Congressional Directory, Webster's New World Dictionary, the AP Stylebook.* But: *"The Careful Writer" and "Modern American Usage."*

See the bibliography for the principal reference works used in preparing this book.

referendum, referendums

reformatory See the **prison, jail** entry.

Reform Judaism See **Jewish congregations**.

refute See the **rebut, refute** entry.

regime See the **government, junta, regime** entry.

regions See the **directions and regions** entry.

reign, rein The leather strap for controlling a horse is a *rein,* hence figuratively: *seize the reins, give free rein to, put a checkrein on.*

Reign is the period a ruler is on the throne: The king began his reign.

release times Follow these guidelines:

TIME SET BY SOURCE: If a source provides material on condition that it not be published or broadcast until a specific time, the story should contain a boldface slug to that effect:

↑ *For Release 10 a.m. EST, time set by source.* ←

MOVEMENT TIME SET BY SOURCE: If a source provides material on condition that it not be moved on any wire read by newspapers or broadcasters until a specific time, the request will be respected. Consult the General Desk if any problems arise.

RELEASE SPECIFIED BY SOURCE: If a source does not specify a particular hour but says material is for release in morning papers, the automatic release time for print and broadcast is 6:30 p.m. Eastern time.

If a source says only that material is for release in afternoon papers, the automatic release time for print and broadcast is 6:30 a.m. Eastern time.

In either case, the story should contain a boldface slug to that effect:

↑ *For Release 6:30 p.m. EST.* ←
↑ *For Release 6:30 a.m. EST.* ←

ENTERPRISE COPY: Stories sent in advance for a specified cycle and date are released for broadcast and morning papers at 6:30 p.m.; 6:30 a.m. if the advance was sent for afternoon papers.

religious affiliations Capitalize the names and the related terms applied to members of the orders: *He is a member of the Society of Jesus. He is a Jesuit.*

religious movements The terms that follow have been grouped under a single entry because they are interrelated and frequently cross denominational lines.

evangelical Historically, *evangelical* was used as an adjective describing dedication to conveying the message of Christ. Today it also is used as a noun, referring to a category of doctrinally conservative Christians. They emphasize the need for a definite, adult commitment or conversion to faith in Christ and the duty of all believers to persuade others to accept Christ.

Evangelicals make up some conservative denominations and are numerous in broader denominations. Evangelicals stress both doctrinal absolutes and vigorous efforts to win others to belief.

The National Association of Evangelicals is an interdenominational, cooperative body of relatively small, conservative Protestant denominations. It has a total of about 2.5 million members and maintains headquarters in Wheaton, Ill.

evangelism The word refers to activity directed outside the church fold to influence others to commit themselves to faith in Christ, to his work of serving others and to infuse his principles into society's conduct.

Styles of evangelism vary from direct preaching appeals at large public meetings to practical deeds of carrying the name of Christ, indirectly conveying the same call to allegiance to him.

The word *evangelism* is derived from the Greek *evangelion*, which means the gospel or good news of Christ's saving action in behalf of humanity.

fundamentalist The word gained usage in an early 20th century fundamentalist-modernist controversy within Protestantism. In recent years, however, *fundamentalist* has to a large extent taken on pejorative connotations except when applied to groups that stress strict, literal interpretations of Scripture and separation from other Christians.

In general, do not use *fundamentalist* unless a group applies the word to itself.

liberal In general, avoid this word as a descriptive classification in religion. It has objectionable implications to many believers.

Acceptable alternate descriptions include *activist, more flexible* and *broadview*.

Moderate is appropriate when used by the contending parties, as is the case in the conflict between the moderate or more flexible wing of the Lutheran Church-Missouri Synod and conservatives, who argue for literal interpretations of biblical passages others consider symbolic.

Do not use the term *Bible-believing* to distinguish one faction from another, because all Christians believe the Bible. The differences are over interpretations.

neo-Pentecostal, charismatic These terms apply to a movement that has developed within mainline Protestant and Roman Catholic denominations since the mid-20th century. It is distinguished by its emotional expressiveness, spontaneity in worship, speaking or praying in "unknown tongues" and healing. Participants often characterize themselves as "spirit-filled" Christians.

Unlike the earlier Pentecostal movement, which led to separate denominations, this movement has swelled within major churches.

Pentecostalism A movement that arose in the early 20th century and separated from historic Protestant denominations. It is distinguished by the belief in tangible manifestations of the Holy Spirit, often in demonstrative, emotional ways such as speaking in "unknown tongues" and healing.

Pentecostal denominations include the Assemblies of God, the Pentecostal Holiness Church, the United Pentecostal Church Inc. and the International Church of the Foursquare Gospel founded by Aimee Semple McPherson.

religious references The basic guidelines:

DEITIES: Capitalize the proper names of monotheistic deities: *God, Allah, the Father, the Son, Jesus Christ, the Son of God, the Redeemer, the Holy Spirit,* etc.

Lowercase pronouns referring to the deity: *he, him, his, thee, thou, who, whose, thy,* etc.

Lowercase *gods* in referring to the deities of polytheistic religions.

Capitalize the proper names of pagan and mythological gods and goddesses: *Neptune, Thor, Venus,* etc.

Lowercase such words as *godawful, goddamn, godlike, godliness, godsend.*

LIFE OF CHRIST: Capitalize the names of major events in the life of Jesus Christ in references that do not use his name: *The doctrines of the Last Supper, the Crucifixion, the Resurrection and the Ascension are central to Christian belief.*

But use lowercase when the words are used with his name: *The ascension of Jesus into heaven took place 40 days after his resurrection from the dead.*

Apply the principle also to events in the life of his mother: *He cited the doctrines of the Immaculate Conception and the Assumption.* But: *She referred to the assumption of Mary into heaven.*

RITES: Capitalize proper names for rites that commemorate the Last Supper or signify a belief in Christ's presence: *the Lord's Supper, Holy Communion, Holy Eucharist.*

Lowercase the names of other sacraments. See the **sacraments** entry.

Capitalize *Benediction* and the *Mass.* But: *a high Mass, a low Mass, a requiem Mass.*

HOLY DAYS: Capitalize the names of holy days. See the **holidays and holy days** entry and separate entries for major Christian and Jewish feasts.

OTHER WORDS: Lowercase *heaven, hell, devil, angel, cherub, an apostle, a priest,* etc.

Capitalize *Hades* and *Satan.*

For additional details, see **Bible**, entries for frequently used religious terms, the entries for major denominations, **religious movements** and **religious titles**.

Religious Society of Friends See **Quakers**.

religious titles The first reference to a clergyman or clergywoman normally should include a capitalized title before the individual's name.

In many cases, *the Rev.* is the designation that applies before a name on first reference. Use *the*

Rev. Dr. only if the individual has an earned doctoral degree (doctor of divinity degrees frequently are honorary) and reference to the degree is relevant.

On second reference to members of the clergy, use only a last name: *the Rev. Billy Graham* on first reference, *Graham* on second. If known only by a religious name, repeat the title: *Pope Paul VI* or *Pope Paul* on first reference, *Pope Paul, the pope* (not Paul) or *the pontiff* on second; *Metropolitan Ireney* on first reference, *Metropolitan Ireney* or *the metropolitan* on second.

Detailed guidance on specific titles and descriptive words such as *priest* and *minister* is provided in the entries for major denominations. In general, however:

CARDINALS, ARCHBISHOPS, BISHOPS: The preferred form for first reference is to use *Cardinal, Archbishop* or *Bishop* before the individual's name: *Cardinal Timothy Manning, archbishop of Los Angeles.* On second reference: *Manning* or *the cardinal.*

Substitute *the Most Rev.* if applicable and appropriate in the context: *He spoke to the Most Rev. Anthony Bevilacqua, archbishop of Philadelphia.* On second reference: *Bevilacqua* or *the archbishop.*

Entries for individual denominations tell when *the Most Rev., the Very Rev.,* etc., are applicable.

MINISTERS AND PRIESTS: Use *the Rev.* before a name on first reference.

Substitute *Monsignor* before the name of a Roman Catholic priest who has received this honor.

Do not routinely use *curate, father, pastor* and similar words before an individual's name. If

they appear before a name in a quotation, capitalize them.

RABBIS: Use *Rabbi* before a name on first reference. On second reference, use only the last name.

NUNS: Always use *Sister,* or *Mother* if applicable, before a name: *Sister Agnes Rita* in all references if the nun uses only a religious name; *Sister Clare Regina Torpy* on first reference if she uses a surname, *Sister Torpy* on second reference.

OFFICEHOLDERS: The preferred first-reference form for those who hold church office but are not ordained clergy in the usual sense is to use a construction that sets the title apart from the name by commas. Capitalize the formal title of an office, however, if it is used directly before an individual's name.

reluctant, reticent *Reluctant* means unwilling to act: *He is reluctant to enter the primary.*

Reticent means unwilling to speak: *The candidate's husband is reticent.*

Reorganized Church of Jesus Christ of Latter Day Saints Not properly described as a *Mormon church.* See the explanation under **Church of Jesus Christ of Latter-day Saints**.

representative, Rep. See **legislative titles** and **party affiliation**.

republic Capitalize *republic* when used as part of a nation's full, formal name: *the Republic of Argentina.*

See **datelines**.

republican, Republican Party *GOP* may be used on second reference.

See the **political parties and philosophies** entry.

Republican Governors Association No apostrophe.

Republican National Committee On second reference: *the national committee, the committee.*

Similarly: *Republican State Committee, Republican County Committee, Republican City Committee, the state committee, the county committee, the city committee, the committee.*

reputation See the **character, reputation** entry.

rescission Not *recision.*

Reserve Capitalize when referring to U.S. armed forces, as in Army Reserve. Lowercase in reference to members of these backup forces: reserves, or reservists.

Reserve Officers' Training Corps The *s'* is military practice. *ROTC* is acceptable in all references.

When the service is specified, use *Army ROTC, Navy ROTC* or *Air Force ROTC,* not *AROTC, NROTC* or *AFROTC.*

resident See the **citizen, resident, subject, national, native** entry.

resistible

restaurateur No *n.* Not *restauranteur.*

restrictive clauses See the **essential clauses, nonessential**

clauses entry.

restrictive phrases See the **essential phrases, nonessential phrases** entry.

Retail Clerks International Union See **United Food and Commercial Workers International Union.**

Reuters The British news agency, part of the public company Reuters Group PLC, is named for Baron Paul Julius von Reuter, the founder.

Based in London, the official name is *Reuters Ltd.,* but it is referred to as *Reuters.*

Rev. When this description is used before an individual's name, precede it with the word *"the"* because, unlike the case with *Mr.* and *Mrs.,* the abbreviation *Rev* does not stand for a noun.

If an individual has a secular title such as *Rep.,* use whichever is appropriate to the context.

See **religious titles.**

revolution Capitalize when part of a name for a specific historical event: *the American Revolution, the Bolshevik Revolution, the French Revolution.*

The Revolution, capitalized, also may be used as a shorthand reference to the *American Revolution.* Also: *the Revolutionary War.*

Lowercase in other uses: *a revolution, the revolution, the American and French revolutions.*

revolutions per minute The abbreviation *rpm* is acceptable on first reference in specialized contexts such as an auto column. Otherwise do not use it until second reference.

revolver See **pistol** and **weapons**.

Rh factor Also: *Rh negative, Rh positive.*

Rhode Island Abbrev.: *R.I.* Smallest of the 50 states in total land area: 1,049 square miles.
See **state names**.

Richter scale See **earthquakes**.

RICO An acronym for *Racketeer Influenced and Corrupt Organizations Act.* Acceptable on second reference, but *anti-racketeering* or *anti-corruption law* is preferred.

riffraff

rifle See **weapons**.

rifle, riffle *To rifle* is to plunder or steal.
To riffle is to leaf rapidly through a book or pile of papers.

right hand (n.) **right-handed** (adj.) **right-hander** (n.)

rightist, ultra-rightist In general, avoid these terms in favor of more precise descriptions of an individual's political philosophy.
As popularly used today, particularly abroad, *rightist* often applies to someone who is conservative or opposed to socialism. It also often indicates an individual who supports an authoritarian government that is militantly anti-communist or anti-socialist.
Ultra-rightist suggests an individual who subscribes to rigid interpretations of a conservative doctrine or to forms of fascism

that stress authoritarian, often militaristic, views.
See **radical** and the **leftist, ultra-leftist** entry.

right of way, rights of way

right-to-work (adj.) A *right-to-work* law prohibits a company and a union from signing a contract that would require the affected workers to be union members.
Federal labor laws generally permit such contracts. There is no federal right-to-work law, but Section 14B of the Taft-Hartley Act allows states to pass such laws if they wish. Many states have done so.
The repeal of Section 14B would have the effect of voiding all right-to-work laws. By itself, the repeal would not require workers to be union members, but in states that now have right-to-work laws, the repeal would open the way to contracts requiring union membership.
See **closed shop** for definitions of various agreements that require union membership.

right wing (n.) But: *right-wing* (adj.), *right-winger* (n.).

Ringling Bros. and Barnum & Bailey Circus Note the *and,* &.
Headquarters is in Washington.

Rio Grande Not *Rio Grande River.* (*Rio* means river.)

rip off (v.) **rip-off** (n., adj.)

river Capitalize as part of a proper name: *the Mississippi River.*

Lowercase in other uses: *the river, the Mississippi and Missouri rivers.*

road Do not abbreviate. See **addresses.**

Roaring '20s See **decades.**

robbery See the **burglary, larceny, robbery, theft** entry.

rock 'n' roll

Rocky Mountains Or simply: *the Rockies.*

roll call (n.) **roll-call** (adj.)

Rollerblade A trademark for a brand of in-line skates.

Rolls-Royce Note the hyphen in this trademark for a make of automobile.

roly-poly

ROM See **Internet** section.

Roman Catholic Church

The church teaches that its bishops have been established as the successors of the apostles through generations of ceremonies in which authority was passed down by a laying-on of hands.

Responsibility for teaching the faithful and administering the church rests with the bishops. However, the church holds that the pope has final authority over their actions because he is the bishop of Rome, the office that it teaches was held by the apostle Peter at his death.

Although the pope is empowered to speak infallibly on faith and morals, he does so only in formal pronouncements that specifically state he is speaking from the chair (*ex cathedra*) of St. Peter. This rarely used prerogative was most recently invoked in 1950, when Pope Pius XII declared that Mary was assumed bodily into heaven.

The Curia serves as a form of governmental cabinet. Its members, appointed by the pope, handle both administrative and judicial functions.

The pope also chooses members of the College of Cardinals, who serve as his principal counselors. When a new pope must be chosen, they meet in a conclave to select a new pope by majority vote. In practice, cardinals are bishops, but there is no requirement that a cardinal be a bishop.

In the United States, the church's principal organizational units are archdioceses and dioceses. They are headed, respectively, by archbishops and bishops, who have final responsibility for many activities within their jurisdictions and report directly to Rome.

The church counts more than 600 million members worldwide. In the United States it has more than 48 million members, making it the largest single body of Christians in the nation.

Roman Catholics believe in the Trinity — that there is one God who exists as three divine persons, the Father, the Son and the Holy Spirit. They believe that the Son became man as Jesus Christ.

In addition to the Holy Eucharist, there are six other sacraments — baptism, confirmation, penance (often called the sacrament of reconciliation), matrimony, holy orders, and the sacrament of the sick (formerly extreme unction).

The clergy below pope are, in

descending order, cardinal, archbishop, bishop, monsignor, priest and deacon. In religious orders, some men who are not priests have the title *brother*.

Capitalize pope when used as a title before a name: *Pope Paul VI, Pope Paul*. Lowercase in all other uses. See the **titles** entry.

The first-references forms for other titles follow. Use only last names on second reference.

Cardinals: *Cardinal Timothy Manning*. The usage *Timothy Cardinal Manning*, a practice traceable to the nobility's custom of identifications such as *William, Duke of Norfolk*, is still used in formal documents but otherwise is considered archaic.

Archbishops: *Archbishop Joseph L. Bernardin*, or *the Most Rev. Joseph L. Bernardin, archbishop of Cincinnati*.

Bishops: *Bishop Bernard J. Flanagan*, or *the Most Rev. Bernard J. Flanagan, bishop of Worcester*.

Monsignors: *Monsignor Joseph E. Vogt*. Do not use the abbreviation *Msgr.* Do not use *the Rt. Rev.* or *the Very Rev.* — this distinction between types of monsignors no longer is made.

Priests: *the Rev. John J. Paret*.

See **religious titles** and **sister** entries.

Romania Not *Rumania*.

Romanian Orthodox Church The Romanian Orthodox Church in America is an autonomous archdiocese of the Romanian Orthodox Church. The Romanian Orthodox Episcopate of America is an autonomous archdiocese within the Orthodox Church in America.

See **Eastern Orthodox churches**.

Roman numerals They use letters (*I, X*, etc.) to express numbers.

Use Roman numerals for wars and to establish personal sequence for people and animals: *World War I, Native Dancer II, King George V, Pope John XXIII, John Jones III*. See the **junior, senior** entry.

Use Arabic numerals in all other cases. See **Arabic numerals** and **numerals**.

In Roman numerals, the capital letter *I* equals 1, *V* equals 5, *X* equals 10, *L* equals 50, *C* equals 100, *D* equals 500 and *M* equals 1,000. Do not use *M* to mean million, as some newspapers occasionally do in headlines.

Other numbers are formed from these by adding or subtracting as follows:

—The value of a letter following another of the same or greater value is added: *III* equals 3.

—The value of a letter preceding one of greater value is subtracted: *IV* equals 4.

Rome The city in Italy stands alone in datelines.

room numbers Use figures and capitalize *room* when used with a figure: *Room 2, Room 211*.

rooms Capitalize the names of specially designated rooms: *Blue Room, Lincoln Room, Oval Office, Persian Room*.

Roquefort cheese, Roquefort dressing A certification mark for a type of blue cheese cured in Roquefort, France.

It is not a trademark.

rosary It is *recited* or *said*, never *read*. Always lowercase.

Rosh Hashana The Jewish new year. Occurs in September or October.

rostrum See the **lectern, podium, pulpit, rostrum** entry.

ROTC Acceptable in all references for *Reserve Officers' Training Corps*.

When the service is specified, use *Army ROTC, Navy ROTC* or *Air Force ROTC*, not *AROTC, NROTC* or *AFROTC*.

round up (v.) **roundup** (n.)

route numbers Do not abbreviate *route*. See **highway designations**.

Royal Dutch-Shell Group of Companies This holding company, based in London and The Hague, owns substantial portions of the stock in numerous corporations that specialize in petroleum and related products. Most have *Shell* in their names.

Among them is Shell Oil Co., a U.S. corporation, with headquarters in Houston.

royal titles See **nobility**.

R.S.V.P. The abbreviation for the French *repondez s'il vous plait*, it means *please reply*.

Rt. Rev. See the entry for an individual denomination.

rubber stamp (n.) **rubber-stamp** (v. and adj.)

rubella Also known as *German measles*.

runner-up, runners-up

running mate

rush hour (n.) **rush-hour** (adj.)

Russia See **Commonwealth of Independent States** entry.

Russian names When a first name in Russian has a close phonetic equivalent in English, use the equivalent in translating the name: *Alexander Solzhenitsyn* rather than *Aleksandr*, the spelling that would result from a transliteration of the Russian letter into the English alphabet.

When a first name has no close phonetic equivalent in English, express it with an English spelling that approximates the sound in Russian: *Nikita*, for example.

For last names, use the English spelling that most closely approximates the pronunciation in Russian.

If an individual has a preference for an English spelling that is different from the one that would result by applying these guidelines, follow the individual's preference.

Women's last names have feminine endings. But use them only if the woman is not married or if she is known under that name (*the ballerina Maya Plissetskaya*). Otherwise, use the masculine form: *Raisa Gorbachev*, not *Gorbacheva*.

Russian names never end in *off*, except for common mistransliterations such as *Rachmaninoff*. Instead, the transliterations should end in *ov*: *Romanov*.

Russian Orthodox Church See **Eastern Orthodox churches**.

Russian Revolution Also: *the Bolshevik Revolution*.

S

Sabbath Capitalize in religious references; lowercase to mean a period of rest.

Sabena Belgian World Airlines A *Sabena airliner* is acceptable in any reference.

Headquarters is in Brussels, Belgium.

saboteur

sacraments Capitalize the proper names used for a sacramental rite that commemorates the life of Jesus Christ or signifies a belief in his presence: *the Lord's Supper, Holy Communion, Holy Eucharist.*

Lowercase the names of other sacraments: *baptism, confirmation, penance* (now often called the *sacrament of reconciliation*), *matrimony, holy orders,* and *the sacrament of anointing the sick* (formerly *extreme unction*).

See entries for the major religious denominations and **religious references**.

sacrilegious

Safeway Stores Inc. Headquarters is in Oakland, Calif.

saint Abbreviate as *St.* in the names of saints, cities and other places: *St. Jude; St. Paul, Minn.; St. John's, Newfoundland; St. Lawrence Seaway.*

But see the entries for **Saint John** and **Sault Ste. Marie**.

Saint John The spelling for the city in New Brunswick.

To distinguish it from *St. John's, Newfoundland.*

salable

SALT See **Strategic Arms Reduction Treaty (START)**

Salt Lake City Stands alone in datelines.

salvo, salvos

SAM, SAMs Acceptable on second reference for *surface-to-air-missile(s).*

San'a It's NOT an apostrophe (') in the Yemen capital's name. It's a reverse apostrophe ('), or a single opening quotation mark.

sandbag (n.) The verbs: *sandbagged, sandbagging.* And: *sandbagger.*

San Diego The city in California stands alone in datelines.

sandstorm See **weather terms**.

sandwich

San Francisco The city in California stands alone in datelines.

sanitarium, sanitariums

San Marino Use alone in datelines on stories from the Republic of San Marino.

Santa Claus

Sardinia Use instead of Italy in datelines on stories from communities on this island.

Saskatchewan A province of Canada north of Montana and North Dakota. Do not abbreviate. See **datelines**.

SAT Use only the initials in referring to the previously designated Scholastic Aptitude Test or the Scholastic Assessment Test.

Satan But lowercase *devil* and *satanic*.

satellites See **spacecraft designations**.

satellite communications The following are some generally used technical terms dealing with satellite communications.
—*uplink* The transmission from the ground to the satellite.
—*downlink* The transmission from the satellite to the ground.
—*foot print* The area on the ground in which a transmission from a particular satellite can be received.
—*earth station* Sending or receiving equipment on the ground for a satellite.
—*transponder* The equipment on a satellite that receives from the ground and sends to the ground. A satellite usually has a number of *transponders*.
—*geosynchronous* A satellite orbit in which the satellite appears to always be in the same place in reference to the Earth. Most communications satellites are in geosynchronous orbits. Also *geostationary*.

Saturday See **days of the week**.

Saturday night special See **weapons**.

Saudi Arabian Oil Co. *Saudi Aramco* is acceptable on second reference. (Formerly the Arabian American Oil Co.)

Sault Ste. Marie, Mich., Sault Ste. Marie, Ontario The abbreviation is *Ste.* instead of *St.* because the full name is *Sault Sainte Marie.*

savings and loan associations They are not banks. Use *the association* on second reference.

savior Use this spelling for all senses, rather than the alternate form, *saviour.*

Scandinavian Airlines System *SAS* is acceptable on second reference.
Headquarters is in Stockholm, Sweden.

scene numbers Capitalize scene when used with a figure: *Scene 2; Act 2, Scene 4.*
But: *the second scene, the third scene.*

scheme Do not use as a synonym for *a plan* or *a project.*

school Capitalize when part

of a proper name: *Public School 3, Madison Elementary School, Doherty Junior High School, Crocker High School.*

scissors Takes plural verbs and pronouns: *The scissors are on the table. Leave them there.*

Scot, Scots, Scottish A native of Scotland is a *Scot.* The people are the *Scots,* not the *Scotch.*

Somebody or something is *Scottish.*

scotch barley, scotch broth, scotch salmon, scotch sour

Scotch tape A trademark for a brand of transparent tape.

Scotch whisky A type of whiskey distilled in Scotland from malted barley. The malt is dried over a peat fire.

Capitalize *Scotch* and use the spelling *whisky* only when the two words are used together.

Lowercase *scotch* standing alone: *Give me some scotch.*

Use the spelling *whiskey* for generic references to the beverage, which may be distilled from any of several grains.

The verb *to scotch* means to stamp out, put an end to.

Scotland Use *Scotland* after the names of Scottish communities in datelines.

See **datelines** and **United Kingdom.**

Scripture, Scriptures Capitalize when referring to the religious writings in the Bible.

See **Bible.**

scuba Lowercased acronym

for *self-contained underwater breathing apparatus.*

sculptor Use for both men and women.

scurrilous

Sea Islands A chain of islands off the coasts of South Carolina, Georgia and Florida.

Islands within the boundaries of South Carolina include Parris Island, Port Royal Island, and St. Helena Island.

Those within Georgia include Cumberland Island (largest in the chain), St. Simons Island and St. Catherines Island (no apostrophes), and Sea Island.

Amelia Island is within the boundaries of Florida.

Several communities have names taken from the island name — Port Royal is a town on Port Royal Island, Sea Island is a resort on Sea Island, and St. Simons Island is a village on St. Simons Island.

In datelines:
PORT ROYAL, S.C. (AP) —
ST. SIMONS ISLAND, Ga. (AP) —

seaman See **military titles.**

Sears, Roebuck and Co. Headquarters is in Hoffman Estates, Ill.

seasons Lowercase *spring, summer, fall, winter* and derivatives such as *springtime* unless part of a formal name: *Dartmouth Winter Carnival, Winter Olympics, Summer Olympics.*

Seattle The city in the state of Washington stands alone in datelines.

second guess (n.) The verb

form: *second-guess*. Also: *second-guesser*.

second hand (n.) **second-hand** (adj. and adv.) *Secondhand Rose had a watch with a second hand that she bought secondhand.*

second-rate (adj.) All uses: *A second-rate play. The play is second-rate.*

second reference When used in this book, the term applies to all subsequent references to an organization or individual within a story.

Acceptable abbreviations and acronyms for organizations frequently in the news are listed under the organization's full name. A few prominent acronyms acceptable on first reference also are listed alphabetically according to the letters of the acronym.

The listing of an acceptable term for second reference does not mean that it always must be used after the first reference. Often a generic word such as *the agency*, *the commission* or *the company* is more appropriate and less jarring to the reader. At other times, the full name may need to be repeated for clarity.

For additional guidelines that apply to organizations, see the **abbreviations and acronyms** entry and **capitalization.**

For additional guidelines that apply to individuals, see **courtesy titles** and **titles.**

secretary Capitalize before a name only if it is an official corporate or organizational title. Do not abbreviate.
See **titles.**

secretary-general With a hyphen. Capitalize as a formal title before a name: *Secretary-General Dag Hammarskjold.*
See **titles.**

secretary of state Capitalize as a formal title before a name.
See **titles.**

secretary-treasurer With a hyphen. Capitalize as a formal title before a name.
See **titles.**

Secret Service A federal agency administered by the Treasury Department.

The *Secret Service Uniformed Division,* which protects the president's residence and offices and the embassies in Washington, formerly was known as the Executive Protective Service.

section Capitalize when used with a figure to identify part of a law or bill: *Section 14B of the Taft-Hartley Act.*

Securities and Exchange Commission *SEC* is acceptable on second reference.

The related legislation is the *Securities Exchange Act* (no *and*).

Security Council (U.N.) *Security Council* may be used on first reference in stories under a United Nations dateline. Use *U.N. Security Council* in other first references.

Retain capitalization of *Security Council* in all references.

Lowercase *council* whenever it stands alone.

Seeing Eye dog A trademark for a guide dog trained by Seeing Eye Inc. of Morristown, N.J.

seesaw

self- Always hyphenate:
self-assured   self-government
self-defense

sell out (v.) **sellout** (n.)

semi- The rules in prefixes apply, but in general, no hyphen. Some examples:
semifinal   semiofficial
semi-invalid   semitropical

semiannual Twice a year, a synonym for *biannual*.
Do not confuse it with *biennial*, which means every two years.

semicolon See entry in **Punctuation** chapter.

semitrailer Or *tractor-trailer* (but not semi-tractor trailer).

senate Capitalize all specific references to governmental legislative bodies, regardless of whether the name of the nation is used: *the U.S. Senate, the Senate, the Virginia Senate, the state Senate, the Senate*.
Lowercase plural uses: *the Virginia and North Carolina senates*.
See **governmental bodies**.
The same principles apply to foreign bodies. See **foreign legislative bodies**.
Lowercase references to nongovernmental bodies: *the student senate at Yale*.

senator, Sen. See **legislative titles** and **party affiliation**.

senatorial Always lowercase.

send off (v.) **send-off** (n.)

senior See the **junior, senior** entry.

senior citizen Use the term sparingly. See **elderly**.

sentences Capitalize the first word of every sentence, including quoted statements and direct questions:
Patrick Henry said, "I know not what course others may take, but as for me, give me liberty or give me death."
Capitalize the first word of a quoted statement if it constitutes a sentence, even if it was part of a larger sentence in the original: *Patrick Henry said, "Give me liberty or give me death."*
In direct questions, even without quotation marks: *The story answers the question, Where does true happiness really lie?*
See **ellipsis** in the **Punctuation** chapter and poetry.

September See **months**.

sergeant See **military titles**.

serial numbers Use figures and capital letters in solid form (no hyphens or spaces unless the source indicates they are an integral part of the code): *A1234567*.

serviceable

service clubs See the **fraternal organizations and service clubs** entry.

service mark A brand, symbol, word, etc. used by a supplier of services and protected by law to prevent a competitor from using it: *Realtor*, for a member of the National Association of Realtors, for example.
When a service mark is used, capitalize it.
The preferred form, however, is to use a generic term unless

the service mark is essential to the story.

See **brand names** and **trademark**.

sesquicentennial Every 150 years.

set up (v.) **setup** (n. and adj.)

7-Eleven Trademark for stores operated and licensed by Southland Corp. Headquarters in Dallas.

Seven Seas Arabian Sea, Atlantic Ocean, Bay of Bengal, Mediterranean Sea, Persian Gulf, Red Sea, South China Sea.

Seven Sisters The colleges are: Barnard, Bryn Mawr, Mount Holyoke, Radcliffe, Smith, Vassar and Wellesley.

Also an outdated nickname for the world's largest privately operated oil companies. They were: British Petroleum, Exxon, Gulf, Mobil, Royal Dutch Shell, Texaco, and Chevron, formerly Standard Oil Co. of California. Chevron has since taken over Gulf and Exxon and Mobil have merged.

Seventh-day Adventist Church The denomination is traceable to the preaching of William Miller of New Hampton, N.Y., a Baptist layman who said his study of the Book of Daniel showed that the end of the world would come in the mid-1840s.

When the prediction did not come true, the Millerites split into smaller groups. One, influenced by visions described by Ellen Harmon, later Mrs. James White, is the precursor of the Seventh-day Adventist practice today.

The church has four con-stituent levels: 1. Local churches. 2. Local conferences of churches for a state or part of a state. 3. Union conferences of a number of local conferences. 4. The General Conference.

The General Conference in Session, which meets every five years, and the General Conference Executive Committee are the highest administrative authorities.

The office of the General Conference, located in Washington, lists U.S. membership at 627,000 and worldwide membership at 5.2 million.

The description *adventist* is based on the belief that a second coming of Christ is near. *Seventh-day* derives from the contention that the Bible requires observing the seventh day of the week as the Sabbath.

Baptism, by immersion, is reserved for those old enough to understand its meaning. Baptism and the Lord's Supper are the only sacraments.

The head of the General Conference holds the formal title of *president*. The formal titles for ministers are *pastor* or *elder*. Capitalize them when used immediately before a name on first reference. On second reference, use only the last name.

The designation *the Rev.* is not used.

See **religious titles**.

7UP Trademark for a brand of soft drink.

Seven Wonders of the World The Egyptian pyramids, the hanging gardens of Babylon, the Mausoleum at Halicarnassus, the temple of Artemis at Ephesus, the Colossus of Rhodes, the statue of Zeus by Phidias at Olympia and the Pharos or lighthouse at Alexandria.

sewage, sewerage *Sewage* is waste matter.

Sewerage is the drainage system.

sex changes Use the pronoun preferred by the individuals who have acquired the physical characteristics (by hormone therapy, body modification, or surgery) of the opposite sex and present themselves in a way that does not correspond with their sex at birth.

If that preference is not expressed, use the pronoun consistent with the way the individuals live publicly.

sexism See the **man, mankind** and **women** entries.

shah Capitalize when used as a title before a name: *Shah Mohammad Reza Pahlavi of Iran.*

The Shah of Iran commonly is known only by this title, which is, in effect, an alternate name. Capitalize *Shah of Iran* in references to the holder of the title; lowercase subsequent references as *the shah.*

The practice is based on the guidelines in the **nobility** entry.

shake up (v.) **shake-up** (n. and adj.)

shall, will Use *shall* to express determination: *We shall overcome. You and he shall stay.*

Either *shall* or *will* may be used in first-person constructions that do not emphasize determination: *We shall hold a meeting. We will hold a meeting.*

For second- and third-person constructions, use *will* unless determination is stressed: *You will*

like it. She will not be pleased.

See the **should, would** entry and **subjunctive mood**.

shape up (v.) **shape-up** (n. and adj.)

Shariah The legal code of Islam. It is roughly comparable to the Talmudic tradition in Judaism.

Shavuot The Jewish Feast of Weeks, commemorating the receiving of the Ten Commandments. Occurs in May or June.

she Do not use this pronoun in references to ships or nations. Use *it* instead.

Sheet Metal Workers International Association The shortened form *Sheet Metal Workers union* is acceptable in all references.

Headquarters is in Washington.

Sheetrock A trademark for a brand of gypsum wallboard.

sheik Use this spelling unless the individual named personally prefers *sheikh.*

shell See **weapons**.

Shell Oil Co. This U.S. company with headquarters in Houston, is part of the Royal Dutch-Shell Group of Companies. The group owns more than half of the stock in Shell Oil.

sheriff Capitalize when used as a formal title before a name. See **titles**.

ships See the **boats, ships** entry.

shirt sleeve, shirt sleeves (n.) **shirt-sleeve** (adj.)

shoeshine, shoestring

shopworn

shortchange

short-lived (adj.) *A short-lived plan. The plan was short-lived.*

short ton Equal to 2,000 pounds. See **ton**.

shot See **weapons**.

shotgun See **weapons**.

should, would Use *should* to express an obligation: *We should help the needy.*

Use *would* to express a customary action: *In the summer we would spend hours by the seashore.*

Use *would* also in constructing a conditional past tense, but be careful:

Wrong: *If Soderholm would not have had an injured foot, Thompson would not have been in the lineup.*

Right: *If Soderholm had not had an injured foot, Thompson would not have been in the lineup.*

See **subjunctive mood**.

showcase, showroom

show off (v.) **showoff** (n.)

shrubs See **plants**.

shut down (v.) **shutdown** (n.)

shut-in

shut off (v.) **shut-off** (n.)

shut out (v.) **shutout** (n.)

(sic) Do not use *(sic)* unless it is in the matter being quoted. To show that an error, peculiar usage or spelling is in the original, use a note to editors at the top of the story, below the summary line but ahead of a byline.

— — —

↑ *EDITORS: The spelling cabob is in the original copy.* ←
     Or:
↑ *EDITORS: The spelling Jorga is correct.* ←

Sicily Use instead of Italy in datelines on stories from communities on this island.

side by side, side-by-side *They walked side by side. The stories received side-by-side display.*

Sierra Nevada, the Not *Sierra Nevada Mountains.* (*Sierra* means mountains.)

sightseeing, sightseer

Simoniz A trademark for a brand of auto wax.

Sinai Not the *Sinai*. But: *the Sinai Desert, the Sinai Peninsula.*

Singapore Stands alone in datelines.

single-handed, single-handedly

sir See **nobility**.

sister Capitalize in all references before the names of nuns.

If no surname is given, the name is the same in all references: *Sister Agnes Rita.*

If a surname is used in first reference, drop the given name on second reference: *Sister Clair Regina Torpy* on first reference, *Sister Torpy* in subsequent references.

Use *Mother* the same way when referring to a woman who heads a group of nuns.

See **religious titles**.

sister-in-law, sisters-in-law

sit down (v.) **sit-down** (n. and adj.)

sit in (v.) **sit-in** (n. and adj.)

sizable

sizes Use figures: *a size 9 dress, size 40 long, 10 1/2B shoes, a 34 1/2 sleeve.*

skeptic See the **cynic, skeptic** entry.

ski, skis, skier, skied, skiing Also: *ski jump, ski jumping.*

Skid Road, Skid Row The term originated as *Skid Road* in the Seattle area, where dirt roads were used to skid logs to the mill. Over the years, *Skid Road* became a synonym for the area where loggers gathered, usually down among the rooming houses and saloons.

In time, the term spread to other cities as a description for sections, such as the Bowery in New York, that are havens for derelicts. In the process, *row* replaced *road* in many references.

Use *Skid Road* for this section in Seattle; either *Skid Road* or *Skid Row* for other areas.

skillful

slang In general, avoid slang, the highly informal language that is outside of conventional or standard usage.

See **colloquialisms; dialect;** and **word selection**.

slash This diagonal line, also known as the *virgule*, may not be transmitted correctly in some computer systems. Substitute a hyphen whenever possible.

slaying See the **homicide, murder, manslaughter** entry.

sledgehammer

sleet See **weather terms**.

sleight of hand

slowdown (n.) Two words in verb form.

slumlord

slush fund

small-arms fire

small-business man

smash up (v.) **smashup** (n. and adj.)

Smithfield Ham A trademark for a ham dry-cured, smoked and aged in Smithfield, Va.

Smithsonian Institution Not *Smithsonian Institute.*

smoke bomb, smoke screen

Smokey Or *Smokey Bear.* Not *Smokey the Bear.*
But: *A smoky room.*

smolder Not **smoulder**.

sneaked Preferred as past tense of *sneak*. Do not use the colloquial *snuck*.

snowdrift, snowfall, snowflake, snowman, snowplow, snowshoe, snowstorm, snowsuit

so called (adv.) **so-called** (adj.)

socialist, socialism See the **political parties and philosophies** entry.

Social Security Capitalize all references to the U.S. system.

The number groups are hyphenated: *123-45-6789*

Lowercase generic uses such as: *Is there a social security program in Sweden?*

social titles See **courtesy titles.**

Society for the Prevention of Cruelty to Animals *SPCA* is acceptable on second reference.

The *American Society for the Prevention of Cruelty to Animals* is limited to the five boroughs of New York City.

The autonomous chapters in other cities ordinarily precede the organization by the name of the city: On first reference, *the Philadelphia Society for the Prevention of Cruelty to Animals*; on second, *the Philadelphia SPCA* or *SPCA* as appropriate in the context.

Society of Friends See **Quakers.**

Society of Professional Journalists (no longer the Society of Professional Journalists,

Sigma Delta Chi). On second reference: *SPJ.*

soft-spoken

software titles Capitalize but do not use quotation marks around such titles as WordPerfect or Windows, but use quotation marks for computer games: *"Where in the World is Carmen Sandiego?"*

solicitor See **lawyer.**

Solid South Those Southern states traditionally regarded as supporters of the Democratic Party.

soliloquy, soliloquies

song titles See **composition titles.**

son-in-law, sons-in-law

SOS The distress signal.
S.O.S (no final period) is a trademark for a brand of soap pad.

sound barrier The speed of sound no longer a true barrier because aircraft have exceeded it. See **Mach number.**

South As defined by the U.S. Census Bureau, the 16-state region is broken into three divisions.

The four *East South Central* states are Alabama, Kentucky, Mississippi and Tennessee.

The eight *South Atlantic* states are Delaware, Florida, Georgia, Maryland, North Carolina, South Carolina, Virginia and West Virginia.

The four *West South Central* states are Arkansas, Louisiana,

Oklahoma and Texas.

There is no official U.S. Census Bureau definition of Southeast.

See **North Central region; Northeast region;** and **West** for the bureau's other regional breakdowns.

south, southern, southeast, southwest See the **directions and regions** entry.

South America See **Western Hemisphere.**

South Carolina Abbrev.: *S.C.* See **state names.**

South Dakota Abbrev.: *S.D.* See **state names.**

Southeast Asia The nations of the Indochinese Peninsula and the islands southeast of it: Cambodia, Indonesia, Laos, Malaysia, Myanmar, Papua New Guinea, the Philippines, Singapore, Thailand and Vietnam.

See **Asian subcontinent** and **Far East.**

Southeast Asia Treaty Organization *SEATO* is acceptable on second reference.

Soviet Union See **Commonwealth of Independent States.**

Space Age It began with the launching of Sputnik 1 on Oct. 4, 1957.

space agency See **National Aeronautics and Space Administration.**

space centers See **John F. Kennedy Space Center** and **Lyndon B. Johnson Space Center.**

spacecraft designations Use Arabic figures and capitalize the name: *Gemini 7, Apollo 11, Pioneer 10.*

spaceship

space shuttle Lowercase *space shuttle,* but capitalize a proper name.

The space shuttle is a reusable winged aircraft capable of carrying people and cargo into Earth orbit. It is designed to take off vertically with the aid of booster rockets. After an orbital mission, re-entry begins with the firing of engines that send the craft back into Earth's atmosphere. The final leg of the return trip is a powerless glide to a landing strip.

spacewalk

Spanish-American War

Spanish names The family names of both the father and mother usually are considered part of a person's full name. In everyday use, customs sometimes vary with individuals and countries.

The normal sequence is given name, father's family name, mother's family name: *Jose Lopez Portillo.*

On second reference, use only the father's family name (*Lopez*), unless the individual prefers or is widely known by a multiple last name (*Lopez Portillo*).

Some individuals use a *y* (for *and*) between the two surnames to ensure that both names are used together (including second references): *Jose Lopez y Portillo.*

A married woman frequently uses her father's name, followed by the particle *de* (for *of*) and her husband's name. A woman named *Irma Perez* who married a man named *Anibal Gutierrez* would be known as *Irma Perez de Gutierrez*. Use *Mrs. Gutierrez* on second reference.

speaker Capitalize as a formal title before a name. Generally, it is a formal title only for the speaker of a legislative body: *Speaker Thomas P. O'Neill.*
See **titles**.

special contexts When this term is used in this book, it means that the material described may be used in a regular column devoted to a specialized subject or when a particular literary effect is suitable.

Special literary effects generally are suitable only in feature copy, but even there they should be used with care. Most feature material should follow the same style norms that apply to regular news copy.

species Same in singular and plural. Use singular or plural verbs and pronouns depending on the sense: *The species has been unable to maintain itself. Both species are extinct.*
See **genus, species**.

speeches Capitalize and use quotation marks for their formal titles, as described in **composition titles**.

speechmaker, speechmaking

speed of sound See **Mach number**.

speeds Use figures. *The car slowed to 7 miles per hour, winds of 5 to 10 miles per hour, winds of 7 to 9 knots, 10-knot wind.*

Avoid extensively hyphenated constructions such as *5-mile-per-hour winds.*

speed up (v.) **speedup** (n. and adj.)

spelling The basic rule when in doubt is to consult this book followed by, if necessary, a dictionary under conditions described in the **dictionary** entry.

Memory Aid: Noah Webster developed the following rule of thumb for the frequently vexing question of whether to double a final consonant in forming the present participle and past tense of a verb:

—If the stress in pronunciation is on the first syllable, do not double the consonant: *combat, combating, combated*; *cancel, canceling, canceled.*

—If the stress in pronunciation is on the second syllable, double the consonant unless confusion would result: *incur, incurred, incurring*. An exception, to avoid confusion with *buss*, is *bus, bused, busing.*

spill, spilled, spilling Not *spilt* in the past tense.

split infinitive See **verbs**.

spokesman, spokeswoman But not *spokesperson*. Use a *representative* if you do not know the sex of the individual.

sport utility vehicle (No plural *s*, no hyphen)

spouse Use when some of the people involved may be men. For example: *physicians and their spouses*, not *physicians and their wives.*

spring See **seasons**.

springtime

sputnik Usually lowercase, but capitalize when followed by a figure as part of a proper name: *Sputnik 1*.

It is Russian for *satellite*.

squall See **weather terms**.

square Do not abbreviate. Capitalize when part of a proper name: *Washington Square*.

squinting modifier A misplaced adverb that can be interpreted as modifying either of two words: *Those who lie often are found out*.

Place the adverb where there can be no confusion, even if a compound verb must be split: *Those who often lie are found out*. Or if that was not the sense: *Those who lie are often found out*.

Sri Lanka Formerly Ceylon. Use *Sri Lanka* in datelines and other references to the nation.

The people may be called either *Sri Lankans* or *Ceylonese*.

Before the nation was called Ceylon, it was Serendip, whence comes the word *serendipity*.

SRO Acceptable on second reference for *standing room only*.

S.S. Kresge Co. Now known as *Kmart*. Headquarters is in Troy, Mich.

SST Acceptable in all references for a *supersonic transport*.

stadium, stadiums Capitalize only when part of a proper name: *Yankee Stadium*.

Stalin, Josef Not *Joseph*.

stall Use care when using *stall* in this sense. When an automobile *stalls*, the engine stops. This may not be true when an airplane *stalls*; it pitches forward or sideways because of a lack of air speed.

stamp, stomp Both are acceptable, but *stamp* is preferred.

stanch, staunch *Stanch* is a verb: *He stanched the flow of blood*.

Staunch is an adjective: *She is a staunch supporter of equality*.

Standard & Poor's Register of Corporations The source for determining the formal name of a business. See **company names**.

The register is published by Standard & Poor's Corp. of New York.

standard-bearer

standard time Capitalize *Eastern Standard Time, Pacific Standard Time*, etc., but lowercase *standard time* when standing alone.

See **time zones**.

stand in (v.) **stand-in** (n. and adj.)

standing room only *SRO* is acceptable on second reference.

stand off (v.) **standoff** (n. and adj.)

stand out (v.) **standout** (n. and adj.)

starboard Nautical for *right*. See **port, starboard** entry.

"The Star-Spangled Banner" But lowercase *the national anthem.*

startup One word (n. and adj.) to describe a new business venture. (An exception to Webster's preference.)

state Lowercase in all *state of* constructions: *the state of Maine, the states of Maine and Vermont.*

Four states — Kentucky, Massachusetts, Pennsylvania and Virginia — are legally commonwealths rather than states. The distinction is necessary only in formal uses: *The commonwealth of Kentucky filed a suit.* For simple geographic reference: *Tobacco is grown in the state of Kentucky.*

Do not capitalize *state* when used simply as an adjective to specify a level of jurisdiction: *state Rep. William Smith, the state Transportation Department, state funds.*

Apply the same principle to phrases such as *the city of Chicago, the town of Auburn,* etc.

See also **state names.**

statehouse Capitalize all references to a specific statehouse, with or without the name of the state: *The Vermont Statehouse is in Montpelier. The governor will visit the Statehouse today.*

Lowercase plural uses: *the Massachusetts and Rhode Island statehouses.*

state names Follow these guidelines:

STANDING ALONE: Spell out the names of the 50 U.S. states when they stand alone in textual material. Any state name may be condensed, however, to fit typographical requirements for tabular material.

EIGHT NOT ABBREVIATED: The names of eight states are never abbreviated in datelines or text: *Alaska, Hawaii, Idaho, Iowa, Maine, Ohio, Texas* and *Utah.*

Memory Aid: Spell out the names of the two states that are not part of the contiguous United States and of the continental states that are five letters or fewer.

ABBREVIATIONS REQUIRED: Use the state abbreviations listed at the end of this section:

—In conjunction with the name of a city, town, village or military base in most datelines. See **datelines** for examples and exceptions for large cities.

—In conjunction with the name of a city, county, town, village or military base in text. See examples in **punctuation** section below. See **datelines** for guidelines on when a city name may stand alone in the body of a story.

—In short-form listings of party affiliation: *D-Ala., R-Mont.* See **party affiliation** entry for details.

Following are the state abbreviations, which also appear in the entries for each state (ZIP code abbreviations in parentheses):

Ala. (AL)	Md. (MD)	N.D. (ND)
Ariz. (AZ)	Mass. (MA)	Okla. (OK)
Ark. (AR)	Mich. (MI)	Ore. (OR)
Calif. (CA)	Minn. (MN)	Pa. (PA)
Colo. (CO)	Miss. (MS)	R.I. (RI)
Conn. (CT)	Mo. (MO)	S.C. (SC)
Del. (DE)	Mont. (MT)	S.D. (SD)
Fla. (FL)	Neb. (NE)	Tenn. (TN)
Ga. (GA)	Nev. (NV)	Vt. (VT)
Ill. (IL)	N.H. (NH)	Va. (VA)
Ind. (IN)	N.J. (NJ)	Wash. (WA)
Kan. (KS)	N.M. (NM)	W.Va. (WV)
Ky. (KY)	N.Y. (NY)	Wis. (WI)
La. (LA)	N.C. (NC)	Wyo. (WY)

(These are the ZIP code abbreviations for the eight states that are not abbreviated in datelines or text: AK (Alaska), HI (Hawaii), ID (Idaho), IA (Iowa), ME (Maine), OH (Ohio), TX (Texas), UT (Utah).

Use the two-letter Postal Service abbreviations only with full addresses, including ZIP code.

PUNCTUATION: Place one comma between the city and the state name, and another comma after the state name, unless ending a sentence or indicating a dateline: *He was traveling from Nashville, Tenn., to Austin, Texas, en route to his home in Albuquerque, N.M. She said Cook County, Ill., was Mayor Daley's stronghold.*

MISCELLANEOUS: Use *New York state* when necessary to distinguish the state from New York City.

Use *state of Washington* or *Washington state* when necessary to distinguish the state from the District of Columbia. (*Washington State* is the name of a university in the state of Washington.)

State of the Union Capitalize all references to the president's annual address.

Lowercase other uses: *"The state of the union is confused,"* the editor said.

state police Capitalize with a state name if part of the formal description for a police agency: *the New York State Police, the Virginia State Police.*

In most cases, state police standing alone is a shorthand reference for *state policemen* rather than a reference to the agency. For consistency and to avoid hairline distinctions about whether the reference is to the agency or

the officers, lowercase the words *state police* whenever they are not preceded by a state name.

See **highway patrol**.

states' rights

statewide

stationary, stationery To stand still is to be *stationary.*

Writing paper is *stationery.*

station wagon

statute mile It equals 5,280 feet, or approximately 1.6 kilometers.

To convert to approximate nautical miles, multiply the number of statute miles by .869.

See **kilometer; knot; mile;** and **nautical mile**.

staunch See the **stanch, staunch** entry.

steady-state theory See **big-bang theory**.

stealth When used in connection with military aircraft, ships and vehicles it means the equipment is masked from various types of electronic detection. Stealth equipment can range from radar wave absorbing paint to electronic jamming devices. Like the *cruise* missile, always lowercase, no quotation marks.

stepbrother, stepfather
Also: *stepsister, stepmother.*

steppingstone

stifling

St. John's The city in the Canadian province of Newfoundland.

Not to be confused with *Saint John, New Brunswick*.

St. Louis The city in Missouri stands alone in datelines.

stockmen's advisory See **weather terms**.

stool pigeon

stopgap

storm See **weather terms**.

storyteller

straight-laced, strait-laced Use *straight-laced* for someone strict or severe in behavior or moral views.

Reserve *strait-laced* for the notion of confinement, as in a corset.

strait Capitalize as part of a proper name: *Bering Strait, Strait of Gibraltar*.

But: *the Bosporus* and *the Dardanelles*. Neither is followed by *Strait*.

straitjacket Not *straightjacket*.

Strategic Arms Reduction Treaty *START* is acceptable on first reference to the treaty as long as it is made immediately clear which is being referred to.

Use the *strategic arms treaty* or *the treaties* in some references to avoid alphabet soup.

There are two treaties, START I (1991) and START II (1993).

Do not confuse with the *Strategic Arms Limitation Treaty* of 1979, known as *SALT*.

Strategic Defense Initiative This is the official name of the research and development work on defense against a nuclear attack. *SDI* is the acronym and is acceptable on second reference. "Star Wars" has become synonymous with both and was derived from the movie series. If used, it must always be within quotation marks.

street Abbreviate only with a numbered address. See **addresses**.

strikebreaker

strong-arm (v., adj.)

strong-willed

student See the **pupil, student** entry.

stylebook One word when referring to the *AP Stylebook* and to *stylebooks* generically.

Styrofoam A trademark for a brand of plastic foam. Use the term plastic foam unless referring specifically to the trademark product.

sub- The rules in prefixes apply, but in general, no hyphen. Some examples:

subbasement	submachine gun
subcommittee	suborbital
subculture	subtotal
subdivision	subzero

subcommittee Lowercase when used with the name of a legislative body's full committee: *a Ways and Means subcommittee*.

Capitalize when a subcommittee has a proper name of its own: *the Senate Permanent Subcommittee on Investigations*.

subject See the **citizen, resident, subject, national, native** entry.

subjunctive mood Use the subjunctive mood of a verb for contrary-to-fact conditions, and expressions of doubts, wishes or regrets:

If I were a rich man, I wouldn't have to work hard.

I doubt that more money would be the answer.

I wish it were possible to take back my words.

Sentences that express a contingency or hypothesis may use either the subjunctive or the indicative mood depending on the context. In general, use the subjunctive if there is little likelihood that a contingency might come true:

If I were to marry a millionaire, I wouldn't have to worry about money.

If the bill passes as expected, it will provide an immediate tax cut.

See the **should, would** entry.

submachine gun See **weapons**.

subpoena, subpoenaed, subpoenaing

Sucaryl A trademark for a brand of noncaloric sweetener.

successor

suffixes See separate listing for commonly used suffixes.

Follow Webster's New World Dictionary for words not in this book.

If a word combination is not listed in Webster's New World, use two words for the verb form; hyphenate any noun or adjective forms.

suit, suite You may have a *suit* of clothes, a *suit* of cards, or be faced with a *lawsuit*.

There are *suites* of music, rooms and furniture.

Sukkot The Jewish Feast of Tabernacles, celebrating the fall harvest and commemorating the desert wandering of the Jews during the Exodus. Occurs in September or October.

summer See **seasons**.

summertime

sun Lowercase. See **heavenly bodies**.

sunbathe The verb forms: *sunbathed, sunbathing.* Also: *sunbather.*

Sun Belt Generally those states in the South and West, ranging from Florida and Georgia through the Gulf states into California.

Sunday See **days of the week**.

super Avoid the slang tendency to use it in place of *excellent, wonderful,* etc.

super- The rules in prefixes apply, but in general, no hyphen. Some frequently used words:

superagency	superhighway
supercarrier	superpower
supercharge	supertanker

As with all prefixes, however, use a hyphen if the word that follows is capitalized: *super-Republican.*

Super Bowl

superconducting super collider

superintendent Do not abbreviate. Capitalize when used as a formal title before a name.
See **titles**.

superior court See **court names**.

supersede

supersonic See **Mach number**.

supersonic transport *SST* is acceptable in all references.

supra- The rules in **prefixes** apply, but in general, no hyphen. Some examples:
supragovernmental supranational

Supreme Court of the United States
Capitalize *U.S. Supreme Court* and also *the Supreme Court* when the context makes the *U.S.* designation unnecessary.

The chief justice is properly the *chief justice of the United States*, not *of the Supreme Court*: *Chief Justice William Rehnquist*.

The proper title for the eight other members of the court is *associate justice*. When used as a formal title before a name, it should be shortened to justice unless there are special circumstances: *Justice Sandra Day O'Connor, Associate Justice Sandra Day O'Connor*.
See **judge**.

supreme courts of the states
Capitalize with the state name (*the New Jersey Supreme Court*) and without the state name when the context makes it unnecessary: *the state Supreme Court, the Supreme Court*.

If a court with this name is not a state's highest tribunal, the fact should be noted. In New York, for example, the Supreme Court is a trial court. Appeals are directed to the Appellate Division of the Supreme Court. The state's highest court is the Court of Appeals.

surface-to-air missile(s) *SAM(s)* may be used on second reference. Avoid the redundant *SAM missiles*.

suspensive hyphenation The form: *The 5- and 6-year-olds attend morning classes.*

swastika

sweat pants, sweat shirt, sweat suit

Swissair Headquarters is in Zurich, Switzerland.

syllabus, syllabuses

synagogue Capitalize only when part of a formal name

Synagogue Council of America See **Jewish congregations**.

synod A council of churches or church officials. See the entry for the denomination in question.

Tabasco A trademark for a brand of hot pepper sauce.

tablecloth

tablespoon, tablespoonfuls Equal to three teaspoons or one-half a fluid ounce.

The metric equivalent is approximately 15 milliliters.

See **liter** and **recipes**.

table tennis See **pingpong**.

tabular matter Exceptions may be made to the normal rules for abbreviations, as necessary to make material fit. But make any abbreviations as clear as possible.

tailspin

tail wind

Taiwan Use *Taiwan*, not *Formosa*, in references to the Nationalist government in Taiwan and to the island itself.

See **China**.

take-home pay

take off (v.) **takeoff** (n. and adj.)

take out (v.) **takeout** (n. and adj.)

take over (v.) **takeover** (n. and adj.)

take up (v.) **takeup** (n. and adj.)

Talmud The collection of writings that constitute the Jewish civil and religious law.

Tammany, Tammany Hall, Tammany Society

tanks Use Arabic figures, separated from letters by a hyphen: *M-60*. Plural: *M-60s*.

tape recording The noun. But hyphenate the verb form: *tape-record*.

Tass Acceptable on first reference for the Russian government's news agency that is officially *ITAR-Tass*. ITAR is an acronym for *Information Telegraph Agency of Russia*. Copy from other parts of the former Soviet Union should carry the logo of the local agency plus *Tass*.

tattletale

teachers college No apostrophe.

team See **collective nouns**.

teammate

teamster Capitalize *teamster* only if the intended meaning is that the individual is a member of the International Brotherhood of Teamsters, Chauffeurs, Warehousemen and Helpers of America.

Teamsters union Acceptable in all references to the *International Brotherhood of Teamsters, Chauffeurs, Warehousemen and Helpers of America.*
See the entry under that name.

tear gas Two words. See also **Chemical Mace**.

teaspoon Equal to one-sixth of a fluid ounce, or one-third of a tablespoon.
The metric equivalent is approximately 5 milliliters.
See **liter**.

teaspoonful, teaspoonfuls Not *teaspoonsful*. See **recipes**.

Technicolor A trademark for a process of making color motion pictures.

teen, teen-ager (n.) **teenage** (adj.) Do not use *teen-aged*. (The hyphen is an exception to Webster's.)

Teflon A trademark for a type of nonstick coating.

telecast (n.) **televise** (v.)

telephone numbers Use figures. The forms: *(212) 621-1500, 621-1500, (212) MU2-1500.* If extension numbers are given: *Ext. 2, Ext. 364, Ext. 4071.*
The parentheses around the area code are based on a format that telephone companies have agreed upon for domestic and international communications.

TelePrompTer A trademark for a type of cuing device.

Teletype A trademark for a brand of teleprinters and teletypewriters.

television program titles Follow the guidelines in **composition titles**.
Put quotation marks around *show* only if it is part of the formal name. The word *show* may be dropped when it would be cumbersome, such as in a set of listings.
In text or listing, treat programs named after the star in any of the following ways: *"The Mary Tyler Moore Show," "Mary Tyler Moore"* or *the Mary Tyler Moore show.* But be consistent in a story or set of listings.
Use quotation marks also for the title of an episode: *"Chuckles Bites the Dust," an episode of "The Mary Tyler Moore Show."*

television station The call letters alone are frequently adequate, but when this phrase is needed, use lowercase: *television station WTEV.*

telex, Telex (n.) A communications system. Use lowercase when not referring to a specific company. Use uppercase only when referring to the company. Never used as a verb.

telltale

temblor See **earthquakes**.

temperature-humidity index See **weather terms**.

temperatures Use figures for all except *zero*. Use a word, not a minus sign, to indicate temperatures below zero.

Right: *The day's low was minus 10.*

Right: *The day's low was 10 below zero.*

Wrong: *The day's low was -10.*

Right: *The temperature rose to zero by noon.*

Right: *The day's high was expected to be 9 or 10.*

Also: *5-degree temperatures, temperatures fell 5 degrees, temperatures in the 30s* (no apostrophe).

Temperatures get *higher* or *lower*, but they don't get *warmer* or *cooler*.

Wrong: *Temperatures are expected to warm up in the area Friday.*

Right: *Temperatures are expected to rise in the area Friday.*

See **Fahrenheit; Celsius;** and **weather terms.**

Ten Commandments Do not abbreviate or use figures.

tenderhearted

tenfold

Tennessee Abbrev.: *Tenn.* See **state names.**

Tennessee Valley Authority *TVA* is acceptable on second reference.

Headquarters is in Knoxville, Tenn.

tera- A prefix denoting 1 trillion units of a measure. Move the decimal point 12 places to the right, adding zeros if necessary, to convert to the basic unit: 5.5 tera-tons = 5,500,000,000,000 tons.

terrace Do not abbreviate. See **addresses.**

Texaco Inc. Headquarters is in White Plains, N.Y.

Texas Do not abbreviate. Second in total land area.
See **state names.**

texts, transcripts Follow normal style guidelines for capitalization, spelling and abbreviations in handling a text or transcript.

Use quotation marks only for words or phrases that were quoted in the text or by the person who spoke.

Identify a change in speakers by starting a paragraph with the new speaker's name and a colon. Use normal second-reference forms if the speaker has been identified earlier; provide a full name and identification if the individual is being mentioned for the first time.

Use *Q:* for *question* and *A:* for *answer* at the start of paragraphs when these notations are adequate to identify a change in speakers.

See **ellipsis** in the **Punctuation** chapter for guidelines on condensing texts and transcripts.

Thai A native or the language of Thailand.

Siam and *Siamese* are historical only.

Use *siamese* for the cat.

Thanksgiving, Thanksgiving Day The fourth Thursday in November.

that (conjunction) Use the conjunction *that* to introduce a dependent clause if the sentence sounds or looks awkward without it. There are no hard-and-fast rules, but in general:

—*That* usually may be omitted when a dependent clause immediately follows a form of the verb *to say*: *The president said he had signed the bill.*

—*That* should be used when a time element intervenes between the verb and the dependent clause: *The president said Monday that he had signed the bill.*

—*That* usually is necessary after some verbs. They include: *advocate, assert, contend, declare, estimate, make clear, point out, propose* and *state.*

—*That* is required before subordinate clauses beginning with conjunctions such as *after, although, because, before, in addition to, until* and *while*: *Haldeman said that after he learned of Nixon's intention to resign, he sought pardons for all connected with Watergate.*

When in doubt, include *that.* Omission can hurt. Inclusion never does.

that, which, who, whom (pronouns) Use *who* and *whom* in referring to people and to animals with a name: *John Jones is the man who helped me.* See the **who, whom** entry.

Use *that* and *which* in referring to inanimate objects and to animals without a name.

See the **essential clauses, nonessential clauses** entry for guidelines on using *that* and *which* to introduce phrases and clauses.

theater Use this spelling unless the proper name is *Theatre*: *Shubert Theatre.*

theft See the **burglary, larceny, robbery, theft** entry.

their, there, they're *Their* is a possessive pronoun: *They went to their house.*

There is an adverb indicating direction: *We went there for dinner.*

There also is used with the force of a pronoun for impersonal constructions in which the real subject follows the verb: *There is no food on the table.*

They're is a contraction for *they are.*

theretofore Use *until then.*

Thermo-Fax A trademark for a brand of photocopy machine.

thermos Formerly a trademark, now a generic term for any vacuum bottle, although one manufacturer still uses the word as a brand name.

Lowercase *thermos* when it is used to mean any vacuum bottle; use *Thermos* when referring to the specific brand.

Third World The economically developing nations of Africa, Asia and Latin America.

Do not confuse with nonaligned, which is a political term. See **nonaligned**.

three-D *3-D* is preferred.

3M The name of the company is Minnesota Mining & Manufacturing. Its products are known under the names *3M* and *Scotch*. The company is popularly known as *3M*. Headquarters is in St. Paul, Minn.

three R's They are: *reading, 'riting and 'rithmetic.*

threesome

throwaway (n. and adj.)

thunderstorm See **weather terms.**

Thursday See **days of the week.**

tidbit

tie, tied, tying

tie in (v.) **tie-in** (n. and adj.)

tie up (v.) **tie-up** (n. and adj.)

time element Use *today, this morning, this afternoon, tonight,* etc., as appropriate in stories for afternoon editions. Use the day of the week elsewhere. See the **today, tonight** and the **tomorrow, yesterday** entries.

Use *Monday, Tuesday,* etc., for days of the week within seven days before or after the current date.

Use the month and a figure for dates beyond this range. See **months** for forms and punctuation.

Avoid such redundancies as *last Tuesday* or *next Tuesday.* The past, present or future tense used for the verb usually provides adequate indication of which Tuesday is meant: *He said he finished the job Tuesday. She will return on Tuesday.*

Avoid awkward placements of the time element, particularly those that suggest the day of the week is the object of a transitive verb: *The police jailed Tuesday.* Potential remedies include the use of the word on (see the **on** entry), rephrasing the sentence, or placing the time element in a different sentence.

time of day The exact time of day that an event has happened or will happen is not necessary in most stories. Follow these guidelines to determine when it should be included and in what form:

SPECIFY THE TIME:
—Whenever it gives the reader a better picture of the scene: Did the earthquake occur when people were likely to be home asleep or at work? A clock reading for the time in the datelined community is acceptable although *predawn hours* or *rush hour* often is more graphic.

—Whenever the time is critical to the story: When will the rocket be launched? When will a major political address be broadcast? What is the deadline for meeting a demand?

DECIDING ON CLOCK TIME: When giving a clock reading, use the time in the datelined community.

If the story is undated, use the clock time in force where the event happened or will take place.

The only exception is a nationwide story or tabular listing that involves television or radio programs. Always use Eastern time, followed by *EDT* or *EST,* and specify whether the program will be broadcast simultaneously nationwide or whether times vary because of separate transmissions for different time zones. If practical, specify those times in a separate paragraph.

ZONE ABBREVIATIONS: Use *EST, CDT, PST,* etc., after a clock time only if:
—The story involves travel or other activities, such as the closing hour for polling places or the

time of a televised speech, likely to affect people or developments in more than one time zone.

—The item involves television or radio programs. (See above.)

—The item is undated.

—The item is an advisory to editors.

CONVERT TO EASTERN TIME? Do not convert clock times from other time zones in the continental United States to Eastern time. If there is high interest in the precise time, add *CDT, PST*, etc., to the local reading to help readers determine their equivalent local time.

If the time is critical in a story from outside the continental United States, provide a conversion to Eastern time using this form:

The kidnappers set a 9 a.m. (3 a.m. EDT) deadline.

See **time zones** for additional guidance on forms.

times Use figures except for *noon* and *midnight*. Use a colon to separate hours from minutes: *11 a.m., 1 p.m., 3:30 p.m.*

Avoid such redundancies as *10 a.m. this morning, 10 p.m tonight* or *10 p.m. Monday night.* Use *10 a.m. today, 10 p.m. today* or *10 p.m. Monday,* etc., as required by the norms in **time element**.

The construction *4 o'clock* is acceptable, but time listings with *a.m.* or *p.m.* are preferred.

See **midnight, noon** and **time zones**.

time sequences Use figures, colons and periods as follows: *2:30:21.65* (hours, minutes, seconds, tenths, hundredths).

Time Warner Inc. See **AOL**

Time Warner Inc.

time zones Capitalize the full name of the time in force within a particular zone: *Eastern Standard Time, Eastern Daylight Time, Central Standard Time,* etc.

Lowercase all but the region in short forms: *the Eastern time zone, Eastern time, Mountain time,* etc.

See **time of day** for guidelines on when to use clock time in a story.

Spell out *time zone* in references not accompanied by a clock reading: *Chicago is in the Central time zone.*

The abbreviations *EST, CDT,* etc., are acceptable on first reference for zones used within the continental United States, Canada and Mexico only if the abbreviation is linked with a clock reading: *noon EST, 9 a.m. PST.* (Do not set off the abbreviations with commas.)

Spell out all references to time zones not used within the contiguous United States: *When it is noon EDT, it is 1 p.m. Atlantic Standard Time and 8 a.m. Alaska Standard Time.*

One exception to the spelled-out form: *Greenwich Mean Time* may be abbreviated as *GMT* on second reference if used with a clock reading.

tiptop

titleholder

titles In general, confine capitalization to formal titles used directly before an individual's name.

The basic guidelines:

LOWERCASE: Lowercase and spell out titles when they are not

UNITED STATES
TIME ZONES

INTERNATIONAL TIME ZONES

International date line

used with an individual's name: *The president issued a statement. The pope gave his blessing.*

Lowercase and spell out titles in constructions that set them off from a name by commas: *The vice president, Nelson Rockefeller, declined to run again. Paul VI, the current pope, does not plan to retire.*

COURTESY TITLES: See the **courtesy titles** entry for guidelines on when to use *Miss, Mr., Mrs., Ms.* or no titles.

The forms *Mr., Mrs., Miss* and *Ms.* apply both in regular text and in quotations.

FORMAL TITLES: Capitalize formal titles when they are used immediately before one or more names: *Pope Paul, President Washington, Vice Presidents John Jones and William Smith.*

A formal title generally is one that denotes a scope of authority, professional activity or academic accomplishment so specific that the designation becomes almost as much an integral part of an individual's identity as a proper name itself: *President Clinton, Sen. Dianne Feinstein, Dr. Marcus Welby, Pvt. Gomer Pyle.*

Other titles serve primarily as occupational descriptions: *astronaut John Glenn, movie star John Wayne, peanut farmer Jimmy Carter.*

A final determination on whether a title is formal or occupational depends on the practice of the governmental or private organization that confers it. If there is doubt about the status of a title and the practice of the organization cannot be determined, use a construction that sets the name or the title off with commas.

ABBREVIATED TITLES: The following formal titles are capitalized and abbreviated as shown when used before a name outside quotations: *Dr., Gov., Lt. Gov., Rep., Sen.* and certain military ranks listed in the **military titles** entry. Spell out all except *Dr.* when they are used in quotations.

All other formal titles are spelled out in all uses.

ROYAL TITLES: Capitalize *king, queen,* etc., when used directly before a name. See individual entries and **nobility**.

TITLES OF NOBILITY: Capitalize a full title when it serves as the alternate name for an individual. See **nobility**.

PAST AND FUTURE TITLES: A formal title that an individual formerly held, is about to hold or holds temporarily is capitalized if used before the person's name. But do not capitalize the qualifying word: *former President Ford, deposed King Constantine, Attorney General-designate Griffin B. Bell, acting Mayor Peter Barry.*

LONG TITLES: Separate a long title from a name by a construction that requires a comma: *Charles Robinson, undersecretary for economic affairs, spoke.* Or: *The undersecretary for economic affairs, Charles Robinson, spoke.*

UNIQUE TITLES: If a title applies only to one person in an organization, insert the word *the* in a construction that uses commas: *John Jones, the deputy vice president, spoke.*

ADDITIONAL GUIDANCE: Many commonly used titles and occupational descriptions are listed separately in this book, together with guidelines on whether and/or when they are capitalized. In these entries, the phrases *before a name* or *immediately before a name* are used to specify that capitalization applies only when a title is not set off from a name by commas.

See **academic titles; composition titles; legislative titles; military titles;** and **religious titles**.

TNT Acceptable in all references for *trinitrotoluene*.

tobacco, tobaccos

Tobago See the **Trinidad and Tobago** entry.

today, tonight Use in direct quotations, in stories intended for publication in afternoon newspapers on the day in question, and in phrases that do not refer to a specific day: *Customs today are different from those of a century ago.*

Use the day of the week in stories intended for publication in morning newspapers and in stories filed for use in either publishing cycle.

See **tonight**.

Tokyo Stands alone in datelines.

tollhouse, tollhouse cookies

Tommy gun Alternate trademark for Thompson submachine gun.

See **weapons**.

tomorrow Use only in direct quotations and in phrases that do not refer to a specific day: *The world of tomorrow will need addi-*

tional energy resources.

Use the day of the week in other cases.

ton There are three different types:

A *short ton* is equal to 2,000 pounds.

A *long ton*, also known as a *British ton*, is equal to 2,240 pounds.

A *metric ton* is equal to 1,000 kilograms, or approximately 2,204.62 pounds.

CONVERSION EQUATIONS:
Short to long: Multiply by .89 (5 short tons x .89 = 4.45 long tons).

Short to metric: Multiply by .9 (5 short tons x .9 = 4.5 metric tons).

Long to short: Multiply by 1.12 (5 long tons x 1.12 = 5.6 short tons).

Long to metric: Multiply by 1.02 (5 long tons x 1.02 = 5.1 metric tons).

Metric to short: Multiply by 1.1 (5 metric tons x 1.1 = 5.5 short tons).

Metric to long: Multiply by .98 (5 metric tons x .98 = 4.9 long tons).

See **metric system**.

See **kiloton** for units used to measure the power of nuclear explosions.

See **oil** for formulas to convert the tonnage of oil shipments to gallons.

tonight All that's necessary is *8 tonight,* or *8 p.m. today.* Avoid the redundant *8 p.m. tonight.*

tornado See **weather terms**.

Toronto The city in Canada

stands alone in datelines.

Tory, Tories An exception to the normal practice when forming the plural of a proper name ending in *y*.

The words are acceptable on second reference to the Conservative Party in Britain and its members.

total, totaled, totaling The phrase *a total of* often is redundant.

It may be used, however, to avoid a figure at the start of a sentence: *A total of 650 people were killed in holiday traffic accidents.*

touch-tone A generic term for a push-button telephone dialing service.

toward Not *towards*.

town Apply the capitalization principles in **city**.

town council Apply the capitalization principles in **city council**.

trade in (v.) **trade-in** (n. and adj.)

trademark A trademark is a brand, symbol, word, etc., used by a manufacturer or dealer and protected by law to prevent a competitor from using it: *Astro-Turf*, for a type of artificial grass, for example.

In general, use a generic equivalent unless the trademark name is essential to the story.

When a trademark is used, capitalize it.

Many trademarks are listed separately in this book, together with generic equivalents.

For questions about trade-

marks not listed in this book, the International Trademark Association, located in New York, is a helpful source of information.

On the Net: www.inta.org/tm-cklst1.htm

See **brand names** and **service marks**.

trade off (v.) **trade-off** (n. and adj.)

traffic, trafficked, trafficking

trampoline Formerly a trademark, now a generic term.

trans- The rules in prefixes apply, but in general, no hyphen. Some examples:

transcontinental	transsexual
transmigrate	transship
transoceanic	trans-Siberian

Also: *trans-Atlantic* and *trans-Pacific*. These are exceptions to Webster's New World in keeping with the general rule that a hyphen is needed when a prefix precedes a capitalized word.

transcripts See the **texts, transcripts** entry.

transfer, transferred, transferring

Transjordan Earlier name for Jordan.

Transportation Communications International Union Formerly the Brotherhood of Railway, Airline and Steamship Clerks, Freight Handlers, Express and Station Employees. *TCU* is acceptable on second reference.

Headquarters is in Rockville, Md.

transsexuals See **sex changes**.

Trans World Airlines A *TWA airliner* is acceptable in any reference.

Headquarters is in New York.

travel, traveled, traveling, traveler

travelogue Not *travelog*.

treasurer Capitalize when used as a formal title immediately before a name. See **titles**.

Caution: The secretary of the U.S. Department of the Treasury is not the same person as the U.S. treasurer.

trees See **plants**.

tribes See the **nationalities and races** entry.

trigger-happy

TriMotor The proper name of a three-engine airplane once made by Ford Motor Co.

Trinidad and Tobago In datelines on stories from this island nation, use a community name followed by either *Trinidad* or *Tobago* — but not both — depending on where the community is located.

Trojan horse, Trojan War

troop, troops, troupe A *troop* is a group of people or animals. *Troops* means several such groups, particularly groups of soldiers.

Use *troupe* only for ensembles of actors, dancers, singers, etc.

tropical depression See **weather terms**.

Truman, Harry S. With a period after the initial. Truman once said there was no need for the period because the S did not stand for a name. Asked in the early 1960s about his preference, he replied, "It makes no difference to me."

AP style has called for the period since that time.

trustee A person to whom another's property or the management of another's property is entrusted.

Do not capitalize if used before a name.

trusty A prison inmate granted special privileges as a trustworthy person.

Do not capitalize if used before a name.

try out (v.) **tryout** (n.)

tsar Use *czar*.

T-shirt

tuberculosis *TB* is acceptable on second reference.

Tuesday See **days of the week**.

tune up (v.) **tuneup** (n. and adj.)

turboprop See **aircraft terms**.

turnpike Capitalize as part of a proper name: *the Pennsylvania Turnpike*. Lowercase *turnpike* when it stands alone.

See **highway designations**.

TV Acceptable as an adjective or in such constructions as *cable TV*. But do not normally use as a noun unless part of a quotation.

Twelve Apostles The disciples of Jesus. An exception to the normal practice of using figures for 10 and above.

20th Century Fox, Twentieth Century Fund, Twentieth Century Limited Follow an organization's practice. See **company names**.

two-by-four Spell out the noun, which refers to any length of building lumber two inches thick by four inches wide.

typhoons Capitalize typhoon when it is part of the name that weather forecasters assign to a storm: *Typhoon Tilda*.

But use *it* and *its* — not *she, her* or *hers* — in pronoun references.

And do not use the presence of a woman's name as an excuse to attribute sexist images of women's behavior to a typhoon.

See **weather terms**.

U
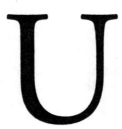

U In Burmese names *U* is an honorific prefix. It means something like Mr., and is used for adult males only. It should not be used. For example, *U Nu* is only *Nu* in all references. Women retain their given names after marriage. No courtesy titles apply.

U-boat A German submarine. Anything referring to a submarine should be *submarine* unless directly referring to a German vessel of World War I or II vintage.

UFO, UFOs Acceptable in all references for *unidentified flying object(s)*.

UHF Acceptable in all references for *ultrahigh frequency*.

Ukrainian Catholic Church See **Eastern Rite churches.**

ukulele

Ulster Historically, one of the four Irish provinces, covering nine counties. Six of the counties became Northern Ireland, three became part of the Republic of Ireland. Avoid use as a synonym for *Northern Ireland*. See **United Kingdom.**

ultra- The rules in **prefixes** apply, but in general, no hyphen. Some examples:

ultramodern	ultrasonic
ultranationalism	ultraviolet

ultrahigh frequency *UHF* is acceptable in all references.

un- The rules in **prefixes** apply, but in general, no hyphen. Some examples:

un-American	unnecessary
unarmed	unshaven

U.N. Used as an adjective, but not as a noun, for United Nations.
See **United Nations.**

Uncle Sam

Uncle Tom A term of contempt applied to a black person, taken from the main character in Harriet Beecher Stowe's novel "Uncle Tom's Cabin." It describes the practice of kowtowing to whites to curry favor.

Do not apply it to an individual. It carries potentially libelous connotations of having sold one's convictions for money, prestige or political influence.

under- The rules in **prefixes** apply, but in general, no hyphen. Some examples:

underdog	undersheriff
underground	undersold

undersecretary One word. See **titles.**

under way Two words in virtually all uses: *The project is under way. The naval maneuvers are under way.*

One word only when used as an adjective before a noun in a nautical sense: *an underway flotilla.*

unemployment rate In the United States, this estimate of the number of unemployed residents seeking work is compiled monthly by the Bureau of Labor Statistics, an agency of the Labor Department.

Each month the bureau selects a nationwide cross section of the population and conducts interviews to determine the size of the U.S. work force. The work force is defined as the number of people with jobs and the number looking for jobs.

The unemployment rate is expressed as a percentage figure. The essential calculation involves dividing the total work force into the number of people looking for jobs, followed by adjustments to reflect variable factors such as seasonal trends.

UNESCO Acceptable on first reference for the *United Nations Educational, Scientific and Cultural Organization*, but a subsequent reference should give the full name.

UNICEF Acceptable in all references for the *United Nations Children's Fund*. The words *International* and *Emergency*, originally part of the name, have been dropped.

unidentified flying object(s) *UFO* and *UFOs* are acceptable in all references.

Uniform Code of Military Justice The laws covering members of the U.S. armed forces.

uninterested See the **disinterested, uninterested** entry.

union Capitalize when used as a proper name of the Northern states during the Civil War: *The Union defeated the Confederacy.*

union names The formal names of unions may be condensed to conventionally accepted short forms that capitalize characteristic words from the full name followed by *union* in lowercase.

Follow union practice in the use of the word *worker* in shortened forms. Among major unions, all except the United Steelworkers use two words: *United Auto Workers, United Mine Workers*, etc.

When *worker* is used generically, make *autoworkers* and *steelworkers* one word in keeping with widespread practice; use two words for other job descriptions: *bakery workers, mine workers.*

See the **local of a union** entry and the individual entries for these unions frequently in the news:

Amalgamated Transit Union
American Federation of Government Employees
American Federation of Labor and Congress of Industrial Organizations
American Federation of Musicians
American Federation of State, County and Municipal Employees
American Federation of Teachers
American Federation of Television and Radio Artists
American Postal Workers Union
Bakery, Confectionery, Tobacco Workers and Grain Millers International Union

Bricklayers, Masons and Plasterers' International Union of America
Brotherhood of Maintenance of Way Employes
Communications Workers of America
Hotel and Restaurant Employees and Bartenders International Union
International Association of Machinists and Aerospace Workers
International Brotherhood of Electrical Workers
International Brotherhood of Painters and Allied Trades of the United States and Canada
International Brotherhood of Teamsters, Chauffeurs, Warehousemen and Helpers of America
International Longshore and Warehouse Union
International Longshoremen's Association
Laborers' International Union of North America
National Association of Letter Carriers
Newspaper Guild, The
Paper, Allied-Industrial, Chemical and Energy Workers International Union
Sheet Metal Workers International Association
Transportation Communications International Union
Union of Needletrades, Industrial and Textile Employees
United Automobile, Aerospace and Agricultural Implement Workers of America
United Brotherhood of Carpenters and Joiners of America
United Electrical, Radio and Machine Workers of America
United Food and Commercial Workers International Union
United Mine Workers of America
United Steelworkers of America

union shop See **closed shop**.

unique It means one of a kind. Do not describe something as *rather unique* or *most unique*.

United Airlines A subsidiary of UAL Corp.
Headquarters is in Chicago.

United Arab Emirates Do not abbreviate, even in datelines.
Use *U.A.E.* (with periods) if quoted matter requires the abbreviation.

United Automobile, Aerospace and Agriculture Implement Workers of America The shortened forms *United Auto Workers* and *United Auto Workers union* are acceptable in all references.
UAW and *Auto Workers* are acceptable on second reference.
Use *autoworker* or *autoworkers* (one word, lowercase) in generic references to workers in the auto industry.
Headquarters is in Detroit.

United Brotherhood of Carpenters and Joiners of America The shortened form *Carpenters union* is acceptable in all references.
Headquarters is in Washington.

United Church of Christ The Evangelical and Reformed Church merged with the Congregational Christian Churches in 1957 to form the United Church of Christ. It has some 1.4 million members.
The word *church* is correctly applied only to an individual local church. Each such church is responsible for the doctrine, min-

istry and ritual of its congregation.

A small body of churches that did not enter the United Church of Christ is known as the National Association of Congregational Churches.

Churches in the association have more than 100,000 members.

Jesus is regarded as man's savior, but no subscription to a set creed is required for membership.

Members of the clergy are known as *ministers*. *Pastor* applies if a minister leads a congregation.

On first reference, use *the Rev.* before the name of a man or woman. On second reference, use only the last name.

See **religious titles**.

United Electrical, Radio and Machine Workers of America

The shortened form *Electrical Workers union* is acceptable in all references.

Headquarters is in New York.

United Food and Commercial Workers International Union

Formed by the merger of the Retail Clerks International Union and the Amalgamated Meat Cutters and Butcher Workmen of North America.

The shortened form *Food and Commercial Workers union* is acceptable in all references.

Headquarters is in Washington.

United Kingdom

It consists of Great Britain and Northern Ireland.

Great Britain (or Britain) consists of England, Scotland and Wales.

Ireland is independent of the United Kingdom.

See **datelines** and **Ireland**.

United Methodist Church

See **Methodist churches**.

United Mine Workers of America

The shortened forms *United Mine Workers* and *United Mine Workers union* are acceptable in all references.

UMW and *Mine Workers* are acceptable on second reference.

Use *mine workers* or *miners*, lowercase, in generic references to workers in the industry.

Headquarters is in Washington.

United Nations

Spell out when used as a noun. Use *U.N.* (no space) only as an adjective.

The periods in *U.N.* for consistency with U.S., are an exception to the first listing in Webster's New World Dictionary.

In datelines:
UNITED NATIONS (AP) —

Use *U.N. General Assembly, U.N. Secretariat* and *U.N. Security Council* in first references not under a United Nations dateline.

General Assembly, the Secretariat and *Security Council* are acceptable in all references under a United Nations dateline and on second reference under other datelines.

Lowercase *the assembly* and *the council* when they stand alone.

See **UNESCO** and **UNICEF**.

United Presbyterian Church in the United States of America

It no longer exists. See **Presbyterian churches** entry.

United Press International

A privately owned news agency formed in 1958 as a merger of United Press and International News Service.

Use the full name on first reference. *UPI* is acceptable on second reference.

The address is 1400 Eye St., Washington, D.C., 20005. The telephone number is (202) 898-8000.

United Rubber, Cork, Linoleum and Plastic Workers of America

The shortened forms *United Rubber Workers* and *United Rubber Workers union* are acceptable in all references.

Capitalize *Rubber Workers* in references to the union or its members.

Use *rubber workers*, lowercase, in generic references to workers in the rubber industry.

Headquarters is in Akron, Ohio.

United Service Organizations

USO is acceptable on second reference.

United States

Spell out when used as a noun. Use *U.S.* (no space) only as an adjective.

For organization with names beginning with the words United States, see entries alphabetized under U.S.

United Steelworkers of America

The shortened forms *United Steelworkers* and *United Steelworkers union* are acceptable in all references.

Capitalize *Steelworkers* in references to the union or its members.

Headquarters is in Pittsburgh.

United Synagogue of America

Not *synagogues*. See **Jewish congregations**.

up- The rules in **prefixes** apply, but in general, no hyphen. Some examples:

upend	upstate
upgrade	uptown

-up Follow Webster's New World Dictionary. Hyphenate if not listed there.

Some frequently used words (all are nouns, some also are used as adjectives):

breakup	makeup
call-up	mix-up
change-up	mock-up
checkup	pileup
cleanup	push-up
close-up	roundup
cover-up	runners-up
crackup	setup
follow-up	shake-up
frame-up	shape-up
grown-up	smashup
holdup	speedup
letup	tie-up
lineup	walk-up
	windup

Use two words when any of these occurs as a verb.

See **suffixes**.

UPI Acceptable on second references for *United Press International.*

uppercase One word (n., v., adj.) when referring to the use of capital letters, in keeping with printers' practice.

upside down (adv.) **upside-down** (adj.) *The car turned upside down. The book is upside-down.*

upstate Always lowercase: *upstate New York.*

upward Not *upwards*.

U.S. Used as an adjective, but not as a noun, for *United States*.

U.S. Air Force See **air force; military academies;** and **military titles**.

US Airways Formerly USAir. Headquarters is in Arlington, Va.

U.S. Army See **army; military academies;** and **military titles.**

U.S. Coast Guard See **coast guard; military academies;** and **military titles.**

U.S. Conference of Mayors The members are the mayors of cities with 30,000 or more residents. See **National League of Cities.**

Use *the conference* or *the mayors' conference* on second reference.

There is no organization with the name *National Mayors' Conference.*

U.S. Court of Appeals The court is divided into 13 circuits as follows:

District of Columbia Circuit.

Federal Circuit.

1st Circuit: Maine, Massachusetts, New Hampshire, Rhode Island, Puerto Rico. Based in Boston.

2nd Circuit: Connecticut, New York, Vermont. Based in New York.

3rd Circuit: Delaware, New Jersey, Pennsylvania, Virgin Islands. Based in Philadelphia.

4th Circuit: Maryland, North Carolina, South Carolina, Virginia, West Virginia. Based in Richmond, Va.

5th Circuit: Louisiana, Mississippi, Texas. Based in New Orleans.

6th Circuit: Kentucky, Michigan, Ohio, Tennessee. Based in Cincinnati.

7th Circuit: Illinois, Indiana, Wisconsin. Based in Chicago.

8th Circuit: Arkansas, Iowa, Minnesota, Missouri, Nebraska, North Dakota, South Dakota. Based in St. Louis.

9th Circuit: Alaska, Arizona, California, Hawaii, Idaho, Montana, Nevada, Oregon, Washington, Guam. Based in San Francisco.

10th Circuit: Colorado, Kansas, New Mexico, Oklahoma, Utah, Wyoming. Based in Denver.

11th Circuit: Alabama, Florida and Georgia. Based in Atlanta.

The courts do not always sit in the cities where they are based. Sessions may be held in other major cities within each region.

REFERENCE FORMS: A phrase such as a *federal appeals court* is acceptable on first reference.

On first reference to the full name, use *U.S. Court of Appeals* or a full name: *8th U.S. Circuit Court of Appeals* or *the U.S. Court of Appeals for the 8th Circuit.*

U.S. Circuit Court of Appeals without a circuit number is a misnomer and should not be used.

In shortened and subsequent references: *the Court of Appeals, the 2nd Circuit, the appeals court, the appellate court(s), the circuit court(s), the court.*

Do not create nonexistent entities such as *the San Francisco Court of Appeals*. Make it *the U.S. Court of Appeals in San Francisco.*

JURISTS: The formal title for the jurists on the court is *judge: U.S. Circuit Judge Homer Thornberry* is preferred to *U.S. Appeals Judge Homer Thornberry,* but either is acceptable.

See **judge.**

U.S. Court of Appeals for the Federal Circuit Commonly

known as the CAFC, it replaced U.S. Court of Claims and U.S. Court of Customs and Patent Appeals. It handles suits against the federal government and appeals involving customs, patents and copyright. It is based in Washington.

U.S. Court of Military Appeals This court, not part of the judicial branch as such, is a civilian body established by Congress to hear appeals from actions of the Defense Department. It is based in Washington.

U.S. Customs Court This court, based in New York City, handles disputes over customs duties that arise at any U.S. port of entry.

U.S. District Courts There are 94. In shortened and subsequent references: *the District Court, the District Courts, the court.*

Judge is the formal title for District Court jurists: *U.S. District Judge Frank Johnson.* See **judge**.

user friendly Avoid. For example: *The system is easy to use,* not *the system is user friendly.*

usher Use for both men and women.

U.S. Information Agency Formerly the U.S. Communication Agency.

Use *U.S. Information Agency* on first reference. Lowercase *the communication agency* or *the agency* in second references.

U.S. Military Academy See **military academies**.

U.S. Navy See **navy; military academies;** and **military titles**.

U.S. Postal Service Use *U.S. Postal Service* or *the Postal Service* on first reference. Retain capitalization of *Postal Service* in subsequent references to the agency.

Lowercase *the service* when it stands alone. Lowercase *post office* in generic references to the agency and to an individual office: *I went to the post office.*

U.S. Postal Service Directory of Post Offices The reference for U.S. place names not covered in this book.

USS For *United States Ship, Steamer* or *Steamship,* preceding the name of a vessel: *the USS Iowa.* In datelines: *ABOARD USS IOWA (AP) —*

U.S. Supreme Court See **Supreme Court of the United States.**

U.S. Tax Court This court handles appeals in tax cases.

USX Corp. Formerly U.S. Steel.

Utah Do not abbreviate. See **state names**.

U-turn (n. and adj.)

V

v. See **verbs**.

vacuum

Valium A trademark for a brand of tranquilizer and muscle relaxant. It also may be called *diazepam*.

valley Capitalize as part of a full name: *the Mississippi Valley.*
Lowercase in plural uses: *the Missouri and Mississippi valleys.*

Vandyke beard, Vandyke collar

Varig Brazilian Airlines Headquarters in Rio de Janeiro.

Vaseline A trademark for a brand of petroleum jelly.

Vatican City Stands alone in datelines.

v-chip

VCR Acceptable in second reference to *videocassette recorder.*

VDT Abbreviation for *video display terminal.* Spell out.

V-E Day May 8, 1945, the day the surrender of Germany was announced, officially ending the European phase of World War II.

vegetables See **food**.

V-8 The engine.

Velcro Trademark for a nylon material that can be pressed together or pulled apart for easy fastening and unfastening. Use a generic term such as fabric fastener.

Venator Group Formerly F.W. Woolworth Co. (The name means *sportsman* in Latin.)

vendor

venereal disease *VD* is acceptable on second reference.

verbal See the **oral, verbal, written** entry.

verbs The abbreviation v. is used in this book to identify the spelling of the verb forms of words frequently misspelled.

SPLIT FORMS: In general, avoid awkward constructions that split infinitive forms of a verb (*to leave, to help*, etc.) or compound forms (*had left, are found out*, etc.)
Awkward: *She was ordered to immediately leave on an assignment.*
Preferred: *She was ordered to leave immediately on an assignment.*

Awkward: *There stood the wagon that we had early last autumn left by the barn.*

Preferred: *There stood the wagon that we had left by the barn early last autumn.*

Occasionally, however, a split is not awkward and is necessary to convey the meaning:

He wanted to really help his mother.

Those who lie are often found out.

How has your health been?

The budget was tentatively approved.

Vermont Abbrev.: *Vt.* See **state names**.

vernacular The native language of a country or place. A vernacular term that has achieved widespread recognition may be used without explanation if appropriate in the context.

Terms not widely known should be explained when used. In general, they are appropriate only when illustrating vernacular speech.

See **colloquialisms** and **dialect**.

verses See **poetry** for guidelines on how to handle verses of poetry typographically.

versus Spell it out in ordinary speech and writing: *The proposal to revamp Medicare versus proposals to reform Medicare and Medicaid at the same time ...* In short expressions, however, the abbreviation *vs.* is permitted: *The issue of guns vs. butter has long been with us.*

For court cases, use *v: Marbury v. Madison.*

vertical takeoff aircraft

See the **V-STOL** and **VTOL** entries.

very high frequency *VHF* is acceptable in all references.

Very Rev. See **Episcopal Church**; **religious titles**; and **Roman Catholic Church**.

Veterans Affairs Formerly Veterans Administration, it became Cabinet level in March 1989 with the full title Department of Veterans Affairs. *VA* (no periods) is still used on second reference.

Veterans Day Formerly Armistice Day, Nov. 11, the anniversary of the armistice that ended World War I in 1918.

The federal legal holiday, observed on the fourth Monday in October during the mid-1970s, reverted to Nov. 11 in 1978.

Veterans of Foreign Wars *VFW* is acceptable on second reference.

Headquarters in Kansas City, Mo.

veto, vetoes (n.) The verb forms: *vetoed, vetoing.*

VHF Acceptable in all references for *very high frequency.*

vice- Use two words: *vice admiral, vice chairman, vice chancellor, vice consul, vice president, vice principal, vice regent, vice secretary.*

Several are exceptions to Webster's New World. The two-word rule has been adopted for consistency in handling the similar terms.

vice president Capitalize or lowercase following the same rules that apply to *president.* See

president and **titles.**
Do not drop the first name on first reference.

vice versa

Victrola A trademark for a brand of record player.

videocassette recorder

videodisc

videotape (n. and v.)

videotex, teletext Not *videotext*. *Videotex* is the generic term for two-way interactive data systems that transmit text and sometimes graphics via telephone lines or cable. User can specify desired information and communicate with host computer or other users through terminal keyboard.
Teletext is a one-way system that transmits text material or graphics via a TV or FM broadcast signal or cable TV system. The user can select material desired but cannot communicate with other users.

vie, vied, vying

vienna bread, vienna coffee, vienna sausages See **food.**

Viet Cong

Vietnam Not *Viet Nam.*

Vietnam War

village Apply the capitalization principles in **city.**

VIP, VIPs Acceptable in all references for *very important person(s).*

Virginia Abbrev.: *Va.* Legally a commonwealth, not a state.
See **state** and **state names.**

Virgin Islands Use with a community name in datelines on stories from the U.S. Virgin Islands. Do not abbreviate.
Identify an individual island in the text if relevant.
See **datelines** and **British Virgin Islands.**

viscount, viscountess See **nobility.**

vitamins Lowercase *vitamin*, use a capital letter and/or a figure for the type: *vitamin A, vitamin B-12.*

V-J Day The day of victory for the Allied forces over Japan in World War II.
It is calculated both as Aug. 15, 1945, the day the fighting with Japan ended, and as Sept. 2, 1945, the day Japan officially surrendered.

V-neck (n. and adj.)

Voice of America *VOA* is acceptable on second reference.

volatile Something that evaporates rapidly. It may or may not be explosive.

Volkswagen of America Inc. The name of the U.S. subsidiary of the German company named *Volkswagen A.G.*
U.S. headquarters is in Auburn Hills, Mich.

volley, volleys

Volunteers in Service to America *VISTA* is acceptable in second reference.

von See **foreign particles**.

voodoo

vote-getter

vote tabulations Always use figures for the totals.

Spell out below 10 in other phrases related to voting: *by a five-vote majority, with three abstentions, four votes short of the necessary two-thirds majority.*

For results that involve fewer than 1,000 votes on each side, use these forms: *The House voted 230-205, a 230-205 vote.*

To make totals that involve more than 1,000 votes on a side easier to read, separate the figures with the word *to* to avoid hyphenated adjectival constructions. See **election returns** for examples.

V-STOL Acceptable on second reference for an aircraft capable of *vertical* or *short takeoff or landing.*

VTOL Acceptable on second reference for an aircraft capable of *vertical takeoff or landing.*

vulgarities See the **obscenities, profanities, vulgarities** entry.

Wac, WAC *Wac* is no longer used by the military but is an acceptable term in a reference to a woman who served in what used to be the *Women's Army Corps*.

WAC is acceptable on second reference to the corps.

Waf, WAF *Waf* no longer is used by the military but is acceptable in a reference to a woman who served in the Air Force.

WAF is acceptable on second reference to *Women in the Air Force*, an unofficial organizational distinction formerly made by the Air Force but never authorized by Congress.

waiter (male) **waitress** (female)

Wales Use *Wales* after the names of Welsh communities in datelines.

See **datelines** and **United Kingdom**.

walk up (v.) **walk-up** (n. and adj.)

Wall Street When the reference is to the entire complex of financial institutions in the area rather than the actual street itself, *the Street* is an acceptable short form.

See **capitalization**.

Wal-Mart

war Capitalize when used as part of the name for a specific conflict: *the Civil War, the Cold War, the Korean War, the Vietnam War, the War of 1812, World War II, Gulf War, Persian Gulf War,* etc.

warden Capitalize as a formal title before a name. See **titles**.

wards Use figures. See **political divisions**.

warhead

war horse, warhorse Two words for a horse used in battle.

One word for a veteran of many battles: *He is a political warhorse.*

warlike

warlord

warrant officer See **military titles**.

wartime

washed-up (adj.)

Washington Abbreviate the state as *Wash.*

Never abbreviate when referring to the U.S. capital.

Use *state of Washington* or *Washington state* and *Washington, D.C.*, or *District of Columbia* when the context requires distinction between the state and the federal district.

See **state** and **state names**.

Washington's Birthday

Capitalize *birthday* in references to the holiday.

The date he was born is computed as Feb. 22. The federal legal holiday is the third Monday in February.

Some states and some organizations refer to it as *Presidents Day* but the formal name has not changed.

wastebasket

waterspout See **weather terms**.

Wave, WAVES

Wave no longer is used by the military but is acceptable in a reference to a woman who served in the Navy.

WAVES is acceptable on second reference to the *Women Accepted for Volunteer Emergency Service*, an organizational distinction made for women during World War II but subsequently discontinued.

weak-kneed

weapons *Gun* is an acceptable term for any firearm. Note the following definitions and forms in dealing with weapons and ammunition:

anti-aircraft A cannon that fires explosive shells. It is designed for defense against air attack. The form: *a 105 mm anti-aircraft gun.*

assault-style weapon Any semiautomatic pistol, rifle or shotgun originally designed for military or police use with a large ammunition capacity. Also, firearms that feature two or more accessories such as a detachable magazine, folding or telescopic stock, silencer, pistol grip, bayonet mount or a device to suppress the flash emitted while shooting in the dark.

artillery A carriage-mounted cannon.

automatic An autoloading action that will fire a succession of cartridges while the trigger is depressed or until the ammunition supply is exhausted. The form: *a .22-caliber automatic.*

buckshot See **shot** below.

bullet The projectile fired by a rifle, pistol or machine gun. Together with metal casing, primer and propellant, it forms a *cartridge*.

caliber A measurement of the diameter of the inside of a gun barrel except for most shotguns. Measurement is in either millimeters or decimal fractions of an inch. The word *caliber* is not used when giving the metric measurement. The forms: *a 9 mm pistol, a .22-caliber rifle.*

cannon A weapon, usually supported on some type of carriage, that fires explosive projectiles. The form: *a 105 mm cannon.*

carbine A short, lightweight rifle, usually having a barrel length of less than 20 inches. The form: *an M-3 carbine.*

cartridge See **bullet** above.

clip A metal container for cartridges, inserted in certain types of firearms.

Colt Named for Samuel Colt, it designates a make of weapon or ammunition developed for Colt handguns. The forms: *a Colt .45-caliber revolver, .45 Long Colt ammunition.*

gauge This word describes the size of a shotgun. Gauge is expressed in terms of the number per pound of round lead balls with a diameter equal to the size of the barrel. The bigger the number, the smaller the shotgun.
Some common shotgun gauges:

Gauge	Interior Diameter
10	.775 inches
12	.729 inches
16	.662 inches
20	.615 inches
28	.550 inches
.410	.410 inches

The .410 actually is a caliber, but commonly is called a gauge.
The forms: *a 12-gauge shotgun, a .410-gauge shotgun.*

howitzer A cannon shorter than a gun of the same caliber employed to fire projectiles at relatively high angles at a target, such as opposing forces behind a ridge. The form: *a 105 mm howitzer.*

machine gun An automatic gun that fires as long as the trigger is depressed. The form: *a .50-caliber Browning machine gun.*

magazine The chamber on a rifle or pistol from which cartridges are fed.

Magnum A trademark for a type of high-powered cartridge with a larger case and a larger powder charge than other cartridges of approximately the same caliber. The form: *a .357-caliber Magnum, a .44-caliber Magnum.*

M-1, M-16 These and similar combinations of a letter and figure(s) designate rifles used by the military. The forms: *an M-1 rifle, an M-16 rifle.*

mortar Device used to launch a mortar shell; it is the shell, not the mortar, that is fired.

musket A heavy, large-caliber shoulder firearm fired by means of a matchlock, a wheel lock, a flintlock or a percussion lock. Its ammunition is a musket ball.

pistol A small firearm or handgun, it can be a single shot, a semiautomatic or a revolver. Its size is measured in calibers. The form: *a .45-caliber pistol.*

revolver A handgun. Its cartridges are held in chambers in a cylinder that revolves. The form: *a .45-caliber revolver.*

rifle A firearm designed or made to be fired from the shoulder and having a rifled bore. It uses bullets or cartridges for ammunition. Its size is measured in calibers. The form: *a .22-caliber rifle.*

Saturday night special The popular name for the type of cheap pistol used for impulsive crimes.

shell The word applies to military or naval ammunition and to shotgun ammunition.

shot Small lead or steel pellets fired by shotguns. A shotgun shell usually contains 1 to 2 ounces of shot. Do not use *shot* interchangeably with *buck-shot*, which refers only to the largest shot sizes.

shotgun A small-arms gun with a smooth bore, sometimes double-barreled. Its ammunition is shot. Its size is measured in gauges. The form: *a 12-gauge shotgun.*

submachine gun A lightweight automatic gun firing handgun ammunition.

weather-beaten

weather bureau See **National Weather Service.**

weatherman The preferred term is *weather forecaster.*

weather terms The following are based on definitions used by the National Weather Service. All temperatures are Fahrenheit.

blizzard Wind speeds of 35 mph or more and considerable falling and/or blowing of snow with visibility near zero.

coastal waters The waters within about 20 miles of the coast, including bays, harbors and sounds.

cyclone A storm with strong winds rotating about a moving center of low atmospheric pressure.
The word sometimes is used in the United States to mean *tornado* and in the Indian Ocean area to mean *hurricane.*

degree-day A unit of measurement describing how much the temperature differs from a standard average for one day. It is usually used to gauge the amount of heating or cooling needed for a building. If the standard average temperature for a day is 65 degrees, then a temperature of 10 below zero for 24 hours yields 75 degree-days.

dust storm Visibility of one-half mile or less due to dust, wind speeds of 30 mph or more.

flash flood A sudden, violent flood. It typically occurs after a heavy rain or the melting of a heavy snow.

flash flood warning Warns that flash flooding is imminent or in progress. Those in the affected area should take necessary precautions immediately.

flash flood watch Alerts the public that flash flooding is possible. Those in the affected area are urged to be ready to take additional precautions if a flash flood warning is issued or if flooding is observed.

flood Stories about floods usually tell how high the water is and where it is expected to crest. Such a story should also, for comparison, list flood stage and how high the water is above, or below, flood stage.
Wrong: *The river is expected to crest at 39 feet.*
Right: *The river is expected to crest at 39 feet, 12 feet above flood stage.*

freeze Describes conditions when the temperature at or near the surface is expected to be below 32 degrees during the growing season. Adjectives such as *severe* or *hard* are used if a cold spell exceeding two days is expected.

A freeze may or may not be accompanied by the formation of frost. However, use of the term *freeze* usually is restricted for occasions when wind or other conditions prevent frost.

freezing drizzle, freezing rain Synonyms for *ice storm.*

frost Describes the formation of very small ice crystals, which might develop under conditions similar to dew except for the minimum temperatures involved. Phrases such as *frost in low places* or *scattered light frost* are used when appropriate. The term *frost* seldom appears in state forecasts unless rather heavy frost is expected over an extensive area.

funnel cloud A violent, rotating column of air that does not touch the ground, usually a pendant from a cumulonimbus cloud.

gale Sustained winds within the range of 39 to 54 mph (34 to 47 knots).

heavy snow It generally means:

a. A fall accumulating to 4 inches or more in depth in 12 hours, or

b. A fall accumulating to 6 inches or more in depth in 24 hours.

high wind Normally indicates that sustained winds of 39 mph or greater are expected to persist for one hour or longer.

hurricane or typhoon A warm-core tropical cyclone in which the minimum sustained surface wind is 74 mph or more.

Hurricanes are spawned east of the international date line. Typhoons develop west of the line. They are known as cyclones in the Indian Ocean.

When a hurricane or typhoon loses strength (wind speed), usually after landfall, it is reduced to *tropical storm* status.

hurricane categories Hurricanes are ranked 1 to 5 according to what is known as the Saffir-Simpson scale of strength:

Category 1 — Hurricane has central barometric pressure of 28.94 inches or more and winds of 74 to 95 mph, is accompanied by a 4-5 foot storm surge and causes minimal damage.

Category 2 — Pressure 28.50 to 28.93 inches, winds from 96 to 110 mph, storm surge 6-8 feet, damage moderate.

Category 3 — Pressure 27.91 to 28.49 inches, winds from 111 to 130 mph, storm surge 9-12 feet, damage extensive.

Category 4 — Pressure 27.17 to 27.90 inches, winds from 131 to 155 mph, storm surge 13-18 feet, damage extreme.

Category 5 — Pressure less than 27.17 inches, winds greater than 155 mph, storm surge higher than 18 feet, damage catastrophic.

Only two *Category 5* storms have hit the United States since record-keeping began: the 1935 Labor Day hurricane that hit the Florida Keys and killed 600 people and Hurricane Camille, which devastated the Mississippi coast in 1969, killing 256 and leaving $1.4 billion damage.

hurricane eye The relatively calm area in the center of the storm. In this area winds are light and the sky often is covered only partly by clouds.

hurricane season The portion of the year that has a relatively high incidence of hurricanes. In the Atlantic, Caribbean and Gulf of Mexico, this is from June through November. In the eastern Pacific, it is May 15 through Nov. 30. In the central Pacific, it is June 1 through Nov. 30.

hurricane tide Same as **storm tide**.

hurricane warning Warns that one or both of these dangerous effects of a hurricane are expected in specified areas in 24 hours or less:
a. Sustained winds of 74 mph (64 knots) or higher, and/or
b. Dangerously high water or a combination of dangerously high water and exceptionally high waves, even though winds expected may be less than hurricane force.

hurricane watch An announcement for specific areas that a hurricane or incipient hurricane conditions may pose a threat to coastal and inland communities.

ice storm, freezing drizzle, freezing rain Describes the freezing of drizzle or rain on objects as it strikes them. *Freezing drizzle* and *freezing rain* are synonyms for *ice storm*.

ice storm warning Reserved for occasions when significant, and possibly damaging, accumulations of ice are expected.

National Hurricane Center The National Weather Service's National Hurricane Center in Miami has overall responsibility for tracking and providing information about tropical depressions, tropical storms and hurricanes in the Atlantic Ocean, Gulf of Mexico, Caribbean Sea and eastern Pacific Ocean.

The service's Central Pacific Hurricane Center in Honolulu is responsible for hurricane information in the Pacific Ocean area north of the equator from 140 degrees west longitude to 180 degrees.

nearshore waters The waters extended to five miles from shore.

nor'easter The term used by the National Weather Service for storms that either exit or move north along the East Coast, producing winds blowing from the northeast.

offshore waters The waters extending to about 250 miles from shore.

sandstorm Visibility of one-half mile or less due to sand blown by winds of 30 mph or more.

severe blizzard Wind speeds of 45 mph or more, great density of falling and/or blowing snow with visibility frequently near zero and a temperature of 10 degrees or lower.

severe thunderstorm Describes either of the following:
a. Winds — Thunderstorm-related surface winds sustained or gusts 50 knots or greater.
b. Hail — Surface hail three-quarters of an inch in diameter or

larger. The word *hail* in a watch implies hail at the surface and aloft unless qualifying phrases such as *hail aloft* are used.

sleet (one form of ice pellet) Describes generally solid grains of ice formed by the freezing of raindrops or the refreezing of largely melted snowflakes. Sleet, like small hail, usually bounces when hitting a hard surface.

sleet (heavy) Heavy sleet is a fairly rare event in which the ground is covered to a depth of significance to motorists and others.

snow avalanche bulletin Snow avalanche bulletins are issued by the U.S. Forest Service for avalanche-prone areas in the western United States.

squall A sudden increase of wind speed by at least 16 knots and rising to 25 knots or more and lasting for at least one minute.

stockmen's advisory Alerts the public that livestock may require protection because of certain combinations of cold, wet and windy weather, specifically cold rain and/or snow with temperatures 45 degrees or lower and winds of 25 mph or higher. If the temperature is in the mid-30s or lower, the wind speed criterion is lowered to about 15 mph.

storm tide Directional wave(s) caused by a severe atmospheric disturbance.

temperature-humidity index The temperature-humidity index indicates the combined effect of heat and air moisture on human

comfort. A reading of 70 or below indicates no discomfort. A reading of 75 would indicate discomfort in half the population and all would feel uncomfortable with a reading of 79. The National Weather Service issues the *THI* between June 15 and Sept. 15.

tidal wave A term often used incorrectly for *seismic sea wave*. These waves are caused by underwater earthquakes, landslides or volcanoes and are sometimes referred to as *great sea waves*. Scientists call them *tsunamis*, a term that is not widely used and should be explained if used.

tornado A violent rotating column of air forming a pendant usually from a cumulonimbus cloud, and touching the ground. It usually starts as a funnel cloud and is accompanied by a loud roaring noise. On a local scale, it is the most destructive of all atmospheric phenomena.

tornado warning Warns the public of an existing tornado or one suspected to be in existence.

tornado watch Alerts the public to the possibility of a tornado.

travelers' advisory Alerts the public that difficult traveling or hazardous road conditions are expected to be widespread.

tropical depression A tropical cyclone in which the maximum sustained surface wind is 38 mph (33 knots) or less.

tropical storm A warm-core tropical cyclone in which the maximum sustained surface winds range from 39 to 73 mph

(34 to 63 knots) inclusive.

typhoon See **hurricane or typhoon** in this listing.

waterspout A tornado over water.

wind chill index Also known as the *wind chill factor*. No hyphen.

The *wind chill* is a calculation that describes the combined effect of the wind and cold temperatures on exposed skin. The *wind chill index* would be minus 22, for example, if the temperature was 15 degrees and the wind was blowing at 25 mph — in other words, a temperature of 22 below zero with no wind.

The higher the wind at a given temperature, the lower the wind chill reading, although wind speeds above 40 mph have little additional cooling effect.

wind shear It is caused when a mass of cooled air rushes downward out of a thunderstorm in what is called a *microburst*, hits the ground and rushes outward in all directions. Wind shear itself is described as a sudden shift in wind direction and speed. A plane flying through a microburst at low altitude, as on final approach or takeoff, would at first experi-

Heat Index Table
Relative Humidity (Percentage)

Air Temp		30	35	40	45	50	55	60	65	70	75	80	85	90	95	100
					Apparent Temperature										
110	-	123	130	137	143	150										
105	-	113	118	123	129	135	142	149								
100	-	104	107	110	115	120	126	132	138	144						
95	-	96	98	101	104	107	110	114	119	124	130	136				
90	-	90	91	93	95	96	98	100	102	106	109	113	117	122		
85	-	84	85	86	87	88	89	90	91	93	95	97	99	102	105	108
80	-	78	79	79	80	81	81	82	83	85	86	86	87	88	89	91
75	-	73	73	74	74	75	75	76	76	77	77	78	78	79	79	80
70	-	67	67	68	68	69	69	70	70	70	70	71	71	71	71	72

Wind Chill Factor Table
Air Temperature

Wind mph	35	30	25	20	15	10	5	0	-5	-10	-15	-20	-25	-30	-35
					Apparent Temperature										
5-	33	27	21	16	12	7	0	-5	-10	-15	-21	-26	-31	-36	-42
10-	22	16	10	3	-3	-9	-15	-22	-27	-34	-40	-46	-52	-58	-64
15-	16	9	2	-5	-11	-18	-25	-31	-38	-45	-51	-58	-65	-72	-78
20-	12	4	-3	-10	-17	-24	-31	-39	-46	-53	-60	-67	-74	-81	-88
25-	8	1	-7	-15	-22	-29	-36	-44	-51	-59	-66	-74	-81	-88	-96
30-	6	-2	-10	-18	-25	-33	-41	-49	-56	-64	-71	-79	-86	-93	-101
35-	4	-4	-12	-20	-27	-35	-43	-52	-58	-67	-74	-82	-89	-97	-105
40-	3	-5	-13	-21	-29	-37	-45	-53	-60	-69	-76	-84	-92	-100	-107
45-	2	-6	-14	-22	-30	-38	-46	-54	-62	-70	-78	-85	-93	-102	-109

Winds of more than 45 mph add little to the chilling.

ence a strong headwind and increased lift, followed by a strong tail wind and sharply decreased lift.

winter storm warning Notifies the public that severe winter weather conditions are almost certain to occur.

winter storm watch Alerts the public to the possibility of severe winter weather conditions.

weather vane

Web See **Internet; World Wide Web.**

Webster's New World College Dictionary See **dictionaries.**

Webster's Third New International Dictionary See **dictionaries.**

Wednesday See **days of the week.**

weekend

weeklong One word as an adjective; an exception to Webster's.

weights Use figures: *The baby weighed 9 pounds, 7 ounces. She had a 9-pound, 7-ounce boy.*

weird, weirdo

Welcome Wagon A trademark of Welcome Wagon International Inc.

well Hyphenate as part of a compound modifier: *She is a well-dressed woman.*
See **hyphen** in the **Punctua-**

tion chapter for guidelines on compound modifiers.

well-being

well-to-do

well-wishers

west, western See the **directions and regions** entry.

West As defined by the U.S. Census Bureau, the 13-state region is broken into two divisions.
The eight *Mountain division* states are Arizona, Colorado, Idaho, Montana, Nevada, New Mexico, Utah and Wyoming.
The five *Pacific division* states are Alaska, California, Hawaii, Oregon and Washington.
See **North Central region; Northeast region;** and **South** for the bureau's other three regional breakdowns.

Western Capitalize for the film or book genre, but lowercase the style of music better known as *country.*

Western Hemisphere The continents of North and South America, and the islands near them.
It frequently is subdivided as follows:

Caribbean The islands from the tip of Florida to the continent of South America, plus French Guiana, Guyana and Suriname on the northeastern coast of South America.
Major island elements are Cuba, Hispaniola (the island shared by the Dominican Republic and Haiti), Jamaica, Puerto Rico, and the West Indies islands.

Central America The narrow strip of land between Mexico and Colombia. Located there are Belize, Costa Rica, El Salvador, Guatemala, Honduras, Nicaragua and Panama.

Latin America The area of the Americas south of the United States where Romance languages (those derived from Latin) are dominant. It applies to most of the region south of the United States except areas with a British heritage: the Bahamas, Barbados, Belize, Grenada, Guyana, Jamaica, Trinidad and Tobago, and various islands in the West Indies. Suriname, the former Dutch Guiana, is an additional exception.

North America Canada, Mexico, the United States and the Danish territory of Greenland. When the term is used in more than its continental sense, it also may include the islands of the Caribbean.

South America Argentina, Bolivia, Brazil, Chile, Colombia, Ecuador, Paraguay, Peru, Uruguay, Venezuela, and in a purely continental sense, French Guiana, Guyana and Suriname. Politically and psychologically, however, the latter three regard themselves as part of the Caribbean.

West Indies An island chain extending in an eastward arc between the southeastern United States and the northern shore of South America, separating the Caribbean Sea from the Atlantic Ocean and including the Bahamas, the Greater Antilles, and the Lesser Antilles.

Major island elements are the nations of Barbados, Grenada, and Trinidad and Tobago, plus smaller islands dependent in various degrees on:

—Britain: British Virgin Islands, Anguilla, and the West Indies Associated States, including Antigua, Dominica, St. Lucia, St. Vincent and St. Christopher-Nevis.

—France: Guadeloupe (composed of islands known as Basse-Terre and Grande-Terre, plus five other islands) and Martinique.

—Netherlands: Netherlands Antilles, composed of Aruba, Bonaire, Curacao, Saba, St. Eustatius and the southern portion of St. Martin Island (the northern half is held by France and is part of Guadeloupe).

—United States: U.S. Virgin Islands, principally St. Croix, St. John and St. Thomas.

West Indies See **Western Hemisphere**.

West Point Acceptable on second reference to the *U.S. Military Academy*.
See **military academies**.
In datelines:
WEST POINT, N.Y. (AP) —

West Virginia Abbrev.: *W.Va.* (no space between *W.* and *Va.*). See **state names**.

wheat It is measured in bushels domestically, in metric tons for international trade.
There are 36.7 bushels of wheat in a metric ton.

wheelchair See **disabled, handicapped, impaired** entry.

wheeler-dealer

whereabouts Takes a singular verb:

His whereabouts is a mystery.

wherever

which See the **essential clauses, nonessential clauses** entry; the **that, which** entry; and the **who, whom** entry.

whip Capitalize when used as a formal title before a name. See **legislative titles** and **titles**.

whiskey, whiskeys Use the spelling *whisky* only in conjunction with *Scotch*.
See the **Scotch whisky** entry.

white-collar (adj.)

White House Do not personify it with phrases such as *the White House said.* Instead, use a phrase such as *a White House official said.*

white paper Two words, lowercase, when used to refer to a special report.

whitewash (n. and v. and adj.)

who, whom Use *who* and *whom* for references to human beings and to animals with a name. Use *that* and *which* for inanimate objects and animals without a name.
Who is the word when someone is the subject of a sentence, clause or phrase: *The woman who rented the room left the window open. Who is there?*
Whom is the word when someone is the object of a verb or preposition: *The woman to whom the room was rented left the window open. Whom do you wish to see?*

See the **essential clauses, nonessential clauses** entry for guidelines on how to punctuate clauses introduced by *who, whom, that* and *which*.

wholehearted

wholesale price index A
measurement of the changes in the average prices that businesses pay for a selected group of industrial commodities, farm products, processed foods and feed for animals.
Capitalize when referring to the U.S. index, issued monthly by the Bureau of Labor Statistics, an agency of the Labor Department.

whole-wheat

who's, whose *Who's* is a contraction for *who is*, not a possessive: *Who's there?*
Whose is the possessive: *I do not know whose coat it is.*

wide- Usually hyphenated. Some examples:

wide-angle	wide-eyed
wide-awake	wide-open
wide-brimmed	

Exception: *widespread.*

-wide No hyphen. Some examples:

citywide	nationwide
continentwide	statewide
countrywide	worldwide
industrywide	

widow, widower In obituaries: A man is *survived by his wife*, or *leaves his wife*. A woman is *survived by her husband*, or *leaves her husband.*
Guard against the redundant *widow of the late.* Use *wife of the late* or *widow of.*

widths See **dimensions**.

wigwag

wildlife

Wilkes-Barre, Pa.

will See the **shall, will** entry and **subjunctive mood**.

Wilson's disease After Samuel A. Wilson, an English neurologist. A disease characterized by abnormal accumulation of copper in the brain, liver and other organs.

Windbreaker A trademark for a brand of wind-resistant sports jacket.

wind chill index See **weather terms**.

window dressing The noun. But as a verb: *window-dress*.

wind-swept

wind up (v.) **windup** (n. and adj.)

wingspan

winter See **seasons**.

wintertime

wiretap, wiretapper The verb forms: *wiretap, wiretapped, wiretapping*.

Wisconsin Abbrev.: *Wis*. See **state names**.

-wise No hyphen when it means *in the direction of* or *with regard to*. Some examples:

clockwise	otherwise
lengthwise	slantwise

Avoid contrived combinations such as *moneywise, religionwise*.

The word *penny-wise* is spelled with a hyphen because it is a compound adjective in which *wise* means *smart*, not an application of the suffix *-wise*. The same for *street-wise* in the *street-wise youth* (an exception to Webster's).

Woman's Christian Temperance Union Not *women's*. *WCTU* is acceptable on second reference.

women Women should receive the same treatment as men in all areas of coverage. Physical descriptions, sexist references, demeaning stereotypes and condescending phrases should not be used.

To cite some examples, this means that:

—Copy should not assume maleness when both sexes are involved, as in *Jackson told news-men* or in *the taxpayer ... he* when it easily can be said *Jackson told reporters* or *taxpayers ... they*.

—Copy should not express surprise that an attractive woman can be professionally accomplished, as in: *Mary Smith doesn't look the part, but she's an authority on ...*

—Copy should not gratuitously mention family relationships when there is no relevance to the subject, as in: *Golda Meir, a doughty grandmother, told the Egyptians today ...*

—Use the same standards for men and women in deciding whether to include specific mention of personal appearance or marital and family situation.

In other words, treatment of the sexes should be evenhanded and free of assumptions and stereotypes. This does not mean that valid and acceptable words such as *mankind* or *humanity* cannot be used. They are proper.

See **courtesy titles; divorcee;** the **man, mankind** entry; and **-persons.**

Women's Army Corps See the **Wac, WAC** entry.

Woolworth's See **Venator Group.**

word-of-mouth (n. and adj.)

word processing (adj.) Do not hyphenate.

words as words The meaning of this phrase, which appears occasionally in this book and similar manuals that deal with words, is best illustrated by an example: In this sentence, *woman* appears solely as a word rather than as the means of representing the concept normally associated with the word.

When italics are available, a word used as a word should be italicized.

Italics are not available to highlight this type of word use on the news wires. When a news story must use a word as a word, place quotation marks around it.

See **plurals.**

word selection In general, any word with a meaning that universally is understood is acceptable unless it is offensive or below the normal standards for literate writing.

This Stylebook lists many words with cautionary notes about how they should be used. The entries in Webster's New World Dictionary provide cautionary notes, comparisons and usage guidelines to help a writer choose the correct word for a particular context.

Any word listed in Webster's New World may be used for the definitions given unless this Stylebook restricts its use to only some definitions recorded by the dictionary or specifies that the word be confined to certain contexts.

If the dictionary cautions that a particular usage is objected to by some linguists or is not accepted widely, be wary of the usage unless there is a reason in the context.

The dictionary provides guidance on many idiomatic expressions under the principal word in the expression. The definition and spelling of underway, for example, are found in the "way" entry.

If it is necessary to use an archaic word or an archaic sense of a word, explain the meaning.

Additional guidance on the acceptability of a word is provided in this book under:

Americanism	**jargon**
colloquialisms	**special contexts**
dialect	**vernacular**
foreign words	

See also the **obscenities, profanities, vulgarities** entry.

workday

workers' compensation

work force

working class (n.) **working-class** (adj.)

workout

workweek

World Bank Acceptable in all references for *International Bank for Reconstruction and Development.*

World Council of Churches This is the main international, interdenominational cooperative body of Anglican, Eastern Orthodox, Protestant and old or national Catholic churches.

The Roman Catholic church is not a member but cooperates with the council in various programs.

Headquarters is in Geneva, Switzerland.

World Court This was an alternate name for the *Permanent Court of International Justice* set up by the League of Nations.

See the entry for the **International Court of Justice**, which has replaced it.

World Health Organization *WHO* is acceptable on second reference.

Headquarters is in Geneva, Switzerland.

World Series Or *the Series* on second reference. A rare exception to the general principles under **capitalization**.

World War I, World War II

worldwide

World Wide Web See **Internet** entry.

worn-out

worship, worshipped, worshipper

worthwhile

would See the **should, would** entry.

wrack See the **rack, wrack** entry.

write in (v.) **write-in** (n. and adj.)

wrongdoing

Wyoming Abbrev.: *Wyo.* See **state names**.

XYZ

Xerox A trademark for a brand of photocopy machine. Never a verb. Use a generic term, such as photocopy.

X-ray (n., v. and adj.) Use for both the photographic process and the radiation particles themselves.

yam Botanically, yams and sweet potatoes are not related, although several varieties of moist-fleshed sweet potatoes are popularly called *yams* in some parts of the United States.

yard Equal to 3 feet.
The metric equivalent is approximately 0.91 meter.
To convert to meters, multiply by 0.91 (5 yards x 0.91 = 4.55 meters).
See **foot; meter;** and **distances**.

year-end (adj.)

yearlong

years Use figures, without commas: *1975.* Use an *s* without an apostrophe to indicate spans of decades or centuries: *the 1890s, the 1800s.*
Years are the lone exception to the general rule in numerals that a figure is not used to start a sentence: *1976 was a very good year.*

See **A.D.; B.C.; centuries; historical periods and events;** and **months**.

yellow journalism The use of cheaply sensational methods to attract or influence readers. The term comes from the "Yellow Kid," a comic strip, in the New York World in 1895.

yesterday Use only in direct quotations and in phrases that do not refer to a specific day: *Yesterday we were young.*
Use the day of the week in other cases.

yesteryear

Yom Kippur The Jewish Day of Atonement. Occurs in September or October.

Young Men's Christian Association *YMCA* is acceptable in all references.
Headquarters is in Chicago.

Young Women's Christian Association *YWCA* is acceptable in all references.
Headquarters is in New York.

youth Applicable to boys and girls from age 13 until 18th birthday. Use *man* or *woman* for individuals 18 and older.

yo-yo Formerly a trademark, now a generic term.

Yukon A territorial section of Canada. Do not abbreviate. Use in datelines after the names of communities in the territory.
See **Canada**.

yule, yuletide

zero, zeros

zero-base budgeting A process that requires an agency, department or division to justify budget requests as if its programs were starting from scratch, or from a base of zero. In theory this assures a review of all programs at budget time.

zigzag

Zionism The effort of the Jews to regain and retain their biblical homeland. It is based on the promise of God in the Book of Genesis that Israel would forever belong to Abraham and his descendants as a nation.
The term is named for Mount Zion, the site of the ancient temple in Jerusalem. The Bible also frequently uses *Zion* in a general sense to denote the place where God is especially present with his people.

ZIP code Use all-caps *ZIP* for *Zoning Improvement Plan*, but always lowercase the word *code*.
Run the five digits together without a comma, and do not put a comma between the state name and the ZIP code: *New York, NY 10020.*

SPORTS GUIDELINES AND STYLE

SPORTS GUIDELINES AND STYLE

In 1983, all sports entries were moved into one section, making the use of the information more convenient.

Perhaps it is also an indication of how the coverage of sports continues to grow and how important it is to the overall news report.

Sports is entertainment. It is big business. It is news that extends beyond games, winners and losers.

It is also statistics — agate.

Writing about sports requires a broad understanding of law and economics and psychology and sociology and mores.

As the appetite grows, so too does the need for writing with style and consistency. The constant is the need to write with clarity and accuracy.

Good sports writing depends on the same writing and reporting tools as any other story.

A stylebook, a sports section of a stylebook, is an aid in reaching that goal.

A note on BC filing of sports items:

The 24-hour BC cycle requires the following procedures to differentiate between (a) AMs games stories (and the optionals that move as leads to them), and (b) game stories designed as new wrapups for PMs:

"AMs" stories should be "BC-Reds-Padres" for the game story and "BC-Reds-Padres, 1st Ld-Writethru," etc., for optionals.

Game "PMs" stories should use the word "Folo" in digest lines and the slug ("BC-Reds-Padres Folo"). When a story carries "Folo" in its slug, it is, by definition, for PMs use. Therefore, it doesn't need "Eds: PMs."

"Folo" is used on PMs versions of game stories only.

On events like major golf and tennis tournaments, when there's a story for PMs papers that will develop with morning action, do it as follows:

^BC-GLF--US Open, Bjt.
^Mickelson holds slim lead after first round<
^Eds: PMs. Changes byline. Will be updated with early action in second round, about 8:30 a.m. EDT.<
^By TIM DAHLBERG=
^AP Sports Writer=
PEBBLE BEACH, Calif. (AP) — xxxxxx

or:

^BC-TEN--Wimbledon, Bjt
^Agassi, Sampras advance; Hingis defeated<
^Eds: PMs. Changes byline. Will be updated with morning matches, about 7 a.m. EDT.<
^By STEPHEN WILSON=
^AP Sports Writer=
WIMBLEDON, England (AP) — xxxxx

SPORTS GUIDELINES AND STYLE

A

Abbreviations Do not spell out the most common abbreviations: NFL, NBA, CART, USAC, AFC, NFC.

All-America, All-American The Associated Press recognizes only one All-America football and basketball team each year. In football, only Walter Camp's selections through 1924, and the AP selections after that, are recognized. Do not call anyone an *All-America* selection unless he is listed on either the Camp or AP roster.

Similarly do not call anyone an *All-America basketball player* unless an AP selection. The first All-America basketball team was chosen in 1948.

Use *All-American* when referring specifically to an individual: *All-American Pat Ewing*, or *He is an All-American.*

Use *All-America* when referring to the team: *All-America team*, or *All-America selection.*

Americas Cup (golf) **America's Cup** (yachting)

archery Scoring is usually in points. Use a basic summary. Example:

(After 3 of 4 Distances)
    1. Darrell Pace, Cincinnati, 914 points.
    2. Richard McKinney, Muncie, Ind. 880.
    3. etc.

AstroTurf A trademark for a type of artificial grass.

athlete's foot, athlete's heart

athletic club Abbreviate as *AC* with the name of a club, but only in sports summaries: *Illinois AC.* See the **volleyball** entry for an example of such a summary.

athletic teams Capitalize teams, associations and recognized nicknames: *Red Sox, the Big Ten, the A's, the Colts.*

athletic director Use the singular *athletic* unless otherwise in a formal title.

auto racing
Follow the forms below for all major auto races:

Examples:
Qualifying:
    ANYTOWN, Fredonia (AP) — Qualifying results Friday for the Fredonia Grand Prix Formula One race on the 3.97-kilometer (2.48-mile) Major Fredonia circuit with driver, country, make of car and qualifying speed:
    1. Ayrton Senna, Brazil, McLaren-Honda, 171.103 kph (108.265 mph).
    2. Alain Prost, France, Ferrari, 170.297 kph (107.919 mph).
    3. etc. for entire starting grid.

Race:
    ANYTOWN, Fredonia (AP) — Results Sunday in the Fredonia Grand Prix over the 3.97-kilometer (2.48-mile) Major Fredonia circuit with driver, country (for U.S. drivers, add hometown), make of car, laps completed, reason out (if any) and winner's average speed:
    1. Ayrton Senna, Brazil, McLaren-Honda, 44 laps, 164.297 kph (101.823 mph).
    2. Alain Prost, France, Ferrari, 44.
    3. Nigel Mansell, Britain, Ferrari, 43.
    4. etc. for entire starting grid, adding all non-finishers as follows:
    23. Bernhard Bergen, Austria, McLaren-Honda, 12, broken axle.

After the final driver, add:
Time of race: 1:52:53.
Margin of victory: 1.7 seconds.
Caution flags: No full-course yellows.
Lead changes: 2 between 2 drivers.
Lap leaders: Senna, 1-34, Boutsen 35-36, Senna 37-44.

For point leaders:
World Driver Leaders
(Points on 9-6-4-3-2-1 basis)
1. Nicki Lauda, Austria, 47 points. 2. Emerson Fitipaldi, Brazil, 53.3. etc.

B

backboard, backcourt, backfield, backhand, backspin, backstop, backstretch, backstroke Some are exceptions to Webster's New World, made for consistency in handling sports stories.

badminton Games are won by the first player to score 21 points, unless it is necessary to continue until one player has a two-point spread. Most matches go to the first winner of two games.
Use a match summary. See **racquetball** for an example.

ball carrier

ballclub, ballpark, ballplayer

baseball
The spellings for some frequently used words and phrases, some of which are exceptions to Webster's New World:

backstop	outfielder
ballclub	passed ball
ballpark	pinch hit (v.)
ballplayer	pinch-hit (n., adj.)
baseline	pinch hitter (n.)
bullpen	pitchout
center field	play off (v.)
center fielder	playoff (n., adj.)
designated hitter	put out (v.) putout (n.)
doubleheader	RBI (s.), RBIs (pl.)
double play	rundown (n.)
fair ball	sacrifice

fastball	sacrifice fly
first baseman	sacrifice hit
foul ball line	shoestring catch
foul tip	shortstop
ground-rule double	shut out (v.)
home plate	shutout (n., adj.)
home run	slugger
left-hander	squeeze play
line drive	strike
line up (v.)	strike zone
lineup (n.)	Texas leaguer
major league(s) (n.)	triple play
major-league (adj.)	twinight doubleheader
major-leaguer (n.)	wild pitch

NUMBERS: Some sample uses of numbers: *first inning, seventh-inning stretch, 10th inning; first base, second base, third base; first home run, 10th home run; first place, last place; one RBI, 10 RBIs. The pitcher's record is now 6-5. The final score was 1-0.*

LEAGUES: Use *American League, National League, American League West, National League East,* or *AL West* and *AL East,* etc. On second reference: *the league, the pennant in the West, the league's West Division,* etc.

BOX SCORES: A sample follows.
The visiting team always is listed on the left, the home team on the right.
Only one position, the first he played in the game, is listed for any player.
Figures in parentheses are the player's total in that category for the season.
Use the *First Game* line shown here only if the game was the first in a doubleheader.
One line in this example — *None out when winning run scored* — could not have occurred in this game as played. It is included to show its placement when needed.

First Game
PHILADELPHIA   **SAN DIEGO**
            ab r h bi   **ab r h bi**

Stone lf	4	0 0 0	Flannry 2	3	0 1 0
GGross lf	0	0 0 0	Gwynn rf	4	0 2 0
Schu 3	4	1 0 0	Garvey 1	4	0 0 0
Samuel 2b	4	0 1 2	Nettles 3b	3	1 1 0
Schmdt 1	4	0 0 0	Royster 3	0	0 0 0
Virgil c	4	2 2 3	McRynl cf	4	0 1 1
GWilson rf	4	0 0 0	Kennedy c	4	0 1 0
Maddoxc	3	0 0 0	Martinez lf	4	1 1 0
Jeltz ss	2	0 0 0	Templtn ss	4	0 2 1
KGross p	3	0 1 0	Dravcky p	2	0 0 0
Tekulve p	0	0 0 0	Bmbry ph	1	0 0 0
			Lefferts p	0	0 0 0
Totals	**32 3 4 3**			**33 2 9 2**	

Philadelphia   010 200 000 - 3
San Diego   000 200 000 - 2
None out when winning run scored.
E. Templeton, GWilson. DP — Philadelpia 2. LOB
— Philadelphia 3, San Diego 6. 2B — Templeton,
Gwynn. HR — Virgil (8).

	IP	H	R	ER	BB	SO
Philadelphia						
KGross W, 4-6	7 1-3	9	2	2	0	3
Tekulve S, 3	1 2-3	0	0	0	1	0
San Diego						
Dravecky L, 4-3	7		4	3	1	2
Lefferts	2		0	0	0	1

HBP — Flannery by KGross. T — 2:13. A-17,740.

LINESCORE:
When a bare linescore summary is required, use this form:

Philadelphia   010 200 000 — 3 4 1
San Diego   000 200 000 — 2 9 1
K. Gross, Tekulve (8) and Virgil; Dravecky, Lefferts
(3) and Kennedy. W - KGross, 4-6. LDravecky, 4-3.
Sv - Tekulve (3). HRs - Philadelphia, Virgil 2 (8).

LEAGUE STANDINGS:
The form:

All Times EDT
NATIONAL LEAGUE

	EAST			
	W	L	Pct.	GB
Pittsburgh	92	69	.571	—
Philadelphia	85	75	.531	61/2
etc.				

	WEST			
	W	L	Pct.	GB
Cincinnati	108	54	.667	—
Los Angeles	88	74	.543	20
etc.				

(Night games not included)
Monday's Results
Chicago 7, St. Louis 5
Atlanta at New York, rain.
Tuesday's Games
Cincinnati (Gullett 14-2 and Nolan 4-4) at New
York (Seaver 12-3 and Matlack 6-1) 2, 6 p.m.
Wednesday's Games
Cincinnati at New York
Chicago at St.Louis, night
Only games scheduled.

In subheads for results and future games, spell out day of the week as: *Tuesday's Games*, instead of *Today's Games*.

basic summary This format for summarizing sports events lists winners in the order of their finish. The figure showing the place finish is followed by an athlete's full name, his affiliation or hometown, and his time, distance, points, or whatever performance factor is applicable to the sport.

If a contest involves several types of events, the paragraph begins with the name of the event.

A typical example:

60-yard dash — 1, Steve Williams, Florida TC, 6.0. 2, Hasley Crawford, Philadelphia Pioneer, 6.1. 3, Mike McFarland, Chicago TC, 6.2. 4, etc.

100 — 1, Steve Williams, Florida TC, 10.1. 2, etc.

Additional examples are provided in the entries for many of the sports that are reported in this format.

Most basic summaries are a single paragraph per event, as shown. In some competitions with large fields, however, the basic summary is supplied under a dateline with each winner listed in a single paragraph. See the **auto racing** and **bowling** entries for examples.

For international events in which U.S. or Canadian competitors are not among the leaders, add them in a separate paragraph as follows:

Also: 14, Dick Green, New York, 6.8. 17, George Bensen, Canada, 6.9. 19, etc.

In events where points, rather than time or distance, are recorded as performances, mention the word points on the first usage only:

1. Jim Benson, Springfield, N.J., 150 points. 2. Jerry Green, Canada, 149. 3. etc.

basketball The spellings of some frequently used words and phrases:

backboard	half-court pass
backcourt	halftime
backcourtman	hook shot
baseline	jump ball

field goal

jump shot

foul line

layup

foul shot

man-to-man

free throw

midcourt

free-throw line

pivotman

frontcourt

play off (v.)

full-court press

playoff (n., adj.)

goaltending

zone

NUMBERS: Some sample uses of numbers: *in the first quarter, a second-quarter lead, nine field goals, 10 field goals, the 6-foot-5 forward, the 6-10 center. He is 6 feet 10 inches tall.*

LEAGUE: *National Basketball Association* or *NBA.*

For subdivisions: *the Atlantic Division of the Eastern Conference, the Pacific Division of the Western Conference,* etc. On second reference: *the NBA East, the division, the conference,* etc.

BOX SCORE: A sample follows. The visiting team always is listed first.

In listing the players, begin with the five starters — two forwards, center, two guards — and follow with all substitutes who played.

Figures after each player's last name denote field goals, free throws, free throws attempted and total points.

Example:

LOS ANGELES (114)

Worthy 8-19 4-6 20, Rambis 4-6 0-0 8, Abdul-Jabbar 6-11 0-0 12, E. Johnson 8-14 3-4 19, Scott 5-14 0-0 10, Cooper 1-5 2-2 4, McAdoo 6-13 0-0 12, McGee 4-7 4-5 14, Spriggs 4-7 0-2 8, Kupchak 3-3 1-2 7. Totals 49-100 14-21 114.

BOSTON (148)

McHale 10-16 6-9 26, Bird 8-14 2-2 19, Parish 6-11 6-7 18, D. Johnson 6-14 1-1 13, Ainge 9-15 0-0 19, Buckner 3-5, 0-0 6, Williams 3-5 0-0 6, Wedman 11-11 0-2 26, Maxwell 1-1 1-2 3, Kite 3-5 1-2 7, Carr 1-3 0-0 3, Clark 1-2 0-0 2. Totals 62-102 17-25 148.

Three-point goals — Wedman 4, McGee 2, Bird, Ainge, Carr. Fouled out — None. Rebounds — Los Angeles 43 (Rambis 9), Boston 63 (McHale 9).

Assists — Los Angeles 28 (E. Johnson 12),

Boston 43 (D. Johnson 10).

Total fouls — Los Angeles 23, Boston 17.

Technicals — Ainge. A — 14,890.

STANDINGS: The format for professional standings:

Eastern Conference
Atlantic Division

	W	L	Pct.	GB
Boston	43	22	.662	—
Philadelphia	40	30	.571	5 1/2
etc.				

In college boxes, the score by periods is omitted because the games are divided only into halves.

UCLA (69)

Jackson 1-6 2-2 4, Maloncon 4-7 2-2 10, Wright 4-7 1-5 9, Gaines 4-6 1-2 9, Miguel 5-10 0-0 10, Butler 2-3 6-8 10, Hatcher 3-8 0-0 6, Immel 2-3 1-1 5, Haley 1-1 4-4 6, Miller 0-2 0-0 0, J. Jones 0-3 0-0 0, Dunlap 0-0 0-0 0. Totals 26-55 17-24 69.

ST. JOHN'S (88)

Berry 10-14 3-5 23, Glass 4-5 3-6 11, Wennington 5-9 4-4 14, Moses 5-6 0-0 10, Mullin 6-11 4-6 16, Jackson 1-3 5-5 7, Stewart 0-3 2-2 2, S. Jones 1-2 2-2 4, Bross 0-1 0-0 0, Rowan 0-2 0-0 0, Shurina 0-0 1-2 1, Coregy 0-0 0-0 0. Totals 32-56 24-32 88.

Halftime — St. John's 48, UCLA 35. Fouled out — None. Rebounds — UCLA 25 (Wright 9), St. John's 39 (Mullin 9). Assists — UCLA 18 (Gaines 5), St. John's 21 (Moses 8). Total fouls — UCLA 22, St. John's 20.

A-15,256

The format for college conference standings:

	Conference			All Games		
	W	L	Pct.	W	L	Pct.
Missouri	12	2	.857	24	4	.857

betting odds Use figures and a hyphen: *The odds were 5-4, he won despite 3-2 odds against him.*

The word *to* seldom is necessary, but when it appears it should be hyphenated in all constructions: *3-to-2 odds, odds of 3-to-2, the odds were 3-to-2.*

bettor A person who bets.

bicycle

billiards Scoring is in points. Use a match summary. Example:

Minnesota Fats, St. Paul, Minn., def. Pool Hall Duke, 150-141.

bobsledding, luge Scoring is in minutes, seconds and tenths of a second. Extend to hundredths if available.

Identify events as *two-man, four-man, men's luge, women's luge.*

Use a basic summary. Example:

Two-man — 1, Jim Smith and Dick Jones, Alaska Sledders, 4:20.77.2, Tom Winner and Joe Finisher, Mountaineers, 4:31.14.3, etc.

bowl games Capitalize them: *Cotton Bowl, Orange Bowl, Rose Bowl,* etc.

bowling Scoring systems use both total points and won-lost records.

Use the basic summary format in paragraph form. Note that a comma is used in giving pinfalls of more than 999.

Examples:

ST. LOUIS (AP) — Second-round leaders and their total pinfalls in the $100,000 Professional Bowlers Association tournament:

1. Bill Spigner, Hamden, Conn., 2,820.
2. Gary Dickinson, Fort Worth, Texas, 2,759.
3. etc.

ALAMEDA, Calif. (AP) — The 24 match play finalists with their won-lost records and total pinfall Thursday night after tour rounds — 26 games — of the $65,000 Alameda Open bowling tournament:

1. Jay Robinson, Los Angeles, 5-3, 5,937.
2. Butch Soper, Huntington Beach, Calif., 3-5, 5,932.
3. etc.

boxing The three major sanctioning bodies for professional boxing are the World Boxing Association, the World Boxing Council and the International Boxing Federation.

Weight classes and titles by organization:

105 pounds – Mini Flyweight, IBF; Strawweight, WBC

108-111 pounds — Junior Flyweight, WBA, IBF; light flyweight, WBC.

112-117 pounds — Flyweight, WBA, WBC, IBF.

115 pounds – Super Flyweight, WBC

118-121 pounds — Bantamweight, WBA, WBC, IBF.

122-125 pounds — Junior featherweight, WBA, IBF, super bantamweight, WBC.

126-129 pounds — Featherweight, WBA, WBC, IBF.

130-134 pounds — Junior lightweight, WBA, IBF; super featherweight, WBC.

135-139 pounds — Lightweight, WBA, WBC, IBF.

140-146 pounds — Junior welterweight, WBA, IBF; super lightweight, WBC.

147-153 pounds — Welterweight, WBA, WBC, IBF.

154-159 pounds — Junior middleweight, WBA, IBF; super welterweight, WBC.

160-174 pounds — Middleweight, WBA, WBC.

160-164 pounds — Middleweight, IBF.

168 pounds — Super middleweight, WBC,IBF.

175-194 pounds — Light heavyweight, WBA, WBC, IBF.

190 pounds — Junior heavyweight, WBA; cruiserweight, WBC, IBF.

Over 190 pounds — Heavyweight, WBA, WBC, IBF.

Some other terms:

kidney punch A punch to an opponent's kidney when the puncher has only one hand free. An illegal punch. If the puncher has both hands free, a punch to the opponent's kidney is legal.

knock out (v.) **knockout** (n. and adj.) A fighter is knocked out if he takes a 10-count.

If a match ends early because one fighter is unable to continue, say that the winner stopped the loser. In most boxing jurisdictions there is no such thing as a technical knockout.

outpointed Not *outdecisioned.*

rabbit punch A punch behind an opponent's neck. It is illegal.

SUMMARIES: Use a match summary.

Some examples, with the fighters' weights after their names and the number of rounds at the end.

Randy Jackson, 152, New York, outpointed Chuck James, 154, Philadelphia, 10.

Muhammad Ali, 220, Chicago, knocked out Pierre Coopman, 202, Belgium, 5.

George Foreman, 217, Hayward, Calif., stopped Joe Frazier, 214, Philadelphia, 2.

TALE OF THE TAPE:
An example:

SAN JUAN, Puerto Rico (AP) — The tale of the tape for the Jean Pierre Coopman-Muhammad Ali world heavyweight championship fight Friday night:

	Coopman	Ali
Age	29	34
Weight	202	220
Height	6-0	6-3
Reach	75	80
Chest Normal	43	44
Chest Expanded	45 1/2	46
Biceps	15	15
Forearm	13	13 1/2
Waist	34 1/2	34
Thigh	25 1/2	26
Calf	15	17
Neck	17	17 1/2
Wrist	7 1/2	8
Fist	12 1/2	13
Ankle	9	9 1/2

SCORING BY ROUNDS:
An example:

NEW YORK (AP) — Scorecards for the Muhammad Ali-Joe Frazier heavyweight title fight Friday night:

Scoring by rounds:

Referee Tom Smith
AAA FFF AAA AFA FFF — A8-7
Judge Bill Swift
AAA FFF FFF AFA FFF — F10-5
Judge Ralph Cohen
AAA FFF FFF FFF AFF — F11-4

Scoring by points system:

Referee Tom Smith
A 10 10 10 10 10 10 10 10 10 10 9 9 9 9 10
F 10 9 9 9 9 9 9 10 10 9 10 10 10 10 10
Total — Ali 146, Frazier 143.

Judge Ralph Cohen
A 10 9 10 10 10 10 10 10 10 10 10 9 9 9 9
F 9 10 10 9 9 9 9 9 10 10 9 10 10 10 10
Total — Ali 145, Frazier 143.

box office (n.) box-office (adj.)

bullfight, bullfighter, bullfighting

bullpen One word, for the place where baseball pitchers warm up, and for a pen that holds cattle.

C

Canada goose Not Canadian goose.

canoeing Scoring is in minutes, seconds and tenths of a second. Extend to hundredths if available.

Use a basic summary. Example:

Canoeing, Men
Kayak Singles, 500 meters

Heat 1 — Rudiger Helm, Germany, 1:56.06. 2. Zoltan Sztanity, Hungary, 1:57.12. 3. etc.

Also: 6. Henry Krawczyk, New York, 2 04.64.

First Repechage — 1, Ladislay Soucek, Czech Republic, 1:53.20. 2. Hans Eich, Germany, 1:54.23. 3. etc.

coach Lowercase in all uses, as a job description, not a formal title. See **titles** in main section.

collective nouns Nouns that denote a unit take singular verbs and pronouns: *class, committee, crowd, family, group, herd, jury, orchestra, team.*

However, team names such as *the Jazz, the Magic, the Avalanche,* take plural verbs.

colt A male horse 4 years and under.

Major College Basketball Conferences
(Football affiliations, where different, are in parentheses.)

AMERICA EAST — Albany, N.Y. (Northeast); Boston University (no program); Delaware (Atlantic 10); Drexel (no program); Hartford (no program); Hofstra (Atlantic 10); Maine (Atlantic 10); New Hampshire (Atlantic 10); Northeastern (Atlantic 10); Stony Brook (Northeast); Towson (Patriot); Vermont (no program).

ATLANTIC 10 — Dayton (Pioneer League); Duquesne (Metro Atlantic); Fordham (Patriot League); George Washington (no program); La Salle (Metro Atlantic); Massachusetts; Rhode Island; Richmond; St. Bonaventure (no program); St. Joseph's (no program); Temple (Big East); Xavier (no program).

ATLANTIC COAST CONFERENCE — Clemson; Duke; Florida State; Georgia Tech; Maryland; North Carolina; North Carolina State; Virginia; Wake Forest.

BIG EAST CONFERENCE — Boston College; Connecticut (Division I-A Independent); Georgetown (Division I-AA Independent); Miami; Notre Dame (Division I-A Independent); Pittsburgh; Providence (no program); Rutgers; St. John's (Division I-AA Independent); Seton Hall (no program); Syracuse; Villanova (Atlantic 10); Virginia Tech; West Virginia.

BIG SKY CONFERENCE — Eastern Washington; Idaho State; Montana; Montana State; Northern Arizona; Portland State; Sacramento State; Weber State.

BIG SOUTH CONFERENCE — Charleston Southern (Division I-AA Independent); Coastal Carolina (no program); Elon (Division I-AA Independent); High Point (no program); Liberty (Division I-AA Independent); North Carolina-Asheville (no program); Radford (no program); Winthrop (no program).

BIG TEN CONFERENCE — Illinois; Indiana; Iowa; Michigan; Michigan State; Minnesota; Northwestern; Ohio State; Penn State; Purdue; Wisconsin.

BIG 12 CONFERENCE — Baylor; Colorado; Iowa State; Kansas; Kansas State; Missouri; Nebraska; Oklahoma; Oklahoma State; Texas; Texas A&M; Texas Tech.

BIG WEST CONFERENCE — Cal Poly-San Luis Obispo (Division I-AA Independent); Cal State Fullerton (no program); Cal State Northridge; Idaho (Sun Belt); Long Beach State (no program); Pacific (no program); UC Irvine (no program); UC Riverside (no program); UC Santa Barbara (no program); Utah State (Division I-A Independent).

COLONIAL ATHLETIC ASSOCIATION — American (no program); George Mason (no program); James Madison (Atlantic 10); North Carolina-Wilmington (no program); Old Dominion (no program); Virginia Commonwealth (no program); William & Mary (Atlantic 10).

CONFERENCE USA — Alabama-Birmingham; Charlotte (no program); Cincinnati; DePaul (no program); East Carolina; Houston; Louisville; Marquette (no program); Memphis; Saint Louis (no program); South Florida (Division I-A Independent); Southern Mississippi; Texas Christian; Tulane.

IVY LEAGUE — Brown; Columbia; Cornell; Dartmouth; Harvard; Pennsylvania; Princeton; Yale.

METRO ATLANTIC ATHLETIC CONFERENCE — Canisius; Fairfield; Iona; Loyola, Md. (no program); Manhattan (no program); Marist; Niagara (no program); Rider (no program); St. Peter's; Siena.

MID-AMERICAN CONFERENCE — Akron; Ball State; Bowling Green; Buffalo; Central Michigan; Eastern Michigan; Kent State; Marshall; Miami (Ohio); Northern Illinois; Ohio; Toledo; Western Michigan.

MID-CONTINENT CONFERENCE — Chicago State (no program); Indiana-Purdue-Indianapolis (no program); Missouri-Kansas City (no program); Oakland, Mich. (no program); Oral Roberts (no program); Southern Utah (Division I-AA Independent); Valparaiso (Pioneer League); Western Illinois (Gateway Conference).

MID-EASTERN ATHLETIC CONFERENCE — Bethune-Cookman; Coppin State (no program); Delaware State; Florida A&M (no program); Hampton; Howard; Maryland-Eastern Shore (no program); Morgan State; Norfolk State; North Carolina A&T; South Carolina State.

MIDWESTERN COLLEGIATE CONFERENCE — Butler (Pioneer League); Cleveland State (no program); Detroit (no program); Illinois-Chicago (no program); Loyola Chicago (no program); Wisconsin-Green Bay (no program); Wisconsin-Milwaukee (no program); Wright State (no program); Youngstown State (Gateway Conference).

MISSOURI VALLEY CONFERENCE — Bradley (no program); Creighton (no program); Drake (Pioneer League); Evansville (no program); Illinois State (Gateway Conference); Indiana State (Gateway Conference); Northern Iowa (Gateway Conference); Southern Illinois (Gateway Conference); Southwest Missouri State (Gateway Conference); Wichita State (no program).

MOUNTAIN WEST CONFERENCE — Air Force; Brigham Young; Colorado State; New Mexico; San Diego State; UNLV; Utah; Wyoming.

NORTHEAST CONFERENCE — Central Connecticut State; Fairleigh Dickinson (no program); Long Island University (no program); Maryland-Baltimore County (no program); Monmouth, N.J.; Mount St. Mary's, Md. (no program); Quinnipiac (no program); Robert Morris; Sacred Heart; St. Francis, N.Y. (no program); St. Francis, Pa.; Wagner.

OHIO VALLEY CONFERENCE — Austin Peay (Pioneer League); Eastern Illinois; Eastern Kentucky; Morehead State (Pioneer League); Murray State; Southeast Missouri; Tennessee-Martin; Tennessee State; Tennessee Tech.

PACIFIC-10 CONFERENCE — Arizona; Arizona State; California; Oregon; Oregon State; Southern California; Stanford; UCLA; Washington; Washington State.

PATRIOT LEAGUE — Army (Conference USA); Bucknell; Colgate; Holy Cross; Lafayette; Lehigh; Navy (Division I-A Independent).

SOUTHEASTERN CONFERENCE — Alabama; Arkansas; Auburn; Florida; Georgia; Kentucky; LSU; Mississippi; Mississippi State; South Carolina; Tennessee; Vanderbilt.

SOUTHERN CONFERENCE — Appalachian State; Chattanooga; College of Charleston; Davidson; East Tennessee State; Furman; Georgia Southern; North Carolina-Greensboro; The Citadel; VMI; Western Carolina; Wofford.

SOUTHLAND CONFERENCE — Lamar; Louisiana-Monroe; McNeese State; Nicholls State; Northwestern State; Sam Houston State; Southeastern Louisiana; Southwest Texas; Stephen F. Austin; Texas-Arlington; Texas-San Antonio.

SOUTHWESTERN ATHLETIC CONFERENCE — Alabama A&M; Alabama State; Alcorn State; Arkansas-Pine Bluff; Grambling State; Jackson State; Mississippi Valley State; Prairie View; Southern University; Texas Southern.

SUN BELT CONFERENCE — Arkansas-Little Rock (no program); Arkansas State; Denver (no program); Florida International (no program); Louisiana Tech; Louisiana-Lafayette; Middle Tennessee; New Mexico State; New Orleans; North Texas; Western Kentucky (Gateway Conference).

TRANS AMERICA ATHLETIC CONFERENCE — Campbell (no program); Central Florida; Florida Atlantic (no program); Georgia State (no program); Jacksonville; Jacksonville State; Mercer (no program); Samford; Stetson (no program); Troy State.

WEST COAST CONFERENCE — Gonzaga (no program); Loyola Marymount (no program); Pepperdine (no program); Portland (no program); St. Mary's, Calif. (Division I-AA Independent); San Diego (Pioneer League); San Francisco (no program); Santa Clara (no program).

WESTERN ATHLETIC CONFERENCE — Boise State; Fresno State; Hawaii; Nevada; Rice; San Jose State; Southern Methodist; Texas-El Paso; Tulsa.

INDEPENDENTS — Belmont (no program); Centenary (no program); Texas-Pan American (no program); Texas A&M-Corpus Christi (no program).

conferences A listing of major college basketball conferences is on the previous page. (Football affiliations, where different, are in parentheses.)

courtesy titles On sports wires, do not use courtesy titles in any reference unless needed to distinguish among those of the same last name. See **courtesy titles** in main section.

cross country No hyphen, an exception to Webster's New World based on the practices of U.S. and international governing bodies for the sport.

Scoring for this track event is in minutes, seconds and tenths of a second. Extended to hundredths if available.

National AAU Championship Cross Country

> Frank Shorter, Miami, 5:25.67; 2. Tom Coster, Los Angeles, 5:30.72; 3. etc.

Adapt the basic summary to paragraph form under a dateline for a field of more than 10 competitors. See the **auto racing** and **bowling** entries for examples.

cycling Use the basic summary format.

D

decathlon Summaries include time or distance performance, points earned in that event and the cumulative total of points earned in previous events.

Contestants are listed in the order of their overall point totals. First name and hometown (or nation) are included only on the first and last events on the first day of competition; on the last day, first names are included only in the first event and in the summary denoting final placings.

Use the basic summary format. Include all entrants in summaries of each of the 10 events.

An example for individual events:

Decathlon (Group A)

> 100-meter dash — 1. Fred Dixon, Los Angeles, 10.8 seconds, 854 points. 2. Bruce Jenner, San Jose State, 11:09, 783. 3. etc.
> Long jump — 1. Dixon, 24-7 (7.34m), 889, 1,743. 2. Jenner, 23-6 (7.17m), 855, 1,638. 3. etc.
> Decathlon final — 1. Bruce Jenner, San Jose State, 8,524 points. 2. Fred Dixon, Los Angeles, 8,277. 3. etc.

discus The disc thrown in track and field events.

diving Use a basic summary. See **skating, figure** for the style on compulsory dives.

E

ERA Acceptable in all references to baseball's *earned run average*.

F

fencing Identify epee, foil and saber classes as: *men's individual foil, women's team foil*, etc.

Use match summary for early rounds of major events, for lesser dual meets and for tournaments.

Use basic summary for final results of major championships.

For major events, where competitors meet in a round-robin and are divided into pools, use this form:

> Epee, first round (four qualify for semifinals) Pool 1 — Joe Smith, Springfield, Mass., 4-1. Enrique Lopez, Chile, 3-2. etc.

figure skating See **skating, figure** for guidelines on the summary form.

filly A female horse under the age of 5.

football The spellings of some frequently used words and phrases:

ball carrier	lineman
ballclub	line of scrimmage
blitz (n., v.)	out of bounds (adv.)
end line	out-of-bounds (adj.)
end zone	pitchout (n.)
fair catch	place kick
field goal	place-kicker
fourth-and-one (adj.)	play off (v.)
fullback	playoff (n., adj.)
goal line	quarterback
goal-line stand	runback (n.)
halfback	running back
halftime	split end
handoff	tailback
kick off (v.)	tight end
kickoff (adj.)	touchback
left guard	touchdown
linebacker	wide receiver

NUMBERS: Use figures for yardage: *The 5-yard line, the 10-yard line, a 5-yard pass play, he plunged in from the 2, he ran 6 yards, a 7-yard gain.* But: *a fourth-and-two play.*

Some other uses of numbers: *The final score was 21-14. The team won its fourth game in 10 starts. The team record is 4-5-1.*

LEAGUE: *National Football League,* or *NFL.*

STATISTICS: All football games, whether using the one- or two-point conversion, use the same summary style.

The visiting team always is listed first.

Field goals are measured from the point where the ball was kicked — not the line of scrimmage. The goal posts are 10 yards behind the goal lines. Include that distance.

Abbreviate team names to four letters or fewer on the scoring and statistical lines as illustrated.

The passing line shows, in order: completions-attempts-had intercepted.

A sample agate package:

Birmingham-Houston, Stats

Birmingham	7	16	0	7	—30
Houston	14	7	0	6	—27

First Quarter
Hou — Harrell 23 pass from Dillon (Fritsch kick), 1:00
Bir — Jones 11 run with lateral after Mason 12 pass from Stoudt (Miller kick), 5:57
Hou — Harrell 6 run (Fritsch kick), 8:07
Second Quarter
Bir — FG Miller 47, 1:13
Bir — Caruth 6 run (Miller kick), 5:49
Hou — Johnson 36 pass from Dillon (Fritsch kick), 12:12
Bir — FG Miller 43, 14:33
Fourth Quarter
Bir — FG Miller 20, 3:42
Bir — Stoudt 1 run (kick failed), 9:09
Hou — Dillon 8 run (pass failed), 13:58
A — 13,202

	Bir	Hou
First downs	21	15
Rushes-yards	46-209	12-70
Passing yards	109	260
Return yards	75	112
Comp-Att	13-24-0	17-33-2
Sacked-Yards Lost	4-23	2-24
Punts	3-38	3-41
Fumbles-lost	1-1	2-0
Penalties-yards	3-25	12-69
Time of Possession	35:57	24:03

INDIVIDUAL STATISTICS
RUSHING—Birmingham, Caruth 23-84, Coles 14-59, Stoudt 8-50, Gant 1-5. Houston, Harrell, 4-34, Fowler 5-26, Dillon 3-10.
PASSING—Birmingham, Stoudt 13-24-0 133. Houston, Dillon 17- 33-2 283.
RECEIVING—Birmingham, Toler 4-53, Jones 3-15, McFadden 2-38, Coles 2-12, Mason, 1-12, Caruth 1-4. Houston, Johnson 5-108, McGee 3-59, McNeil 3-36, 2-27, Sanders 3-29. Verdin 1-24.
MISSED FIELD GOALS—Houston, Fritsch 32.

The rushing and receiving paragraph for individual leaders shows attempts and yardage gained. The passing paragraph shows completions, attempts, number of attempts intercepted, and total yards gained.

STANDINGS: The form for **professional standings:**
American Conference
East

	W	L	T	Pct.	PF	PA
Baltimore	10	4	0	.714	395	269
New England	9	5	0	.643	387	275
Etc.						

The form for college **conference standings**:

	Conference					All games			
	W	L	T	Pts.	OP	W	L	T	Pts. OP
UCLA	6	1	0	215	123	8	2	1	326 233
Etc.									

In college conference standings, limit team names to nine letters or fewer. Abbreviate as necessary.

fractions Put a full space between the whole number and the fraction. Do not separate with a *thin* symbol.

G

game plan

gelding A castrated male horse.

golf Some frequently used terms and some definitions:

Americas Cup No possessive.

birdie, birdies One stroke under par.

bogey, bogeys One stroke over par. The past tense is *bogeyed.*

caddie

eagle Two strokes under par.

fairway

Masters Tournament No possessive. Use *the Masters* on second reference.

tee, tee off

U.S. Open Championship Use *the U.S. Open* or *the Open* on second reference.

NUMBERS: Some sample uses of numbers:

Use figures for handicaps: *He has a 3 handicap; a 3-handicap golfer, a handicap of 3 strokes; a 3-stroke handicap.*

Use figures for par listings: *He had a par 5 to finish 2-up for the round, a par-4 hole; a 7-under-par 64, the par-3 seventh hole.*

Use figures for club ratings: *a No. 5 iron, a 5-iron, a 7-iron shot, a 4-wood.*

Miscellaneous: *the first hole, the ninth hole, the 10th hole, the back nine, the final 18, the third round. He won 3 and 2.*

ASSOCIATIONS: *Professional Golfers' Association of America* (note the apostrophe) or *PGA.* Headquarters is in Palm Beach Gardens, Fla. Members teach golf at golf shops and teaching facilities across the country.

The *PGA Tour* is a separate organization made up of competing professional golfers. Use *tour* (lowercase) on second reference.

The PGA conducts the PGA Championship, the PGA Seniors' Champion-ship, and the Ryder Cup matches as well as other golf championships not associated with the PGA Tour.

The *Ladies Professional Golfers Association* (no apostrophe, in keeping with LPGA practice) or *LPGA.*

SUMMARIES — Stroke (Medal) Play: List scores in ascending order. Use a dash before the final figure, hyphens between others.

On the first day, use the player's score for the first nine holes, a hyphen, the player's score for the second nine holes, a dash and the player's total for the day:

First round:
Jack Nicklaus   35-35 — 70
Johnny Miller   36-35 — 71
Etc.

On subsequent days, give the player's scores for each day, then the total for all rounds completed:

Second round:
Jack Nicklaus   70-70 — 140
Johnny Miller   71-70 — 141
Etc.

Final round, professional tournaments, including prize money:

Jack Nicklaus, $30,000   70-70-70-68 — 278
Johnny Miller, $17,500   71-70-70-69 — 280

Use hometowns, if ordered, only on national championship amateur tournaments. Use home countries, if ordered, only on major international events such as the British Open. If used, the hometown or country is placed on a second line, indented one space:

Arnold Palmer   70-69-68-70—277
    United States
Tony Jacklin   71-70-70-70—281
    England

The form for cards:

Par out   444 343 544-35
Watson out   454 333 435-34
Nicklaus out   434 243 544-33
Par in   434 443 454-35 — 70
Watson in   434 342 443-31 — 65
Nicklaus in   433 443 453-33 — 66

SUMMARIES — Match Play: In the first example that follows, the *and 1* means that the 18th hole was skipped because Nicklaus had a 2-hole lead after 17. In the second, the match went 18 holes. In the third, a 19th hole was played because the golfers were tied after 18.

Jack Nicklaus def. Lee Trevino, 2 and 1.
Sam Snead def. Ben Hogan, 2-up.
Arnold Palmer def. Johnny Miller, 1-up (19).

Grey Cup The Canadian Football League's championship game.

Gulfstream Park The racetrack.

gymnastics Scoring is by points. Identify events by name: *sidehorse, horizontal bars*, etc.

Use a basic summary. Example:

Sidehorse — 1. John Leaper, Penn State, 8.8 points. 2. Jo Jumper, Ohio State, 7.9. 3. Etc.

H

halfback

handball Games are won by the first player to score 21 points or, in the case of a tie breaker, 11 points. Most matches go to the first winner of two games.

Use a match summary. Example:

Bob Richards, Yale, def. Paul Johnson, Dartmouth, 21-18, 21-19.
Tom Brenna, Massachusetts, def. Bill Stevens, Michigan, 21-19, 17-21, 21-20.

handicaps Use figures, hyphenating adjectival forms before a noun: *He has a 3 handicap, he is a 3-handicap golfer, a handicap of 3 strokes, a 3-stroke handicap.*

hit and run (v.) **hit-and-run** (n. and adj.) *The coach told him to hit and run. He scored on a hit-and-run. She was struck by a hit-and-run driver.*

hockey The spellings of some frequently used words:

blue line	play off (v.)
crease	playoff (n., adj.)
face off (v.)	power play
faceoff (n., adj.)	power-play goal
goalie	red line
goal line	short-handed
goal post	slap shot
goaltender	two-on-one break
penalty box	

The term *hat trick* applies when a player has scored three goals in a game. Use it sparingly, however.

LEAGUE: *National Hockey*

League or *NHL*.

For NHL subdivisions: *the Central Division of the Western Conference, the division, the conference*, etc.

SUMMARIES: The visiting team always is listed first in the score by periods.

Note that each goal is numbered according to its sequence in the game.

The figure after the name of a scoring player shows his total goals for the season.

Names in parentheses are players credited with an assist on a goal.

The final figure in the listing of each goal is the number of minutes elapsed in the period when the goal was scored.

Philadelphia	3 0 0 —3
Edmonton	2 2 1 —5

First period — 1, Philadelphia, Rick Sutter 1 (Ron Sutter, Smith),:46. 2, Edmonton, Coffey 10 (Huddy, Kurri), 4:22 (pp). 3, Philadelphia, Bergen 4 (Zezel, Crossman), 6:38 (pp). 4, Philadelphia, Craven 4 (Smith, Marsh), 11:32 (sh). 5, Edmonton, Huddy 3 (Coffey, Kurri), 18:23 (pp). Penalties — Poulin, Phi (high-sticking), 3:31; Hughes, Edm (high-stocking), 5:17; Messier, Edm (slashing), 5:59; Crossman, Phi, double minor (holding-unsportsmanlike conduct), 8:32; Hospodar, Phi (slashing), 16:38.

Second period — 6, Edmondton, Anderson 10,:21. 7, Edmonton, Gretzky 15 (Coffey, Huddy), 12:53 (pp). Penalties —Tocchet, Phi (roughing),:48; Fogolin, Edm (roughing),:48; Paterson, Phi (hooking), 12:11; Allison, Phi (slashing), 17:39; Hunter, Edm (roughing),17:39; Lowe, Edm (holding), 18:02; Crossman, Phi (holding), 19:07; Hunter, Edm (holding), 20:00.

Third Period — 8 Edmonton, Gretzky 16 (Messier, Anderson), 3:422 (pp). Penalties — Hospodar, Phi (hooking), 2:46; Hunter, Edm (kneeing), 7:58.

Shots on goal — Philadelphia 10-6-7 23. Edmonton 10-12-1 32.

Penalty shots — Ron Sutter, Phi, 8:47 1st (missed).

Goalies — Philadelphia, Lindbergh at 8:56 2nd; re-entered at start of 3rd, 10-9) Edmonton, Fuhr (23-20). A —17,498. Referee — Kerry Fraser.

STANDINGS: The form:

Eastern Conference
Atlantic Division

	W	L	T	Pts.	GF	GA
Philadelphia	47	10	14	108	314	184
NY Islanders	45	17	9	99	310	192
Etc.						

horse races Capitalize their formal names: *Kentucky Derby, Preakness, Belmont Stakes*, etc.

horse racing Some frequently used terms and their definitions:

colt A male horse 4 years old and under.

horse A male horse over 4 years old.

gelding A castrated male horse.

filly A female horse under the age of 5.

mare A female horse 5 years and older.

stallion A male horse used for breeding.

broodmare A female horse used for breeding.

furlong One-eighth of a mile. Race distances are given in furlongs up through seven furlongs, after that in miles, as in *one-mile, 1/1-16 miles.*

entry Two or more horses owned by same owner running as a single betting interest. In some states two or more horses trained by same person but having different owners also are coupled in betting.

mutuel field Not *mutual field*. Two or more horses, long shots, that have different owners and trainers. They are coupled as a single betting interest to give the field not more than 12 wagering interests. There cannot be more than 12 betting interests in a race. The bettor wins if either horse finishes in the money.

half-mile pole The pole on a race track that marks one-half mile from the finish. All distances are measured from the finish line, meaning that when a horse reaches the quarter pole, he is one-quarter mile from the finish.

bug boy An apprentice jockey, so-called because of the asterisk beside the individual's name in a program. It means that the jockey's mount gets a weight allowance.

horses' names Capitalize. See **animals** in main section.

I

IC4A See **Intercollegiate Association of Amateur Athletes of America**.

indoor (adj.) **indoors** (adv.) *He plays indoor tennis. He went indoors.*

Intercollegiate Association of Amateur Athletes of America In general, spell out on first reference.

A phrase such as *IC4A tournament* may be used on first reference, however, to avoid a cumbersome lead. If this is done, provide the full name later in the story.

J

judo Use the basic summary format by weight divisions for major tournaments; use the

match summary for dual and lesser meets.

K

Kentucky Derby *The Derby* on second reference. An exception to normal second-reference practice. Plural is *Derbies*.

See **capitalization** in main section.

L

lacrosse Scoring in goals, worth one point each.

The playing field is 110 yards long. The goals are 80 yards apart, with 15 yards of playing area behind each goal.

A match consists of four 15-minute periods. Overtimes of varying lengths may be played to break a tie.

Adapt the summary format in **hockey**.

Ladies Professional Golf Association No apostrophe after *Ladies*. In general, spell out on first reference.

A phrase such as *LPGA tournament* may be used on first reference to avoid a cumbersome lead. If this is done, provide the full name later in the story.

left hand (n.) **left-handed** (adj.) **left-hander** (n.)

M

marathon Use the formats illustrated in the **cross country**

and **track and field** entries.

mare A female horse 5 years and older.

match summary This format for summarizing sports events applies to one vs. one contests such as tennis, match play golf, etc.

Give a competitor's name, followed either by a hometown or by a college or club affiliation. For competitors from outside the United States, a country name alone is sufficient in summaries sent for domestic use.

Jimmy Connors, Belleville, Ill., def. Manuel Orantes, Spain, 2-6, 6-3, 6-2, 6-1.

metric system See main section.

motorboat racing Scoring may be posted in miles per hour, points or laps, depending on the competition.

In general, use the basic summary format. For some major events, adapt the basic summary to paragraph form under a dateline. See the **auto racing** entry for an example.

motorcycle racing Follow the formats shown under **auto racing**.

N

National Association for Stock Car Auto Racing Or *NASCAR.*

National Collegiate Athletic Association Or *NCAA.*

numerals See the main sec-

tion on general use and entries on **betting odds**, **handicaps** and **scores**.

O

odds See **betting odds**.

Olympics Capitalize all references to the international athletic contests: *the Olympics, the Winter Olympics, the Olympic Games, an Olympic-size pool.*

Lowercase *the games* in second refenence.

P

pingpong A synonym for *table tennis.*

The trademark name is *Ping-Pong.*

play off (v.) **playoff, playoffs** (n. and adj.) The noun and adjective forms are exceptions to Webster's New World Dictionary, in keeping with widespread practice in the sports world.

postseason, preseason No hyphen.

R

racket Not *racquet,* for the light bat used in tennis and badminton.

racquetball Amateur games are played to 15 points in a best-of-three match. Professional matches are played to 11 points, unless it is necessary to continue until one player has a two-point spread. Most matches go to the winner of three of five games.

Use a match summary.

record Avoid the redundant *new record.*

right hand (n.) **right-handed** (adj.) **right-hander** (n.)

rodeo Use the basic summary format by classes, listing points.

rowing Scoring is in minutes, seconds and tenths of a second. Extend to hundredths if available.

Use a basic summary. An example, for a major event where qualifying heats are required:

Single Sculls Heats (first two in each heat qualify for Monday's quarterfinals, losers go to repechage Friday): Heat 1 — 1, Peter Smith, Australia, 4:24.7. 2. Etc. Heat 2 — 1, John Jones, Canada, 4:26.3. 72, Etc.

runner-up, runners-up

S

scores Use figures exclusively, placing a hyphen between the totals of the winning and losing teams: *The Reds defeated the Red Sox 4-3, the Giants scored a 12-6 football victory over the Cardinals, the golfer had a 5 on the first hole but finished with a 2-under-par score.*

Use a comma in this format: *Boston 6, Baltimore 5.*

See individual listings for each sport for further details.

skating, figure Scoring includes both ordinals and points.

Use a basic summary. Example:

ples:
Men
(After 3 compulsory figures)
Sergei Volkov, Russia, 19-5 ordinals, 44.76 points. 2, John Curry, Britain, 21.5, 44.96. 3, Etc.
Women's Final
Dorothy Hamill, Riverside, Conn., 9.0 ordinals, 215 points; 2, Dianne de Leeuw, Netherlands, 20.0, 236; 3, Etc.

skating, speed Scoring is in minutes, seconds and tenths of a second. Extend to hundredths if available.

Use a basic summary.

ski, skis, skier, skied, skiing Also: *ski jump, ski jumping.*

skiing Identify events as: *men's downhill, women's slalom,* etc. In ski jumping, note style where two jumps and points are posted.

Use a basic summary. Example:

90-meter special jumping — 1, Karl Schnabel, Austria, 320 and 318 feet, 234.8 points. 2, Toni Innauer, Austria, 377-299, 232.9. 3, Etc. Also; 27, Bob Smith, Hanover, N.H., 312-280, 201. 29, Etc.

soccer The spellings of some frequently used words and phrases:

AFC (Asian Football Confederation)

Bundesliga (German League first division)

CAF (Confederation Africaine de Football; refer to as the governing body of African soccer rather than spelling out French acronym)

Champions League

coach (also known as *manager* on British teams and *technical director* on some Latin American teams)

CONCACAF (Confederation of North and Central American and Caribbean Football — use full name somewhere in story)

CONMEBOL (Confederacion Sudamerica de Futbol; refer to as South America's governing body rather than spelling out Spanish acronym)

Cup Winners Cup

FIFA (Federation International de Football Association, FIFA acceptable as first reference, refer to as the international soccer football governing body rather than spelling out French acronym)

friendly (use *exhibition game* on U.S. wires)

forward (*striker* for international wires)

goalkeeper (*goalie* is acceptable but goaltender is not)

midfielder

offside

penalty area (sometimes penalty box — do not refer to solely as box on U.S. wires)

MLS (Major League Soccer, MLS acceptable on first reference)

OFC (Oceania Football Confederation)

Serie A (Italian League first division)

sideline (*touchline* for international wires)

UEFA (Union of European Football Associations)

In summaries and key lines for international wires, the home team is listed first; on U.S. wires, the visiting team is listed first

SUMMARY:
At Saint-Denis, France
Italy   0 2 – 2
France 2 0 – 2
(France won 4-3 on penalty kicks)
First half -- 1, France, Zidane 4 (Djorkaeff), 12th minute. 2,
France, Deschamps (penalty kick), 45th minute.
Second half -- 3, Italy, own goal, 88th minute. 4, Italy, R. Baggio 6
(D. Baggio), 90th minute.
First overtime -- None.
Second overtime -- None.
Penalty kicks -- France 4 (Zidane G, Lizarazu NG, Trezeguet G, Henry
G, Blanc G); Italy 3 (Baggio G, Albertini NG, Costacurta G, Vieri G, Di
Biagio NG).
Yellow Cards -- Italy, Del Piero, 26th minute; Bergomi, 28th;
Costacurta, 113th. France, Guivarc'h, 53rd minute; Deschamps, 63rd.
Referee -- Dallas (Scotland). Linesmen -- Grigores-

cu (Romania),
Warren (England).
A --77,000
Lineups
Italy -- Gianluca Pagliuca; Giuseppe Bergomi, Fabio Cannavaro, Alessandro Costacurta, Paolo Maldini; Francesco Moriero, Dino Baggio (Demetrio Albertini, 52nd), Luigi Di Biagio, Gianluca Pessotto (Angelo Di Livio, 90th); Christian Vieri, Alessandro Del Piero (Roberto Baggio, 67th).
France -- Fabien Barthez; Lilian Thuram, Laurent Blanc, Marcel Desailly, Bixente Lizarazu; Didier Deschamps, Emmanuel Petit, Zinedine Zidane, Christian Karembeu (Thierry Henry, 65th); Stephane Guivarc'h (David Trezeguet, 65th), Youri Djorkaeff.

Lineup order is goalkeepers, defenders, midfielders, forwards.

Separate the different positions with semicolons and the players within a position with commas.

STANDINGS: The form for U.S. wires:

Italian League
At A Glance
By The Associated Press
All Times EST
Division One

Team	W	L	T	G	A	Pts
Fiorentina	12	4	2	34	18	38
Lazio of	10	3	5	37	20	35

Sunday's Games=
Bologna 2, AC Milan 3
Internazionale of Milan 5, Cagliari 1
Juventus of Turin 2, Perugia 1
Sunday, Jan. 31
Lazio of Rome at Bari, 8:30 a.m.
Juventus of Turin at Cagliari, 8:30 a.m.
Vicenza at Fiorentina, 8:30 a.m.

The form for international wires:

Scores and standings move in separate files.

Schedule has times GMT instead of EST or EDT.

Schedule lists home teams first.

Sunday, Jan. 31
Bari vs. Lazio of Rome, 0130
Cagliari vs. Juventus of Turin, 0130
Fiorentina vs. Vicenza, 0130

Standings have a different style, starting with *GP* (games played), changing header from *T* (ties) to *D* (draws) and putting draws between wins and losses instead of after.

Italian League Standings
By The Associated Press

Division One						
Team	GP	W	D	L	GF GA	Pts
Fiorentina	18	12	4	2	34 18	38
Lazio of Rome	18	10	3	5	37 20	35

sports editor Capitalize as a formal title before a name. See **titles** in main section.

sports sponsorship If the sponsor's name is part of the sports event, such as *Pepsi 500* or *Buick Open*, use the name in the title. If there is a previously established name commonly accepted for the event — *Orange Bowl, Sugar Bowl* — use that name even if it currently has a corporate sponsor. *Orange Bowl*, not *FedEx Orange Bowl*. However, mention the sponsor in an editor's note at the end of the copy:

Eds: The event is sponsored by FedEx.

stadium, stadiums Capitalize only when part of a proper name: *Yankee Stadium*.

swimming Scoring is in minutes, if appropriate, seconds and tenths of a second. Extend to hundredths if available.

Most events are measured in metric units.

Identify events as *men's 440-meter relay, women's 100-meter backstroke*, etc., on first reference. Condense to *men's 440 relay, women's 100 backstroke* on second reference.

See the **track and field** entry for the style on relay teams and events where a record is broken

Use a basic summary. Examples, where qualifying heats are required:

Men's 200-meter Backstroke Heats (fastest eight qualify for final Saturday night) heat 1 — 1, John Naber, USC, 2:03.25; 2, Zoltan Verraszio, Hungary, 2:03.50; 3. Etc.

For diving events, adapt the **skating, figure** entry.

T

table tennis See **pingpong**.

tennis The scoring units are points, games, sets and matches.

A player wins a point if his opponent fails to return the ball, hits it into the net or hits it out of bounds. A player also wins a point if his opponent is serving and fails to put the ball into play after two attempts (*double faults*, in tennis terms).

A player must win four points to win a game. In tennis scoring, both players begin at *love*, or zero, and advance to 15, 30, 40 and game. (The numbers *15, 30* and *40* have no point value as such — they are simply tennis terminology for *1 point, 2 points* and *3 points*.) The server's score always is called out first. If a game is tied at 40-all, or *deuce*, play continues until one player has a two-point margin.

A set is won if a player wins six games before his opponent has won five. If a set becomes tied at five games apiece, it goes to the first player to win seven games. If two players who were tied at five games apiece also tie at six games apiece, they normally play a tiebreaker — a game that goes to the first player to win seven points. In some cases, however, the rules call for a player to win by two games.

A match may be either a best-of-three contest that goes to the first player or team to win two sets, or a best-of-five contest that goes to the first player or team to win three sets.

Set scores would be reported this way: *Chris Evert Lloyd defeated Sue Barker 6-0, 3-6, 6-4.* Indicate tiebreakers in parentheses after the set score: *7-6, (11-9)*.

SUMMARIES: Winners always are listed first in agate summaries. An example:

Men's Singles
First Round

Jimmy Connors, Belleville, Ill., def. Manuet Orantes, Spain, 2-6, 6-3, 6-2, 6-1.

Bjorn Borg, Sweden, def. Jim Green, New York (default).

Arthur Ashe, New York, def. James Peters, Chicago, 6-3, 4-3 (retired).

track and field Scoring is in distance or time, depending on the event.

Most events are measured in metric units. For those meets that include feet, make sure the measurement is clearly stated, as in *men's 100-meter dash, women's 880-yard run*, etc.

For time events, spell out *minutes* and *seconds* on first reference, as in *3 minutes, 26.1 seconds*. Subsequent times in stories and all times in agate require a colon and decimal point: *3:34.4*. For a marathon, it would be *2 hours, 11 minutes, 5.01 seconds* on first reference then the form *2:12:4.06* for later listings.

Do not use a colon before times given only in seconds and tenths of a second. Use progressions such as *6.0 seconds, 9.4, 10.1*, etc. Extend times to hundredths, if available: *9.45*.

In running events, the first event should be spelled out, as in *men's 100-meter dash*. Later references can be condensed to phrases such as *the 200, the 400*, etc.

For hurdle and relay events, the progression can be: *100-meter hurdles, 200 hurdles*, etc.

For field events — those that do not involve running — use these forms: *26 1/2 for 26 feet, one-half inch; 25-10 1/2 for 25 feet, 10 1/2 inches*, etc.

In general, use a basic summary. For the style when a record is broken, note the mile event in the example below. For the style in listing relay teams, note 1,000-meter relay.

60-yard dash — 1, Steve Williams, Florida TC, 6.0 2, Hasley Crawford, Philadelphia Pioneer, 6.2 3, Mike McFarland, Chicago TC. 6.2 3. Etc.

100 — 1, Steve Williams, Florida TC 10.1. 2. Etc.

Mile — 1, Filbert Bayi, Tanzania, 3:55.1, meet record, old record 3:59, Jim Beatty, Los Angeles TC. Feb. 27, 1963; 2. Paul Cummings, Beverly Hills TC. 3:56.1; 3, Etc.

Women's 880 — 1, Johanna Forman, Falmouth TC. 2:07.9. 2. Etc.

1,600-meter relay — 1, St. John's, Jon Kennedy, Doug Johnson, Gary Gordon, Ordner Emanuel, 3:21.9. 2. Brown, 3:23.5. 3. Fordham, 3:24.1. 4. Etc.

Team scoring — Chicago TC 32. Philadelphia Pioneer 29, Etc.

Where qualifying heats are required:

Men's 100-meter heats (first two in each heat qualify for Friday's semifinals): Heat 1 — 1, Steve Williams, Florida TC. 10.1. 2. Etc.

V

volley, volleys

volleyball Games are won by the first team to score 15 points, unless it is necessary to continue until one team has a two-point spread.

Use a match summary. Example:

National AAU Men's Volleyball
First Round

New York AC def. Illinois AC 15-7, 12-15, 19-17.

Vesper Boat Club, Philadelphia, def. Harvard 15-7, 15-8.

W

water polo Scoring is by goals. List team scores. Example:

World Water Polo Championship
First Round

United States 7, Canada 1

Britain 5, France 3
Etc.

water skiing Scoring is in points. Use a basic summary. Example:

World Water Skiing Championships
Men

Overall — 1, George Jones, Canada, 1,987 points. 2, Phil Brown, Britain, 1,756. 3, Etc.
Slalom — 1, George Jones, Canada, 73 buoys (two rounds). 2, Etc.

weightlifting Identify events by weight classes. Where both pounds and kilograms are available, use both figures with kilograms in parentheses, as shown in the examples.

Use a basic summary. Example:

Flyweight (114.5 lbs.) — 1, Zygmont Smalcerz, Poland, 744 pounds (337.5 kg). 2, Lajos Szuecs, Hungary, 728 (330 kg). 3, Etc.

World Series Or *the Series* on second reference. A rare exception to the general principles under **capitalization**.

wrestling Identify events by weight division.

Y

yachting Use a basic summary, identifying events by classes.

yard Equal to 3 feet.
The metric equivalent is approximately 0.91 meter.
To convert to meters, multiply by 0.91 (5 yards x 0.91 = 4.55 meters).
See **foot; meter;** and **distances.**

yard lines Use figures to indicate the dividing lines on a footbal field and distance traveled: *4-yard line, 40-yard line, he plunged*

in from the 2, he ran 6 yards, a 7-yard gain.

yearling An animal 1 year old or in its second year. The birthdays of all thoroughbred horses arbitrarily are set at Jan. 1. On that date, any foal born in the preceding year is reckoned 1 year old.

BUSINESS GUIDELINES AND STYLE

BUSINESS GUIDELINES AND STYLE

This section of the Stylebook is designed to help AP reporters cover business and economic news accurately and clearly.

It includes an explanation of how to write one of the most common business stories, the quarterly earnings report issued by all publicly held corporations. And there are alphabetical definitions of business and economic terms and jargon.

A word of caution.

As with any specialty, technical terms and economic argot permeate the business world. Avoid jargon. Define technical terms. Do not assume your reader knows their meaning. Stories about corporations, business executives and economic trends increasingly are spreading beyond the business pages. We must cover these stories so they can be understood by the general public.

Covering Corporate Earnings Reports

Federal law requires all corporations whose stock is publicly traded to report revenues and profits or losses each three months in an income statement. This is what business is all about, whether a corporation made money or lost it, and why. These statements are usually released on the major public relations wire services, PR Newswire or Business Wire, during an earnings "season," a three- or four-week period that begins roughly two weeks after the end of each quarter.

Each of these stories should include certain basic information.

The lead should tell the reader what the company does, if it is not a household word, and should give the increase or decline of profits, either in percentage or absolute terms, along with the reason. Profits are synonymous with income and earnings.

The story should also include the company's revenues, which is sometimes called sales.

Comparisons of profits or losses and revenues/sales should be made with the same period a year earlier. For example, the third quarter of this year compared to the third quarter of last year. This reduces seasonable variations that affect many businesses.

Another important figure to include is earnings-per-share, which is simply the profit divided by the number of shares of stock outstanding. Company statements often express this figure as "primary" or "basic" and "fully diluted." AP uses "fully diluted" as a more meaningful figure. Earnings per share is used by analysts to compare companies.

Finally, include the year-to-date figures for all of the above. The only quarter when this isn't done is the first quarter.

Include comments on the corporation's performance from the chief executive or outside analysts, and any background that puts the performance in perspective.

Note: AP has traditionally focused such stories on "net" earnings, which are the profits left over after all expenses have been paid. But in recent years, Wall Street analysts have been much more concerned with operating earnings, which are net earnings excluding one-time "extraordinary" gains or charges which distract from the performance of the core business.

Operating earnings may exclude the costs of a big reorganization, such as severance payments to laid-off workers or penalties for breaking leases on factories that are closed. They also exclude things like taxes and interest.

Operating earnings per share is a key measure for Wall Street securities analysts.

Here's why, weeks before the earnings reports, analysts issue predictions for this figure, and these predictions are compiled into a "consensus" figure by research companies such as First Call/Thompson Financial.

On the day of the report, investors compare the consensus prediction for operating earnings per share with the actual number and the stock price often moves up or down based on whether the company meets, fails to meet or exceeds expectations.

When AP says in a story "Company X's performance beat Wall Street analysts' predictions," this is the number we're referring to.

Caution: Before you report on a company's earnings expectations, confirm both the consensus prediction for operating earnings per share and actual operating earnings per share with an analyst. That's because the operating earnings per share is not a precise accounting term and can vary from company to company.

If a company has no extraordinary events, operating earnings and net earnings can be identical.

"Operating earnings" is sometimes confused with "earnings from continuing operations."

Continuing operations is a subset of operations. It refers to business units that existed in the past and will exist in the future.

It excludes "discontinued operations" which represent businesses that have been sold or shut down in the past year. Companies often downplay earnings of these operations since they are no longer relevant to future profits.

If extraordinary charges or gains weigh so heavily on the results that using net earnings in the lead would ignore the news, you do not have to do so. In this case, operating earnings will be the more important number and may be used in the lead.

Not good:
XYZ Data Co.'s net profits grew 864 percent in the fourth quarter due largely to the costs of its purchase a year ago of the International Widget Co.

Excluding the acquisition costs, XYZ earnings rose a modest 8 percent.

Better:
XYZ Data Co.'s profits rose a modest 8 percent in the fourth quarter, excluding a big corporate acquisition a year ago, thanks to a boost in sales of its new line of handheld computers.

The company earned $100 million, or 10 cents per share, compared to $92.5 million, or 8 cents a share, a year ago, excluding the cost of the November 1997 purchase of International Widget Co. When the purchase costs are added, XYZ's net income for the fourth quarter of 1997 was just $10.37 million.

The most immediate reaction to a financial report is the movement of the company's stock. This should be included in our earnings stories.

Major factors that influence a stock price:

1. Did the company meet, exceed or miss analyst predictions?

2. Did the shares rise or fall sharply in the days before the report in anticipation of factor No. 1? If so, they could go in the opposite direction after the report comes out. (Remember, many investors buy on the rumor, sell on the news.)

3. Did the company issue a statement predicting future profits? Losses?

INTERNATIONAL BUREAUS

Currency Conversions

International writers should report results in domestic currencies first, then give U.S. dollars for current period results only. There's no need to covert last year's results to dollars.

If the company doesn't give its own conversion to dollars, you'll have to do it. You should use the foreign exchange rate on the last day of the quarter, not today's exchange rate.

Different Accounting Rules

In some countries, companies don't report every quarter. The reports may come out every six months or even annually. Many foreign companies don't report "net earnings" or "earnings per share." Some report "earnings before taxes." If that's all they report, call them to see if they will give you net earnings. If they won't, use whatever number seems closest.

Foreign companies that sell shares in the United States (called American depository receipts) often issue a separate earnings statement using American accounting standards. Use this when you can.

Here's a concise example of an earnings story that doesn't include any one-time factors, followed by one that does.

Wal-Mart's quarterly profits up 23 percent, but fears of slowdown hurt stock

By RACHEL BECK
AP Business Writer

NEW YORK (AP) — Wal-Mart Stores Inc.'s fourth-quarter profits rose 23 percent from a year ago, fueled by strong sales growth at its U.S. superstores and operations abroad.

While the results reported Tuesday by the world's largest retailer were slightly above expectations, its stock fell about 3 percent on concerns that its growth may slow in the coming year.

Wal-Mart earned $1.92 billion, or 43 cents a share, for the quarter ended Jan. 31, compared with $1.56 billion, or 35 cents a share, a year ago. That's above the 42 cents a share that analysts had forecast.

Quarterly sales totaled $51.39 billion, an increase of 26 percent over the $40.79 billion in the same period a year ago. Sales at stores open at least a year, an industry gauge of performance, rose 6.3 percent.

Sales at its Wal-Mart stores rose 12.6 percent in the quarter, boosted by gains at its Supercenters, which combine discount and grocery stores. Sales at its Sam's Club warehouse stores increased 7.4 percent.

International sales gained about 164 percent, fueled by strength in its Mexican, Canadian, British and Puerto Rican divisions.

During the quarter, Wal-Mart named Lee Scott as president and chief executive officer, replacing David Glass who will remain at the company for a year as chairman of the executive committee of the board of directors.

Scott, who was Wal-Mart's chief operating officer and vice chairman, had been tapped about a year ago to succeed Glass.

The company also took some significant steps during the quarter to beef up its Internet operations.

In December, Wal-Mart teamed up with America Online Inc. to create an Internet service provider (ISP) and offer discounted Web access to people who currently may not have an affordable phone hookup in towns near its 2,500 stores. The name and price of the ISP have not yet been released.

In January, the company relaunched www.Walmart.com, which now stocks more than 600,000 items and offers services, such as travel reservations. It also formed a new Internet company with venture-capital firm Accel Partners, which will work to enhance the giant retailer's Web site.

While Wal-Mart continues to outpace most of its rivals with its sharp growth, there were fears that its pace may slow in the coming year.

The Federal Reserve boosted interest rates four times in the last year to fend off inflationary pressures — and may raise rates further. That has raised concerns that consumer spending may slow in the coming months.

"That's the real issue affecting all retailers right now," said Jeffrey Feiner, a retail analyst at Lehman Brothers Inc.

Wal-Mart also said that it will continue aggressively cutting prices, which the company calls "rollbacks." But such promotions will be more difficult in the coming year because of high raw material prices, increased labor costs and strengthening of Asian currencies.

The "rollbacks" have been one of Wal-Mart's key marketing strategies to woo shoppers into its stores.

Wal-Mart's shares fell 68 3/4 cents to $57.18 3/4 in trading at 4:30 p.m. on the New York Stock Exchange. The Bentonville, Ark.-based retailer's stock was down as low as $55 in early trading.

For the year, Wal-Mart earned $5.58 billion, or $1.25 a share, compared to $4.43 billion, or 99 cents a share, in 1998. Sales for the year were $165 billion, an increase of 20 percent over the previous year.

Here's an earnings story that includes significant one-time events.

Lilly earnings soar despite tumbling Prozac sales

INDIANAPOLIS (AP) — Eli Lilly's fourth-quarter profit rose 20 percent as declining sales of the antidepressant Prozac were offset by stronger demand for the company's osteoporosis and antipsychotic drugs.

Excluding one time gains and losses, the Indianapolis-based drug firm's operating income rose to $671.7 million, or 61 cents per share, up from $567.3 million or 51 cents per share a year ago.

Results matched Wall Street estimates, according to First Call/Thomson Financial.

Including one-time events, such as wholesalers who stocked up on drugs due to Y2K concerns, Lilly earned $786.3 million or 71 cents per share.

Sales rose 7 percent to $2.82 billion from $2.64 billion. Prozac sales dropped 13 percent to $645.2 million.

Prozac has been the nation's top selling antidepressant for the past decade. But sales have fallen recently due to new competitors.

Helping offset the decline in Prozac was the antipsychotic drug Zyprexa, which saw a sales increase of 36 percent to $587.7 million.

Sales of Evista, an osteoporosis drug, jumped 39 percent to $112.1 million.

For all of 1999, excluding one-time events, Lilly's net income rose 16 percent to $2.52 billion, or $2.28 per share, up from $2.1 billion, or $1.87 per share, in 1998. Sales rose 8 percent to $10.0 billion, up from $9.24 billion.

Shares of Lilly rose $1.50 to $64.25 in trading on the New York Stock Exchange.

BUSINESS GUIDELINES AND STYLE

A

accounts payable Current liabilities or debts of a business which must be paid in the near future (within one year).

accounts receivable Amounts due to a company for merchandise or services sold on credit. These are short-term assets.

acquisitions The process of buying or acquiring some asset. The term can refer to the purchase of a block of stock or, more often, to the acquisition of an entire company.

agricultural parity The ratio between the price a farmer buys and sells, calculated from the same base period when farm incomes were considered equivalent to income standards of the economy.

antitrust Any law or policy designed to encourage competition by curtailing monopolistic power and unfair business practices.

appreciation Increase in value of property, as opposed to *depreciation*.

arbitrage Buying currency, commercial bills or securities in one market and selling them at the same time in another to make a profit on the price discrepancy.

asset Current cash and other items readily converted into cash, usually within one year.

asset, fixed Plant, land, equipment, long-term investments that cannot be readily liquefied without disturbing the operation of the business.

B

balance sheet A listing of assets, liabilities and net worth showing the financial position of a company at the specific time. A bank balance sheet is generally referred to as a statement of condition.

balloon mortgage A mortgage whose amortization schedule will not extinguish the debt by the end of the mortgage term, leaving a large payment (called balloon payment) of the remaining principal balance to be paid at that time.

bankruptcy An individual or organization, acting voluntarily or by court order, liquidates its assets and distributes the proceeds to creditors.

Various filings under U.S. Bankruptcy Code:

Chapter 7 — Sometimes referred to as straight bankruptcy, this filing usually leads to liquidation of a company. A company in Chapter 7 proceedings is able to continue to operate under the direction of a court trustee until the matter is settled. If the company can resolve its problems and settle with creditors in the interim, it may not have to be liquidated.

Chapter 11 — The most common form of bankruptcy, this action frees a company from the threat of creditors' lawsuits while it reorganizes its finances. The debtor's reorganization plan must be accepted by a majority of its creditors. Unless the court rules otherwise, the debtor remains in control of the business and its assets.

Chapter 12 — This is an extension of Chapter 11, designed to help debt-burdened family farms. It allows family farmers to operate under bankruptcy court protection while paying off creditors.

Chapter 13 — Called the "wage earner" bankruptcy, this is available to individuals who promise to repay as many creditors as possible from available income.

basis point The movement of interest rates or yields expressed in hundredths of a percent.

bear market A period of generally declining stock prices.

bearer bond A bond for which the owner's name is not registered on the books of the issuing company. Interest and principal is thus payable to the bond holder.

bearer stock Stock certificates that are not registered in any name. They are negotiable without endorsement and transferable by delivery.

Big Board Acceptable on second reference for the *New York Stock Exchange.*

blue chip stock Stock company known for its long-established record of making money and paying dividends.

bond ratings Grades assigned by credit-rating agencies to corporate and municipal debt securities, based on the borrower's expected ability to repay. The higher the grade, the lower the interest rate a borrower must pay.

The two major Wall Street credit rating firms are Moody's Investors Service Inc. and Standard & Poor's bond ratings. Both issue a variety of grades. Standard & Poor's bond ratings, for example, include 10 basic grades: in order, AAA, AA, A and BBB, given to borrowers with the strongest ability to repay; BB, B, CCC, CC and C, for more speculative securities, and D, for securities that are in payment default.

bonds See **loan terminology**.

book value The difference between a company's assets and liabilities.

The *book value per share* of common stock is the *book value* divided by the number of common shares outstanding.

brand names When they are used, capitalize them.

Brand names normally should be used only if they are essential to a story.

Sometimes, however, the use of a brand name may not be essential but is acceptable because it lends an air of reality to a story: *He fished a Camel from his shirt pocket* may be preferable to the less specific cigarette.

Brand name is a non-legal term for *service mark* or *trademark*. See entries under those words in the main section.

bull market A period of generally increasing market prices.

bullion Unminted precious metals of standards suitable for coining.

C

capital When used in a financial sense, *capital* describes money, equipment or property used in a business by a person or corporation.

capital gain, capital loss The difference between what a *capital* asset cost and the price it brought when sold.

cents Spell out the word *cents* and lowercase, using numerals for amounts less than a dollar: *5 cents, 12 cents*. Use the $ sign and decimal system for larger amounts: *$1.01, $2.50*.

central bank A bank having responsibility for controlling a country's monetary policy.

charge off A loan that no longer is expected to be repaid and is written off as a bad debt.

Chicago Board of Trade The largest commodity trading market in the United States.

Chicago Board Options Exchange (CBOE) An exchange set up by the Chicago Board of Trade.

closely held corporation A corporation in which stock shares and voting control are concentrated in the hands of a small number of investors, but for which some shares are available and traded on the market.

Co. See **company**.

collateral Stock or other property that a borrower is obliged to turn over to a lender if unable to repay a loan.

See **loan terminology**.

commercial paper One of the various types of short-term negotiable instruments whereby industrial or finance companies obtain cash after agreeing to pay a specific amount of money on the date due.

commodity The products of mining or agriculture before they have undergone extensive processing.

commodities futures contract A contract to purchase or sell a specific amount of a given commodity at a specified future date.

common stock, preferred stock An ownership interest in a corporation.

If other classes of stock are outstanding, the holders of common stock are the last to receive dividends and the last to receive payments if a corporation is dissolved. The company may raise or lower common stock dividends as its earnings rise or fall.

When preferred stock is outstanding and company earnings are sufficient, a fixed dividend is paid. If a company is liquidated, holders of preferred stock receive payments up to a set amount before any money is distributed to holders of common stock.

company, companies Use *Co.* or *Cos.* when a business uses either word at the end of its proper name: *Ford Motor Co., American Broadcasting Cos.* But: *Aluminum Company of America.*

If *company* or *companies* appears alone in second reference, spell the word out.

The forms for possessives: *Ford Motor Co.'s profits, American Broadcasting Cos.' profits.*

See main section for specific company names.

company names Consult the company or Standard & Poor's Register of Corporations if in doubt about a formal name. Do not, however, use a comma before *Inc.* or *Ltd.*

Do not use all capital letter names unless the letters are individually pronounced: *CRX, USX.* Others should be uppercase and lowercase.

conglomerate A corporation that has diversified its operations, usually by acquiring enterprises in widely varied industries.

consumer credit Loans extended to individuals or small businesses usually on an unsecured basis, and providing for monthly repayment. Also referred to as installment credit or personal loans.

convertible bond See **loan terminology**.

Corp. See **corporation**.

corporate names See **company names**.

corporation An entity that is treated as a person in the eyes of the law. It is able to own property, incur debts, sue and be sued.

Abbreviate *corporation* as *Corp.* when a company or government agency uses the word at the end of its name: *Gulf Oil Corp., the Federal Deposit Insurance Corp.*

Spell out *corporation* when it occurs elsewhere in a name: *the Corporation for Public Broadcasting.*

Spell out and lowercase *corporation* whenever it stands alone.

The form for possessives: *Gulf Oil Corp.'s profits.*

cost-plus

coupon See **loan terminology** for its meaning in a financial sense.

cross rate The rate of exchange between two currencies calculated by referring to the rates between each and a third currency.

D

debt service The outlay necessary to meet all interest and principal payments during a given period.

default The failure to meet a financial obligation, the failure to make payment either of principal or interest when due or a breach or nonperformance of the terms of a note or mortgage.

deflation A decrease in the general price level, which results from a decrease in total spending relative to the supply of available goods on the market. Deflation's immediate effect is to increase purchasing power.

depreciation The reduction in the value of capital goods due to wear and tear or obsolescence.

Estimated depreciation may be deducted from income each year as one of the costs of doing business.

discount Interest withheld when a note, draft or bill is purchased.

discount rate The rate of interest charged by the Federal Reserve on loans it makes to member banks. This rate has an influence on the rates banks then charge their customers.

dividend In a financial sense, the word describes the payment per share that a corporation distributes to its stockholders as their return on the money they have invested in its stock.

See **profit terminology**.

dollars Always lowercase. Use figures and the $ sign in all except casual references or amounts without a figure: *The book cost $4. Dad, please give me a dollar. Dollars are flowing overseas.*

For specified amounts, the word takes a singular verb: *He said $500,000 is what they want.*

For amounts of more than $1 million, use up to two decimal places. Do not link the numerals and the word by a hyphen: *He is worth $4.35 million. He is worth exactly $4,351,242. He proposed a $300 billion budget.*

The form for amounts less than $1 million: *$4, $25, $500, $1,000, $650,000.*

See **cents**.

Dow Jones & Co. The company publishes the Wall Street Journal and Barron's National Business and Financial Weekly. It also operates the Dow Jones News Service.

For stock market watchers, it provides the Dow Jones industrial average, the Dow Jones transportation average, the Dow Jones utility average, and the Dow Jones composite average.

Headquarters is in New York.

downside risk The probability that the price of an investment will fall.

dumping The selling of a product in a foreign market at a price lower than the domestic price. It is usually done by a monopoly when it has such a large output that selling entirely in the domestic market would substantially reduce the price.

durable goods Long-lasting goods such as appliances that are bought by consumers.

E

employee Not *employe*.

equity When used in a financial sense, *equity* means the value of property beyond the amount that is owed on it.

A *stockholder's equity* in a corporation is the value of the shares he holds.

A *homeowner's equity* is the difference between the value of the house and the amount of the unpaid mortgage.

Eurodollar A U.S. dollar on deposit in a European bank, including foreign branches of U.S. banks.

extraordinary loss, extraordinary income See **profit terminology**.

F

factor A financial organization whose primary business is purchasing the accounts receivable of other firms, at a discount, and taking the risk and responsibilities of making collection.

Fannie Mae A publicly held company traded on the New York Stock Exchange that helps provide money for home mortgages, primarily conventional mortgages, by buying residential mortgages for its investment portfolio and packaging pools of mortgages from lenders.

The nickname *Fannie Mae* is acceptable, but somewhere in the story the company should be identified as the *Federal National Mortgage Association*.

Federal Farm Credit System The federally chartered cooperative banking system that provides most of the nation's agricultural loans. The system is cooperatively owned by its farm borrowers and is made up of the regional banks that issue operating and mortgage loans through local land bank associations and production credit associations.

federal funds, federal funds rate Money in excess of what the Federal Reserve says a bank must have on hand to back up deposits. The excess can be lent overnight to banks that need more cash on hand to meet their reserve requirements. The interest rate of these loans is the *federal funds rate*.

Federal Home Mortgage Corp. See **Freddie Mac** entry.

Federal National Mortgage Association See **Fannie Mae** entry.

firm A business partnership is correctly referred to as a *firm*: *He joined a law firm.*

Do not use *firm* in references to an incorporated business entity. Use *the company* or *the corporation* instead.

fiscal, monetary *Fiscal* applies to budgetary matters.

Monetary applies to money supply.

fiscal year The 12-month period that a corporation or governmental body uses for bookkeeping purposes.

The federal government's fiscal year starts three months ahead of the calendar year — fiscal 1984, for example, ran from Oct. 1, 1983, to Sept. 30, 1984.

float Money that has been committed but not yet credited to an account, like a check that has been written but has not yet cleared.

f.o.b. Acceptable on first reference for **free on board**.

force majeure A condition permitting a company to depart from the strict terms of a contract because of an event or effect that can't be reasonably controlled.

401(k) (no space)

Freddie Mac A government-chartered organization formed to help provide money for home mortgages by buying mortgages from lenders such as banks and repackaging them as investment securities.

Freddie Mac, a publicly held company traded on the New York Stock Exchange, packages conventional mortgages as well as FHA mortgages.

The nickname *Freddie Mac* is acceptable, but somewhere in the story, the company should be identified as the *Federal Home Mortgage Corp.*

freely floating Describes an exchange rate that is allowed to fluctuate in response to supply and demand in the foreign markets.

full faith and credit bond See **loan terminology**.

futures *Futures* contracts are agreements to deliver a quantity of goods, generally commodities, at a specified price at a certain time in the future. *Options*, which also are widely traded on the nation's commodities exchanges, give buyers the right but not the obligation to buy or sell something at a certain price within a specified period.

The purpose of the futures exchanges is to transfer the risk of price fluctuations from people who don't want the risk, such as farmers or metals processors, to speculators who are willing to take a gamble on making big profits.

Major U.S. commodities markets are the Chicago Board of Trade, Chicago Mercantile Exchange, New York Mercantile Exchange, the Commodity Exchange in New York, the New York Cotton Exchange, and the Coffee, Sugar and Cocoa Exchange.

G

general obligation bond See **loan terminology**.

H

hedging A method of selling for future delivery whereby a dealer protects himself from falling prices between the time he buys a product and the time he resells or processes it. A miller, for example, who buys wheat to convert to flour, will sell a similar quantity of wheat he doesn't own at near the price at which he bought his own. He will agree to deliver it at the same time his flour is ready for market. If at that time the price of wheat and therefore flour has fallen, he will lose on the flour but can buy the wheat at a low price and deliver it at a profit. If prices have risen, he will make an extra profit on his flour which he will have to sacrifice to buy the wheat for delivery. But either way he has protected his profit.

holding company A company whose principal assets are the securities it owns in companies that actually provide goods or services.

The usual reason for forming a holding company is to enable one corporation and its directors to control several companies by holding a majority of their stock.

I

Inc. See **incorporated**.

income See **profit terminology**.

incorporated Abbreviate and capitalize as *Inc.* when used as a part of a corporate name. It usually is not needed, but when it is used, do not set off with commas: *J.C. Penney Co. Inc. announced* ...

See **company names**.

Index of Leading Economic Indicators A composite of 10 economic measurements developed to help forecast shifts in the direction of the U.S. economy.

It is compiled by the Conference Board, a private business-sponsored research group, which

took it over from the Commerce Department in 1995.

inflation A sustained increase in prices. The result is a decrease in the purchasing power of money.

There are two basic types of inflation:

—*Cost-push inflation* occurs when rising costs are the chief reason for the increased prices.

—*Demand-pull inflation* occurs when the amount of money available exceeds the amount of goods and services available for sale.

infrastructure An economy's capital in the form of roads, railways, water supplies, educational facilities, health services, etc., without which investment in factories can't be fully productive.

International Monetary Fund *IMF* is acceptable on second reference. Headquarters is in Washington.

A supply of money supported by subscriptions of member nations, for the purpose of stabilizing international exchange and promoting orderly and balanced trade. Member nations may obtain foreign currency needed, making it possible to correct temporary maladjustments in their balance of payments without currency depreciation.

L

leverage The use of borrowed assets by a business to enhance the return of the owner's equity. The expectation is that the interest rate charged will be lower than the earnings made on the money.

leveraged buyout A corporate acquisition in which the bulk of the purchase price is paid with borrowed money. The debt then is repaid with the acquired company's cash flow, with money raised by the sale of its assets or by the later sale of the entire company.

liabilities When used in a financial sense, the word means all the claims against a corporation.

They include accounts payable, wages and salaries due but not paid, dividends declared payable, taxes payable, and fixed or long-term obligations such as bonds, debentures and bank loans.

See **assets**.

liquidation When used in a financial sense, the word means the process of converting stock or other assets into cash.

When a company is liquidated, the cash obtained is first used to pay debts and obligations to holders of bonds and preferred stock. Whatever cash remains is distributed on a per-share basis to the holders of common stock.

liquidity The ease with which assets can be converted to cash without loss in value.

loan terminology Note the meanings of these terms in describing loans by governments and corporations:

bond A certificate issued by a corporation or government stating the amount of a loan, the interest to be paid, the time for repayment and the collateral pledged if payment cannot be made. Repayment generally is not due for a long period, usually seven years or more.

collateral Stock or other property that a borrower is obligated to turn over to a lender if unable to repay a loan.

commercial paper A document describing the details of a short-term loan between corporations.

convertible bond A bond carrying the stipulation that it may be exchanged for a specific amount of stock in the company that issued it.

coupon A slip of paper attached to a bond that the bondholder clips at specified times and returns to the issuer for payment of the interest due.

debenture A certificate stating the amount of a loan, the interest to be paid and the time for repayment, but not providing collateral. It is backed only by the corporation's reputation and promise to pay.

default A person, corporation or government is in default if it fails to meet the terms for repayment.

full faith and credit bond An alternate term for general obligation bond, often used to contrast such a bond with a moral obligation bond.

general obligation bond A bond that has had the formal approval of either the voters or their legislature. The government's promise to repay the principal and pay the interest is constitutionally guaranteed on the strength of its ability to tax the population.

maturity The date on which a bond, debenture or note must be repaid.

moral obligation bond A government bond that has not had the formal approval of either the voters or their legislature. It is backed only by the government's "moral obligation" to repay the principal and interest on time.

municipal bond A general obligation bond issued by a state, country, city, town, village, possession or territory, or a bond issued by an agency or authority set up by one of these governmental units. In general, interest paid on municipal bonds is exempt from federal income taxes. It also usually is exempt from state and local taxes if held by someone living within the state of issue.

note A certificate issued by a corporation or government stating the amount of a loan, the interest to be paid and the collateral pledged in the event payment cannot be made. The date for repayment is generally more than a year after issue but not more than seven or eight years later. The shorter interval for repayment is the principal difference between a note and a bond.

revenue bond A bond backed only by the revenue of the airport, turnpike or other facility that was built with the money it raised.

Treasury borrowing A *Treasury bill* is a certificate representing a loan to the federal government that matures in three, six or 12 months. A *Treasury note* may mature in one to 10 years or

more. A *Treasury bond* matures in seven years or more.

M

margin The practice of purchasing securities in part with borrowed money, using the purchased securities as collateral in anticipation of an advance in the market price. If the advance occurs, the purchaser may be able to repay the loan and make a profit. If the price declines, the stock may have to be sold to settle the loan. The margin is the difference between the amount of the loan and the value of the securities used as collateral.

monetary See the **fiscal, monetary** entry.

moral obligation bond See **loan terminology**.

municipal bond See **loan terminology**.

N

Nasdaq The name of the computerized trading network that used to be known as the National Association of Securities Dealers Automated Quotations system.

National Labor Relations Board *NLRB* is acceptable on second reference.

net income, net profit See **profit terminology**.

New York Stock Exchange

NYSE is acceptable on second reference as an adjective. Use *the stock exchange* or *the exchange* for other references.

note For use in a financial sense, see **loan terminology**.

O

option The word means an agreement to buy or sell something, such as shares of stock, within a stipulated time and for a certain price.

A *put option* gives the holder the right to sell blocks of 100 shares of stock within a specified time at an agreed-upon price.

A *call option* gives the holder the right to buy blocks of 100 shares of stock within a specified time at an agreed-upon price.

over the counter A term for the method of trading when securities are not listed on a recognized securities exchange.

P

preferred stock See the **common stock, preferred stock** entry.

price-earnings ratio The price of a share of stock divided by earnings per share for a 12-month period. Ratios in AP stock tables reflect earnings for the most recent 12 months.

For example, a stock selling for $60 per share and earning $6 per share would be selling at a price-earnings ratio of 10-to-1.

See **profit terminology**.

PricewaterhouseCoopers

prime rate A benchmark rate used by banks to set interest charges on a variety of corporate and consumer loans, including some adjustable home mortgages, revolving credit cards and business loans. Banks set the rate based on their borrowing costs, as reflected by the interest on short-term Treasury securities in the bond market.

profit-taking (n. and adj.) Avoid this term. It means selling a security after a recent rapid rise in price. It is inaccurate if the seller bought the security at a higher price, watched it fall, then sold it after a recent rise but for less than he bought it. In that case, he would be cutting his losses, not taking his profit.

profit terminology Note the meanings of the following terms in reporting a company's financial status. Always be careful to specify whether the figures given apply to quarterly or annual results.

The terms, listed in the order in which they might occur in analyzing a company's financial condition:

revenue The amount of money a company took in, including interest earned and receipts from sales, services provided, rents and royalties.

The figure also may include excise taxes and sales taxes collected for the government. If it does, the fact should be noted in any report on revenue.

sales The money a company received for the goods and services it sold.

In some cases the figure includes receipts from rents and royalties. In others, particularly when rentals and royalties make up a large portion of a company's income, figures for these activities are listed separately.

gross profit The difference between the sales price of an item or service and the expenses directly attributed to it, such as the cost of raw materials, labor and overhead linked to the production effort.

income before taxes Gross profits minus companywide expenses not directly attributed to specific products or services. These expenses typically include interest costs, advertising and sales costs, and general administrative overhead.

net income, profit, earnings The amount left after taxes have been paid.

A portion may be committed to pay preferred dividends. Some of what remains may be paid in dividends to holders of common stocks. The rest may be invested to obtain interest revenue or spent to acquire new buildings or equipment to increase the company's ability to make further profits.

To avoid confusion, do not use the word *income* alone — always specify whether the figure is *income before taxes* or *net income.*

The terms *profit* and *earnings* commonly are interpreted as meaning the amount left after taxes. The terms *net profit* and *net earnings* are acceptable synonyms.

earnings per share (or **loss per share**, for companies posting a net loss) The figure obtained by dividing the number of outstanding shares of common stock into the amount left after dividends have been paid on any preferred stock.

dividend The amount paid per share per year to holders of common stock. Payments generally are made in quarterly installments.

The dividend usually is a portion of the earnings per share. However, if a company shows no profit during a given period, it may be able to use earnings retained from profitable periods to pay its dividend on schedule.

return on investment A percentage figure obtained by dividing the company's assets into its net income.

extraordinary loss, extraordinary income An expense or source of income that does not occur on a regular basis, such as a loss due to a major fire or the revenue from the sale of a subsidiary. Extraordinary items should be identified in any report on the company's financial status to avoid creating the false impression that its overall profit trend has suddenly plunged or soared.

protective tariff A duty high enough to assure domestic producers against any effective competition from foreign producers.

R

receivership A legal action in which a court appoints a *receiver* to manage a business while the court tries to resolve problems that could ruin the business, such as insolvency. *Receivership* is often used in federal bankruptcy court proceedings. But it also can be used for nonfinancial troubles such as an ownership dispute.

In bankruptcy proceedings, the court appoints a trustee called a *receiver* who attempts to settle the financial difficulties of the company while under protection from creditors.

recession A falling-off of economic activity that may be a temporary phenomenon or could continue into a depression.

retail sales The sales of retail stores, including merchandise sold and receipts for repairs and similar services.

A business is considered a *retail store* if it is engaged primarily in selling merchandise for personal, household or farm consumption.

revenue See **profit terminology**.

revenue bond See **loan terminology**.

revolving credit Describes an account on which the payment is any amount less than the total balance, and the remaining balance carried forward is subject to finance charges.

rollover The selling of new securities to pay off old ones coming due or the refinancing of an existing loan.

S

savings and loan associations They are not banks. Use *the association* on second reference.

service mark A brand, symbol, word, etc. used by a supplier of services and protected by law to prevent a competitor from using it: *Realtor*, for a member of the National Association of Realtors, for example.

When a service mark is used, capitalize it.

The preferred form, however, is to use a generic term unless the service mark is essential to the story.

See **brand names** and **trademark**.

short An investment term used to describe the position held by individuals who sell stock that they do not yet own by borrowing from their broker in order to deliver to the purchaser.

A person selling short is betting that the price of the stock will fall.

short covering The purchase of a security to repay shares of a security borrowed from a broker.

short sale A sale of securities that are not owned by the sellers at the time of sale but which they intend to purchase or borrow in time to make delivery.

small-business man

spinoff (n.) A distribution that occurs when the company forms a separate company out of a division, a subsidiary or other holdings. The shares of the new company are distributed proportionately to the parent company holders.

spot market A market for buying or selling commodities or foreign exchange for immediate delivery and for cash payment.

spot price The price of a commodity available for immediate sale and delivery. The term is also used to refer to foreign exchange transactions.

Standard & Poor's Register of Corporations The source for determining the formal name of a business. See **company names**.

The register is published by Standard & Poor's Corp. of New York.

stockbroker

stock index futures Futures contracts valued on the basis of indexes that track the prices of a specific group of stocks. The most widely traded is the future based on the Standard & Poor's 500-stock index. Speculators also trade options on index futures.

stock market prices Use fractions rather than decimals, spelling out the fraction if it is not linked with a figure: *The stock went up three-quarters of a point. The stock went up 1 1/2 points.*

T

trademark A trademark is a brand, symbol, word, etc., used by a manufacturer or dealer and protected by law to prevent a competitor from using it: *Astro-Turf*, for a type of artificial grass, for example.

In general, use a generic equivalent unless the trademark name is essential to the story.

When a trademark is used, capitalize it.

Many trademarks are listed separately in this book, together with generic equivalents.

The International Trademark Association, located in New York, is a helpful source of information about trademarks.

See **brand names** and **service marks**.

Treasury bills, Treasury bonds, Treasury notes See **loan terminology**.

U

union names The formal names of unions may be condensed to conventionally accepted short forms that capitalize characteristic words from the full name followed by *union* in lower-case.

Follow union practice in the use of the word *worker* in shortened forms. Among major unions, all except the *United Steelworkers* use two words: *United Auto Workers, United Mine Workers*, etc.

See entry in main section for more detail and references.

W

Wall Street When the reference is to the entire complex of financial institutions in the area rather than the actual street itself, *the Street* is an acceptable short form.

See **capitalization**.

wholesale price index A measurement of the changes in the average price that businesses pay for a selected group of industrial commodities, farm products, processed foods and feed for animals.

Capitalize when referring to the U.S. index, issued monthly by the Bureau of Labor Statistics, an agency of the Labor Department.

Y

yield In a financial sense, the annual rate of return on an investment, as paid in dividends or interest. It is expressed as a percentage obtained by dividing the market price for a stock or bond into the dividend or interest paid in the preceding 12 months.

See **profit terminology**.

A GUIDE TO PUNCTUATION

A GUIDE TO PUNCTUATION

There is no alternative to correct punctuation. Incorrect punctuation can change the meaning of a sentence, the results of which could be far-reaching.

Even if the meaning is not changed, bad punctuation, however inconsequential, can cause the reader to lose track of what is being said and give up reading a sentence.

The basic guideline is to use common sense.

—Punctuation is to make clear the thought being expressed.

—If punctuation does not help make clear what is being said, it should not be there.

"The Elements of Style" by E.B. White and William Strunk Jr. is a bible of writers. It states:

"Clarity, clarity, clarity. When you become hopelessly mired in a sentence, it is best to start fresh; do not try to fight your way through against terrible odds of syntax. Usually what is wrong is that the construction has become too involved at some point; the sentence needs to be broken apart and replaced by two or more shorter sentences."

This applies to punctuation. If a sentence becomes cluttered with commas, semicolons and dashes, start over.

These two paragraphs are full of commas and clauses; all of it equals too much for the reader to grasp:

The Commonwealth Games Federation, in an apparent effort to persuade other nations to ignore the spiraling boycott, ruled Sunday that Budd, a runner who has had a storied past on and off the track, and Cowley, a swimmer who competes for the University of Texas, were ineligible under the Commonwealth Constitution to compete for England in the 10-day event to be held in Edinburgh, Scotland, beginning July 24.

The decision on Budd, who has been the object of a number of demonstrations in the past, and Cowley followed an earlier announcement Sunday by Tanzania that it was joining Nigeria, Kenya, Ghana and Uganda in boycotting the games because of Britain's refusal to support economic sanctions against South Africa's white-led government.

PUNCTUATION MARKS AND HOW TO USE THEM

ampersand (&) Use the ampersand when it is part of a company's formal name: *Baltimore & Ohio Railroad, Newport News Shipbuilding & Dry Dock Co.*

The *ampersand* should not otherwise be used in place of *and*.

apostrophe (') Follow these guidelines:

POSSESSIVES: See the **possessives** entry in main section.

PLURAL NOUNS NOT ENDING IN S: Add 's: *the alumni's contributions, women's rights.*

PLURAL NOUNS ENDING IN S: Add only an apostrophe: *the churches' needs, the girls' toys, the horses' food, the ships' wake, states' rights, the VIPs' entrance.*

NOUNS PLURAL IN FORM, SINGULAR IN MEANING: Add only an apostrophe: *mathematics' rules, measles' effects.* (But see INANIMATE OBJECTS below.)

Apply the same principle when a plural word occurs in the formal name of a singular entity: *General Motors' profits, the United States' wealth.*

NOUNS THE SAME IN SINGULAR AND PLURAL: Treat them the same as plurals, even if the meaning is singular: *one corps' location, the two deer's tracks, the lone moose's antlers.*

SINGULAR NOUNS NOT ENDING IN S: Add 's: *the church's needs, the girl's toys, the horse's food, the ship's route, the VIP's seat.*

Some style guides say that singular nouns ending in s sounds such as *ce, x,* and *z* may take either the apostrophe alone or 's. See SPECIAL EXPRESSIONS, but otherwise, for consistency and ease in remembering a rule, always use 's if the word does not end in the letter s: *Butz's policies, the fox's den, the justice's verdict, Marx's theories, the prince's life, Xerox's profits.*

SINGULAR COMMON NOUNS ENDING IN S: Add 's unless the next word begins with s: *the hostess's invitation, the hostess' seat; the witness's answer, the witness' story.*

SINGULAR PROPER NAMES ENDING IN S: Use only an apostrophe: *Achilles' heel, Agnes' book, Ceres' rites, Descartes' theories, Dickens' novels, Euripides' dramas, Hercules' labors, Jesus' life, Jules' seat, Kansas' schools, Moses' law, Socrates' life, Tennessee Williams' plays, Xerxes' armies.* (An exception is *St. James's Palace.*)

SPECIAL EXPRESSIONS: The following exceptions to the general rule for words not ending in s apply to words that end in an s sound and are followed by a word that begins with s: *for appearance' sake, for conscience' sake, for goodness' sake.* Use 's otherwise: *the appearance's cost, my conscience's voice.*

PRONOUNS: Personal interrogative and relative pronouns have separate forms for the possessive. None involves an apostrophe: *mine, ours, your, yours, his, hers, its, theirs, whose.*

Caution: If you are using an apostrophe with a pronoun, always double-check to be sure that the meaning calls for a contraction: *you're, it's, there's, who's.*

Follow the rules listed above in forming the possessives of other pronouns: *another's idea, others' plans, someone's guess.*

COMPOUND WORDS: Applying the rules above, add an apostrophe or *'s* to the word closest to the object possessed: *the major general's decision, the major generals' decisions, the attorney general's request, the attorneys general's request.* See the **plurals** entry for guidelines on forming the plurals of these words.

Also: *anyone else's attitude, John Adams Jr.'s father, Benjamin Franklin of Pennsylvania's motion.* Whenever practical, however, recast the phrase to avoid ambiguity: *the motion by Benjamin Franklin of Pennsylvania.*

JOINT POSSESSION, INDIVIDUAL POSSESSION: Use a possessive form after only the last word if ownership is joint: *Fred and Sylvia's apartment, Fred and Sylvia's stocks.*

Use a possessive form after both words if the objects are individually owned: *Fred's and Sylvia's books.*

DESCRIPTIVE PHRASES: Do not add an apostrophe to a word ending in *s* when it is used primarily in a descriptive sense: *citizens band radio, a Cincinnati Reds infielder, a teachers college, a Teamsters request, a writers guide.*

Memory Aid: The apostrophe usually is not used if *for* or *by* rather than *of* would be appropriate in the longer form: *a radio band for citizens, a college for teachers, a guide for writers, a request by the Teamsters.*

An *'s* is required however, when a term involves a plural word that does not end in *s*: *a children's hospital, a people's republic, the Young Men's Christian Association.*

DESCRIPTIVE NAMES: Some governmental, corporate and institutional organizations with a descriptive word in their names use an apostrophe; some do not. Follow the user's practice: *Actors' Equity, Diners Club, the Ladies' Home Journal, the National Governors' Association.* See separate entries for these and similar names frequently in the news.

QUASI POSSESSIVES: Follow the rules above in composing the possessive form of words that occur in such phrases as *a day's pay, two weeks' vacation, three days' work, your money's worth.*

Frequently, however, a hyphenated form is clearer: *a two-week vacation, a three-day job.*

DOUBLE POSSESSIVE: Two conditions must apply for a double possessive — a phrase such as *a friend of John's* — to occur: 1. The word after *of* must refer to an animate object, and 2. The word before *of* must involve only a portion of the animate object's possessions.

Otherwise, do not use the possessive form of the word after *of*: *The friends of John Adams mourned his death.* (All the friends were involved.) *He is a friend of the college.* (Not *college's,* because *college* is inanimate).

Memory Aid: This construction occurs most often, and quite naturally, with the possessive forms of personal pronouns: *He is a friend of mine.*

INANIMATE OBJECTS: There is no blanket rule against creating a possessive form for an inanimate object, particularly if the object is treated in a personified sense. See some of the earlier examples, and note these: *death's call, the wind's murmur.*

In general, however, avoid excessive personalization of inanimate objects, and give preference to an *of* construction when it fits the makeup of the sentence. For example, the earlier references to *mathematics' rules* and *measles' effects* would better be phrased: *the rules of mathematics, the effects of measles.*

OMITTED LETTERS: *I've, it's, don't, rock 'n' roll, 'tis the season to be jolly. He is a ne'er-do-well.* See **contractions** in main section.

OMITTED FIGURES: *The class of '62. The Spirit of '76. The '20s.*

PLURALS OF A SINGLE LETTER: *Mind your p's and q's. He learned the three R's and brought home a report card with four A's and two B's. The Oakland A's won the pennant.*

DO NOT USE: For plurals of numerals or multiple-letter combinations. See **plurals**.

brackets [ ] They cannot be transmitted over news wires. Use parentheses or recast the material.

See **parentheses**.

colon (:) The most frequent use of a colon is at the end of a sentence to introduce lists, tabulations, texts, etc.

Capitalize the first word after a colon only if it is a proper noun or the start of a complete sentence: *He promised this: The company will make good all the losses.* But: *There were three considerations: expense, time and feasibility.*

EMPHASIS: The colon often can be effective in giving emphasis: *He had only one hobby: eating.*

LISTINGS: Use the colon in such listings as time elapsed (*1:31:07.2*), time of day (*8:31 p.m.*), biblical and legal citations (*2 Kings 2:14; Missouri Code 3:245-260*).

DIALOGUE: Use a colon for dialogue. In coverage of a trial, for example:
Bailey: What were you doing the night of the 19th?
Mason: I refuse to answer that.

Q AND A: The colon is used for question-and-answer interviews:
Q: Did you strike him?
A: Indeed I did.

INTRODUCING QUOTATIONS: Use a comma to introduce a direct quotation of one sentence that remains within a paragraph. Use a colon to introduce long quotations within a paragraph and to end all paragraphs that introduce a paragraph of quoted material.

PLACEMENT WITH QUOTATION MARKS: Colons go outside quotation marks unless they are part of the quotation itself.

MISCELLANEOUS: Do not combine a dash and a colon.

comma (,) The following guidelines treat some of the most frequent questions about the use of commas. Additional guidelines on specialized uses are provided in separate entries such as **dates** and **scores**.

For detailed guidance, consult the punctuation section in the back of Webster's New World Dictionary.

IN A SERIES: Use commas to separate elements in a series, but do not put a comma before the conjunction in a simple series: *The flag is red, white and blue. He would nominate Tom, Dick or Harry.*

Put a comma before the concluding conjunction in a series, however, if an integral element of the series requires a conjunction: *I had orange juice, toast, and ham and eggs for breakfast.*

Use a comma also before the concluding conjunction in a complex series of phrases: *The main points to consider are whether the athletes are skillful enough to compete, whether they have the stamina to endure the training, and whether they have the proper mental attitude.*

See the **dash** and **semicolon** entries for cases when elements of a series contain internal commas.

WITH EQUAL ADJECTIVES: Use commas to separate a series of adjectives equal in rank. If the commas could be replaced by the word *and* without changing the sense, the adjectives are equal: *a thoughtful, precise manner; a dark, dangerous street.*

Use no comma when the last adjective before a noun outranks its predecessors because it is an integral element of a noun phrase, which is the equivalent of a single noun: *a cheap fur coat* (the noun phrase is *fur coat*); *the old oaken bucket; a new, blue spring bonnet.*

WITH NONESSENTIAL CLAUSES: A nonessential clause must be set off by commas. An essential clause must not be set off from the rest of a sentence by commas.

See the **essential clauses, nonessential clauses** entry in the main section.

WITH NONESSENTIAL PHRASES: A nonessential phrase must be set off by commas. An essential phrase must not be set off from the rest of a sentence by commas.

See the **essential phrases, nonessential phrases** entry in the main section.

WITH INTRODUCTORY CLAUSES AND PHRASES: A comma is used to separate an introductory clause or phrase from the main clause: *When he had tired of the mad pace of New York, he moved to Dubuque.*

The comma may be omitted after short introductory phrases if no ambiguity would result: *During the night he heard many noises.*

But use the comma if its omission would slow comprehension: *On the street below, the curious gathered.*

WITH CONJUNCTIONS: When a conjunction such as *and, but* or *for* links two clauses that could stand alone as separate sentences, use a comma before the conjunction in most cases: *She was glad she had looked, for a man was approaching the house.*

As a rule of thumb, use a comma if the subject of each clause is expressly stated: *We are visiting Washington, and we also plan a side trip to Williamsburg. We visited Washington, and our senator greeted us personally.* But no comma when the subject of the two clauses is the same and is not repeated in the second: *We are visiting Washington and plan to see the White House.*

The comma may be dropped if two clauses with expressly stated subjects are short. In general, however, favor use of a comma unless a particular literary effect is desired or if it would distort the sense of a sentence.

INTRODUCING DIRECT QUOTES: Use a comma to introduce a complete one-sentence quotation within a paragraph: *Wallace said, "She spent six months in Argentina and came back speaking English with a Spanish accent."* But use a colon to introduce quotations of more than one sentence. See **colon**.

Do not use a comma at the start of an indirect or partial quotation: *He said the victory put him "firmly on the road to a first-ballot nomination."*

BEFORE ATTRIBUTION: Use a comma instead of a period at the end of a quote that is followed by attribution: *"Rub my shoulders," Miss Cawley suggested.*

Do not use a comma, however, if the quoted statement ends with a question mark or exclamation point: *"Why should I?" he asked.*

WITH HOMETOWNS AND AGES: Use a comma to set off an individual's hometown when it is placed in apposition to a name: *Mary Richards, Minneapolis, and Maude Findlay, Tuckahoe, N.Y., were there.*

If an individual's age is used, set it off by commas: *Maude Findlay, 48, Tuckahoe, N.Y., was present.*

WITH PARTY AFFILIATION, ACADEMIC DEGREES, RELIGIOUS AFFILIATIONS: See separate entries under each of these terms.

NAMES OF STATES AND NATIONS USED WITH CITY NAMES: *His journey will take him from Dublin, Ireland, to Fargo, N.D., and back. The Selma, Ala., group saw the governor.*

Use parentheses, however, if a state name is inserted within a proper name: *The Huntsville (Ala.) Times.*

WITH YES AND NO: *Yes, I will be there.*

IN DIRECT ADDRESS: *Mother, I will be home late. No, sir, I did not take it.*

SEPARATING SIMILAR WORDS: Use a comma to sepa-rate duplicated words that otherwise would be confusing: *What the problem is, is not clear.*

IN LARGE FIGURES: Use a comma for most figures greater than 999. The major exceptions are: street addresses (*1234 Main St.*), broadcast frequencies (*1460 kilohertz*), room numbers, serial numbers, telephone numbers, and years (*1876*). See separate entries under these headings.

PLACEMENT WITH QUOTES: Commas always go inside quotation marks.

See **semicolon**.

compound adjectives See the **hyphen** entry.

dash (—) Follow these guidelines:

ABRUPT CHANGE: Use dashes to denote an abrupt change in thought in a sentence or an emphatic pause: *We will fly to Paris in June — if I get a raise. Smith offered a plan — it was unprecedented — to raise revenues.*

SERIES WITHIN A PHRASE: When a phrase that otherwise would be set off by commas contains a series of words that must be separated by commas, use dashes to set off the full phrase: *He listed the qualities — intelligence, humor, conservatism, independence — that he liked in an executive.*

ATTRIBUTION: Use a dash before an author's or composer's name at the end of a quotation: *"Who steals my purse steals trash." —Shakespeare.*

IN DATELINES:
NEW YORK (AP) — The city is broke.

IN LISTS: Dashes should be used to introduce individual sections of a list. Capitalize the first word following the dash. Use peri-

ods, not semicolons, at the end of each section. Example: *Jones gave the following reasons:*
—He never ordered the package.
—If he did, it didn't come.
—If it did, he sent it back.
WITH SPACES: Put a space on both sides of a dash in all uses except the start of a paragraph and sports agate summaries.

ellipsis (...) In general, treat an ellipsis as a three-letter word, constructed with three periods and two spaces, as shown here.

Use an ellipsis to indicate the deletion of one or more words in condensing quotes, texts and documents. Be especially careful to avoid deletions that would distort the meaning.

Brief examples of how to use ellipses are provided after guidelines are given. More extensive examples, drawn from the speech in which President Nixon announced his resignation, are in the sections below marked CONDENSATION EXAMPLE and QUOTATIONS.

SPACING REQUIREMENTS: In some computer editing systems the thin space must be used between the periods of the ellipsis to prevent them from being placed on two different lines when they are sent through a computer that handles hyphenation and justification.

Leave one regular space — never a thin — on both sides of an ellipsis: *I ... tried to do what was best.*

PUNCTUATION GUIDELINES: If the words that precede an ellipsis constitute a grammatically complete sentence, either in the original or in the condensation, place a period at the end of the

last word before the ellipsis. Follow it with a regular space and an ellipsis: *I no longer have a strong enough political base. ...*

When the grammatical sense calls for a question mark, exclamation point, comma or colon, the sequence is word, punctuation mark, regular space, ellipsis: *Will you come? ...*

When material is deleted at the end of one paragraph and at the beginning of the one that follows, place an ellipsis in both locations.

CONDENSATION EXAMPLE: Here is an example of how the spacing and punctuation guidelines would be applied in condensing President Nixon's resignation announcement:
Good evening. ...
In all the decisions I have made in my public life, I have always tried to do what was best for the nation. ...
... However, it has become evident to me that I no longer have a strong enough political base in Congress.
... As long as there was a base, I felt strongly that it was necessary to see the constitutional process through to its conclusion, that to do otherwise would be ... a dangerously destabilizing precedent for the future.

QUOTATIONS: In writing a story, do not use ellipses at the beginning and end of direct quotes:
"It has become evident to me that I no longer have a strong enough political base," Nixon said.
Not *"... it has become evident to me that I no longer have a strong enough political base ... ,"* Nixon said.

HESITATION: An ellipsis also may be used to indicate a pause or hesitation in speech, or a thought that the speaker or writer does not complete. Substitute a dash for this purpose, however, if the context uses ellipses to indicate that words actually spoken or written have been deleted.

SPECIAL EFFECTS: Ellipses also may be used to separate individual items within a paragraph of show business gossip or similar material. Use periods after items that are complete sentences.

exclamation point (!) Follow these guidelines:

EMPHATIC EXPRESSIONS: Use the mark to express a high degree of surprise, incredulity or other strong emotion.

AVOID OVERUSE: Use a comma after mild interjections. End mildly exclamatory sentences with a period.

PLACEMENT WITH QUOTES: Place the mark inside quotation marks when it is part of the quoted material: *"How wonderful!" he exclaimed. "Never!" she shouted.*

Place the mark outside quotation marks when it is not part of the quoted material: *I hated reading Spenser's "Faerie Queene"!*

MISCELLANEOUS: Do not use a comma or a period after the exclamation mark:

Wrong: *"Halt!", the corporal cried.*

Right: *"Halt!" the corporal cried.*

hyphen (-) Hyphens are joiners. Use them to avoid ambiguity or to form a single idea from two or more words.

Some guidelines:

AVOID AMBIGUITY: Use a hyphen whenever ambiguity would result if it were omitted: *The president will speak to small-business men.* (*Businessmen* normally is

one word. But *the president will speak to small businessmen* is unclear.)

Others: *He recovered his health. He re-covered the leaky roof.*

COMPOUND MODIFIERS: When a compound modifier — two or more words that express a single concept — precedes a noun, use hyphens to link all the words in the compound except the adverb *very* and all adverbs that end in *-ly*: *a first-quarter touchdown, a bluish-green dress, a full-time job, a well-known man, a better-qualified woman, a know-it-all attitude, a very good time, an easily remembered rule.*

Many combinations that are hyphenated before a noun are not hyphenated when they occur after a noun: *The team scored in the first quarter. The dress, a bluish green, was attractive on her. She works full time. His attitude suggested that he knew it all.*

But when a modifier that would be hyphenated before a noun occurs instead after a form of the verb *to be*, the hyphen usually must be retained to avoid confusion: *The man is well-known. The woman is quick-witted. The children are soft-spoken. The play is second-rate.*

The principle of using a hyphen to avoid confusion explains why no hyphen is required with *very* and *-ly* words. Readers can expect them to modify the word that follows. But if a combination such as *little-known man* were not hyphenated, the reader could logically be expecting *little* to be followed by a noun, as in *little man.* Instead, the reader encountering *little known* would have to back up mentally and make the compound connection on his own.

TWO-THOUGHT COM-POUNDS: *serio-comic, socio-economic.*

COMPOUND PROPER NOUNS AND ADJECTIVES: Use a hyphen to designate dual heritage: *Italian-American, Mexican-American.*

No hyphen, however, for *French Canadian* or *Latin American.*

PREFIXES AND SUFFIXES: See the **prefixes** and **suffixes** entries, and separate entries for the most frequently used prefixes and suffixes.

AVOID DUPLICATED VOWELS, TRIPLED CONSONANTS: Examples: *anti-intellectual, pre-empt, shell-like.*

WITH NUMERALS: Use a hyphen to separate figures in **odds, ratios, scores**, some **fractions** and some **vote tabulations**. See examples in entries under these headings.

When large numbers must be spelled out, use a hyphen to connect a word ending in *-y* to another word: *twenty-one, fifty-five*, etc.

SUSPENSIVE HYPHENATION: The form: *He received a 10- to 20-year sentence in prison.*

parentheses ( ) In general, use parentheses around logos, as shown in the **datelines** entry, but otherwise be sparing with them.

Parentheses are jarring to the reader. Because they do not appear on some news service printers, there is also the danger that material inside them may be misinterpreted.

The temptation to use parentheses is a clue that a sentence is becoming contorted. Try to write it another way. If a sentence must contain incidental material, then commas or two dashes are frequently more effective. Use these alternatives whenever possible.

There are occasions, however, when parentheses are the only effective means of inserting necessary background or reference information. When they are necessary, follow these guidelines:

WITHIN QUOTATIONS: If parenthetical information inserted in a direct quotation is at all sensitive, place an editor's note under a dash at the bottom of a story alerting copy desks to what was inserted.

PUNCTUATION: Place a period outside a closing parenthesis if the material inside is not a sentence (*such as this fragment*).

(*An independent parenthetical sentence such as this one takes a period before the closing parenthesis.*)

When a phrase placed in parentheses (*this one is an example*) might normally qualify as a complete sentence but is dependent on the surrounding material, do not capitalize the first word or end with a period.

MATERIAL FROM OTHER AREAS: If a story contains information from outside the datelined city, put the material in parentheses only if the correspondent in the datelined community was cut off from incoming communications. See **dateline selection**.

INSERTIONS IN A PROPER NAME: Use parentheses if a state name or similar information is inserted within a proper name: *The Huntsville (Ala.) Times*. But use commas if no proper name is involved: *The Selma, Ala., group saw the governor.*

NEVER USED: Do not use parentheses to denote a political figure's party affiliation and jurisdiction. Instead, set them off with commas, as shown under **party affiliation**.

Do not use (*cq*) or similar notation to indicate that an unusual spelling or term is correct. Include the confirmation in an editor's note at the top of a story.

periods (.) Follow these guidelines:

END OF DECLARATIVE SENTENCE: *The stylebook is finished.*

END OF A MILDLY IMPERATIVE SENTENCE: *Shut the door.*

Use an exclamation point if greater emphasis is desired: *Be careful!*

END OF SOME RHETORICAL QUESTIONS: A period is preferable if a statement is more a suggestion than a question: *Why don't we go.*

END OF AN INDIRECT QUESTION: *He asked what the score was.*

MANY ABBREVIATIONS: For guidelines, see the **abbreviations and acronyms** entry. For the form of frequently used abbreviations, see the entry under the full name, abbreviation, acronym or term.

INITIALS: *John F. Kennedy, T.S. Eliot* (No space between *T.* and *S.*, to prevent them from being placed on two lines in typesetting.)

Abbreviations using only the initials of a name do not take periods: *JFK, LBJ.*

ELLIPSIS: See **ellipsis**.

ENUMERATIONS: After numbers or letters in enumerating elements of a summary: *1. Wash the car. 2. Clean the basement.* Or: *A. Punctuate properly. B. Write simply.*

PLACEMENT WITH QUOTATION MARKS: Periods always go inside quotation marks. See **quotation marks.**

question mark (?) Follow these guidelines:

END OF A DIRECT QUESTION: *Who started the riot?*

Did he ask who started the riot? (The sentence as a whole is a direct question despite the indirect question at the end.)

You started the riot? (A question in the form of a declarative statement.)

INTERPOLATED QUESTION: *You told me — Did I hear you correctly? — that you started the riot.*

MULTIPLE QUESTION: Use a single question mark at the end of the full sentence:

Did you hear him say, "What right have you to ask about the riot?"

Did he plan the riot, employ assistants, and give the signal to begin?

Or, to cause full stops and throw emphasis on each element, break into separate sentences: *Did he plan the riot? Employ assistants? Give the signal to begin?*

CAUTION: Do not use question marks to indicate the end of indirect questions:

He asked who started the riot. To ask why the riot started is unnecessary. I want to know what the cause of the riot was. How foolish it is to ask what caused the riot.

QUESTION AND ANSWER FORMAT: Do not use quotation marks. Paragraph each speaker's words:

Q: Where did you keep it?
A: In a little tin box.

PLACEMENT WITH QUOTATION MARKS: Inside or outside, depending on the meaning:

Who wrote "Gone With the Wind"?

He asked, "How long will it take?"

MISCELLANEOUS: The question mark supersedes the comma that normally is used when supplying attribution for a quotation: *"Who is there?" she asked.*

quotation marks (" ") The basic guidelines for open-quote marks (") and close-quote marks ("):

FOR DIRECT QUOTATIONS: To surround the exact words of a speaker or writer when reported in a story:

"I have no intention of staying," he replied.

"I do not object," he said, "to the tenor of the report."

Franklin said, "A penny saved is a penny earned."

A speculator said the practice is "too conservative for inflationary times."

RUNNING QUOTATIONS: If a full paragraph of quoted material is followed by a paragraph that continues the quotation, do not put close-quote marks at the end of the first paragraph. Do, however, put open-quote marks at the start of the second paragraph. Continue in this fashion for any succeeding paragraphs, using close-quote marks only at the end of the quoted material.

If a paragraph does not start with quotation marks but ends with a quotation that is continued in the next paragraph, do not use close-quote marks at the end of the introductory paragraph if the quoted material constitutes a full sentence. Use close-quote marks, however, if the quoted material does not constitute a full sentence. For example:

He said, "I am shocked and horrified by the incident.

"I am so horrified, in fact, that I will ask for the death penalty."

But: *He said he was "shocked and horrified by the incident."*

"I am so horrified, in fact, that I will ask for the death penalty," he said.

DIALOGUE OR CONVERSATION: Each person's words, no matter how brief, are placed in a separate paragraph, with quotation marks at the beginning and the end of each person's speech:

"Will you go?"

"Yes."

"When?"

"Thursday."

NOT IN Q-and-A: Quotation marks are not required in formats that identify questions and answers by *Q*: and *A*:. See the **question mark** entry for example.

NOT IN TEXTS: Quotation marks are not required in full texts, condensed texts or textual excerpts. See **ellipsis**.

COMPOSITION TITLES: See the **composition titles** entry for guidelines on the use of quotation marks in book titles, movie titles, etc.

NICKNAMES: See the **nicknames** entry.

IRONY: Put quotation marks around a word or words used in an ironical sense: *The "debate" turned into a free-for-all.*

UNFAMILIAR TERMS: A word or words being introduced to readers may be placed in quotation marks on first reference:

Broadcast frequencies are measured in "kilohertz."

Do not put subsequent references to *kilohertz* in quotation marks.

See the **foreign words** entry.

AVOID UNNECESSARY FRAGMENTS: Do not use quotation marks to report a few ordinary words that a speaker or writer has used:

Wrong: *The senator said he would "go home to Michigan" if he lost the election.*

Right: *The senator said he would go home to Michigan if he lost the election.*

PARTIAL QUOTES: When a partial quote is used, do not put quotation marks around words that the speaker could not have used.

Suppose the individual said, *"I am horrified at your slovenly manners."*

Wrong: *She said she "was horrified at their slovenly manners."*

Right: *She said she was horrified at their "slovenly manners."*

Better when practical: Use the full quote.

QUOTES WITHIN QUOTES: Alternate between double quotation marks (" or ") and single marks (' or '):

She said, "I quote from his letter, 'I agree with Kipling that "the female of the species is more deadly than the male," but the phenomenon is not an unchangeable law of nature,' a remark he did not explain."

Use three marks together if two quoted elements end at the same time: *She said, "He told me, 'I love you.'"*

PLACEMENT WITH OTHER PUNCTUATION: Follow these long-established printers' rules:

—The period and the comma always go within the quotation marks.

—The dash, the semicolon, the question mark and the exclamation point go within the quotation marks when they apply to the quoted matter only. They go outside when they apply to the whole sentence.

See **comma**.

semicolon (;) In general, use the semicolon to indicate a greater separation of thought and information than a comma can convey but less than the separation that a period implies.

The basic guidelines:

TO CLARIFY A SERIES: Use semicolons to separate elements of a series when individual segments contain material that also must be set off by commas:

He leaves a son, John Smith of Chicago; three daughters, Jane Smith of Wichita, Kan., Mary Smith of Denver, and Susan, wife of William Kingsbury of Boston; and a sister, Martha, wife of Robert Warren of Omaha, Neb.

Note that the semicolon is used before the final *and* in such a series.

Another application of this principle may be seen in the cross-references at the end of entries in this book. Because some entries themselves have a comma, a semicolon is used to separate references to multiple entries, as in: *See the* **felony, misdemeanor** *entry;* **pardon, parole, probation;** *and* **prison, jail**.

See the **dash** entry for a different type of connection that uses dashes to avoid multiple commas.

TO LINK INDEPENDENT CLAUSES: Use semicolon when a coordinating conjunction such as *and, but* or *for* is not present: *The package was due last week; it arrived today.*

If a coordinating conjunction is present, use a semicolon before it only if extensive punctuation also is required in one or more of the individual clauses: *They pulled their boats from the water, sandbagged the retaining walls, and boarded up the windows; but even with these precautions, the island was hard-hit by the hurri-cane.*

Unless a particular literary effect is desired, however, the better approach in these circumstances is to break the independent clauses into separate sentences.

PLACEMENT WITH QUOTES: Place semicolons outside quotation marks.

BIBLIOGRAPHY

BIBLIOGRAPHY

Following are reference books used in the preparation of The Associated Press Stylebook. They are the accepted reference sources for material not covered by the Stylebook.

First reference for spelling, style, usage and foreign geographic names:
Webster's New World College Dictionary, Fourth Edition, IDG Books.

Second reference for spelling, style and usage:
Webster's Third New International Dictionary of the English Language, Unabridged; G. & C. Merriam Co., Springfield, Mass.

Second reference for foreign geographic names:
National Geographic Atlas of the World, National Geographic Society, Washington, D.C.

First reference for place names in the 50 states:
National 5-Digit ZIP Code and Post Office Directory; U.S. Postal Service, Washington, D.C.

For aircraft names:
Jane's All the World's Aircraft; Jane's Yearbooks, London, and Franklin Watts Inc., New York.

For military ships:
Jane's Fighting Ships; Jane's Yearbooks, London, and Franklin Watts Inc., New York.

For non-military ships:
Lloyd's Register of Shipping; Lloyd's Register of Shipping Trust Corp. Ltd., London.

For railroads:
Official Railway Guide — Freight Service, and Official Railway Guide — Passenger Service, Travel Edition; Official Railway Guide, New York.

For federal government questions:
Official Congressional Directory; U.S. Government Printing Office, Washington.

For foreign government questions:
Political Handbook of the World; McGraw-Hill Book Co., New York.

For the formal name of a business:
Standard & Poor's Register of Corporations, Directors and Executives; Standard & Poor's Corp., New York.

For religion questions:

Handbook of Denominations in the United States; Abingdon Press, Nashville, Tenn., and New York.

Yearbook of American and Canadian Churches; Abingdon Press, Nashville, Tenn., and New York, for the National Council of Churches of Christ in the U.S.A., New York.

Other references consulted in the preparation of the AP Stylebook:

Bernstein, Theodore M. *The Careful Writer: A Modern Guide to English Usage*. Atheneum, 1965.

Bernstein, Theodore M. *More Language That Needs Watching*. Channel Press, 1962.

Bernstein, Theodore M. *Watch Your Language*. Atheneum, 1958.

Cappon, Rene J. *The Word*. The Associated Press, 1982; second edition, 1991.

Follett, Wilson (edited and completed by Jacques Barzun). *Modern American Usage*. Hill & Wang, 1966.

Fowler, H.W. *A Dictionary of Modern English Usage*. Oxford University Press, 1965.

The Chicago Manual of Style, 14th Edition. University of Chicago Press, 1995.

Morris, William and Morris, Mary. *Harper Dictionary of Contemporary Usage*. Harper & Row, 1975; second edition, 1985.

Newton, Harry, *Newton's Telecom Dictionary*, 15th Edition, Miller Freeman, Inc., 1999.

Shaw, Harry. *Dictionary of Problem Words & Expressions*. McGraw-Hill Book Co., 1975.

Skillin, Marjorie E. and Gay, Robert M. *Words Into Type*. Prentice-Hall Inc., 1974.

Strunk, William Jr. and White, E.B. *The Elements of Style*, second edition. The Macmillan Co., 1972.

Also consulted were the stylebooks of the Boston Globe, Indianapolis News, Kansas City Star, Los Angeles Times, Miami Herald, Milwaukee Journal Sentinel, Newsday, New York Times, Wilmington (Del.) News-Journal, and the U.S. Government Printing Office.

BRIEFING ON
MEDIA LAW

FOREWORD

What follows is not a textbook on libel. It is a guide for The Associated Press staff. It explains fundamental principles of libel law and relevant First Amendment principles for working writers and editors.

This manual will not make the reader an expert on libel or on the First Amendment. It will, we hope, make everyone aware of what libel is and how to avoid it.

Underlying all the guidance in this book is one basic rule for the AP staff: If a legal problem develops with a story, or if guidance is needed in the handling of a story, consult the General Desk. Nothing in the manual alters this rule.

The law of libel is a matter of state law and, as is the case with all other matters of state law, it is neither universal, nor static. While the First Amendment principles which guide the state laws of libel are universally applicable to all the states, each state is free to craft its own laws against libel, within the First Amendment boundaries. Few generalities about the law of libel apply universally to all the states.

The past 30 years have ushered in dramatic change in the First Amendment principles governing libel. New interpretations go on, especially in the arena of cyberspace. What has not and does not change is our promise to ourselves to be accurate and to be fair.

For his help with this manual we are indebted to the late General News Editor Samuel G. Blackman.

LOUIS D. BOCCARDI
President and
Chief Executive Officer

INTRODUCTION

Associate Justice John Marshall Harlan remarked that "the law of libel has changed substantially since the early days of the Republic."

And it has changed substantially since he made that observation.

But the working journalist remembers: The news stories that generate the most claims of injury to reputation — the basis of libel — are run-of-the-mill. Perhaps 95 of 100 libel suits are in that category and result from publication of charges of crime, immorality, incompetence or inefficiency. A Harvard Nieman report makes the point: "The gee-whiz, slam-bang stories usually aren't the ones that generate libel, but the innocent-appearing, potentially treacherous minor yarns from police courts and traffic cases, from routine meetings and from business reports."

Most suits based on relatively minor stories result from factual error or inexact language — for example, getting the plea wrong or making it appear that all defendants in a case face identical charges. Many libel suits arise in the context of reporting court and police news, especially criminal courts. Problems can arise in stories about crime and in identifying a suspect where there has been no arrest or where no charge has been made.

Libel even lurks in such innocent-appearing stories as birth notices and wedding announcements. As Turner Catledge, former managing editor of *The New York Times*, noted in his book, "My Life and the Times," "Sometimes people will call in the engagement of two people who hate each other, as a practical joke." The fact that some New York newspapers have had to defend suits for such announcements illustrates the care and concern required in every editorial department.

The lesson is twofold: one, there is no substitute for accuracy, and, two, news organizations may face legal challenges to what they publish — even when they have accurately reported statements made by someone else, as in the case of a phony engagement announcement. When the press reports that person X has leveled libelous accusations against person Y, unless a privilege discussed below applies, the press may be held to account not only for the truth of the fact that the allegations were made, but also for the steps taken to verify the truth of the accusations. When accusations are made against a person, it is always well to investigate the truth of the accusations as well as to try for balancing comment which has some relation to the original charges. Irrelevant countercharges can lead to problems with the person who made the first accusation. Always bear in mind that a newspaper can be held responsible in defamation for republishing the libelous statement made by another.

This handbook outlines the law of libel, in general, and provides more details of the law as it specifically applies in Texas, Illinois, California and New York. While certain privileges, such as the privilege for neutral reportage, are not universally recognized, the law in every state is always evolving — the courts of any particular state may decide to recognize a privilege they had not recognized before.

Chapter 1
WHAT IS LIBEL?

At its most basic, libel means injury to reputation. Each state, however, has adopted its own definition of the term *libel*. In some states libel is distinguished from *slander*, in that a libel is written, or otherwise printed, whereas a slander is spoken; in either case, the term *defamation* generally includes both terms. Words, pictures, cartoons, photo captions and headlines can all give rise to a claim for libel.

In Illinois, libel is defined as "the publication of anything injurious to the good name or reputation of another, or which tends to bring him into disrepute." Illinois is an example of a state that makes no distinction between slander and libel.

In New York, a libelous statement is one which tends to expose a person to hatred, contempt or aversion or to induce an evil or unsavory opinion of him in the minds of a substantial number of people in the community.

In Texas, where libel is defined by statute, a "libel is a defamation expressed in written or other graphic form that tends to blacken the memory of the dead or that tends to injure a living person's reputation and thereby expose the person to public hatred, contempt or ridicule, or financial injury or to impeach any person's honesty, integrity, virtue, or reputation or to publish the natural defects of anyone and thereby expose the person to public hatred, ridicule, or financial injury." In California, where libel is also defined by statute, libel is a *false* and *unprivileged* publication by writing, printing, picture, effigy or other fixed representation which exposes any person to hatred, contempt, ridicule or obloquy, or which causes him to be shunned or avoided or which injures him in his occupation.

California is an example of a state that distinguishes substantively between libel and slander. In California, a slander, also defined by statute, is a false and unprivileged publication, orally uttered (including over the radio) which: (1) charges a person with committing a crime or with having been indicted, convicted or punished for a crime; (2) alleges that a person is infected with a contagious or loathsome disease; (3) imputes a person is generally unqualified to perform his job or tends to lessen the profits of someone's profession, trade or business; (4) imputes impotence or want of chastity, or (5) by natural consequence charges actual damage. The definition of slander is thus more narrow than that of libel in California — so the speaker you quote may not be guilty of slander, but your written publication of the same matter may constitute a libel.

Finally, many states, such as California, draw a distinction between a libel which defames the plaintiff without reference by extrinsic explanatory matter and a libel which requires reference to extrinsic matters. A claim for damages based on a statement that is not libelous without reference to extrinsic matter usually must be accompanied by a showing of specific damages suffered. A claim based on libel that does not require external reference can generally stand without a showing of specific damage.

Chapter 2

LIABILITY FOR REPUBLICATION

A common misconception regarding the law of libel is that the publisher of a true and accurate quote of a statement containing libelous allegations is immune from suit if the quoted statement was actually made and was accurately transcribed by the reporter.

In many circumstances, however, a newspaper can be called to task for republishing the libelous statement of another. For example, even when it comes to the reporting of the fact that a plaintiff has filed a libel suit against a defendant, a newspaper could, in certain circumstances, be held responsible for repeating the libel that gave rise to the suit. In most states, a "fair report privilege" shields the publisher of an accurate and impartial report of the contents of legal papers which have commenced a libel action. (See Chapter 3.) In some states, however, the fair report privilege does not attach to the contents of legal papers until a case goes to trial or some other specified judicial action takes place. Thus, publication of the pleadings in a libel case before the specified judicial action takes place could give rise to a fresh claim for libel.

On the other hand, there are some instances where a newspaper will be justified in republishing the statements of another. First, there is the fair report privilege. Additionally, many states recognize that newspapers under the pressure of daily deadlines often rely on the research of other reputable newspapers in republishing news items originally appearing in the other newspapers. In such cases, reliance on a reputable newspaper or news agency is recognized as a defense to a libel claim. Of course, this justification ceases to exist if the republisher had or should have had substantial reason to question the accuracy or good faith of the original story. In some states, this defense is even further modified where the plaintiff is a public figure or public official, in which case the republisher is justified unless it had *actual* knowledge that the original statement was, in fact, false or published with a belief it was probably false, i.e., recklessly.

Liability for republication of another's materials is an area of the law of libel whose limits have been tested recently by the advent of the Internet. Should online access providers be held liable as though they were the "publishers" of the material published everyday on the Internet by the millions of individuals with access to the Internet? Although the question has not yet been fully resolved, the trend seems to be to either relieve the access providers of any liability, or to hold them responsible only for publication of those matters which they actually know to be false or probably false (as where someone calls the service to complain).

Chapter 3
PRIVILEGES

In addition to the substantive defenses described later, in Chapter 4, certain privileges, grounded in both constitutional and state law, limit the ability of a plaintiff to successfully prosecute a libel claim. When an article raises any libel concerns, an editor or reporter should consider whether or not any of the following privileges apply to the publication. If any privileges do apply, the reporter and editor should consider whether the circumstances of the contemplated publication match the circumstances under which the privilege will attach.

1. Opinion

The rationale behind the *opinion privilege* is that only statements that can be proven true or false are capable of defamatory meaning and that statements of "opinion" cannot, by their nature, be proven true or false. As the Supreme Court decision, *Gertz v. Robert Welch Inc.*, 418 U.S. 323 (1974), which recognized the constitutional dimension of the opinion privilege, stated, "there is no such thing as a false idea." In a more recent case, *Milkovich v. Lorain Journal Co.*, 497 U.S. 1 (1990), the Supreme Court attempted to clarify how an opinion was to be distinguished from a fact. *Milkovich* is widely thought of by legal commentators, however, to have added more confusion than clarity to the question. After *Milkovich*, some states have turned to their own state constitutions as providing basis for the opinion privilege and have thus attempted to avoid the *Milkovich* confusion. One such state, New York, has gone so far as to declare that its state constitution affords more protection for expression of opinion than the U.S. Constitution does — at least under the *Milkovich* standards. Texas, on the other hand, has claimed to have adopted the *Milkovich* holding.

One test for distinguishing fact from opinion that appears to be followed in many states, even after the *Milkovich* decision, asks: (1) whether the statement has a precise core of meaning on which a consensus of understanding exists; (2) whether the statement is verifiable; (3) whether the textual context of the statement would influence the average reader to infer factual content; and (4) whether the broader social context signals usage as either fact or opinion.

In New York, a statement of opinion based on accurately stated and reported facts is not actionable. Likewise, statements incapable of being proven false are considered protected expressions of opinion, as are epithets, satire, parody and hyperbole.

Under these principles, calling a doctor a "rotten apple," for example, was incapable of being proved true or false and was therefore protected as an expression of opinion. Similarly, a statement that plaintiff lacked "talent, ambition, initiative" was a nonactionable expression of opinion. A letter to the editor published in a scientific journal submitted by the International Primate Protection League and which warned that a multinational corporation's plans for establishing facilities to conduct hepatitis research using chimpanzees could well wind up spreading hepatitis to the rest of the chimpanzee population was, given its overall context, protected as opinion.

Where the facts underlying the opinion are reported inaccurately and would adversely affect the conclusion drawn by the average reader concerning the opinion expressed, however, the publication may give rise to a claim for libel in New York. Moreover, accusations of criminal or illegal activity, even when couched in the form of opinion, are not protected by the opinion privilege. Finally, to be protected under the opinion privilege in New York, the content, tone and apparent purpose of the statement should signal the reader that the statement reflects the author's opinion.

In Illinois, the test for distinguishing a fact from opinion is whether the statement clearly discloses the factual basis on which it depends. If so, the statement is pure opinion. If the statement suggests or appears to rely on undisclosed facts, it will be considered a statement of fact. Illinois courts assess the totality of the circumstances in which the statement appears. A statement is not protected in Illinois by the opinion privilege if it implies the existence of undisclosed facts which are both false and defamatory. In addition, false statements of fact, even when couched in terms of opinion, are capable of defamatory meaning. In Illinois, if a statement is provably false, it may be actionable unless the language is clearly "loose, figurative or hyperbolic."

In Illinois, the statement that a sports commentator was a "liar" without reference to specific facts was protected as opinion. Taken in the total context of an article, the statement that plaintiff was "neo-Nazi" was protected as opinion. Likewise, a statement calling a plaintiff a "commie," suggesting that he does not understand the subject he teaches and that he is "not traveling with a full set of luggage," was also protected as opinion. Statements accusing doctors of being "cancer con-artists," of practicing "medical quackery," and of promoting "snake oil remedies," were also protected. A newspaper column and editorial characterizing a nudist pageant as "pornography" and as "immoral" were also protected.

In California, after *Milkovich*, the state's highest court held that a false assertion of fact could be libelous even though couched in terms of opinion, although statements that are clearly satirical, rhetorical, or hyperbolic continue to be protected. The same court also declared, in another case, that no "categorical exception for opinion exists independently under California Law" (*Kahn v. Bower*, 1991). This is in direct contrast to New York's approach.

Another court in California held that three questions should be considered to distinguish opinion from fact: (1) does the statement use figurative or hyperbolic language that would negate the impression that the statement is serious? (2) does the general tenor of the statement negate the impression that the statement is serious? (3) can the statement be proved true or false? Under this test, a television commentator's statement that a manufacturer's product "didn't work" was not an opinion because, despite the humorous tenor of the comment, it did not use figurative or hyperbolic language, it could reasonably be understood as asserting an objective fact that could be proven true or false. Likewise, a statement made in a newspaper interview that plaintiff was an "extortionist" was not protected as opinion.

Before *Milkovich*, courts in Texas had held that only false statements of fact were actionable in libel. After *Milkovich*, at least one court has held that there is no separate constitutional privilege for opinion and that opinions or ideas may be actionable if they imply false statements of objective fact.

Thus, before *Milkovich*, a Texas court found that a statement in an editorial that the prosecution's burden of proof of guilt "is no excuse for cheating" was protected as opinion. Likewise, the characterization of a fluoridation opponent as a "quack" and an "imported fearmonger" was protected as opinion.

After *Milkovich*, statements that plaintiffs were incompetent pilots and troublemakers, when made in the context of a public issue, were protected opinions. On the other hand, the statement that a stockbroker was going to lose his license, was in big trouble with the SEC and would never work again as a broker, was not protected as opinion, but was, in fact, actionable.

The common thread to these variations is that opinions that are offered in a context that presents the facts on which the opinion is based are generally not actionable. On the other hand, opinions that imply the existence of undisclosed, defamatory facts (i.e., if *you* knew what *I* know) are more likely to be actionable. In addition, a statement that is capable of being proven true or false, regardless of whether it is expressed as an opinion or as an exaggeration or even hyperbole, may be actionable.

One example offered by a prominent commentator on libel law illustrates the point:

"Suppose the opinion is, 'I think X must be an alcoholic,' and there are no underlying facts stated. It would be reasonable for a reader to conclude that the writer knew facts that would justify such a comment — that X drank often, alone and compulsively, for example. If these facts are defamatory, that is, false and damaging to reputation, the comment will be considered defamatory also. Had underlying, accurate facts been supplied — 'that X drinks three martinis every night on the club car which is why I think he must be an alcoholic' — the comment would be protected." (Sanford, *Libel and Privacy*, Second Edition, 1994.)

2. Fair Comment and Criticism

The fair comment and criticism privilege long predates the constitutional opinion privilege and continues, in most states, to exist as an independent matter of state law. The right of fair comment has been summarized as follows: "Everyone has a right to comment on matters of public interest and concern, provided they do so fairly and with an honest purpose. Such comments or criticism are not libelous, however severe in their terms, unless they are written maliciously. Thus it has been held that books, prints, pictures and statuary publicly exhibited, and the architecture of public buildings, and actors and exhibitors are all the legitimate subjects of newspapers' criticism, and such criticism fairly and honestly made is not libelous, however strong the terms of censure may be." (*Hoeppner v. Dunkirk Pr. Co.*, 1930.)

Some states, such as Texas, have recognized the fair comment privilege as a matter of statutory law. The Texas statute protects reasonable and fair comment or criticism of the official acts of public officials and of other matters of public concern when published for general information.

In Illinois, the fair comment privilege applies to statements of opinion, relating to an act, not an individual. The statements of opinion must include their factual predicate and relate to a matter of public interest. A recent Illinois court, however, has held that this privilege was supplanted by the U.S. constitutional opinion privilege (i.e., *Gertz* and *Milkovich*) — thus placing in doubt the continued existence of this privilege.

3. Fair Report

Under the fair report privilege, a fair and accurate report of a public proceeding cannot provide grounds for a libel suit. In New York the fair report privilege is a matter of statute. According to the statute, a fair and substantially accurate report of an official judicial or legislative proceeding cannot be the basis for defamation action. In order to qualify for the privilege, however, the account must be substantially accurate and fair. The privilege can still apply where the publisher edits out portions of an official report, provided that what is published is still substantially accurate. At least one New York trial court has even applied this fair report privilege to a news report based on information provided by police sources.

Pursuant to the Texas fair report statute, the privilege applies to "a fair, true and impartial account" of: (a) judicial proceedings; (b) an official proceeding to administer the law; (c) all executive and legislative proceedings; and (d) the proceedings of public meetings dealing with public purposes. In this context, the phrase "fair, true and impartial account" means a substantially true account. This privilege relieves a news organization of responsibility for determining the underlying truth of the statements made in these contexts, precisely because the very fact that these comments were made is newsworthy and important regardless of whether they are actually true. Once again, however, this privilege is limited to statements made in the contexts as defined.

California also has a statute recognizing a privilege for a fair and true report in a public journal of a judicial, legislative or other public official proceeding, including a report of anything said in the course thereof. California also recognizes a privilege for a fair and true report of a public meeting, which includes press conferences.

In Illinois, a report of a governmental proceeding is privileged unless the report significantly alters the defamatory meaning of the statements made by government officials. The privilege may not apply if the defamatory statement itself does not appear in the public record.

Statements made outside the court by police or a prosecutor or an attorney may or may not qualify as privileged, depending on what state you are in and on the circumstances in which the statements are made. Some states only extend the privilege to such out of court statements if made by specified top officials.

In New York and some other states, court rules provide that the papers filed in matrimonial actions are sealed and thus not open to inspection by the general public. It is not clear whether the fair report privilege will attach to publication of the contents of such papers, which by court rule, or order of the judge, are to be kept confidential.

In one case where this very situation arose, the vice president of a company filed a libel suit in New York alleging that he was fired because a newspaper published his wife's charges of infidelity set forth in divorce proceedings. The newspaper responded that its report was a true and fair account of court proceedings. The New York Court of Appeals rejected that argument on grounds that the law makes details of marital cases secret because spatting spouses frequently make unfounded charges.

The lesson of this case is that information gleaned from "confidential" court documents might not be covered under the fair report privilege. In such a case, the paper will be put to the test of proving that it made a reasonable effort to determine the truth of the allegations before publishing them.

There are other "traps" to be aware of when relying on this privilege. For example, statements made on the floor of convention sessions or from speakers' platforms organized by private organizations may not be privileged under the fair report privilege. Strictly speaking, conventions of private organizations are not "public and official proceedings" even though they may be forums for discussions of public questions.

Similarly, while statements made by the president of the United States or a governor in the course of executive proceedings have absolute privilege for the speaker (even if false or defamatory), the press' privilege to report all such statements is not always absolute. For example, President Kennedy once was asked at a news conference what he was going to do about "two well-known security risks" in the State Department. The reporter gave names when the president asked for them. The AP published the names because it was in the public interest to report the incident fully.

No suits resulted. In contrast, after a civil rights march, George Wallace, then governor of Alabama, appeared on a television show and said some of the marchers were members of communist and communist-front organizations. He gave some names, which newspapers carried. Some libel suits resulted.

4. Neutral Reportage

The lack of recognition, in many states, of the *neutral reportage* privilege is a sad fact of which all reporters and editors should be aware. The neutral reportage privilege protects a fair, true and impartial account of a newsworthy event. Neutral reportage is, of course, a basic tenet of good journalism and, as such, is a good practice to follow regardless of whether it is an officially recognized privilege in your state.

California is one of the few states that has recognized the neutral reportage privilege. The privilege is available when the plaintiff is a public figure, the defamatory statement is made by one who is a party to a public controversy and the publication is accurate and neutral. One California court applying the privilege found that a newspaper's account of an accusation that a police officer had improperly obtained a false confession to a crime from a person later released as innocent was not actionable where the newspaper also printed the officer's denial of the charge.

Although Texas does not officially recognize the neutral report privilege, at least one recent case has recognized the principle of the neutral reportage privilege, without naming it as such. In that case, *KTRK Television v. Felder*, 1997, the court held that a story which accurately reported that parents of school children had accused a school teacher of physically threatening and verbally abusing their children was substantially true regardless of whether the allegations themselves were accurate.

Similarly, while New York state courts do not recognize a privilege for neutral reportage, a federal court in New York state has actually found a neutral reportage privilege grounded in the U.S. Constitution. As the court described the neutral reportage privilege in this case, "when a responsible, prominent organization ... makes serious charges against a public figure, the First Amendment protects the accurate and disinterested reporting of those charges, regardless of the reporter's private views regarding their validity." (*Edwards v. National Audubon Society*, 2d Cir. 1977.) Subsequent cases have held that the neutral reportage privilege will not apply when the author of an article appears to espouse or concur in the charges made by others and that the privilege is limited to cases involving public figures.

Chapter 4
DEFENSES

When contemplating publication of a statement that might raise a libel claim, a publisher would do well to consider the defenses available and the requirements of each defense. The several defenses available to news organizations charged with committing libel are listed below.

1. Not Capable of Defamatory Meaning

The first and most obvious defense to an actual or threatened libel suit is that the language complained of "is not capable of defamatory meaning." Generally, statements accusing someone of being a criminal, an adulterer, insane or infected with a loathsome disease are considered "capable of defamatory meaning." However, to determine whether any particular statement is susceptible of defamatory meaning, reference must be made to the definition of libel adopted in the relevant state.

Whether or not any given statement is "capable of defamatory meaning" depends additionally on the entire circumstances in which the statement arises as well as the state whose law governs. For example, a New York court found that a statement identifying an attorney as a "flashy entertainment lawyer" was not, without more, defamatory. Likewise, in New York, allegations of drunkenness, use of "political clout" to gain governmental benefit, membership in the "Mafia," communist affiliation or that someone has cancer *may or may not* be defamatory, depending on the circumstances of the case.

In Illinois, a court found that even though an allegation that an employee made unauthorized phone calls amounted to an allegation of misconduct on the job, the statement was not, without more, defamatory, because the allegation did not amount to an indictable criminal offense punishable by imprisonment. On the other hand, an Illinois court did find defamatory the statement that an employee was selling illegal drugs at work.

In California, a court has held that it is defamatory *per se* to call someone a communist. Another California court, however, has cautioned that whether or not a statement is defamatory depends on the social climate at the time the statement is made. That court held that it was not defamatory in 1968 to say that someone was a member of the John Birch Society and an extremist, but implied that it would be defamatory to say that someone was a member of the Ku Klux Klan.

In Texas, a statement may be false, abusive and unpleasant without being defamatory. For example, a Texas court held that describing someone as resembling a "hard boiled egg," referring to baldness and pudginess, was not defamatory. Likewise, describing a political candidate as a "radical," "backed and financed by big-shot labor bosses" was not considered defamatory in Texas. On the other hand, an insinuation that a person is connected with gambling and prostitution was found to be defamatory. The assertion that a person who had made an allegation against another of child molestation had fabricated and since recanted the allegation was defamatory when no recantation had, in fact, been made.

2. Truth

A public official and a public figure and a private individual involved in a matter of public concern all will have to prove the statement is false in order to prevail on their libel claim. (The states are divided on whether and in what circumstances the private individual will have to prove falsity if the matter is not one of public concern.) While it is true that most libel plaintiffs will have to prove that the statement about which they complain is false, as a practical matter a libel defendant's best defense is that the statement is true. In most states, such as New York, truth is a complete and unconditional defense to a civil action for libel. In California a true statement is simply not actionable in defamation — even if published maliciously.

In New York, "substantial accuracy" is the test for truth or falsity. In California, proving "truth" requires proof that the substance or the sting of the defamatory charge is true. This does not require proof of the literal truth of every word in the publication.

In Texas, truth is considered an absolute privilege by Texas statute. Texas, too, employs the "substantial truth" test. In other words, the statements must not only be literally false, they must be substantially false — the alleged defamatory statement must be more damaging to the plaintiff's reputation, in the mind of the average listener, than a truthful statement would have been. If the gist of the statement is true or undisputed, variance with respect to matters of secondary importance can be disregarded.

Under the Illinois state constitution, truth is a defense to all actions for libel "when published with good motives and for justifiable ends." The "good motives" limitation would violate the U.S. Constitution, however, where a public figure is involved, but where a private individual is involved, it may still be valid.

3. Fault

As a matter of constitutional law, under Gertz v. Robert Welch, Inc. (1974), some showing of fault on the part of defendant is a predicate to any recovery in a defamation action. Accordingly, another defense available to any newspaper or reporter accused of libel is that they did not act with the requisite degree of fault. The level of "fault" that the plaintiff must prove will vary depending on who the plaintiff is. When determining fault, reference will be made to the standards of conduct generally adhered to in the circumstances.

Public Figures. If the plaintiff is a public figure or public official, the plaintiff must establish by clear and convincing evidence that the publication was made with actual malice. That is the rule of New York Times v. Sullivan (1964). Although "actual malice" is a constitutional requirement, states have, within the constitutional boundaries, developed their own ways of determining whether actual malice has been shown.

New York courts have thus stated that actual malice looks to the subjective state of mind of the publisher at the time of publication. It inquires into whether the publisher believed the statement was false or whether he published it with reckless disregard for its truth, or with awareness of a high probability that the statement was false. Generally speaking, it is difficult for a plaintiff to show that a newspaper published a story with actual malice.

In Texas, actual malice is the making of a statement with knowledge that it is false, or with "reckless disregard" of whether it is true. Reckless disregard means a high degree of awareness of probable falsity. To prove reckless disregard, the plaintiff must present sufficient evidence to permit the conclusion that the defendant entertained serious doubts as to the truth of the publication. Moreover, in Texas, malice cannot be inferred from the frequency of a publisher's criticism of a public official's performance, nor does the fact that statements are taken out of context establish actual malice.

In Illinois, the actual malice rule requires a libel plaintiff to show with convincing clarity that the defendant entertained serious doubts as to the truth of the publication. As one Illinois court stated, actual malice is shown only when a reporter's investigation "has revealed either insufficient information to support the allegations in good faith or information which creates substantial doubt as to the truth of published allegations." (*Wanless v. Rothballer, 115 Ill.2d 158, 508 N.E.2d 316, 332, 1986.*)

Private Individuals. The U.S. Supreme Court has not addressed the standard by which a newspaper's actions will be judged where the plaintiff is a private figure. Many state courts, however, have held that a negligence standard of liability applies. In Texas, if the plaintiff is not a public figure, then the newspaper defendant's standard will be judged by a negligence standard, i.e., whether the defendant should have known, through the exercise of reasonable care, that a statement was false when the defamatory matter is one of private concern.

New York, on the other hand, has held that if the plaintiff is a private individual involved in a matter of legitimate public concern, the plaintiff must establish by a preponderance of the evidence that the publication was made in a grossly irresponsible manner without due regard for the standards of information gathering and dissemination ordinarily followed by responsible parties involving similar matters. The focus in such a case is on objective standards, not the defendant's state of mind.

While there is a lot of subtle variation in this area of the law which concerns lawyers, the bottom line for reporters and editors is that if the plaintiff is a public figure or public official, the plaintiff will bear a high burden of proof in making out his claim. If the plaintiff is a private individual, however, who happens to be involved in a matter of legitimate public concern, the plaintiff's burden of proof may, in some states, be somewhat eased. If the claim is brought by a private individual not involved in matters of legitimate public concern, however, the burden of proof for the plaintiff will definitely be eased. Accordingly, there are more risks to publishing matters not of legitimate public concern about private individuals than to publishing matters that are of public concern, especially where they involve public figures or public officials.

Chapter 5

SUPREME COURT DECISIONS REGARDING LIBEL LAW

What follows is an overview of the First Amendment principles guiding the libel law. The constitutional trend here outlined has a direct impact on which of the aforementioned defenses newspaper libel defendants are most likely to have to rely.

In a series of decisions commencing in 1964, the Supreme Court established important First Amendment protections for the press in the libel area. But in more recent decisions, the tide has been running against the press. While the full impact of the later decisions is not yet clear, a review of the rulings since the mid-1960s shows the trend.

1. Public Officials and Public Figures

In The New York Times case, the Supreme Court ruled in March 1964 that public officials cannot recover damages for a report related to official duties unless they prove actual malice. To establish actual malice, the official was required to prove that at the time of publication, those responsible for the story knew it was false or published it with reckless disregard of whether it was true or false. The decision reversed two $500,000 libel verdicts returned in Alabama against The New York Times and four black ministers. The court said:

"The constitutional guarantees (the First and 14th Amendments) require, we think, a federal rule that prohibits a public official from recovering damages for a defamatory falsehood relating to his official conduct unless he proves that the statement was made with 'actual malice' — that is, with knowledge that it was false or with reckless disregard of whether it was false or not."

This does not give newspapers absolute immunity against libel suits by officials who are criticized. But it does mean that when a newspaper publishes information about a public official and publishes it without actual malice, it should be spared a damage suit even though some of the information may be wrong.

The court said it considered the case "against the background of a profound national commitment to the principle that debate on public issues should be uninhibited, robust and wide-open, and that it may well include vehement, caustic and sometimes unpleasantly sharp attacks on government and public officials."

The ruling in The New York Times case with respect to public officials was extended by the Supreme Court in June 1967 to apply also to public figures in The Associated Press v. Walker. In so holding, the court reversed a $500,000 libel judgment won by former Maj. Gen. Edwin A. Walker in a Texas state court against the AP.

The AP reported that Walker had "assumed command" of rioters at the University of Mississippi and "led a charge of students against federal marshals" when James H. Meredith was admitted to the university in September 1962. Walker alleged those statements to be false.

In ruling for the AP, the court found: "Under any reasoning, Gen. Walker was a public man in whose public conduct society and the press had a legitimate and substantial interest."

The rulings in The New York Times and The Associated Press cases were constitutional landmark decisions for freedom of the press and speech. They offered safeguards not previously defined. But they did not confer license for defamatory statements or for reckless disregard of the truth.

The Associated Press decision made an additional important distinction. In the context of a case with which The Associated Press case had been consolidated, the Supreme Court upheld an award granted to Wallace Butts, former athletic director of the University of Georgia, against Curtis Publishing Co. The suit was based on an article in the Saturday Evening Post accusing Butts of giving his football team's strategy secrets to an opposing coach prior to a game between the two schools.

The court found that Butts was a public figure, but said there was a substantial difference between the two cases. Justice Harlan said: "The evidence showed that the Butts story was in no sense 'hot news' and the editors of the magazine recognized the need for a thorough investigation of the serious charges. Elementary precautions were, nevertheless, ignored."

Justice Warren, in a concurring opinion, referred to "slipshod and sketchy investigatory techniques employed to check the veracity of the source." He said the evidence disclosed "reckless disregard for the truth."

The differing rulings in The Associated Press and the Saturday Evening Post cases should be noted carefully. The Associated Press-Walker case concerned "hot news"; the Saturday Evening Post-Butts story was investigative reporting of which journalists are doing more and more.

Extension of The New York Times rule in another case was based on a column by Drew Pearson which characterized a candidate for the United States Senate as "a former small-time bootlegger." The jury held that the accusation related to the private sector of the candidate's life. Reversing this judgment, the Supreme Court said: "We therefore hold as a matter of constitutional law that a charge of criminal conduct, no matter how remote in time or place, can never be irrelevant to an official's or a candidate's fitness for office for purposes of application of the 'knowing falsehood or reckless disregard' rule of New York Times v. Sullivan." (*Monitor Patriot v. Roy, 401 U.S. 265, 1971.*)

Another case was brought by a Chicago captain of detectives against Time magazine, which had quoted from a report of the U.S. Civil Rights Commission without making clear that the charges of police brutality were those of the complainant whose home was raided and not the independent findings of the commission. The court described the commission's documents as "bristling with ambiguities" and said that Time did not engage in a "falsification" sufficient to sustain a finding of actual malice. (*Time, Inc. v. Pape, 401 U.S. 279 , 1971.*)

The progression of The New York Times and The Associated Press cases was interrupted, however, in June 1974 with the Supreme Court's decision in the case of Gertz v. Robert Welch Inc. Gertz, a lawyer of prominence in Chicago, had been attacked in a John Birch Society publication as a communist. There were additional accusations as well. Gertz sued and won a libel verdict in his favor. The Supreme Court upheld the verdict, noting that he was neither a public official nor a public figure.

The Gertz decision opened the door to giving courts somewhat wider leeway in determining whether someone was a public person. This case also opened the way to giving state courts the right to assess what standard of liability should be used in testing whether a publication about a private individual is actionable. It insisted, however, that *some* degree of fault, at least negligence, be shown. As a result, some state courts have established a *negligence* standard (whether a reasonable person would have done the same thing as the publisher under the circumstances). The New York courts follow a *gross negligence* test when the matter published is of public concern. Others still observe the *actual malice* test in suits by private individuals against the press.

More recently, in the case Time v. Firestone, the Supreme Court again appears to have restricted the "public figure" and "public issue" standards. The case stemmed from Time magazine's account of the divorce of Russell and Mary Alice Firestone. The magazine said she had been divorced on grounds of "extreme cruelty and adultery." The court made no finding of adultery. She sued.

She was a prominent social figure in Palm Beach, Fla., and held press conferences in the course of the divorce proceedings. Yet the Supreme Court said she was not a public figure because "she did not assume any role of special prominence in the affairs of society, other than perhaps Palm Beach society, and she did not thrust herself to the forefront of any particular public controversy in order to influence resolution of the issues involved in it."

As in the Gertz case, the Firestone decision further cleared the way for increased application of a negligence standard — a standard less severe than the actual malice standard that was at the base of The New York Times v. Sullivan and The Associated Press v. Walker.

Supreme Court decisions, starting with Gertz and extending through Firestone and more recent cases, have consistently narrowed the class of people to be treated as public figures under the Times-Sullivan and AP-Walker standards.

Two 1979 rulings by the Supreme Court illustrate the narrowing of the protections that seemed so wide only a few years earlier:

Sen. William Proxmire of Wisconsin was sued for $8 million by Ronald Hutchinson, a research scientist who had received several public grants, including one for $50,000. Proxmire gave Hutchinson a "Golden Fleece" award, saying Hutchinson "has made a fortune from his monkeys and in the process made a monkey of the American taxpayer." Hutchinson sued. The Supreme Court found that despite the receipt of substantial public funds, Hutchinson was not a public figure. The court also ruled that Proxmire's news release was not protected by congressional immunity. (*Hutchinson v. Proxmire, 443 U.S. 111, 1979.*)

Ilya Wolston pleaded guilty in 1957 to criminal contempt for failing to appear before a grand jury investigating espionage. A book published in 1974 referred to these events. Wolston alleged that he had been libeled. In ruling on Wolston v. Reader's Digest, the Supreme Court said that he was not a public figure. The court said people convicted of crimes do not automatically become public figures. Wolston, the court said, was thrust into the public spotlight unwillingly.

In effect, the court extended the Firestone concept of *unwilling notoriety* to criminal as well as civil cases. Thus the pattern through Gertz, Firestone, Proxmire and Reader's Digest is clear. The New York Times rule has been left standing but it is slowly being whittled away by exceptions.

The Supreme Court is rejecting the notion that a person can be a public figure simply because of the events that led to the story at issue. The court is saying that public figure means people who seek the limelight, who inject themselves into public debate, etc. The court is saying that involvement in a crime, even a newsworthy one, does not make one a public figure.

This narrowing of the definition of who is a public figure also means that the broad protections that came out of The New York Times and The Associated Press cases apply to fewer numbers of the people who are written about in the news.

Moreover, the broad protections of "knowing falsity" and "reckless disregard of the truth" set out in The New York Times and The Associated Press cases are being replaced in state after state with simple negligence standards. In other words, the plaintiff, now adjudged to be a private citizen because of the recent rulings, need only prove that the press was negligent, not reckless.

The difference is more than semantic. This development suggests that press lawyers will be relying more on some of the old standbys as defenses — plaintiff's inability to prove falsity, privilege, fair comment — and this puts the ball right back with editors and reporters.

2. Private Figure/Public Concern

Fortunately, however, this trend has been at least partially abridged by the Supreme Court's decision in Philadelphia Newspapers v. Hepps. In that decision, the Court held that where a newspaper has published statements on a matter of public concern, even a private figure plaintiff cannot prevail without showing the statements at issue are false. This case provides that the common law rule requiring a defendant to prove truth is supplanted by a constitutional requirement that the plaintiff demonstrate falsity when the statements involved are of public concern.

3. Discovery

A 1979 Supreme Court ruling, Herbert v. Lando, meanwhile, has had a significant impact on what materials a libel plaintiff can compel a news organization to disclose. The case ruled that retired Army Lt. Col. Anthony Herbert, a Vietnam veteran, had the right to inquire into the editing process of a CBS "60 Minutes" segment, produced by Barry Lando, which provoked his suit. Herbert had claimed the right to do this so that he could establish actual malice.

The decision formalizes and calls attention to something that was at least explicit in The New York Times case: that a plaintiff had the right to try to prove the press was reckless or even knew that what it was printing was a lie. How else could this be done except through inquiry about a reporter's or editor's state of mind?

The ruling reminds plaintiffs' lawyers that they can do this. This, no doubt, may be responsible for far more of this kind of inquiry than the press has had to face before.

4. Summary Judgment

There was a footnote in the Proxmire case that has had a marked effect on the way libel cases are litigated. Footnote 9 questioned the practice of dismissing libel actions early in the course of litigation. The lower courts have paid serious attention to this footnote, with the result that more and more libel actions are being tried before a jury.

In a 1986 decision, Anderson v. Liberty Lobby, however, the Supreme Court held that summary judgment should be granted in libel actions against public officials and public figures unless the plaintiff can prove actual malice with "convincing clarity" or by "clear and convincing evidence." This rule should facilitate the early dismissal of unmeritorious claims without the expense and burden of proceeding to trial.

5. Opinion Privilege

More recently, in Milkovich v. Lorain Journal Co. (1990), the Supreme Court made clear that even statements of opinion may constitute libel if "sufficiently factual to be proven true or false." The Milkovich case therefore took away the opinion defense to libel that had been adopted by many lower courts. Although the decision did not alter the rules relating to public figures and events described above (for example, the requirement of actual malice), the case may lead to more jury trials in libel suits, particularly where the person bringing the suit is a private individual.

6. Damages

The huge jury verdicts that often result have caused much concern among legal commentators and the press. A number of remedies have been proposed, including statutory caps on both compensatory and punitive damages. A 1996 non-press Supreme

Court case, holding that some excessive damage verdicts might violate the Constitution, holds out some promise of relief.

An indication that the Supreme Court is facing this problem in the libel area appeared in its 1984 opinion in Bose v. Consumers Union. Bose Corp. sued Consumer Reports over its publication of disparaging comments concerning Bose's loudspeaker systems and obtained a damage judgment of about $211,000. The Court of Appeals, after a careful review of the record, reversed the judgment. The Supreme Court endorsed this process, underscoring the need for appellate courts in libel cases to make an independent review of the record — a standard of scrutiny that does not apply in most other appeals. For the foreseeable future, the press will continue to rely on the willingness of the appeals courts to overturn excessive jury verdicts.

SUMMARY OF FIRST AMENDMENT RULES

The gist of the principles established in the cases discussed above may be summarized as follows:

A. The Public Official Rule: The press enjoys a great protection when it covers the affairs of public officials. In order to successfully sue for libel, a public official must prove actual malice. This means the public official must prove that the editor or reporter had knowledge that the facts were false or acted with reckless disregard of the truth. (See Chapters 5 and 7).

B. The Public Figure Rule: The rule is the same for public figures and public officials. That is, a public figure must prove actual malice. The problem is that it is very difficult in many cases to predict who will be classified as a public figure. (See Chapters 5 and 7). In general, there are two types of public figures:

1. General Purpose Public Figure: This is an individual who has assumed the role of special prominence in the affairs of society and occupies a position of persuasive power and influence. An example is the entertainer Jay Leno.

2. Limited Purpose Public Figure: This is a person who has thrust himself or herself into the vortex of a public controversy in an attempt to influence the resolution of the controversy. An example would be a vocal scientist who has lectured and published articles in an attempt to influence a state legislature to ban fluoridation of water.

C. The Private Figure Rule: A private figure is defined in the negative: someone who is not a public figure. The rule of law for libel suits brought by private figures varies from state to state. The variations fall into three general categories:

1. A number of states follow the same rule for private figures and public figures. They require private figures to prove actual malice. These states include Alaska, Colorado, Indiana and New Jersey.

2. At least one state, New York, requires private figures to prove that the publisher acted in a "grossly irresponsible manner" when the matter published is of public concern.

3. Most states require private figures to prove only "negligence." Negligence is difficult to define. As a rule of thumb, a careless error on the part of the journalist could be found to constitute negligence.

Chapter 6
PUBLIC AND PRIVATE PLAINTIFFS

Determination of whether a plaintiff is a public figure plays a crucial role in determining the degree of fault the plaintiff will have to attribute (by proof) to the defendant. As it has been noted, the Supreme Court has, in recent years, narrowed its definition of who is a public figure. The party accused of committing libel will bear the burden of establishing whether the plaintiff is a public or a private figure. As with the rest of the law of libel, whether a plaintiff is a public figure or official varies from state to state.

1. Public Figures

In New York, a public figure is one who has thrust himself or herself into the vortex of a public issue or controversy or has taken affirmative steps to attract public attention. Public figures have included: candidates for public office; religious groups; a belly dancer; and a "stripper for God."

In Texas, a public figure is one who has assumed a role of prominence in the affairs of society. Texas courts generally ask three questions in order to determine whether someone is a limited purpose public figure: (1) is the controversy truly a public controversy? (i.e., (a) are people talking about the controversy *and* (b) are people other than those immediately involved in the controversy likely to feel the impact of its resolution?); (2) does the plaintiff have more than a trivial or tangential role in the controversy?; (3) is the alleged defamation *relevant* to the plaintiff's participation in the controversy? Under this standard, an abortion protester on a public street in the vicinity of an abortion clinic was considered a limited purpose public figure, as was a zoologist who appeared on television shows and gave interviews on his controversial work.

In California, a public figure is one who has voluntarily and actively sought, in connection with any matter of public interest, to influence resolution of the issues involved. At least one court in California has held that once one becomes a public figure, one retains that status "to the end of his days." For a limited purpose public figure, the public figure status generally continues as long as the specific issues for which public status was achieved continues.

A former city attorney who was also a civic leader and an attorney for a corporation organized to recall members of a city council was a public figure, under the California test. Others who have been found to be public figures have included: (1) a licensed clinical psychologist who conducted "nude marathon" group therapy sessions; (2) an author and television personality; (3) the founder of a well-known drug rehabilitation program; (4) a prominent and outspoken feminist author; (5) a candidate for city council; and (6) the owner, operator and manager of a radio station.

On the other hand, a public school teacher whose participation in public controversy did not exceed that which she was required to by school district regulations (except that she responded to media inquiries), was not a public figure in California. Similarly, a corporation which conducted a closeout sale for a landmark department store was not a public figure simply because it was doing business with a party to a controversy.

A note on corporations: In New York, the same standards that determine whether an individual is a public figure apply to corporations. In Texas, at least one court has asked three questions in order to determine whether a corporation is a public or a private figure: (1) what level of notoriety does the corporation enjoy among the average individuals in the relevant geographic area? (2) what is the nature of the corporation's business? and (3) what is the frequency and intensity of media scrutiny that the corporation normally receives? For example, a British corporation that did not deal in consumer goods and had not received significant past publicity was a private figure for the purposes of a libel claim.

2. Public Officials

In New York, public officials are those who are elected or appointed to office and who appear to have substantial responsibility for control over public and governmental affairs. Judges, police officers, state troopers and corrections officers have all been held to be public officials under this standard.

In Texas, the following criteria are relevant to determining whether a plaintiff is a public official: (1) the public interest in the public position held by the plaintiff; (2) the authority possessed by the plaintiff to act on behalf of a government entity; (3) the amount of governmental funds controlled by the plaintiff; (4) the number of employees the official supervises; (5) the amount of contact between the plaintiff and the public, and (6) the extent to which the plaintiff acts in a representative capacity for the governmental entity or has any direct dealings with the government.

Under this standard, (1) a county sheriff, (2) a Child Protective Services specialist with authority to investigate charges of child abuse, remove children from their homes and place them in foster care, (3) an undercover narcotics agent employed by the state's law enforcement agency, (4) a ranking officer in charge of a narcotics squad of four men, (5) an individual who was a high school athletic director, head football coach and teacher, and (6) an assistant regional administrator of a branch office of the Securities and Exchange Commission and even a part-time city attorney, have all been found to be public officials.

Under the same test, the following persons were found not to be public officials: (1) a high school teacher; (2) a prominent member of two private organizations affiliated with a state university; (3) a former special counsel for a court of inquiry into county fund management; (4) a court reporter; and (5) an appointed justice of the peace (where the article appeared in a city where plaintiff was not justice of the peace and did not refer to plaintiff's official capacity).

In California, a public official is one who has, or appears to the public to have, substantial responsibility for or control over the conduct of governmental affairs. In California, people found to be public officers have included a police officer, an assistant public defender, and an assistant district attorney.

As a final note, for the plaintiff to be considered a public official for purposes of a libel claim, the article will probably have to address, at some point, the plaintiff's official status and that status must be in some way relevant to the article.

Chapter 7
MISCELLANEOUS

1. Defamation of the Dead
Most states do not recognize a cause of action for defamation of the dead. Many states, do, however, permit an ongoing libel suit to continue after the death of the complaining person. For example, in New York no one can bring a cause of action for defamation of a deceased person unless they can demonstrate that their own reputation has been damaged by the defamation of the deceased. If the action is commenced before the plaintiff's death, however, it may be continued. Substantially, the same rules apply in California. In Texas, too, the libel claim will survive if filed before the plaintiff dies. In Illinois, in contrast, actions for defamation do not survive death of *either* party (i.e., plaintiff or defendant) regardless of whether the action had been commenced before the party's death.

2. Group Libel
Most states appear not to authorize actions for libel based on defamation of a group. In Illinois, for example, a court dismissed an action by nine members of a 23-lawyer defense team which team the defendant newspaper had described as "as craven a group of lawyers as I've seen." The case was dismissed because it did not include all the members of the defense team.

New York does not permit libel actions alleging defamation of a group. Rather, the plaintiff must be able to show that the comments respecting the group actually defame its individual members. Factors considered by courts making this determination include: (1) the size of the group; (2) the degree of organization of the group, and (3) the prominence of the group and its individual members.

In California, an individual plaintiff may not maintain an action for defamation directed against a class of persons to which he belongs, unless those to whom the communication is directed understand the communication as applying to the plaintiff. A California court has also commented that whether group libel actions are ever allowed is "highly questionable at best." Similarly, in Texas, an individual may not recover damages for defamation of a large group of which he or she is a member where nothing in the defamation singles out the plaintiff in particular.

Chapter 8
APPLYING THE RULES

We already have defined libel and explained the defenses available to the press. Let's now look at some applications.

In a society in which standards of right living are recognized by most people, any accusation that a member of society has violated such standards may be injurious. Members of a community establish in the minds of others an estimate of what they are believed to be. Injury to that reputation may mean business, professional or social ruin.

One court decision put the matter this way:

"The law of defamation is concerned only with injuries to one's reputation....

"Embarrassment and discomfort no doubt came to her from the publication, as they would to any decent woman under like circumstances. Her own reaction, however, has no bearing upon her reputation. That rests entirely upon the reactions of others. We are unable to find anything in this article which could appreciably injure plaintiff's reputation." (*Kimmerle v. New York Evening Journal Inc., 262 N.Y. 99*)

The traditional rule was that defamation was concerned only with injuries to one's reputation. That rule was altered in 1974 by the Gertz case, which held that emotional distress is also an element of damages in libel.

In order to be libelous, it is not necessary that a publication impute criminal activity. The following was held to be libelous:

"Pauper's Grave For Poor Child"

"Unless financial aid is forthcoming immediately, the body of a 4-year-old boy who was run over Tuesday will be interred in Potter's Field, burying ground of the homeless, friendless and penniless, who die or are killed in New York City. The parents of this youngster are in dire financial straits, and at this writing have no alternative but to let their son go to his final rest in a pauper's grave."

The court said:

"It is reasonably clear, therefore, that in some cases it may be a libel if the plaintiff has been written up as an object of pity .... The reason is that in libel the matter is defamatory not only if it brings a party into hatred, ridicule or contempt by asserting some moral discredit upon his part, but also if it tends to make him be shunned or avoided, although it imputes no moral turpitude to him." (*Katapodis v. Brooklyn Spectator Inc., 28 7 N.Y. 17*).

A publication that does not discredit a person as an individual may nonetheless damage a person's professional status.

A story stated that after a youth's body had been taken from the waters in which he had been swimming, he was pronounced dead by a doctor. Later the youth was revived. The doctor sued because of the implication that he had been unable to determine whether a person was living or dead.

Similarly, a publication may affect a business. Companies are naturally sensitive to news stories that reflect on their business prospects and practices. There have been many such news stories in the fields of environmental and consumer protection. The issues are complicated, and the legal aspects are not always clear. Formal charges and allegations should be reported precisely and fairly.

Likewise, there is no alternative to precision in reporting any criminal charge.

An essential element of an action for libel is that the complainant be identifiable to a third party. Nevertheless, the omission of names will not, in itself, provide a shield against a claim for libel. As was pointed out earlier, there may be enough details for the person to be recognizable.

A story may, by the use of a general description or name, make a charge capable of defamatory meaning against an organized group. It is possible that any member of the group could try to bring an action on the story.

In most states, the individual will have to be able to prove that the story is about the plaintiff, rather than the group as a whole. If the plaintiff succeeds, however, and the material is capable of defamatory meaning and not privileged, then the question turns to proof of truth and "fault."

Can the truth of the charge be established by documents, by testimony from trustworthy people or by material from privileged sources? It may not be enough to show that somebody gave you the unprivileged information. The issue turns on the truth of the charge itself and your investigation and attempts to verify the charge.

Another potential libel pitfall is the mistaken identity case, when, for example, a famous individual is confused with a person bearing a similar name who gets into a scrape. Petty thieves running afoul of the law may give the names of famous people — often old-time athletes — in the hope of getting leniency from a judge. If a newspaper reports that the famous person was arrested, the famous person may object to the report.

Another mistaken identity situation might arise when a non-famous person, John Doe, is arrested and is subsequently identified in news reports about the arrest as "John Doe, the high school teacher." If the John Doe who was arrested was really John Doe, the lawyer, and John Doe the high school teacher really exists, he probably will not be pleased with the news report.

Chapter 9
POINTS TO REMEMBER

When you have any concerns about any particular statement or opinion, the first question to ask is whether it is capable of defamatory meaning. Second, does it refer to a specific, identifiable individual? Third, do any privileges apply? Does the opinion privilege apply? What about the fair report privilege? Does the state recognize any other privilege? (e.g., one for fair comment and criticism of public officials? Or the neutral report privilege?) Fourth, is the individual identified a public figure or a public official? Fifth, is the topic of the article one of public concern? Finally, what investigation was done in the preparation of the article and what sources does the article rely on?

—Remember, once the AP has published a story, only a **KILL** transmitted on a wire can definitively remove copy that is problematic in terms of the paragraph above, or which contains other very serious errors. Remember also that a KILL can be applied to a portion of a story. It is not necessary to KILL an entire item simply to remove one paragraph of the story. The KILL can be applied to only a portion of the story.

—If a privilege applies, remember that the privilege does not remove the need for careful reporting and the use of editorial judgment. In many cases, courts have held that it is up to the jury to decide whether a particular publication was a fair and true report or whether there was "actual malice."

—Remember to be careful of descriptive phrases that may give rise to cases of mistaken identity. A report that "an elderly janitor for a local school" was arrested could lead to suits from every elderly janitor in the school district.

—Remember that the fact that police are questioning someone about a crime does not necessarily justify the label *suspect*. Witnesses are obviously also questioned about a crime. Additionally, depending on the circumstances, the fact that a detective tells you that someone is a suspect will not always be privileged as a fair report. For example, several of the news organizations which reported that an individual was considered a suspect in planting the bomb that exploded in Atlanta during the 1996 Olympic Games have been sued by the man.

—Pictures and captions must be as accurate and objective as news stories. Pictures and their captions can also give rise to a claim of libel.

CHAPTER 10

PROCEDURES FOR HANDLING KILLS AND CORRECTIVES

This chapter summarizes how to make critical corrections to stories that have already moved, and how to remove them completely or temporarily from the news report if needed. We use KILLS, ELIMINATIONS, WITHHOLDS, CORRECTIVES and CLARIFICATIONS in these cases. The rules for the use of these items are more complex than for ordinary corrections,

which are described in the Filing Practices section of this Stylebook.

The General Desk in New York or the deputy managing editor/administration must approve a KILL, ELIMINATION, CORRECTIVE or CLARIFICATION before it is filed. The New York Photo Desk must be consulted for photo problems.

In many cases, the story involved may have been transmitted over more than one service. Any corrective action must be taken on all services where the story moved.

1. WITHHOLDS, ELIMINATIONS, and KILLS

ELIMINATIONS AND KILLS are used to permanently remove from the wire

material that is still "alive" -- usually, copy that has been transmitted in the current 24-hour cycle. For material transmitted in a previous cycle, use a CORRECTIVE or CLARIFICATION.

An **ELIMINATION** advises an AP member not to use a story at all in its publication and to remove it from its Web site. It may be used when the entire basis of the story is found to be wrong.

KILLS have the same effect as eliminations, but are used on stories with very serious errors or that are potentially libelous. A KILL informs a member that the story, or part of a story, must not be used. When a story needs to be removed from the wire for legal reasons, use a KILL rather than an ELIMINATION.

WITHHOLDS are used to temporarily remove from the report a story that may or may not be incorrect, and which we're in the process of checking.

If the check finds that the story was correct as originally filed, an advisory canceling the WITHHOLD and releasing the story can be filed.

If, while the story is withheld, we obtain information that would change the story slightly, an advisory should be filed noting the changes. The advisory should be followed quickly with a writethru incorporating the changes.

If the story is found to be substantially in error or potentially libelous, the WITHHOLD should be followed by an ELIMINATION or a KILL.

2. FORMATS FOR WITHHOLDS, ELIMINATIONS and KILLS

For print and online services, Workbench templates and the formats below should be used. For broadcast services, follow broadcast style.

Datelines on withholds, eliminations and kills should be the same as on the original stories. Withholds, eliminations and kills should carry the same category code as the original story (*a* for national news stories, *n* for state news stories, *s* for sports, etc.).

WITHHOLDS, ELIMINATIONS and KILLS should be filed to print, broadcast and online sites at the same time.

WITHHOLDS

The form for a WITHHOLD is:
^BC-Gold Find, WITHHOLD, a0680
^WITHHOLD<
DENVER — Withhold BC-Gold Find, a0680. Authorities say the miner's story has been questioned.
^The AP<

The form to release a story that has previously been WITHHELD is:
^BC-Gold Find, WITHHOLD ADVISORY, a0680
^WITHHOLD ADVISORY<
DENVER — The story BC-Gold Find, filed as a0680, is available for use. The miner's story has been confirmed. (Or: The story BC-Gold, filed as a0680, has been confirmed. A new version with additional information will be sent shortly.)
^The AP<

ELIMINATIONS

The form for an ELIMINATION for print and online wires is:

^BC-Practical Joke, ELIMINATION, a0240
^BULLETIN ELIMINATION<
BOSTON — Eliminate BC-Practical Joke, a0240. It cannot be confirmed.
^The AP<

On print wires, but NOT on online wires, follow the BULLETIN ELIMINATION immediately with an advisory. State whether a substitute story is planned:

^BC-Practical Joke, ELIMINATION Advisory, a0240
Editors: The BOSTON story about the practical joke, a0240, has been eliminated. It cannot be confirmed.
A sub story will be filed shortly. (Or: No sub will be filed.)
^The AP<

KILLS

A KILL should say succinctly what was wrong with the original story -- for example, "Smith was charged with robbery, not murder." Do not make any legal conclusions in the KILL - e.g., "the story is potentially libelous" - when transmitting the KILL.

The form for a KILL:

^BC-Smith Charged, KILL, a0720
^BULLETIN KILL<
NEW YORK — Kill BC-Smith Charged, a0720. Smith was charged with robbery, not murder.
^The AP<

If only part of a story is killed, it should be followed by a writethru, eliminating the offending paragraph. The form for a partial kill is:

^BC-Smith Charged, KILL, a0720
^BULLETIN KILL<
NEW YORK — Kill graf 7 of BC-Smith Charged, a0720. Smith was not convicted last year of armed robbery.
^The AP<

On print wires, but NOT on online wires, follow the KILL immediately with an advisory. State whether a substitute story is planned:

^BC-Smith Charged, KILL Advisory, a0720
^Editors:<
The New York story BC-Smith Charged, a0720, has been killed. Smith was charged with robbery, not murder.
A kill is mandatory.
Make certain the story is not published.
A substitute story will be filed shortly. (Or: No substitute story will be filed.)
^The AP<

Repeat the kill advisory approximately 12 hours later:

^BC-Smith Charged, KILL Advisory<
^Editors:
The New York story BC-Smith Charged, filed Monday as a0720, has been killed. Smith was charged with robbery, not murder.
A kill is mandatory.
Make certain the story is not published.
A substitute story was filed as a0741, slugged BC-Smith Charged, 2nd Ld-Writethru. (Or: No substitute story was filed.)
^The AP

If a substitute story is filed, mark it as the next lead-writethru to the previous story. Include a nonpublishable editor's note advising that it replaces an earlier story that was KILLED.

The form is:

^BC-Smith Charged, 4th Ld-Writethru,
^Eds: SUBS 7th graf pvs, which was killed, to CORRECT that Smith was charged last year with armed robbery but was not convicted. No pickup.<

3. DISREGARDS
Use a DISREGARD to advise members of material sent inadvertently, including old stories, duplicate stories and copy not meant for online or print wires. The advisory should say why the material should be disregarded.

The form:

^BC-Turkey-Quake Survivors, DISREGARD, a0704,
^Editors:
Disregard BC-Turkey-Quake Survivors, a0704. The story moved in a previous cycle. (Or: The material is not intended for use in this service.)
^The AP<

4. CORRECTIVES and CLARIFICATIONS
A CORRECTIVE is a publishable story that acknowledges an error in a story and sets the record straight.

Do not be hasty in transmitting a CORRECTIVE. When you take the step of transmitting a CORRECTIVE, it is important to ensure that the correction is actually warranted, that it corrects all aspects of the story that may need correction and that the correction itself is accurate.

Transmission of a CORRECTIVE does not necessarily safeguard the AP against legal action. In fact, transmission of a CORRECTIVE may itself have legal consequences because it formally acknowledges an error.

You should be aware of any legal requirement in your state setting a time within which a correction must appear.

CORRECTIVES and CLARIFICATIONS should identify the previous incorrect story by slug, transmission number and date. They should carry the dateline and category code of the original story. For print and online services, use Workbench templates and the formats below. For broadcast services, follow broadcast style.

The format for a corrective:

^BC-Fed-Indictments, CORRECTIVE
^Eds: Members who used a0620, BC-Fed-Indictments, sent Oct. 22 under a New York dateline, are asked to use the following story.<

NEW YORK (AP) — In an Oct. 22 story about federal indictments of city officials, The Associated Press reported erroneously the name of one of those indicted. The correct name is Joseph Arnold, not John Arnold.

The proper form for a CORRECTIVE story often will be the straightforward statement that a previous AP report contained an error. However, where the AP did not originate the error, the CORRECTIVE should make that clear. For instance, "The Associated Press, quoting state police, on Tuesday identified a man charged with embezzlement as Reginald Smith. The correct name of the man charged was Robert Smith."

When the original story cited a member as a source, consult with the member. We will usually cite the member in the corrective. If the original story used member material as a source but did not attribute it to the member, we sometimes handle the corrective as if the AP itself made the error. Consult local or New York news managers if necessary.

CLARIFICATIONS

A clarification is a publishable story used to clarify or expand upon a previous story which, while factually correct, may be unfair or subject to misinterpretation.

A clarification must NOT be used as a substitute for a kill or a corrective. The clarification is used to provide background or detail in the interest of clarity or fairness. It is not used to correct factual errors in copy.

The format:

^BC-Air Fares, CLARIFICATION, a0710

^Eds: Members who used BC-Air Fares, a0710 of May 8, may wish to use the following, which explains that not all fares on domestic flights are subject to change.<

WASHINGTON (AP) _ In a story May 8, The Associated Press reported that fares on domestic flights will increase beginning in April. Fares will increase for flights in the continental United States, but not for flights to Hawaii and Alaska.

5. Sending KILLS, ELIMINATIONS, WITHHOLDS, CORRECTIVES AND CLARIFICATIONS

Every KILL, ELIMINATION, WITHHOLD, CORRECTIVE and CLARIFICATION must be sent to the same services as the original story. To ensure that distribution is complete, the news editor in charge of the bureau or desk where the problem arose should fully advise the General Desk of all services to which the original item was sent.

The General Desk, Broadcast News Center, AP Digital, Graphics and Photos are responsible for ensuring that these items are filed wherever necessary in their services.

6. Report Requirements

Any time that a kill or corrective is filed, the bureau chief or news editor must prepare and maintain a file containing the following:

1. Wire copy of the original story and of the KILL and ELIMINATION that was sent. Include material transmitted on broadcast.

2. Wire copy of the substitute story, CORRECTIVE or CLARIFICATION filed.

3. A copy of any source material used by the writer or editor in preparation of the story, including member clip, reporter's notes and the like.

In addition, a factual letter stating why the story was KILLED or ELIMINATED should be sent to the deputy managing editor. This statement should be prepared either by the bureau chief or the news editor, in consultation with the staff members involved. If legal action is a possibility, this explanation should not be prepared without prior consultation with the deputy managing editor.

The letter should include relevant details not covered above, such as any contact with outsiders on the matter.

The letter should be a factual report of what happened. It is not the place for extraneous comments about staff members or bureau procedures. Nor is it the place for apologies, nor any legal or factual speculation or conclusions.

Do not make any response to any letter or other communication in connection with any case where legal action seems possible, especially if a lawyer is involved, without first consulting the deputy managing editor.

CHAPTER 11

ACCESS TO PLACES AND INFORMATION

1. The First Amendment Right of Access
Courtrooms - Criminal Proceedings

In 1980, in Richmond Newspapers v. Virginia, the Supreme Court ruled that, under the First Amendment, criminal trials are presumptively open to the public and the media and may be closed only when it is necessary to protect some interest that outweighs the interest in access. A trial judge must articulate findings, on the record, to support any closure. This decision marked the first time in the nation's history that the right to find out what a branch of government is doing had been afforded direct and specific constitutional protection.

In 1982, in Globe Newspapers v. Superior Court, the Supreme Court recognized that the constitutional right of access to criminal trials applies even with respect to a sex-offense trial involving a victim who is a minor. The court struck down a statute mandating closure in such cases. While it said that the states have a significant interest in protecting minors who are victims of sexual assault from the trauma of testifying in open court, the Supreme Court held that trial judges must determine on a case-by-case basis whether this interest outweighs the presumption of openness and stated that any closure order must be "narrowly tailored to protect that interest" without unduly infringing on First Amendment rights.

The Supreme Court further held in 1984 in Press-Enterprise v.

Superior Court that the constitutional right of access to criminal trials encompasses the right to attend jury selection.

In 1986, in a second case, called Press-Enterprise v. Superior Court, the Supreme Court ruled that the First Amendment right of access attaches to preliminary hearings in a criminal case unless specific findings are made on the record to demonstrate that closure is essential to preserve higher values and is narrowly tailored to serve that interest. If the interest asserted is the defendant's right to a fair trial, the preliminary hearing may not be closed unless there is a "substantial probability" that the right to a fair trial will be prejudiced by publicity that closure would prevent and that reasonable alternatives to closure cannot adequately protect the right to a fair trial.

The AP has distributed the following statement to be read in court by its reporters when confronted with an attempt to close a criminal proceeding.

The statement allows the reporter, when permitted to address the court, to state the basic press position and to seek time for counsel to appear to make the legal argument.

The following statement can be read verbatim, although if any parts are not applicable to a specific case, they can be changed or omitted.

> May it please the Court, I am (name) of The Associated Press (or newspaper). I respectfully request the opportunity to register on the record an objection to the motion to close this proceeding to the public and to representatives of the news media. The Associated Press (or newspaper) requests a hearing at which its counsel may present to the court legal authority and arguments that closure in this case is improper.
>
> The United States Supreme Court has now firmly held that the press and the public have a constitutional right to attend criminal trials and pretrial proceedings and may not be excluded unless the court makes findings on the record that closure is required to preserve higher values and is narrowly tailored to serve those values. There is, therefore, a presumption of openness which is firmly rooted in the Constitution and essential to proper functioning of the criminal justice system.
>
> The Associated Press (or newspaper) takes the position that the defendant should be required to make the following showing in order to prevail on a motion to close this proceeding:
>
> First, the defendant must demonstrate that by conducting this proceeding in public the defendant's right to a fair trial will be prejudiced by publicity which closure would prevent. The defendant must demonstrate therefore that disclosures made in this hearing will prejudice the case and that these disclosures would not otherwise be brought to the attention of potential jurors.

Second, the defendant must demonstrate that none of the alternatives to an order closing this proceeding would effectively protect the right to a fair trial. Among the alternatives available to protect the defendant's rights are: a careful and searching voir dire, continuance, severance, change of venue, peremptory challenges, sequestration and admonition of the jury.

Third, the defendant must demonstrate that closure will be effective in protecting the right to a fair trial. In the present case there has already been substantial publicity concerning the facts. The defendant must demonstrate that any prejudice to the right of a fair trial would result from publicity given to disclosures made in this proceeding, and not to previously published facts or allegations.

Finally, the defendant must establish that reasonable alternatives to closure cannot adequately protect the defendant's fair trial rights.

The Associated Press (or newspaper) believes that there has been substantial public interest generated by this case. The public has a right to be informed of future developments, and the court should avoid any impression that justice is being carried on in secrecy. The public has a right to know how the court system is handling criminal matters, what kind of deals may be struck by prosecutors and defense lawyers, what kind of evidence may be kept from the jury, and what sort of police or prosecutorial acts or omissions have occurred. For these reasons, The Associated Press (or newspaper) objects to the motion for closure and respectfully requests a hearing in which it can present full legal arguments and authority.

Courtrooms - Civil Proceedings

The Supreme Court has never addressed the question of whether there is a First Amendment right of access to civil trials and pretrial proceedings. Several federal appeals courts, employing the reasoning of the Supreme Court's criminal trial access decisions, have ruled that both civil trials and pretrial proceedings are presumptively open to the press and public.

Court Documents

Both the First Amendment and state and federal common law also provide a right of access to various court documents, like the complaint, the answer, motions and legal briefs. There are, however, reasons that a judge may legitimately WITHHOLD a particular court document from the public. What is important to remember in this context, however, is that the *presumption* is that the press and the public have the right to access the document. In the absence of a statute directing that the document be kept confidential (as in most matrimonial actions), the Court must have a legitimate reason for keeping the document confidential.

2. The Freedom of Information Act (FOIA)

The federal Freedom of Information Act, originally passed by Congress in 1966 and amended periodically since, allows any citizen or any foreign national resident in the United States to request any records from the executive branch of the federal government.

It does not cover Congress or the federal courts or state or local governments. All Cabinet agencies, independent agencies, regulatory commissions and government-owned corporations are covered.

The president and his immediate staff are exempt but the Executive Office of the president and the Office of the Management and Budget are covered.

Records include all documents, papers, reports, and letters in the government's possession. The term "record" also has been ruled to cover films, photographs, sound recordings and computer tapes, but not physical objects that cannot be reproduced.

A 1996 law expanded the FOIA to require federal agencies, whenever possible, to share data in a specific format, such as on computer diskette or CD-ROM. The Electronic FOIA also broadened citizen access to government by placing more information online.

There are nine exemptions in the act that agencies may — but are not obliged to — claim as a basis for withholding records. Those exemptions have generated voluminous litigation.

Different agencies have responded in different ways to FOIA requests based on issues ostensibly already settled in court.

If you want an item, ask for it. Let the government decide whether it has any grounds or willingness to deny your request. Even an exempt document can be released at the government's discretion.

Because of the various exemptions and a lack of manpower assigned to implement the act, there are often long delays in getting documents, which often contain large blacked-out portions.

Here are a few elementary steps, among many available, that might help avoid those problems:

—Call the public information office of the federal agency you believe has the records before filing your request to make sure you have the right agency and the right address for filing it. Ask them whether they will release what you are seeking without FOIA request.

—Be as specific as possible about what you want. Give the dates, titles, authors and addresses for document and letters if you know them. In your letter, provide your telephone number and offer to supply any other information which might help narrow the search.

—Even if you are using the letterhead stationery of a news organization, state specifically that you are a reporter for that organization and plan to use the material in news stories. The act does not require you to state your purpose, but disclosures in the public interest are eligible for fee waivers, exemption waivers and in some cases expedited handling.

—Request a waiver of search and copying fees. In case the

waiver is denied, set a limit on the amount you will pay, such as $100, without the agency's obtaining your prior, specific consent.

—If you want field office files checked as well as those at head-quarters, be sure to specifically request that. Some agencies, such as the FBI, will not do that unless asked.

—Request that the agency cite specific exemptions for each item or portion of an item if it decides to deny any part of the re-quested release.

—If your initial request is denied, file an administrative appeal. Some agencies take a very different view on appeal. The denial let-ter will specify to whom the appeal must be sent.

—In appeal letters, argue the case for public benefit from dis-closure; several exemptions request a balancing effort between pri-vacy and public interests, and appellate reviewers may be more likely to exercise their right to waive an exemption if a good case is made.

These are only a few examples of the steps that will improve your chances of success. You may want to consult FOIA experts or manuals before proceeding.

An FOI Service Center is maintained by The Reporters Com-mittee for Freedom of the Press, 1735 Eye Street, N.W., Suite 504, Washington, D.C. 20006. The committee publishes a 32-page pamphlet with sample FOIA letters and appeal forms as well as analyses of the act. The committee also maintains a toll-free hot-line (1-800-F-FOI-AID), 24 hours a day, seven days a week, with attorneys available to provide FOIA advice.

The U.S. Department of Justice publishes an annual "Freedom of Information Case List" which reviews recent cases, contains up-to-date copies of the relevant statutes and, most important, the "Justice Department Guide to the FOIA," which gives the current government understanding of what is covered and not covered by each exemption. This document, published each September, is available for purchase from the Superintendent of Documents, U.S. Government Printing Office, Washington, D.C. 20402.

Another view of current law on each exemption as well as a step-by-step guide to the process, with sample request and appeal letters, is contained in "Litigation Under the Federal Freedom of Information Act and Privacy Act," 14th edition, edited by Allan Adler and published by The American Civil Liberties Union Foun-dation. Individual copies are available for $40 from: Publications Department, American Civil Liberties Union Foundation, 122 Maryland Avenue, N.E., Washington, D.C. 20002.

It is advisable to check on specific state freedom of information laws.

Each individual state also has its own freedom of information laws that apply to state and local government agencies.

Chapter 12
THE RIGHT OF PRIVACY

The right of privacy is a doctrine that has been developing in the past century. Its roots are often traced to an article entitled, "The Right to Privacy," which appeared in the Harvard Law Review in 1890, and was co-authored by Louis D. Brandeis, who later became a Supreme Court justice. The article asserted, "The press is overstepping in every direction the obvious bounds of propriety and decency." The article argued that these excesses ought to be deterred through the recognition of a distinct cause of action that would protect the individual's "right of privacy." As a Supreme Court justice, Brandeis later wrote:

"The makers of our Constitution undertook to secure conditions favorable to the pursuit of happiness. They recognized the significance of man's spiritual nature, of his feelings and of his intellect. They knew that only a part of the pain, pleasure and satisfactions of life are to be found in material things. They sought to protect Americans in their beliefs, their thoughts, their emotions and their sensations. They conferred, as against the government, the right to be let alone — the most comprehensive of rights and the right most valued by civilized men." (*Olmstead v. United States*, 277 *U.S.* 438, 478, Brandeis, J. dissenting.)

Since the writing of the article, innumerable legal commentators have debated whether such a cause of action ought to be recognized at all. From this debate, four distinct forms of the "right of privacy" cause of action have arisen: (1) misappropriation of name or likeness for commercial purpose; (2) public disclosure of private facts; (3) unreasonable intrusion upon seclusion; and (4) false light in the public eye. In recent times, these causes of action have taken on significance to the press as plaintiffs have attempted to avoid the heavy burdens of proof placed on the libel plaintiff by alleging an invasion of a form of the right of privacy, instead.

1. Misappropriation of Name or Likeness
The first form of invasion of privacy recognized by the courts was misappropriation of the name or likeness of a living person for purposes of trade or advertising without that person's consent. In recent years, some states have included voice as well as name or likeness. The First Amendment does provide for at least some exceptions to such a right of privacy — as where a candidate for public office includes his opponent's name and likeness in campaign advertisements.

2. Public Disclosure of Private Facts
Generally speaking, a claim for public disclosure of private facts complains about (1) publicity, (2) which the reasonable person would find highly offensive, (3) concerning private information about the plaintiff. Some states also require that the information

published not concern or relate to a legitimate public interest. The states that recognize this cause of action generally make exceptions for public figures and for persons involved in matters of public concern. In 1967, however, the Supreme Court held that the First Amendment "command[s] nothing less than that states may not impose sanctions for the publication of truthful information contained in official records for public inspection." (*Cox Broadcasting Corp. v. Cohn, 420 U.S. 469, 1975*.) So, at least to the extent that the private facts are a matter of public record, no cause of action for public disclosure will lie.

3. Intrusion Upon Seclusion

A claim for unreasonable intrusion upon seclusion alleges that a defendant intentionally committed an unreasonable and highly offensive intrusion upon another's interest in solitude or seclusion, either as to the plaintiff's physical person or the plaintiff's private affairs or concerns. Intrusion claims commonly arise in three contexts: (1) surreptitious surveillance; (2) trespass of property, and (3) instances where consent to enter a private setting for one purpose has been exceeded (as where a reporter gains access to information under false pretenses).

Although plaintiffs have often complained about a picture of them that was taken, if the picture was taken in a public place, there will generally be no cause of action for intrusion. If the picture is taken in or around the plaintiff's home, however, the plaintiff may have a cause of action for intrusion. This cause of action has been raised recently and with increasing frequency by plaintiffs who are photographed or videotaped by news agencies accompanying on-duty police officers.

Recently, the family of a health care corporation executive successfully obtained an injunction against the elaborate efforts of a particular news organization to obtain information about the family. In this case the court held, "[c]onduct that amounts to a persistent course of hounding, harassment and unreasonable surveillance, even if conducted in a public or semi-public place, may nevertheless rise to the level of invasion of privacy based on intrusion upon seclusion."

4. False Light

A claim for false light basically complains about publicity that places the plaintiff in a false light in the public eye. Some states hold that the publicity must be of a kind that would be highly offensive to a reasonable person. One form in which such a claim occasionally arises occurs where an opinion or utterance is falsely attributed to the plaintiff. In another version of the claim, plaintiff's picture is used to illustrate an article to which he has no reasonable connection, as where the picture of an honest taxi driver is used to illustrate an article about the cheating propensities of cab drivers.

The Supreme Court of the United States ruled in January 1967 that the constitutional guarantees of freedom of the press are applicable to claims for invasion-of-privacy by false light involving reports of newsworthy matters. The ruling arose out of a reversal by the Supreme Court of a decision of a New York court that an article with photos in Life magazine reviewing a play, "The Desperate Hours," violated the privacy of a couple who had been held hostage in a real-life incident. In illustrating the article, Life posed the actors in the house where the real family had been held captive.

The family alleged violation of privacy by false light in the public eye, saying the article gave readers the false impression that the play was a true account of their experiences. Life said the article was "basically truthful."

The court said:

"The line between the informing and the entertaining is too elusive for the protection of [freedom of the press]. Erroneous statement is no less inevitable in such case than in the case of comment upon public affairs, and in both, if innocent or merely negligent, it must be protected if the freedoms of expression are to have the 'breathing space' that they 'need to survive.'

"We create grave risk of serious impairment of the indispensable service of a free press in a free society if we saddle the press with the impossible burden of verifying to a certainty the facts associated in a news article with a person's name, picture or portrait, particularly as related to non-defamatory matter."

The court added, however, that these constitutional guarantees do not extend to "knowing or reckless falsehood." A newspaper still may be liable for invasion of privacy if the facts of a story are changed deliberately or recklessly, or "fictionalized." As with The New York Times and The Associated Press decisions in the field of libel, "The Desperate Hours" case does not confer a license for defamatory statements or for reckless disregard of the truth.

5. State Recognition of the Right to Privacy

States vary widely both in terms of their acceptance of any of these right to privacy claims and in terms of the rules governing any such claims. Of the four forms of the "privacy" cause of action, New York only recognizes the claim for misappropriation of name or likeness for commercial purposes. Texas recognizes claims for intrusion upon seclusion, public disclosure of private facts and misappropriation of name or likeness for commercial purposes. The California state constitution recognizes the right of privacy and California therefore recognizes all four forms of the right of privacy cause of action. Although there is some disagreement among Illinois courts regarding whether to recognize the tort of intrusion upon seclusion, it can be generally said that Illinois, too, recognizes all four forms of the right of privacy.

In light of the development of the right of privacy, it can be generally said that when people become involved in a news event, voluntarily or involuntarily, they forfeit the right to privacy. Similarly, a person somehow involved in a matter of legitimate public interest, even if not a bona fide spot news event, normally can be written about with safety.

However, this is different from publication of a story or picture that dredges up the sordid details of a person's past and has no current newsworthiness. Paul P. Ashley, then president of the Washington State Bar Association, said in a talk on this subject at a meeting of The Associated Press Managing Editors Association:

"The essence of the wrong will be found in crudity, in ruthless exploitation of the woes or other personal affairs of private individuals who have done nothing noteworthy and have not by design or misadventure been involved in an event which tosses them into an arena subject to public gaze."

6. Examples

Here are details of a few cases brought in the name of right of privacy:

—In a case against a Chicago newspaper, an Illinois trial court held that a mother had stated a cause of action for invasion of privacy where she alleged that she told the newspaper reporter that she did not want to make any public statement about her son's death and where the reporter nevertheless remained in the private hospital room with the mother, recorded her grief-stricken last words to her son and subsequently published a picture of the son's dead body and the mother's "last words" to her son.

—A leading case centering on publication of details of a person's past concerned a man who, as a child prodigy in 1910, had attracted national attention. In 1937, The New Yorker magazine published a biographical sketch of the "child prodigy" in his adult years. He alleged invasion of privacy by public disclosure of private facts.

The court said "he had cloaked himself in obscurity but his subsequent history, containing as it did the answer to the question of whether or not he had fulfilled his early promise, was still a matter of public concern. The article ... sketched the life of an unusual personality, and it possessed considerable popular news interest."

The court said further:

"We express no comment on whether or not the newsworthiness of the matter printed will always constitute a complete defense. Revelations may be so intimate and so unwarranted in view of the victim's position as to outrage the community's notions of decency. But when focused upon public characters, truthful comments upon dress, speech, habits, and the ordinary aspects of personality will usually not transgress this line. Regrettably or not, the misfortunes and frailties of neighbors and 'public figures' are subjects of considerable interest and discussion to the rest of the population. And when such are the mores of the community, it would be unwise for a court to bar their expression in the newspapers, books, and magazines of the day."

—The unsavory incidents of the past of a former prostitute, who had been tried for murder, acquitted, married and lived a respectable life, were featured in a motion picture. She sued for invasion of privacy by public disclosure of private facts. The court ruled that the use of her name in the picture and the statement in advertisements that the story was taken from true incidents in her life violated her right to pursue and obtain happiness.

Some courts have ruled that a person who is recognizable in a picture of a crowd in a public place is not entitled to the right of privacy, but if the camera singled him out for no news-connected reason, then his privacy might be invaded.

Another example of spot news interest: A child was injured in an auto accident in Alabama. A newspaper took a picture of the scene before the child was removed and ran it. That was spot news. Twenty months later a magazine used the picture to illustrate an article. The magazine was sued for public disclosure of private facts and lost the case, the court ruling that 20 months after the accident the child was no longer "in the news."

In another case, a newspaper photographer in search of a picture to illustrate a hot weather story took a picture of a woman sitting on her front porch. She wore a house dress, her hair in curlers, her feet in thong sandals. The picture was taken from a car parked across the street from the woman's home. She sued, charging invasion of privacy by intrusion upon seclusion and public disclosure of private facts. A court, denying the newspaper's motion for dismissal of the suit, said the scene photographed "was not a particularly newsworthy incident," and the limits of decency were exceeded by "surreptitious" taking and publishing of pictures "in an embarrassing pose."

Chapter 13
COPYRIGHT GUIDELINES

Copyright is the right of authors to control the reproduction and use of their creative expressions that have been fixed in tangible form. The types of creative expression eligible for copyright protection include literary, graphic, photographic, audiovisual, electronic and musical works. In this context, "tangible forms" range from film to computer disks to material posted on the Internet. Personal letters or diaries may be protected by copyright even though they may not have been published and may not contain a copyright notice.

Not all uses of copyright material constitute infringement. The broadest limitation on the reach of copyright law is that *ideas and facts are never protected by a copyright*. Rather, the copyright pertains only to the literary, musical, graphic or artistic form in which an author expresses intellectual concepts.

This page can show the distinction between protected expression and nonprotected ideas and facts. Despite the copyright protecting this page, a subsequent author is free to report the facts it contains. The subsequent author may not, however, employ the same or essentially the same combination of words, structure, and tone, which comprises the expression of those facts.

While copyright generally prohibits the use of another's protected expression, the doctrine of "fair use" permits, in certain circumstances, the use of copyright material without its author's permission.

To determine whether a particular use is fair, courts are required to evaluate and balance such factors as: (1) the purpose of the use; (2) the nature of the copyright work that is used; (3) the amount and substantiality of the portion used in relation to the copyright work as a whole; and (4) the effect of the use upon the potential value of the copyright work.

News reporting, criticism, and comment are favored purposes under the fair-use doctrine, but "scooping" a copyright holder's first use of previously unpublished material is not. Note, though, that "purpose" is only one of the fair-use factors. Thus, a use for a proper purpose may nevertheless constitute an infringement if other factors weigh against that use's being fair.

Here are some general guidelines:

First, fair use is more likely to be found if the copyrighted work is informational rather than fictional.

Second, fair use is more likely to be found if the copyrighted work is published as opposed to unpublished.

Third, the greater the amount of the copyrighted work used, the less likely that a court will characterize the use as fair. The use of an entire copyrighted work is almost never fair. Size alone, however, is not decisive; courts have found uses not to be fair when the portion used was small but so important that it went to the heart of the copyrighted work.

Fourth, uses that decrease any potential market for the copyrighted work tend not to be fair. For instance, if a literary critic reproduces all five lines of a five-line poem, the potential market for the poem will be diminished because any reader of the critic's piece can also obtain a copy of the poem for free.

The First Amendment provides no greater right to use copyrighted materials than those provided by the copyright law. Moreover, proper attribution cannot transform an infringing use into a fair one.

In using copyright material in a news story or column, writers should make sure that no more of a copyrighted work than is necessary for a proper purpose is used, and that the work is not used in a way that impairs its value.

It is always possible to obtain permission from the copyright holder. Reporters and editors having questions about whether their use in a news story or column of copyright material is a fair use should review these factors. No mathematical formula can yield the answer.

PHOTO CAPTIONS

PHOTO CAPTIONS

Nearly all AP captions follow a simple formula:

• The first sentence of the caption describes what the photo shows, in the present tense, and states where and when the photo was made.

• The second sentence of the caption gives background on the news event or describes why the photo is significant.

• Whenever possible, try to keep captions to no more than two concise sentences, while including the relevant information. Try to anticipate what information a newspaper editor or reader will need.

THIS IS AN EXAMPLE OF THE STANDARD AP CAPTION:

The Mississippi River flows through a hole in the Sny Island, Ill., levee, flooding farmland and homes 10 miles south of Quincy, Ill., Sunday, July 25, 1993. About 2,000 people were evacuated from the 44,000 acres that flooded. (AP Photo/Bill Waugh)

DO NOT use DESCRIPTIVE OVERLINES such as:

1. **SAFE AT SECOND**—For a baseball play at second base, or **PRESI-DENT ADDRESSES WOMEN**—For a presidential speech to a women's group. Regular captions have **NO** overlines.

INSTRUCTIVE OVERLINES will be used in the following cases:

1. For **FILE PHOTOS** the word **FILE** will be the **OVERLINE**.

Example: FILE—New York Knicks' Patrick Ewing is bowled over by Charlotte Hornets' Larry Johnson in this May 12, 1993, file photo during the NBA playoffs in New York. (AP Photo/Ron Frehm, File)

2. For **ADVANCES** the **OVERLINE** is the word **ADVANCE** and the **RE-LEASE DATE**. Do not use story slugs or writer's name in the **OVERLINE**.

Example: ADVANCE FOR MAY 15-16—Sean Smith, a fish culturist at Vermont's new fish hatchery in Grand Isle, Vt., one of the Lake Champlain islands, moves young rainbow trout on May 4, 1993, to a new tank. (AP Photo/Toby Talbot)

3. For **SPECIALS** the **OVERLINE** should be the word **SPECIAL** and the name of the publication. Do not use the authorizing editor in the **OVERLINE**. Also, if the city is **not** part of the formal title of the publication's name, add it.

Example: SPECIAL FOR THE CLEVELAND PLAIN DEALER— Diana Holmes participates in the second day of the 66th annual National Spelling Bee in Washington Thursday, June 3, 1993. (AP Photo/Ron Edmonds)

4. For **EMBARGOED** photos the **OVERLINE** should be the word **EMBARGOED** with the **RELEASE TIME AND DATE**. Also, add **HFR** (Hold for Release) in the **SUPPLEMENTAL CATEGORY** field of the **NAA/IPTC** header for embargoed photos for same day release.

Example: EMBARGOED UNTIL 9 P.M. EDT, June 1, 1993—Jan Smith, right, leaves the courtroom at the Travis County courthouse with friends Tuesday, June 1, 1993, in Austin, Texas, after her assailant William Johnson was found guilty of assault. (AP Photo/Austin American Statesman, Chuck Johnson)

The **DATE**, including the day of the week, day and year must appear in the body of all captions if known. If only the year and/or month is known, use that. Do not say "recently." In file photos use the date the photo was originally shot, if known. If the date is not known get as close as you can even if only the year is known. If the date is unknown state **"undated photo"** in the body of the caption and in the **INSTRUCTIONS** field of the **NAA/IPTC** header.

The **SIGNOFF** for an AP staffer or stringer is, in parentheses, **AP Photo** followed by a slash and the name of the photographer. Don't use **str** or **stf. Example: (AP Photo/Rick Bowmer)**. If the name of the photographer is not known or needs to be withheld, the signoff is: **(AP Photo)**.

MEMBER PHOTO SIGNOFF: (AP Photo/USA Today, Anne Ryan).

HANDOUT PHOTO SIGNOFF: (AP Photo/General Motors). If photographer is known: **(AP Photo/General Motors, John Smith)**.

POOL PHOTO SIGNOFF: (AP Photo/Bill Waugh, Pool). For pool photos, do not name the newspaper or agency that shot for the pool in the caption signoff. However, put the name of the organization that shot the pool in the **BYLINE TITLE** field of the NAA/IPTC header.

SPECIALS PHOTO SIGNOFF for photo shot by AP: **(AP Photo/Al Smith)**. If made by member's own photographer: **(Chicago Tribune Photo/Bill James)**.

FILE PHOTO SIGNOFF: (AP Photo/Lenny Ignelzi, File). If the name of the photographer who shot the file photo is not known the signoff should be: **(AP Photo/File)**

AP GRAPHIC SIGNOFF: (AP Graphic/Karl Tate).

HANDOUT GRAPHIC SIGNOFF: (AP Graphic/AccuWeather).

TV FRAMEGRAB PHOTO SIGNOFF: (AP Photo/CNN)

MANDATORY CREDITS, OUTS, CORRECTION INFORMATION and **EDITOR'S NOTES** do not appear in the caption box. They appear in the **INSTRUCTIONS** field in the NAA/IPTC header.

CAPTIONS FOR TRANSMIT POINTS WITH LEAF II TRANSMITTERS AND EXTERNAL LEAF COMPANDERS: Retain the old slug style, but adopt the new style for the body of the caption. Note the new style signoff for the caption writer, day of the week/time and byline title.

Example: [S OH CSA103 BBN REDS CARDINALS] Cincinnati Reds base runner Willie Greene is out at home as St. Louis Cardinals catcher Hector Villanueva gets set to make the tag during the fourth inning in Cincinnati Thursday, June 3, 1993. (AP Photo/Al Behrman)(ab52127stf)

CAPTIONS FOR TRANSMIT POINTS LEAF II TRANSMITTERS WITHOUT COMPANDERS AND ANALOG DRUM TRANSMITTERS: Use the new style for the body of the caption. Retain the picture number and dateline. Note the new style signoff for the caption writer, day of the week/time and byline title. Retain the story slug.

Example: (CSA103) Cincinnati Reds baserunner Willie Greene is out at home as St. Louis Cardinals catcher Hector Villanueva gets set to make the tag during the fourth inning in Cincinnati Thursday, June 3, 1993. (AP Photo/Al Behrman) (ab52127stf)1993 SLUG: BBNReds Cardinals

CAPTION CORRECTIONS, ADDITIONS, ELIMINATIONS

An AP captions **CORRECTION** is moved when a simple and nonlibelous error occurs in a caption. Examples would be a misspelled name, wrong hometown, sports score or slug. The procedure AP uses to file a caption correction form on PhotoStream is to point out the information that is being corrected in the **INSTRUCTIONS** field of the NAA/PTC header and write a corrected caption in publishable form. The word **CORRECTION** and the original photo's **TRANS REFERENCE** number are added to the **OBJECT NAME** field in the NAA/PTC header. The form is followed by the photo again with a corrected publishable caption noting so in the **IN-**

STRUCTIONS field of the NAA/PTC header. The same procedure is followed for an AP caption **ADDITION**.

An AP caption **ADDITION** is moved when the original caption is incomplete but otherwise accurate. An AP caption **ADDITION** may add the name of someone in the photo or other important background information.

An AP caption **ELIMINATION** is moved for an acceptable photo that has a caption field that misrepresents the photo or is in bad taste. When this occurs, an AP caption **ELIMINATION** form is moved alerting members. Then the photo is rerun with the corrected caption using procedures for an AP caption **CORRECTION** transmission.

PHOTO KILLS AND ELIMINATIONS

An AP photo **KILL** is moved on PhotoStream and DataStream for a photo that is objectionable and calls into question the threat of legal action, libel or copyright. Photo **KILLS** move in consultation with the New York Photos desk supervisor and senior photo management.

An AP photo **ELIMINATION** is moved on PhotoStream and DataStream for a photo that carries no threat of legal action but is objectionable for other reasons, such as error, poor taste or inaccuracy. When these occur, either an AP photo **KILL** or **ELIMINATION** is moved, alerting members.

NAA/IPTC HEADER FIELDS

Byline: The Byline field lists the name of the person who made the photo.

Byline Title: The Byline Title field lists the title of the person who made the photo.

Caption: The Caption field is the text that accompanies the photo, containing the who, what, when, where and why information.

Caption Writer: The Caption Writer field lists the initials of all the people who wrote or edited the caption, header fields or image file. This includes toning and pixel editing.

Category: The Category field lists codes that aid in a more detailed search. (See category definitions in this section.)

City: The City field lists where the photo was originally made. For file photos, do not use the transmission point's city.

Country: The Country field lists the three-letter country code where the photo was originally made. For file photos, do not put the transmission point's country.

Create Date Time: The Create Date Time field is the date the photo was originally made. For file photos, use the date the photo was originally made, if known. If the complete date is not known, Leafdesk 8.3 software will allow the field to be left blank. The field will not accept a partial date. The time is not needed.

Credit: The Credit field is the name of the service transmitting the photo.

Headline: The Headline field lists keywords to aid in a more detailed search for a photo.

Instructions: The Instructions field lists special notations that apply uniquely to a photo, such as file photo, correction, advance or outs.

Object Name: The Object Name field lists the story slug associated with a photo. For photos without a story, Associated Press photographers or photo editors will make up a logical slug to aid in a search and note it as a "stand-alone photo" in the INSTRUCTIONS field of the NAA/PTC header. If a related story moves on DataStream, the photo will be retransmitted with the appropriate OBJECT NAME to match the story.

Routing: The Routing field is used by The Associated Press to route photos on to PhotoStream.

Source: The Source field lists who is the original provider of a photo, such as: AP, an AP member, pool photo provider or handout photo provider.

State: The State field lists the state where the photo was originally made. Use U.S. postal code abbreviations. For file photos, do not use the transmission point's state.

Supp Categories: The Supplemental Categories field lists codes that aid in a more detailed search for a photo. (See supplemental categories definitions in this section.)

Trans Reference: The Trans Reference field lists a call letter/number combination associated with a photo. It includes an originating transmit point's call letters and picture number from that point's sequence of offerings for a given day. Example: NY105.

AP Caption and NAA/IPTC Header
Quick Reference Guide

```
┌─────────────────────────────────────────────────────────┐
│ ▣▤▤▤▤▤▤▤▤▤▤▤ Header - See Instructions ▤▤▤▤▤▤▤▤▤▤ ▣ │
│                                                           │
│ Ⓐ  [ Caption        ▼] 🅘 ▣    Show: [ Preferred Fields ▼]│
│    ┌──────────────────────────────────────────────────┐⇧│
│    │ Montreal Expos' Sean Berry, right, is congratulated│ │
│    │ by third base coach Jerry Manuel as Berry rounds  │ │
│    │ the bases after hitting the first of two solo     │ │
│    │ home runs for the night in the Expos' 11-3 victory│ │
│    │ over the Colorado Rockies at Denver's Mile High   │ │
│    │ Stadium Wednesday, Sept. 1, 1993. (AP             │ │
│    │ Photo/Jack Dempsey)                               │⇩│
│    └──────────────────────────────────────────────────┘ │
└─────────────────────────────────────────────────────────┘
```

	Field	Value
Ⓑ	Create DateTime ▼ 🅘	09/01/93
Ⓒ	Category ▼ 🅘	S
Ⓓ	Supp Categories ▼ 🅘	BBN
Ⓔ	Object Name ▼ 🅘	EXPOS ROCKIES
Ⓕ	Routing ▼ 🅘	ALL
Ⓖ	Source ▼ 🅘	AP
Ⓗ	Credit ▼ 🅘	AP
Ⓘ	Byline ▼ 🅘	JACK DEMPSEY
Ⓙ	Byline Title ▼ 🅘	STR
Ⓚ	Country ▼ 🅘	USA
Ⓛ	State ▼ 🅘	CO
Ⓜ	City ▼ 🅘	DENVER
Ⓝ	Instructions ▼ 🅘	BEST QUALITY AVAILABLE
Ⓞ	Caption Writer ▼ 🅘	TEB DZ
Ⓟ	Trans Reference ▼ 🅘	DXS102
Ⓠ	Headline ▼ 🅘	SEAN BERRY JERRY MANUEL

[Prefs...] [Clear Prefs] [Copy All] [Edit] [Done]

Ⓐ Caption text

Ⓑ Date photo was originally made whether spot or file.

Ⓒ A--News, F--Business, I--International, S--Sports, V--Advisory

Ⓓ Codes to aid in search.

Ⓔ Story slug. If no story, make up logical slug.

Ⓕ Codes AP uses to route photos onto PhotoStream.

Ⓖ Name of original provider of the photo.

Ⓗ Name of service transmitting photo.

Ⓘ Name of person who made photo.

Ⓙ Title of person who made photo.

Ⓚ Country code where photo was made.

Ⓛ State postal code where photo was made.

Ⓜ Name of city where photo was made.

Ⓝ Any special information or editors' notes.

Ⓞ Initials of people who wrote or edited caption, header, pixels or toned.

Ⓟ Unique call letter/number combination and date of transmission in numerical form.

Ⓠ Logical keywords to aid in a search for a photo.

SUPPLEMENTAL CATEGORIES

GENERAL:
ADV Advance
APN APNewsfeatures
ENT Entertainment, celebrities (don't use the word people)
FEA Feature pictures of a non-news nature
FILE File photo
HFR Hold for Release (embargoed photos for same day release)
MAP Map or graphic
NAT National Geographic package
OBIT Obituary
PM Internal filing code used to batch-move photos at beginning of daily cycle.
SPF Special Features package
SPCL Special
WEA Weather

NEWS EVENTS:
CVN National political conventions
ELN For election cycles only
XGR State legislatures

SPORTS:
BBA Professional baseball (American League)
BBN Professional baseball (National League)
BBO Professional baseball (minor league or related to neither league)
BBC College baseball
BKN NBA basketball
BKC Men's college basketball
BKW Women's college basketball
BKO Other basketball including high school and semipro
BOX Boxing
CAR Racing (car, speedboat or motorcycle)
FBN NFL Football
FBC College football
FBO Other football including high school and semipro
GLF Golf
GYM Gymnastics
HKN NHL hockey
HKC College hockey
HKO Other hockey including high school and minor league
OLY Olympics
RAC Racing (animals)
RUN Track and Field
SKI Skiing
SOC Soccer
TEN Tennis

FILING THE WIRE

FILING THE WIRE

These guidelines are intended to help editors handle copy easily and efficiently.

Codes in the heading of a story tell the computer where to send it, how quickly it should be moved out, and in what format.

See:
Coding Requirements
   File Name
      Priority Codes
      Category Codes
      Format Identifiers
Keyword Slug Line
      Version Section
      Reference Number Section

Filing the Wire: Coding Requirements

The **file name** consists of a letter of the alphabet and four numbers. The letter is called the **Service Level Designator** and shows the type of service the file belongs to. Usually stories are numbered in sequence. But some stories or fixtures — digests, advances and AP Photo and Graphic Updates, for example — are given predetermined numbers. The first AP News Digest of the new cycle, for instance, is always a9000 or p9000 on the high-speed lines.

These are the letters and types of service most common in nationwide transmissions:

a — Spot news.
b — Advances.
c — Standing features.
f — News designed primarily for financial pages.
s — Sports copy.

Other letters used by the AP include:
h — Special sports report for smaller newspapers.
p — Spot news, special packaging.
r — Race report.
t — Sports, special packaging.
u — Special stock and markets package.

Priority codes are used by the AP to assure that stories are sent in the order of their urgency. At newspapers, the codes can be used by computer systems to determine the order in which stories come to an editor's attention.

The principal priority codes, in order of urgency, and their use:
f —Flash, highest priority, used for flashes only.
b — NewsAlerts, Bulletins, first adds to bulletins, kill notes.
u — Urgent, high-priority copy, including all writethrus containing corrections. It must be used on all items that carry an *Urgent* slug. It also may be used on items that lack this slug but must move on an urgent basis.
r — Stories of a routine nature.
d — Deferred priority: Used on spot copy that can be delayed.
a — For weekday advances designed for use more than 12 hours after transmission. (Hold-for-release material sent for use less than 12 hours after transmission carries a spot news priority.)
s — For Sunday advances designed for use more than 12 hours after transmission.

Category codes help newspapers sort copy into various categories. For example, domestic stories may go in one place in the queue, Washington stories in another, and foreign stories somewhere else.

The principal category codes and their uses:
a — Domestic, non-Washington, general news items.
b — Special events.
d — Food, diet. For use primarily on standing advance features on food, recipes and the like. Frequently used with stories on c-level DataStream.
e — Entertainment features, reviews, fixtures and coverage of scheduled entertainment events. Spot general news involving the entertainment industry or people carries the **a** or **n** category.
f — News copy, regardless of dateline, designed primarily for use on financial pages. When a major story of financial interest moves as part of the general news service it should have a regular category code such as a. If it has also moved on a financial wire,

editors should be advised that the same story has been routed to both financial desks and general news desks.

i — International items, including stories from the United Nations, U.S. possessions, and undated roundups keyed to foreign events.

j — Lottery results only. (Stories about lotteries or lottery winners carry standard news category codes.)

k — Commentary. Material designed primarily for editorial and op-ed pages; editorial roundups.

l — Selected "lifestyle" copy.

n — Stories of state or regional interest under domestic datelines. If a regional item has a Washington dateline, use the w category. If a regional item has an international dateline, use the i category. If a regional item is designed primarily for financial pages use the f category and if it is designed primarily for the sports pages, use the s category.

o — Weather tables and forecast fixtures. Do not use on weather stories.

p —Political copy.

q — Use only for result or period score of a single sports event. The code is designed to help newspaper computer systems build a list of scores or ignore individual scores and wait for transmissions that group them.

s — Sports stories, standings, results of more than one event.

v —Advisories about stories that may carry any of the category letters. This code is used primarily for news digests, news advisories, lists of transmitted advances and indexes.

w — Washington-datelined stories. Change to the *a* or *i* category code if a subsequent lead shifts to a different city.

The **format identifier** is comprised of two letters, which appear after the category code.

Use **bx** if the item is intended to be set in body type or standard text.

Use **bt** if the item is intended to be set in body type and contains even one tabular line.

Use **at** if the item is intended to be set in agate type and contains even one tabular line.

Use **ax** if the item is intended to be set in agate type but contains no tabular lines.

a0625
uwbx
^BC-Budget Surplus

s0357
rsat
^BC-NBA-Celts-Knicks, Box

Special note to members: Format Identifiers on DataStream

The letters **bx**, **at**, etc., shown in the examples above do not appear on DataStream. However, they help generate non-printing characters that are sent in this location to convey the same information about whether the item is meant to be set in agate or body type and whether it contains tabular material.

Filing the Wire: Keyword Slugline

Every news item in the AP report has a **keyword slug line**.
Every keyword slug line must have at least a keyword section. Up to three other sections, as shown in the examples that follow, are used when necessary.
The commas that appear in the example are critical for operations of many AP computers. ↑
The **keyword section** of the line consists of a cycle designator

KEYWORD SECTION
(A Cycle Designator and a Keyword.)

Comma defines end of the section.
No space before the word count.

a0401
dw

↑ BC-Congress, 300 ←

Always end with a WORD COUNT
and the flush left symbol.

KEYWORD **Strive for brevity and uniqueness.**
Maximum 21 characters.

Always a hyphen.

CYCLE DESIGNATOR

Always start with a boldface arrow.

and a keyword or keywords. A boldface symbol or upper-rail (⌐ or ^) precedes the cycle designator. This is followed by the cycle designator, a hyphen and the keyword. A comma marks the end of the section.

Because the keyword section provides the basic identification of a story for automatic linkup routines, it must be repeated in exactly the same form on all subsequent leads, adds, inserts, subs, etc. filed for a story.

The cycle designator is always BC-, to indicate that the story may be used by morning or afternoon newspapers.

The **keyword** clearly indicates the content of the story.

It should not be longer than 21 letters. (Rule of thumb: *If you have to count the letters, the keyword is too long.*)

Use of easily recognized abbreviations and acronyms, such as *Scotus* for the Supreme Court of the United States and *Xgr* for legislature, is encouraged. (Also, the keyword of an item sent on a state service contains the postal code for the state of origin.)

The computer produces a word count at the end of the line.

When writing or editing a story, editors can use the word count key to determine how long a story is.

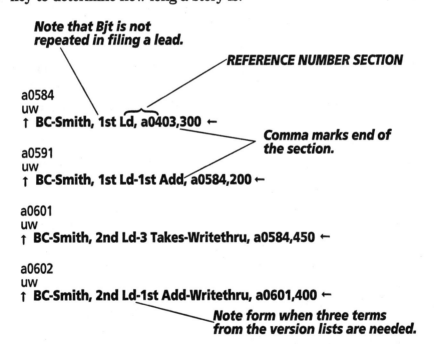

Note that Bjt is not repeated in filing a lead.

REFERENCE NUMBER SECTION

a0584
uw
↑ BC-Smith, 1st Ld, a0403,300 ←

Comma marks end of the section.

a0591
uw
↑ BC-Smith, 1st Ld-1st Add, a0584,200 ←

a0601
uw
↑ BC-Smith, 2nd Ld-3 Takes-Writethru, a0584,450 ←

a0602
uw
↑ BC-Smith, 2nd Ld-1st Add-Writethru, a0601,400 ←

Note form when three terms from the version lists are needed.

The **reference number** is the transmission number used on a previous take of a story. List only one in a keyword line.

Follow these norms:

Cite the number of the most recent lead if you are sending a new lead. If you are filing an add, cite only the transmission number on the immediately preceding take of the story.

If a story has moved in many pieces and you think editors should have more reference numbers than the one in the keyword line, list them on a line below the keyword slug line.

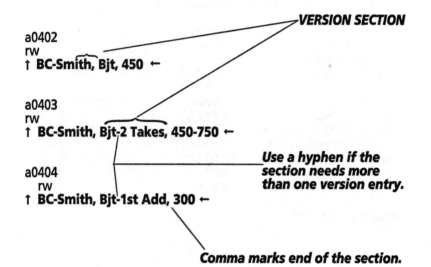

VERSION SECTION

a0402
rw
↑ BC-Smith, Bjt, 450 ←

a0403
rw
↑ BC-Smith, Bjt-2 Takes, 450-750 ←

Use a hyphen if the section needs more than one version entry.

a0404
rw
↑ BC-Smith, Bjt-1st Add, 300 ←

Comma marks end of the section.

The **version section** of the keyword slug line is designed to give editors and computer systems a quick indication of whether to place an item at the top, bottom or middle of previous takes sent under the same keyword.

The terms that follow are the only ones that should appear in the version section of a keyword slug line. When more than one term is necessary, separate them with a hyphen. Use figures as indicated.

The version vocabulary is broken into two lists. Do not use more than one of the items from this first list in a keyword slug line. If a term from the second list is needed, it must follow any term from this list:

Bjt
1st Ld, 2nd Ld, 10th Ld, etc.
Adv 01, Adv 31, etc.
Advisory
HFR (Hold for Release)
KILL
WITHHOLD
ELIMINATION
CORRECTIVE
CLARIFICATION

A term from the second list may stand alone in the version section if no term from the first list is needed. Some stories require two terms from the second list. If that is the case, the order in which the terms appear is not critical, but they must be separated by a hyphen. The second list:

2 Takes, 3 Takes, etc.
1st Add, 2nd Add, etc.
Writethru
Box (Sports only)

FILING PRACTICES

BC FILING

AP news moves in a 24-hour cycle. For U.S. papers, the cycle begins at midnight Eastern time on national wires, and usually at midnight local time on state wires. On World Service wires, the cycle starts at midnight GMT.

Each story is filed on a "24-hour" basis, with a single lead sequence from midnight to midnight. The first story after midnight on a major fire, for example, might be slugged BC-Fire. As the story develops, it might be slugged BC-Fire, 1st Ld-Writethru by 8 a.m., BC-Fire, 4th Ld-Writethru by 1 p.m., BC-Fire, 6th Ld-Writethru by 6 p.m. and BC-Fire, 10th Ld-Writethru by 11 p.m. After midnight, the new-cycle story will once again be simply BC-Fire.

On a developing story, it's important to retain the same basic slug ("BC-Fire" in this case) whenever possible from cycle to cycle. Don't switch, for example, from "BC-Fire" to "BC-Inferno." If a slug must change because of the nature of the story, start a new numbering sequence with the new slug and make reference to the earlier series:

^BC-Town Burns
^Eds: Incorporates BC-Block Burns

For U.S. members, if a story is developing strongly beyond midnight and still needs to be updated for late AMs papers, the lead sequence can be continued past the start of the new cycle. In the example above, the story might be BC-Fire, 12th Ld-Writethru by 1 a.m. and BC-Fire, 13th Ld-Writethru by 2 a.m. When it's late enough that AMs papers are no longer publishing (about 4 a.m. Eastern time), begin the new-cycle sequence, sending the new story for use by PMs papers as BC-Fire. In such a case, the story for PMs and all subsequent leads in PMs time will carry an "Eds: PMs" label (see below: Filing Practices: "Eds: AMs" and "Eds: PMs")

Keeping copy fresh

Just because there is a single BC numbering sequence from midnight to midnight doesn't mean an important story should remain the same in approach. The new BC story moving after midnight should take a different approach to the copy that moved in time for AMs. The version of the story moving in late afternoon - the story aimed at AMs -- should take a different approach to what PMs papers have published.

PMs papers aren't publishing after 4 p.m. EST or EDT, but the leads moved before that time with PMs in mind should continue to be updated even after that hour for Web and broadcast needs, until the version of the story aimed at AMs papers is ready.

Day of the week

BC style is to use the day of the week in spot copy. However, if a spot story is something of a feature, it makes sense to lower the time element to the second graf to make the story more useable for both AMs and PMs papers.

Corrections and clarifications

Stories can be written through for the purpose of correcting them only in the same 24-hour cycle in which they originally moved. (Exception: If a developing story is continuing to be written through with a running lead sequence past the midnight hour, it can still be written through.

If, say, at 5 a.m., an error is discovered in a story that moved at 8 p.m., do a new BC- story, noting in an "Eds:" note that it corrects an error in the version of the story moved in the previous cycle. There may also be a need, in AMs time, for a corrective to the original story. The same approach applies to clarifications.

See also the **Procedures** section of the **Briefing on Media Law**.

Refiling Sunday copy for Monday PMs

Some U.S. state bureaus refile, for Monday PMs papers, a number of stories that moved Saturday for Sunday and Sunday for Monday. Under BC filing they can still be refiled, with a note saying "Eds: Originally moved for Sunday AMs." They may, of course, be modified slightly to lower the time element or make updates. (In such a case, say "Eds: A version moved for Sunday AMs.")

FILING PRACTICES

ADDS
In filing an add, place below the keyword slug line a slug that lists:

—The name of the datelined community followed by a colon. (Use UNDATED if the item does not have a dateline. The name of the community usually is adequate; include the state or country name only if needed to avoid confusion.)

—The last two words of the previous take.

uw
^BC-Air Fares, 1st Ld-1st Add, a0584<
^WASHINGTON: this year.<

ADVANCE SLUGS
Stories transmitted in advance on nationwide services require a minimum of two additional slugs.

The first allows the computer systems to key on the item. Use the notation Adv followed by the two-digit release date shown in the keyword line.

The second slug line specifies the release date in more detail.

aw
^BC-New Team, ADV15-2 Takes<
^Adv03<
^For release in AM newspapers of Monday, May 15 and thereafter<

Any other slugs on the story follow the three shown here.

Be sure to use the *a* priority code if the advance is for weekday release, the s priority code if it is for Sunday release.

When filing a series use a consistent keyword but differentiate the parts by use of a Roman numeral.

^BC-Regulators I, Adv10-3 Takes<
^BC-Regulators II, Adv11-3 Takes<

For weekend or two-day advances:

^BC-CA--Balance of Power, Adv09-10,930<
^Adv09-10<
^For release weekend editions of May 9-10 and thereafter<

Even though AP files news in a 24-hour cycle for use by AM or PM newspapers, advances can still be targeted if desired for AM or PM use.

ADVISORIES
Advisories include a wide range of items, from the news digests or budgets to one paragraph items saying a certain story or photo is in the works or has moved.

All advisories carry the *v* category code. Most advisories have the word Advisory in the version field, separated from the keyword by a comma. Some fixture advisories also have a three-letter identifier in the keyword line to make them easier to find.

Spot news advisories with information on a particular story should have a keyword the same as the story.

General information advisories may simply use *BC-Advisory* in the keyword.

uv
^BC-Air Fares, Advisory
EDITORS:
The embargo on BC-Air Fares, a0432, has been broken. The story is available for immediate use.
The AP<

Bjt TAGS

Use the "Bjt" tag the first time a budgeted story moves in the 24-hour cycle. Do not use on subsequent versions, except for the first "Eds: AMs" version of a budgeted story, which does require a "Bjt."

^BC-Fire, Bjt, 4th Ld-Writethru
^Fire destroys six city blocks<
^Eds: AMs.

BOLDFACE FOR SLUGS

Use the upper-rail key to create boldface for all slug lines illustrated in the Stylebook.

Some terminal screens display the symbol for boldface with a character that looks like this: ↑

Others use a character that looks like this: ^

BULLETINS

A decision on whether to slug a story *bulletin* or *urgent* rests with the supervisor. The *bulletin* slug always must be used judiciously.

A *bulletin* should be kept short. Usually, one or two publishable sentences will be all that is needed to get a story started.

A *bulletin* should not carry a word count, byline, photo or graphics plans, editor's note or summary line. (One exception: an undated bulletin should carry a byline or *By The Associated Press*.)

A *bulletin* is always preceded by an *APNewsAlert*, which is a one-line nonpublishable headline. (See **NewsAlerts** entry.)

bi
^BC-Quake<
^BULLETIN<

An *urgent* slug, with an urgent priority, is adequate for adds to a bulletin.

BYLINES

Except for prefixes such as *Mac, Mc, Le,* or *De* (writer's preference) and *Sr.* or *Jr.,* a writer's name is entirely in capital letters.

The standard underline for full-time AP employees is *Associated Press Writer.* Abbreviate *Associated Press* to *AP* for specialty underlines such as *AP Sports Writer* and *AP Special Correspondent.*

Bylines and underlines are transmitted in boldface and marked for centering:

^By F. JOSEF HEBERT=
^Associated Press Writer=

^By RICHARD N. OSTLING=
^AP Religion Writer=

^By CHARLES J. HANLEY=
^AP Special Correspondent=

For undated stories when a writer's name is not used:

^By The Associated Press=

For dual bylines, center the word and on a separate line between the names as follows:

^By SAMPLE AUTHOR=
^and=
^EXAMPLE WRITER=
^Associated Press Writers=

When a story has been written by someone who is not an AP employee, a byline without an underline is adequate.

When a writer works for a newspaper, use the byline with the name of the newspaper:
^By NEWSPAPER WRITER=
^Hometown Citizen-Times=

CENTERING SYMBOL

Some terminal screens display the symbol with a character that looks like this: <->

Others use a character that looks like this: =

Place a centering symbol at the end of all bylines and underlines to bylines.

See the example under the **bylines** entry in this section.

CHANGING DATELINES

The designation of *2nd, 3rd, 4th Ld,* etc. continues in sequence even if the dateline changes on a story.

If a new lead does shift the dateline, follow the keyword line with a "changes dateline" slug:

ua
^BC-Air Fares, 6th Ld-Writethru, a0910<
^Changes dateline from WASHINGTON.<

Do not use the term "Precede."

CLARIFICATIONS
For a full explanation, see **Procedures** section of the **Briefing on Media Law**. The format:

^BC-Air Fares, CLARIFICATION, a0710
^Eds: Members who used BC-Air Fares, a0710 of May 8, may wish to use the following, which explains that not all fares on domestic flights are subject to change.<
WASHINGTON (AP) — In a story May 8, The Associated Press reported that fares on domestic flights will increase beginning in April. Fares will increase for flights in the continental United States, but not for flights to Hawaii.

To send a clarification, do not simply type the format shown here. Use the template in Reporter's Workbench to format it precisely. This is essential for archive and other purposes. To use the template, open the story for which you are doing a clarification, click Templates, click Kill or Correct This Story and select what you want to do.

CORRECTIONS
Always use the priority code *u.*
Use a writethru with an editor's note explaining specifically the location of the correction and what it is.

uw
BC-Air Fares, 2nd Ld-Writethru, a0403<
Eds: To CORRECT airline from American to TWA, sub 20th graf: The company ... until then.
WASHINGTON (AP) —

Always give the reason for a correction. Be specific. Do not use vague phrases such as *to correct a figure* — give the correct figure and the one it replaces. If correcting a typo, say, for instance, "to correct spelling of 'adequate.'" The objective is to let editors who may be on deadline know the severity of the error without having to go back to the original copy.

CORRECTIVES
For a full explanation, see **Procedures** section of the **Briefing on Media Law**. The format:

^BC-Fed-Indictments, CORRECTIVE
^Eds: Members who used a0620, BC-Fed-Indictments, sent Oct. 22 under a New York dateline, are asked to use the following story.<

NEW YORK (AP) — In an Oct. 22 story about federal indictments of city officials, The Associated Press reported erroneously the name of one of those indicted. The correct name is Joseph Arnold, not John Arnold.

To send a corrective, do not simply type the format shown here. Use the template in Reporter's Workbench to format it precisely. This is essential for archive and other purposes. To use the template, open the story for which you are doing a corrective, click Templates, click Kill or Correct This Story and select what you want to do.

CREDIT LINES

Use credit lines at the end of a story to note staffers who contributed to the story other than the byliner. Place them under an indented three-underscore line. Do not begin them with *Editor's Note:*

‾‾‾
Associated Press writers John Jones and Susan Smith in Omaha, special correspondent Jane Brown in Paris and researcher Jim Doe contributed to this report.

DASH LINES

Use a line of three dashes to separate individual items sent within the same story file, such as several datelined stories in a package of briefs. Dashes also should be used on a separate line after a publishable editor's note.

The dash line may:

— Begin with a paragraph mark. No special symbol is required at the end.

— Begin with an upper rail, and end with a quad left or center symbol.

DISREGARDS

For a full explanation, see **Procedures** section of the **Briefing on Media Law**.

Use this to advise of material sent on the wire inadvertently, including old stories, duplicate stories and copy not meant for the wires. The advisory should say why the material should be disregarded.

The form:

^BC-Turkey-Quake Survivors, DISREGARD, a0704, ^Editors:
Disregard BC-Turkey-Quake Survivors, a0704. The story moved in a previous cycle.
^The AP<

Do not simply type the format shown here. Use the template in Reporter's Workbench to format it precisely. This is essential for archive and other purposes. To use the template, open the story to be disregarded, click Templates, click Kill or Correct This Story and select what you want to do.

"Eds: AMs" and "Eds: PMs"

The movement of the new version of a developing story aimed at AMs or PMs should be pointed out to editors in two ways:
— On a digest and/or a Package Advisory, if the story is mentioned there.
— With an "Eds: AMs" note or "Eds: PMs" note on the story itself.

The "Eds: PMs" note is used only in early PMs time (usually around 1-6 a.m.). It's used to designate the version of a story aimed at PMs papers when the story has been developing over the midnight cycle divide, or when a story broke very soon after midnight and the earlier copy was likely to have been used by AMs papers.

<u>Example of a story developing over the midnight barrier:</u>
The wire carries BC-Fire, 9th Ld-Writethru at 11 p.m., BC-Fire, 10th Ld-Writethru at 2 a.m. and the desk is ready at 3 a.m. to send the new story for PMs. Include "Eds: PMs" on the 3 a.m. story with the PMs approach (and on all subsequent leads aimed at PMs):

^BC-Fire, Bjt<
^Fire destroys three city blocks<
^Eds: PMs.

(There's no writethru number because this is the start of a new lead sequence. The previous sequence was carried over, past the midnight barrier, from the previous cycle.)

<u>Example of a story developing shortly after midnight:</u>
BC-Fire, a new and important story, moves at 12:30 a.m. It is led with BC-Fire, 1st Ld-Writethru at 1 a.m., BC-Fire, 2nd Ld-Writethru at 2 a.m. and the desk is ready at 3 a.m. to send the new story for PMs. Include "Eds: PMs" on the 3 a.m. story with the PMs approach (and on all subsequent leads aimed at PMs):

^BC-Fire, Bjt, 3rd Ld-Writethru<
^Fire destroys three city blocks<
^Eds: PMs.

(The 3 a.m. story will be BC-Fire, 3rd Ld-Writethru. The story started entirely in the current cycle so a single lead sequence is used throughout the cycle.)
The "Eds: AMs" note is used only in AMs time, usually late afternoon. It's used to designate the version of a story aimed at AMs papers when the story has been developing during PMs time. Suppose, for example, that BC-Fire, 3rd Ld-Writethru moves at 6 a.m., BC-Fire, 7th Ld-Writethru moves at 4 p.m. and the desk is ready

now at 5 p.m. to send the new story for AMs. Include "Eds: AMs" on the 5 p.m. story with the AMs approach (and on all subsquent leads aimed at AMs):

^BC-Fire, 8th Ld-Writethru
^Fire destroys three city blocks<
^Eds: AMs.

"Eds: AMs" should be used only when making a substantial change in the approach or content of a story. If a story runs at 9 a.m. and is written through at 5 p.m. to add minor information, the writethru should not carry an "Eds: AMs."

Use precisely the format "Eds: AMs." and "Eds: PMs." The note should be letter-perfect for computer systems to identify it:

Eds: AMs.
Eds: PMs. Updates with court testimony.

On a very fast-moving story, in order to make clear that newspapers on deadline can go to bed, use a separate advisory to highlight the change in approaches.

<u>Example:</u>

^BC-Governor's Illness, Advisory<
Editors: BC-Governor's Illness, 7th Ld-Writethru will stand for AMs. Upcoming is a new story for PMs papers, BC-Governor's Illness.

Items marked "Eds: AMs" or "Eds: PMs" signify in themselves a story with a new approach. There is no need to say in addition that the lead "Recasts previous."

Other information can be added on merits after "Eds: AMs" or "Eds: PMs." If the lead only rejigs the story, or adds non-critical quotes or details, "Eds: AMs" or "Eds: PMs" is enough. But if the lead adds, say, the first quotes from the other side of a controversial issue, or other material of substantial importance, mention it so editors are aware that this version of the story is more than just a new approach.

This will happen relatively rarely, though, in an "Eds: AMs" or "Eds: PMs" situation. Important details will normally be added to the running series of leads on a story, not held for an "AMs" or "PMs" redo.

ELIMINATIONS

For a full explanation, see **Procedures** section of the **Briefing on Media Law**.

The format:

^BC-Practical Joke, ELIMINATION, a0240
^BULLETIN ELIMINATION
BOSTON—Eliminate the Practical Joke story, filed as a0240. It cannot be confirmed.
    ^The AP<

On print wires, but NOT on online wires, follow the BULLETIN ELIMINATION immediately with an advisory. State whether a substitute story is planned:

^BC-Practical Joke, ELIMINATION Advisory, a0240,
Editors: The BOSTON story about the practical joke, a0240, has been eliminated. It cannot be confirmed.
A sub story will be filed shortly. (Or: No sub will be filed.)
    ^The AP<

Do not simply type the format shown here. Use the template in Reporter's Workbench to format it precisely. This is essential for archive and other purposes. To use the template, open the story to be eliminated, click Templates, click Kill or Correct This Story and select what you want to do.

FLASHES
Use as an underline immediately below the APNewsAlert slug on the rare occasion when an APNewsAlert represents a transcendent development.
A flash carries an *f* priority code, a dateline and attribution if appropriate. The format:

fa
^BC-APNewsAlert<
^FLASH<
SPACE CENTER, HOUSTON — Man lands on the moon.

(See **NewsAlerts**)

FLUSH LEFT SYMBOL
Some terminal screens display the flush left symbol with a character that looks like this: <-
Others use a character that looks like this: <

GLANCES
Glances are brief listings of information that accompany a story, although some may occasionally stand alone.
Glances and other layering devices, such as biographical boxes, chronologies, lists and highlights, are always undated and carry a line referring to the main story.

rw
^BC-Budget-Dollar-Glance,100<
^Where the money comes from, and where it goes<
^With BC-Budget, Bjt<
^By The Associated Press

Where the federal government gets a typical dollar and where it goes:

WHERE IT COMES FROM:

Individual income taxes, 48 cents; Social Security, Medicare and other payroll taxes, 34 cents; corporate income taxes, 10 cents.

Layering devices provide expanded detail, give editors a way to dress up a page and serve as points of entry for readers.

They should be listed with related stories on digests and advisories.

HOLD-FOR-RELEASE SLUGS

In assigning priority codes and writing the keyword line, treat as spot copy any story that is for release within the current filing cycle at a set time or that is to be released upon movement of a wire note advising that the story can be used.

All embargoed copy contains *HFR* (Hold for Release) in the version field of the keyword line. A hyphen separates *HFR* from other information in the version field.

Place the necessary cautions about release on a second slug line immediately under the keyword slug line. For example:

rw
^BC-XX- -State of the Union, HFR-4 takes< (where **XX** is the state postal code; no postal code for national services)
^HOLD FOR RELEASE, expected about noon EST.

Or:

da
^BC-XX- -Statistics, HFR<
^For release 6:30 p.m. EST.

Also see the **release times** entry.

INSERTS

Make inserts with writethru leads, with an editor's note saying what is being updated.

INTERNET CITATIONS

Place them at the ends of stories, under an indented three-underscore line. Example:

‾‾‾
On the Net: www.whitehouse.gov/report

If there is other material to put at the end of a story, such as the names of other staffers contributing, put the Internet citation last.

KILLS

For a full explanation, see **Procedures** section of the **Briefing on Media Law**. The format:

^BC-Smith Charged, KILL, a0720
^BULLETIN KILL<
NEW YORK — Kill BC-Smith Charged, a0720. Smith was charged with robbery, not murder.
 ^The AP<

If only part of a story is killed, it should be followed by a writethru, eliminating the offending paragraph. The form for a partial kill is:

^BC-Smith Charged, KILL, a0720
^BULLETIN KILL<
NEW YORK — Kill graf 7 of BC-Smith Charged, a0720. Smith was not convicted last year of armed robbery.
 ^The AP<

On print wires, but NOT on online wires, follow the KILL immediately with an advisory. State whether a substitute story is planned:

^BC-Smith Charged, KILL Advisory, a0720
^Editors:<
The New York story BC-Smith Charged, a0720, has been killed. Smith was charged with robbery, not murder.
A kill is mandatory.
Make certain the story is not published.
A substitute story will be filed shortly. (Or: No substitute story will be filed.)
 ^The AP<

Repeat the kill advisory approximately 12 hours later:

^BC-Smith Charged, KILL Advisory<
^Editors:
The New York story BC-Smith Charged, filed Monday as a0720, has been killed. Smith was charged with robbery, not murder.
A kill is mandatory.
Make certain the story is not published.
A substitute story was filed as a0741, slugged BC-Smith Charged, 2nd Ld-Writethru. (Or: no substitute story was filed.)
 ^The AP<

Do not simply type the format shown here. Use the template in Reporter's Workbench to format it precisely. This is essential for archive and other purposes. To use the template, open the story to be killed, click Templates, click Kill or Correct This Story and select what you want to do.

If a substitute story is filed, mark it as the next lead-writethru to the previous story. Include a nonpublishable editor's note advising that it replaces an earlier story that was KILLED.
The form is:

^BC-Smith Charged, 4th Ld-Writethru,
^Eds: SUBS 7th graf pvs, which was killed, to CORRECT that Smith was charged last year with armed robbery but was not convicted. No pickup.<

LEADS
With the exception of breaking stories, all leads should be writethrus with editor's notes saying what is being updated.
File a new lead to a story whenever developments warrant. Provide a nonpublishable editor's note explaining the reason for the lead, such as:

^Eds: UPDATES 2nd graf with new figures.<

The designation of *2nd, 3rd, 4th Ld*, etc., continues in sequence even if the dateline changes. See the **Changing Datelines** entry.

LOGOS
Follow the dateline by the AP logo enclosed in parentheses without spaces. Put spaces on both sides of the dash that follows:

LOS ANGELES (AP) — An earthquake struck the city today.

Logos are not used in digest and advisory lines.

MORE LINES
A MORE indication, if needed at the conclusion of a take of copy, should begin with an upper rail:
^MORE<

NEWSALERTS
A one-line, nonpublishable headline that briefly reports a development about to move as a bulletin or urgent. If a NewsAlert is filed, do not also file a similar advisory. A NewsAlert must be followed quickly by a bulletin or urgent.
NewsAlerts should have a *b* priority and an *a, f, i, s* or *w* category code, depending on the desk of origin. They should always carry the simple slug: **^BC-APNewsAlert.**
The text should include a dateline. It should also include attri-

bution in cases where it is appropriate to clarify the source of the information.

A sample:

^BC-APNewsAlert<
HOLLYWOOD, Fla. — Joe DiMaggio dies, his lawyer says.

NONPUBLISHABLE EDITOR'S NOTES
Editor's notes not intended for publication should begin flush left with an upper rail symbol and end with a flush left symbol.

Do not precede a nonpublishable editor's note with a paragraph symbol.

^Eds: UPDATES 2nd graf with new figures.<

See also **Publishable Editor's Notes**.

NONTRANSMITTING SYMBOLS
The following are symbols that should not be used in standard AP wire transmissions.

Some of the symbols can be sent and received by some computers but are not generally used because they are not available throughout the newspaper industry or may act as control characters to make a computer perform a function rather than print a character.

accent marks Do not use them; they cause garbled copy in some newspaper computers.

asterisk * Rarely translates and in many cases cannot be sent by AP computers or received by newspaper computers.

at sign @ Does not exist. In computer addresses, use (at). Example: *president(at)whitehouse.gov.*

brackets [ ] Rarely translates and in many cases cannot be sent by AP computers or received by newspaper computers. Use parentheses.

bullets • Do not use because they cannot be transmitted without causing problems with some newspaper computers. Use dashes instead.

cent ¢ Does not exist. Spell out.

equals = This is the control symbol for centering. In some computers it can be translated and printed but it is best spelled out.

percent % Rarely translates and in many cases cannot be sent by AP computers or received by newspaper computers.

pound sign £ or **#** Frequently a control character. Rarely translates and in many cases cannot be sent by AP computers or received by newspaper computers.

slash / Many newspapers translate the slash into other characters or use it as a control symbol. Substitute a hyphen whenever possible. If it is necessary to use a *slash* in a story, as in the case of Internet addresses, include a nonpublishable editor's note explaining that the *slash* may not be transmitted correctly in some member computing systems.

tilde ~ Do not use the symbol. If necessary for Internet addresses, write out the word and put it in parentheses.

underscore _ Do not use the symbol. If necessary for Internet addresses, write out the word and put it in parentheses.

Others:
Symbols for start-of-header, start-of-text, end-of-text, end-of-transmission and the like cannot be printed and when contained in text may confuse computers. To use in text they have to be spelled out or abbreviated in regular characters: "start-of-text," "stx."

Symbols and combinations of characters and symbols used by languages other than English generally can be transmitted or received only by AP and newspaper computers programmed for those languages. Leave the symbols off or use generally accepted equivalents. For example, German umlauts are represented using two regular letters when they are needed: In "Goethe," the "oe" is the "o" with an umlaut.

Typesetting symbols such as tab-line-indicators, tab-field-indicators, en, em, thin should only be used to set tabular copy. Spell out when used in text. They may or may not print and might confuse a computer.

Other typefaces such as *italic* cannot be sent on AP news wires.

PACKAGE ADVISORIES
If a story is strongly developing and a digest isn't scheduled for a couple of hours, use a Package Advisory to bring together all the elements of a story. Package Avisories also provide a place to tell members about how AP is covering a story; to advise on coverage plans; and to draw attention to exceptional AP work.

Example:

^BC-Nasdaq 5,000, Package Advisory
^Editors:
Our package for AMs newspapers:

STORY:

NEW YORK — It started 29 years ago as a way to measure the progress of fledgling companies too small or weak for the prestigious New York Stock Excnange. On Thursday, the Nasdaq Stock Market's composite index soared to its first close above 5,000, cementing its role as the top-performing and fastest-growing barometer of the U.S. stock market.

Slug BC-Nasdaq 5,000, 4th Ld-Writethru, version for AMs papers. Sent as a0861. 600 words.

By Business Writer Eileen Glanton.

SIDEBAR:

BC-Nasdaq-Chronology, milestones in the Nasdaq composite index. 250 words.

GRAPHIC:
NASDAQ 5000, Chart shows percentage change in the Dow and Nasdaq since February 1971.

PHOTO:
AP Photo NYR114, interior view of Nasdaq's Market Site showing 5,000.
    ^The AP<

PREVIOUS-CYCLE COPY
Top copy from the previous 24-hour cycle should be repeated after the new cycle begins at midnight, unless a new-cycle version has been written.

Use this format to repeat a story without change from the previous cycle:

^BC-Terminal Tower<
Eds: Also moved in previous cycle

PUBLISHABLE EDITOR'S NOTES
Publishable editor's notes follow the summary line and should begin with a paragraph symbol, followed by:
    —The words *EDITOR'S NOTE* in all caps.
    —A space, a dash and a space.
    —The text of the note.

Do not put the note in parentheses or use an upper rail at the start of the note.

EDITOR'S NOTE — This is the second installment of a three-part series on governmental agencies.

SUMMARY LINES
All stories should have summary lines giving the essence of what a story is about.

A summary line should be no more than one line in length and is on the line immediately below the keyword line. (If there is an editor's note, it follows the summary line.) Only the first word and proper nouns are capitalized. Follow story style in spelling out numbers.

rw
^BC-Air Fares<
^Air fares going up a Hopkins airport<

TABLES

The construction of tables is an art that is often laborious and time-consuming. The following rules are designed to help build simple stories:

I. Every story or file that has even one line of tabular material in it must have a tabular format identifier in the priority-category code line.

The identifier may be *bt* for body-tabular or *at* for agate-tabular, but it MUST be there.

Examples: *mbt, mat.*

II. Every tabular line must begin with a tab line indicator symbol called a *tli.*

III. Immediately before the first character of the first tabulated column there must be a tab field indicator symbol represented by a *tfi.* There must be at least one space between the last character of the first column following the *tli* and the *tfi* preceding the first tabbed column.

Example:
tliReagantfi000 000 00
tliVerylongnametfi000 000 00

IV. The number of the columns and the width of the entire format are restricted by how they will fit in a newspaper and not by the margin of the services on which they are being sent. A good rule of thumb is to use as many abbreviations as possible while keeping the table understandable.

The basic rule for AP tables is that a line in an agate table may not exceed 392 units and lines in a body type table cannot exceed 293.

Each letter and number has a unit count. By totaling the units of all of the characters you will find whether the table will fit.

The unit count is fixed and does not change for the various newspaper type fonts. Theoretically it will fit all.

Here are the counts:

A -14	a -11	T -13	t -7
B -14	b -11	U -15	u -11
C -13	c -13	V -14	v -11
D -15	d -11	W -18	w -15
E -15	e -10	X -15	x -11
F -14	f -7	Y -15	y -11
G -15	g -11	Z -12	z -9
H -15	h -11		
I -8	i -6	0 -9	1 -9
J -11	j -7	2 -9	3 -9
K -15	k -11	4 -9	5 -9
L -13	l -6	6 -9	7 -9

M -18	m -18	8 -9	9 -9
N -15	n -11	, -6	. -6
O -14	o -10		
P -14	p -11	EM18	
Q -14	q -11	EN9	
R -15	r -9	Thin6	
S -11	s -9	Fractions18	

As you can see from the above table, all characters are not 18, nine or six units, but vary. However, you can use *em, en* and *thin* symbols to get within one unit of a character's width.

By figuring out how to set the line with the most characters, you can get the basic table width and all other lines should fall properly into place.

You can put in the *em, en* or *thin* symbols manually but frequently the standard AP computer will do it adequately once the file is stored in the system.

URGENTS

A decision on whether to slug a story *URGENT* rests with the supervisor.

Always place an urgent slug immediately below the keyword line.

The word **URGENT** should be preceded by an upper rail, all caps and flush left on a line by itself. A story with an urgent slug should always have an urgent priority code. The urgent priority code also may be used if an item is not urgent but needs to be moved on an urgent basis.

The slugging of a typical urgent:

ui
^BC-Quake<
^URGENT<

For the first break on an *urgent* story, the initial urgent should be no more than three or four paragraphs, followed by subsequent takes to form an *urgent* series. Subsequent urgent-caliber developments on the story should also be filed as an *urgent* series, or as a short, *urgent* lead picking up into the previous story. Writethrus adding other significant developments on a major story may also be slugged *urgent*, and need not be broken up into takes. But use care in using the *urgent* slug on long writethrus. The material may well call for a new, short *urgent*.

WITHHOLDS

For a full explanation, see **Procedures** section of the **Briefing on Media Law.**

The form for a WITHHOLD is:

^BC-Gold Find, WITHHOLD, a0680
^WITHHOLD

DENVER — Withold BC-Gold, filed as a0680. Authorities say the miner's story has been questioned.
^The AP<

Do not simply type the formats shown here. Use the template in Reporter's Workbench to format it precisely. This is essential for archive and other purposes. To use the template, open the story to be withheld, click Templates, click Kill or Correct This Story and select what you want to do.

WORD COUNTS
Most computers automatically put in the word count.

If the word count is not automatic, put it in at the end of the keyword line immediately following the final comma, without a space.

WRITETHRUS
Writethrus are used to update or correct a story, and to combine separate takes of a bulletin or urgent series.

uw
^BC-Governor's Illness, 2nd Ld-Writethru, a0584<
EDS: Combine a0579, a0581 and a0582, adds new comments.

PROOFREADERS' MARKS

¶ ATLANTA (AP)—The organization   indent for paragraph

said Thursday. It was the first   paragraph

the last attempts.   no paragraph

With this the president tried

the Jones Smith company is not   transpose

over a period of sixty or more years   use figures

there were 9 in the group.   spell it out

Ada, Oklahoma is the hometown   abbreviate

The Ga man was the guest of   don't abbreviate

prince edward said it was his   uppercase

as a result This will be   lowercase

the ac cuser pointed to them   remove space

In these times it is necessary   insert space

the order for the later devices   retain

The ruling a fine example   insert word

according to the this source   delete

boldface, center

flush right

flush left

insert comma

insert apostrophe

insert quotation marks

insert period

hyphen

dash

ABOUT THE AP

On an early morning in May 1848, 10 men representing six New York City newspapers sat around an office table of the New York Sun. They had been in session for more than an hour and all that time they had been in stubborn argument.

At issue was the costly collection of news by telegraphy. The newly invented telegraph made transmission of news possible by wire but at costs so high that the resources of any single paper would be strained.

David Hale of the Journal of Commerce argued that only a joint effort between New York's papers could make telegraphy affordable and effectively prevent telegraph companies from interfering in the newsgathering process. To get news from the west and from abroad, Hale argued, newspapers had to work together if the public was to be served with increasingly wider coverage of the United States and the world.

Although reluctant at first, the six highly competitive papers agreed to the historic plan, and The Associated Press was born.

The Associated Press assumed its modern legal form in 1900 when AP incorporated as a not-for-profit cooperative under the Membership Corporation Law of New York state.

The AP membership elects the board of directors, AP's governing body.

Today the not-for-profit cooperative (www.ap.org) is the world's largest news organization, providing coverage of news, sports, business, weather, entertainment, politics and technology in text, audio, video, graphics and photos to 15,000 news outlets with a daily reach of more than one billion people around the world. Its services are distributed by satellite and the Internet to more than 120 nations. AP is also a leader in developing and marketing newsroom technology.

AP's news services, with headquarters in New York City, have 241 bureaus worldwide and more than 3,500 employees.

AP's main news departments include:

General Desk

General Desk supervisors oversee the minute-to-minute coordination of all of AP's news operations.

National News

The National Desk is responsible for the AP's spot national news report. The National News department also includes the National Reporting Team, the Arts and Entertainment staff, the Computer-Assisted Reporting staff, the West and South regional wires, AP Weekly Features and the State Summaries desk.

Washington

The Washington bureau is responsible for coverage of the federal government and national issues. With a staff of 150, it is AP's largest domestic bureau.

Business News

The AP's business news department covers major business developments including economic indicators, industry regulation, earnings and mergers. It is also looking for good reads on how people and companies make money and workplace trends. A special unit covers technology.

Newsfeatures

The mission of Newsfeatures writers and editors is to produce high-quality national and international enterprise stories; participate in coverage of major spot stories; and to produce and direct AP's religion coverage and much of its science and medical coverage.

Sports

To meet a growing demand for expanded sports coverage, AP in 1946 established the first news agency wire dedicated entirely to sports. By 1977 the media devoted so much editorial space and air time to sports that AP was operating a 1,050-word-a-minute sports wire around the clock and also publishing a widely circulated annual AP Sports Almanac. Today, the sports wire and all other wires move at approximately 9,600 words a minute.

International Desk

In 1849, Daniel Craig established the AP's first foreign bureau in Halifax, Nova Scotia. That one-man AP foreign staff has grown into a global network numbering more than 500. The International Desk directs all international news coverage. It edits world news for U.S. members and sends news, sports and financial copy to more than 8,500 World Service subscribers abroad. It relies on U.S. bureaus for fast coverage of World Service-interest stories.

World Services

AP's World Service distributes news and photos to more than 8,500 international subscribers and translates the report into four languages. AP is part of a joint venture with Dow Jones & Co., publishers of the Wall Street Journal, Barron's and the Dow Jones News Services to publish Dow Jones Newswires, which are marketed and sold outside the United States to banks, brokers, and other businesses, as well as major media. The DJ Newswires draw on the combined editorial resources of AP, Dow Jones and a specialized staff of reporters and editors.

Graphics

The Graphics Department provides maps, charts, diagrams and graphic art for newspaper and Web use. The department's coordinators and artists work closely with reporters and editors, and also do their own research — which can often help a reporter. The Graphics Department is broken up into beats: international, national, sports, business and features/enterprise. The beats are covered by a coordinator and an artist.

News and Information Research Center

The News and Information Research Center offers AP reporters everything from news articles to complete dossiers on people or businesses. Many resources are available online 24 hours a day. NIRC staff members will research more complicated requests.

Elections and Polling

The AP is a leading force in U.S. polling and elections. AP conducts its own pre-election polls and trains staffers to assess polls. On election nights, AP offers the most extensive voting results and delivery systems in the nation and its own exit poll analysis.

Editorial Training

The editorial training department works to enhance the news and writing skills of AP newspeople and supervisors.

State News

The state news department guides the organization and structure of bureaus in the United States.

Photos

In 1927, AP started a fledgling news picture service. Today, AP operates the most sophisticated picture collection distribution system of any news organization. The classic film and chemical photo process has been replaced by the process of digital picture handling. With a worldwide staff of more than 400, AP Photos provides images to illustrate AP stories and Web presentations, stand-alone photos, photo enterprise packages and a variety of special services. Most photos moved on AP circuits are digital photos. AP's photo archive offers ready access to past photos. The AP Photo Archive holds some 700,000 photos. Any user anywhere in the world can enter the archive via the Internet, browse the picture file by using search criteria and download selected pictures in a matter of minutes.

Broadcast

Between 1933 and 1941, AP supplied written news to radio stations owned by newspaper members only when the news was of "transcendent importance." In 1941, the AP launched a separate broadcast wire, making the company the first news organization to operate a broadcast news circuit 24 hours a day, seven days a week. That development has led to such contemporary broadcast services as AP Network News, All News Radio, Associated Press Television News (APTN), Sports Network Televison (SNTV), AP GraphicsBank and the Electronic News Production System, a computer system for television newsrooms around the world. APTN and SNTV are based in London. The bulk of AP's other broadcast services and the administrative staff are housed at the Broadcast News Center in Washington, D.C. The BNC puts out a scripted national broadcast report used by thousands of stations. Around the United States, broadcast editors based in the AP's control bureaus parallel that national effort with written state reports.

Today, 4,500 television and radio stations depend on AP's information technology, text stories, audio, video, graphics, and photo services for their on-air and online products and services.

Communications

From the establishment of the first permanent leased news wire in 1875 to satellite transmission of the news to development of the digital darkroom, AP's technical staff has pioneered services that have repeatedly advanced technology in the news industry. Its worldwide staff of 500 is based in New York with technical centers that serve as a technological backbone in Kansas City, Mo., and in Cranbury, N.J. Cranbury includes a research and development unit.

Financial Markets

The AP has provided stock tables to the newspaper industry since the early 1920s. More than 900 newspapers now publish stock prices supplied by The Associated Press through AP's Grand Central Stocks or StocksExpress services.

Membership

The Newspaper Membership department, based at New York headquarters, oversees relations with newspaper members in the U.S. Broadcast Services in Washington, D.C., does the same for television and radio stations.

AP's Nontraditional Businesses

Changes in the newspaper and broadcast industry challenge AP to stay ahead in the race to provide information to members and to their readers, listeners and viewers. As services to newspapers and broadcast stations have matured, AP has found nontraditional revenue sources to support further expansion of its worldwide newsgathering operations.

AP's Business Development department serves as an umbrella for nontraditional services. Its Information Services unit sells to clients such as governments and corporations, offering regular news services and a group of subject-specific news wires tailored to each client's industry and news needs.

AP also supplements its newsgathering operations from the sale of photos to nonmembers through AP's Wide World subsidiary.

Another subsidiary, AP Telecommunications, provides members and nonmembers data and network communication technologies.

AP's AdSEND group speeds advertisements from agencies and retailers to newspapers in hours, and even minutes when needed. Ads created on computer are sent by modem or satellite using AP AdSEND software and technology to major newspapers around the United States and abroad.

In response to publishers' increasing interest in the Internet and the World Wide Web, AP in 1995 formed the Multimedia Services department to develop The WIRE, a multimedia news site that AP members can integrate into their own Web sites. AP packages news, photos, graphics, audio and video of the day's top news stories into compelling presentations for use online. Multimedia Services operates in tandem with AP Digital, a division created in 2000 to provide news and information to Web sites, wireless operators and other new media applications. AP Digital is the company's conduit to the Internet. It brings together The WIRE, AP Online and MegaSports to provide a variety of linked Internet products and tickers for members and commercial subscribers.

HEADQUARTERS
The Associated Press
50 Rockefeller Plaza
New York, N.Y. 10020
(212) 621-1500

Following are telephone numbers for frequently called departments and desks at the AP's headquarters in New York City. The area code is 212.

AP Enterprise	621-1830	New York City Bureau	621-1670
Business News	621-1680	Photo Desk	621-1900
Digital Stocks	621-1540	Race Desk	621-1638
General Desk	621-1600	Service Desk	621-1595
Graphics Desk	621-1905	Sports Desk	621-1630
International Desk	621-1663	World Service	621-1750

U.S. Bureaus

Following are telephone numbers for AP bureaus in the United States.

750 West 2nd Ave., Suite 102
Anchorage, **Alaska** 99501
(907) 272-7549

505 N. Third St., Suite 120
Phoenix, **Arizona** 85004
(602) 258-8934

10802 Executive Center Dr., Suite 100
Little Rock, **Arkansas** 72211-4377
(501) 225-3668

221 S. Figueroa
Los Angeles, **California** 90012-2501
(213) 626-1200

1390 Market St., Suite 318
San Francisco, **California** 94102
(415) 621-7432

1444 Wazee St., Suite 130
Denver, **Colorado** 80202-1395
(303) 825-0123

55 Farmington Ave., Suite 402
Hartford, **Connecticut** 06105-3711
(860) 246-6876

2021 K. St., N.W., Suite 606
Washington, **D.C.** 20006-1082
(202) 776-9400

9100 N.W. 36th St.
Miami, **Florida**, 33178
(305) 594-5825

One CNN Center, South Tower
Atlanta, **Georgia** 30303-2705
(404) 522-8971

News Building
605 Kapiolani Blvd.
Honolulu, **Hawaii** 96813
(808) 536-5510

10 S. Wacker Drive, Suite 2525
Chicago, **Illinois** 60606-7407
(312) 781-0500

Star News Building
251 N. Illinois St., Suite 1600
P.O. Box 1950
Indianapolis, **Indiana** 46204
(317) 639-5501

Insurance Exchange Building
505 Fifth Ave., Suite 1000
Des Moines, **Iowa** 50309-2315
(515) 243-3281

Courier-Journal Building
525 West Broadway
Room 407-A
Louisville, **Kentucky** 40202
(502) 583-7718

1515 Poydras St.
New Orleans, **Louisiana** 70112
(504) 523-3931

222 St. Paul Place, Suite 400
Baltimore, **Maryland** 21202
(410) 539-3524

184 High St.
Boston, **Massachusetts** 02110
(617) 357-8100

300 River Place, Suite 2400
Detroit, **Michigan** 48207
(313) 259-0650

Business and Technical Center
511 11th Ave. South, Suite 404
Minneapolis, **Minnesota** 55415
(612) 332-2727

Capitol Towers
125 Congress St., Suite 1330
Jackson, **Mississippi** 39201-3311
(601) 948-5897

215 West Pershing Rd., Suite 221
Kansas City, **Missouri** 64108-4300
(816) 421-4844

Room C West Building
1300 Cedar St., P.O. Box 5810
Helena, **Montana** 59604-5810
(406) 442-7440

909 N. 96th St., #104
Omaha, **Nebraska** 68114
(402) 391-0031

5 Blake St.
Concord, **New Hampshire** 03301
P.O. Box 1200
Concord, **New Hampshire** 03302-1200
(603) 224-3327

50 West State St., Suite 1114
Trenton, **New Jersey** 08608
(609) 392-3622

The Journal Center
5130 San Francisco Road NE, Suite A
Albuquerque, **New Mexico** 87109-4640
(505) 822-9022

645 Albany-Shaker Rd.
P.O. Box 11010
Albany, **New York** 12211-0010
(518) 458-7821

50 Rockefeller Plaza
New York, **New York** 10020
(212) 621-1670

4020 West Chase Blvd.
Raleigh, **North Carolina** 27607
(919) 833-8687

1103 Schrock Road, Suite 300
Columbus, **Ohio** 43229
(614) 885-2727

Central Park One
525 Central Park Drive, Suite 202
Oklahoma City, **Oklahoma** 73105
(405) 525-2121

121 S.W. Salmon St., Suite 1450
Portland, **Oregon** 97204-2924
(503) 228-2169

One Franklin Plaza, Suite 250
Philadelphia, **Pennsylvania** 19102
(215) 561-1133

1311 Marion Street
P.O. Box 101101
Columbia, **South Carolina** 29201
(803) 799-6418

330 N. Main Ave., #303
Sioux Falls, **South Dakota** 57101-1125
(605) 332-2111

215 Centerview Dr.
Brentwood, **Tennessee** 37027
(615) 373-9988

4851 LBJ Freeway, Suite 300
Dallas, **Texas** 75244-6002
(972) 991-2100

30 E. 1st South, Suite 200
Salt Lake City, **Utah** 84111
(801) 322-3405

700 East Main St., Suite 1380
Richmond, **Virginia** 23219-2684
(804) 643-6646

201 Boren Ave. North
P.O. Box 2144
Seattle, **Washington** 98109
(206) 682-1812

500 Virginia St. East, Suite 1150
Charleston, **West Virginia** 25301-2135
(304) 346-0897

Journal Square
918 N. Fourth St.
Milwaukee, **Wisconsin** 53203-1596
(414) 225-3580

AP PUBLICATIONS

AP STYLEBOOK The journalist's "bible." AP member newspapers, broadcast members and journalism departments of member schools—$7.75 per copy, plus postage. A special assessment can be made for the charges to AP member newspapers. Bookstores serving AP member schools—$9.75 per copy. All others—$11.75 per copy. Payment in full must accompany these orders. For shipping and handling, add $4.00 for up to nine books, $8.00 for orders of 10 or more.

AP GUIDE TO NEWS WRITING In this revised edition of what was formerly titled **The Word**, author Jack Cappon, AP general news editor, explains the essentials of top-quality newswriting and demonstrates techniques to give your stories clarity, precision and polish — and avoid wordiness. AP members may order the **AP Guide to News Writing** for $12 a copy, plus $3.50 shipping. An assessment can be made for the charges. All others may order by calling 1-800-338-3282 or accessing www.petersons.com.

AP GUIDE TO PHOTOJOURNALISM This revised and updated edition of **The Picture**, by Brian Horton, goes beyond the basics of lenses and exposure times to offer a rare, insider's perspective on the art and craft of photojournalism. Using some 200 photographs from AP archives, he provides useful instruction on technical considerations, but also deals with the less tangible, indispensable elements of content, style, and the creative process. AP members may order the **AP Guide to Photojournalism** for $12 a copy, plus $3.50 shipping. All others may order by calling 1-800-722-4726.

MANUAL DE TECNICAS DE REDACCION PERIODISTICA

A handbook of writing techniques designed for Spanish-language print and broadcast journalists. An important guide for anyone who writes professionally in Spanish—or wants to learn how the professionals do it— **Manual de Tecnicas** covers the fundamentals of journalism: writing the lead, sources and quotes, structure and connections, writing with "color," basic vocabulary, often misused terms, use and overuse of data, and much, much more. The spiral-bound book, written in Spanish by the same rules it preaches, is a practical guide backed by AP's long and prestigious experience in journalism.

AP members can order **Manual de Tecnicas** for $11.95 a copy, including shipping. (Members can be assessed directly.) All others may order the book for $13.95, plus $2.95 shipping for up to 10 copies; $5.95 for more than 10. Prepayment is required.

AP BROADCAST NEWS HANDBOOK The revised edition of the **AP Broadcast News Handbook**, a 476-page soft-cover book, deals with the practical aspects of writing and delivering news in all electronic media. The **Handbook**, by Brad Kalbfeld, provides expert guidelines on how to find, research, write, edit, produce, and deliver authoritative, accurate, and engaging news stories in the studio or from the field. It also offers indispensable advice on key technical aspects of the job, from how to handle a microphone to how wire services work AP members may order the **AP Broadcast News Handbook** for $15 a copy, plus $3.50 shipping. All others may order by calling 1-800-722-4726.

apbookstore.com

Copies of **The Associated Press Stylebook** and other AP reference books, maps and posters can be ordered online at **http://www.apbookstore.com** on a secure site. However, if you prefer to order by mail, please fill out this form and enclose your check payable to **AP Books**, The Associated Press, 50 Rockefeller Plaza, New York, NY 10020.

ORDER FORM

Name
Organization
Address
City, State and ZIP Code
Phone Number

☐ **Please assess, we are AP members.**

PRODUCT	QTY	TOTAL
AP Stylebook $11.75/copy; $9.75 for college bookstores; $7.75 AP members Shipping: $4.00 for up to nine books; $8.00 for 10 or more	____	____
AP Guide to News Writing $12 a copy for AP members; $3.50 for shipping	____	____
AP Guide to Photojournalism $12 a copy for AP members; $3.50 for shipping	____	____
Manual de Tecnicas $13.95/copy; $11.95 for AP members Shipping: $2.95 for up to ten books; $5.95 for more than 10	____	____
AP Broadcast News Handbook $15 a copy for AP members; $3.50 for shipping	____	____

SHIPPING: _____

ORDER TOTAL: _____

(Checks payable to AP Books.)